BANGLADESH

45⁵⁰

2021
NEW
EDITIONS

U P L

IN HOMAGE TO THE CHANGEMAKERS
IN OUR WORLD OF KNOWLEDGE

Making of a Nation

AN ECONOMIST'S TALE

MAKING OF A NATION BANGLADESH

NURUL ISLAM

University
Press
Limited

The University Press Limited
Red Crescent House (Level 6)
61 Motijheel Commercial Area
Dhaka 1000, Bangladesh
Phone: (+8802) 9565441, 57160710
Mobile: 01917733741
E-mail: info@uplbooks.com.bd
Website: www.uplbooks.com

Fourth impression, August 2021
First published, 2003

Cover design by Mohammad Sajjadur Rahman

ISBN 978 984 506 125 4

Published by Mahrukh Mohiuddin, The University Press Limited, Red Crescent House (Level 6), 61 Motijheel C/A, Dhaka 1000. This book has been set in Times New Roman. Designer: Babul Chandra Dhar and produced by Abarton, 354 Dilu Road, New Eskaton, Moghbazar, Dhaka. Printed at the Akota Offset Press, 119 Fakirapool, Dhaka, Bangladesh.

*I dedicate this book to
my wife, children and grandchildren.*

Contents

PART II: BUILDING A STATE

Glossary

Agartala Conspiracy Case Capital of Indian eastern state of Tripura, wherein Pakistan had alleged that Sheikh Mujib entered into a conspiracy with India to overthrow Pakistan government.

Aman, Aus, Boro Seasonal varieties of rice crop.

Awami League The political party which won in 1970 elections in Pakistan and led the war of independence in 1971.

Bangladesh Nationalist Party The political party founded by Ziaur Rahman in 1977.

BAKSAL Bangladesh Krishak (Peasants) Sramik (Workers) Awami League set up by Sheikh Mujib in 1975 as the single political party in Bangladesh.

National Awami Party Splinter group of Awami League, led by Maulana Abdul Hamid Khan Bhasani.

PKSF A foundation for financing microcredit NGOs engaged in promoting rural employment.

Rakkhi Bahini A para-military force created by Sheikh Mujib to aid police forces in the maintenance of law and order.

Preface

This book is in three parts. The first part deals with the unfolding struggle with Pakistan on economic issues leading to the birth of Bangladesh in December 1971. The second part analyses a few selected economic policies and developments during the first few years (1972-1975) of Bangladesh's existence under the government of Bangabandhu Sheikh Mujibur Rahman. The third part discusses a few policy issues of current concern.

Much has been written on both the pre-1972 struggle, first for autonomy and then, for independence, as well as on the postindependence era of Sheikh Mujib. This book differs from others in two respects. Firstly, it is not an empirical analysis of economic developments but analyses economic policies and issues. Secondly, it is written from the point of view of one who either participated in or observed from close quarters the evolution and the formulation of policies.

The first part analyses the role that economists played in raising public awareness about economic policy issues which dominated the divide between East and West Pakistan. It delineates their engagement in debates and negotiations with policymakers and economists of West Pakistan as well as the support they provided to the political movements in East Pakistan. In choosing among the policy issues, incidents and debates of that period, I have used the following criteria: they either have relevance or lessons for today; they represented landmarks in the evolution of East/West economic relations and they deserve to be revisited in the interest of a better appreciation of the economic history of Bangladesh or I was personally closely involved with them. During the period 1972-1975, as a member of the economic policymaking team, I was learning to assist governing a country we had claimed for ourselves. There were many segments of the evolving process of decision making on economic policies which have not been written. I have tried to fill up the gap as best as I can.

The interpretation of some policy issues and developments has been subject to considerable controversy, which continues even today. Postindependence developments have not been recounted by many an insider. There are few left among the participants who can claim a first-hand knowledge of events. I hope that my analysis contributes to the debate from an insider's point of view; I have attempted to fill the gaps in facts and interpretation as I perceived them. Bangladesh is a highly fractured society; our views are strong and our feelings and emotions run very high. At this distance of time, there is room for my generation to strive for objectivity and a dispassionate look at the past. I hope I have been able to do so.

I had earlier written a book detailing some aspects of my experience as the Deputy Chairman of the Bangladesh Planning Commission (1972-1975). The present study goes beyond that one and covers additional issues. Moreover, it elaborates on what happened "behind the scenes" in the course of the decision making process, and includes glimpses into the role of personalities and individuals. I hope that this will provide a better appreciation of why choices were made.

The analysis of the major issues and incidents in the first two parts of the book are based on reports and documents of the period, many of them unpublished, and on my notes. I have reproduced a very small selection among the hitherto unpublished documents as well as communications not available in the public domain. A few events analysed here are based on my recollections, supplemented by discussions with others who have some knowledge about them. Accounts of my personal interactions with individuals are entirely my own. This is specifically true of Chapters 5 and 7.

The third part of the book moves away from the past. It attempts to study the present in the light of the past, with implications for the future. The issues I discuss often appear prominently in the current debates on economic policies in Bangladesh. I believe that they will continue to engage national debates for some years to come. My observations and analysis are intended to stimulate debate.

Even though this book is about the economic issues and events before and after the independence of Bangladesh, I have added two chapters, one at the beginning of the book and another in the last part, which include a rough sketch of my professional life at different points of time. The intention is to give readers an idea about my background and training — as an introduction to my involvement in the events and policies that are analysed in the book. This book is largely about the past but also to some degree about the present and future. I belong to the past generation but the book is written also for the current and future generations. I have introduced myself and in the process, also provided a glimpse of the state of economic profession in those early days. I hope this will enable the readers to understand the lens through which I interpret the issues and unfolding events.

In spite of my best efforts, I cannot guarantee the absence of minor mistakes in reporting some events or specific dates. In some cases, I have omitted details of a few incidents or individuals, about which I was not absolutely sure. References to individuals, both dead and alive, have been made in many places. In several cases, even though I have avoided mentioning names, I may have still provided enough indications to recognise the individuals concerned. It is possible that some of my observations may offend or contradict the perceptions of others; some would feel ill served by my accounts. To all, I offer my apologises. But I claim no higher truth than my perceptions.

Who is the audience of this book? This is not an academic treatise. It is meant for a wider public, including formal and informal economists. As for the historical part of this book, it is written on the assumption that history matters and that it often repeats itself. There are economists who are playing a role in today's public policy. For them, history, as narrated here, maybe of some interest. Readers belonging to my generation are vanishing rapidly. A few of them may find in it a reminder of their times, specially during the period 1956-71. There is a second group who grew up mainly during the post-1960 period. They belong to the transitional period traversing the years before and after independence. To this group, this is a recount of issues and policies which they heard about but which, at that time, they could not quite comprehend or appreciate the implications thereof. They may find it interesting to read about them from the point of view of one who was involved in these events. Lastly, there is the generation which grew up during the 1970s and after; the vast majority of the younger generation of today belong to this category. To this last group, the first part of this book is the history of a period about which they occasionally get "snapshots" from their elders. Most of them have very little interest in the story prior to 1975 and for that matter, prior to the 1990s. I hope that there may yet be some amongst them and among their posterity who might be interested in the history of economic policies which drove the independence movement as well as those which dominated the immediate postindependence period. Some of them might even be interested to learn about them in the context of economic ideas and perspectives of the time. It may remind them that frequently current issues are embedded or have their counterparts in the past and are likely to persist or reemerge in their future. The last part is expected to be of interest to all of these aforementioned groups since it deals with current issues and is likely to be relevant in the future.

This book covers issues and events which involve relations, in different periods of time, with two other South Asian countries i.e. India and Pakistan. The first part includes events and issues relating to Pakistan in its early years. I am not fully aware of how the younger generation of Pakistan today views this period nor what analysis or perspective they have been provided by their historians. I assume that it would be very different from what is provided here. In the light of interest that the Hamoodur Rahman Commission's report has aroused at least in some circles in Pakistan, it appears that they may like to know what "the other side" thinks about the background economic issues.

The book in the second and third parts has devoted sections on Indo-Bangladesh economic relations, both historical and current. The subject is of topical interest and importance in both countries for most people in Bangladesh, and one hopes, at least, for some in India. I participated in the evolution of bilateral relations during the period 1972-1975. As far as I know, none of my Indian counterparts have written on this subject. I have also dealt with a few aspects of the current relationship between the two countries and the implications for the future. I have ventured into this analysis with the expectation that, as I am away from the current scene, I may claim some detachment.

Many friends have encouraged me to write this book. I am specially grateful to Hasan Imam who read all the chapters in several drafts painstakingly until the bitter end, making comments on the arguments, style and language and greatly helped me to revise the book. A.R. Khan, in spite of his heavy preoccupations, was generous enough to read some chapters and made very valuable suggestions for improvement. Both A.R. Khan and Hasan Imam, witnessed or shared my trials and tribulations as my colleagues at PIDE/BIDS and the Bangladesh Planning Commission. My daughter, Roumeen Islam, as my best critic, helped me to think through my approach and conceptualise the main messages of the book. She commented on and helped rewrite a few critical chapters. Saad Andaleeb read carefully earlier drafts of several chapters and offered extensive comments on content and style. Kabiruddin Ahmed and Akhter Mahmood read selected chapters and made useful comments.

I would be remiss in my duty if I do not record how my nine year old granddaughter, Leila, from time to time, corrected my typing and spelling on the computer.

Finally, I would like to express my sincere thanks and appreciation to Vicky Lee of IFPRI, who went out of her way to assist me in getting the manuscript ready, for her patience in deciphering my unintelligible notes.

Washington, D.C., 2003   **Nurul Islam**

Part I
BIRTH OF A NATION

Chapter 1

PROLOGUE:
AN ECONOMIST IN THE MAKING

At midnight on 25th March 1971, the last nail was driven into the coffin of Undivided Pakistan. On that night, which has earned a place for itself in history, the Pakistan army unleashed a brutal assault on the civilian population of East Pakistan — innocent men, women, and children. It committed atrocities on a scale unprecedented in the recent history of colonial states. Countless people were killed; ten million refugees fled to India. The Bangladesh freedom fighters, under the leadership of the government in exile, organised their resistance and fought back. India, faced with a staggering burden of refugees and a looming danger of sociopolitical destabilisation in its Eastern states, stepped in, to help East Pakistan. The final stage in the struggle for independence had begun.

It all started in the early days of Pakistan. The government had decided to introduce Urdu, the language of the minority population living in West Pakistan, as the official language of the state. This was an unwarranted attack on East Pakistan's cultural and linguistic heritage — an attempt to deny the use of its mother tongue in the affairs of the state Bengali — a rich language with a literature renowned in the Indian subcontinent. Predictably, East Pakistanis opposed this measure. Protests led by students in East Pakistan were forcefully subdued — there was bloodshed. The Language Movement that followed, snowballed and fuelled the demand for a shift in the balance of political power in favour of East Pakistan. West Pakistan resisted and was unyielding. Its army seized power and established its unchallenged authority. The process of disenfranchisement of East Pakistan was completed.

For almost two decades, East Pakistan was in the grip of economic stagnation; disparities with West Pakistan widened while resources were transferred from the less developed East to the more developed West Pakistan. Tension mounted and events moved fast. East Pakistan demanded full autonomy and control over its own resources and over the management of its economy under the leadership of Bangabandhu Sheikh Mujibur Rahman, who launched his *Six-Points Programme* — a charter for the realisation of East Pakistan's political and economic rights. The economists of East Pakistan, among whom I numbered, joined the movement interpreting, and elaborating on the relevant economic issues, and raising public awareness about the economic basis of our surging nationalism. We assisted Bangabandhu Sheikh Mujibur Rahman and his associates; we engaged in contentious debates with our counterparts in West Pakistan. After a few years of stonewalling, negotiations for a settlement with East Pakistan were haltingly started and abruptly aborted by West Pakistan, paving the way for the fateful crackdown by the army on 25th March 1971.

After nine months of war, wading through death and destruction, Bangladesh was born on December 16, 1971. Challenges facing the new nation were daunting. But our expectations were high. We vowed that we would overcome all obstacles. Several of us economists, joined Bangabandhu Sheikh Mujibur Rahman[1] in building the economic foundations of the new state. Achievements and failures bringing fulfilment and frustrations respectively, awaited us in the years to follow. Barely four years were to pass before the political landscape in the nation changed and new, different regimes followed. Many fresh challenges emerged. Yet even until today adequate responses to some of these challenges have kept eluding us. Many promises that we made to ourselves as the people of a new nation continue to remain unfulfilled.

***

Every nation's future, the set of choices it makes and the choices it can make are inextricably linked to its history — to its past. The funny thing about history though, is that the eye of the beholder matters.

---

[1] Hereafter in the succeeding chapters referred to as Sheikh Mujib.

First, which facts are chosen in telling the story determines which angle one emphasises. Second, a simple recital of the facts alone cannot explain a people's evolution. In what follows, I will interpret the past, sometimes as a passive spectator, sometimes as an active participant, but always trying to the best of my ability to give a balanced view of events. My bias will be to focus on the evolution of economic policies leading to and after the emergence of Bangladesh. This is the sphere where I feel I can bring value to the analysis of what happened and how we got where we are today. Yet to do this convincingly, in order to help reader look through the lens which I used to view Bangladesh's past and present, and simply because I would get greater fulfilment in telling my story — I must explain how it all started for me.

My passage from early youth to succeeding years saw the flowering of Bangladeshi nationalism. As a student, I was a passive spectator, aware of the gathering ferment. Yet my transformation was rapid and I was drawn from the calm of academia into confrontation with West Pakistan on economic issues that dominated the East-West divide. But I must start at the beginning of the process, and introduce my professional background and training, and the intellectual milieu in which I lived and served.

I was born in Chittagong where I was educated until I left for Presidency College in Kolkata to be a first year student in the B.A. programme. Yet, political events intervened to cut this sojourn short. After the first year (1946-47), I was forced to leave in the face of India's partition and its bloody aftermath. In August 1947, I joined Dhaka University where I completed my M.A. in Economics.

The Economics Department of Dhaka University was by then almost wholly depleted of senior and well trained teachers who had mostly been Hindus and who therefore had found it necessary to migrate to India after the partition. This staff was replaced by teachers recruited from local colleges and from amongst those who had freshly obtained their M.A. degrees from the Department. These new recruits were not of the calibre and experience needed to teach a solid economics programme at the University. As students, those of us who were determined to learn, had no choice but to teach ourselves, which we did with a great deal of effort. Luckily, the field did not remain completely barren. We were fortunate to have two teachers who had returned recently after the completion of higher studies abroad: A.F.A. Husain, educated at the London School of Economics, who joined in 1948; and M.N. Huda, with a Ph.D. in Agricultural Economics from Cornell University, who joined in 1949.

My time at Dhaka University was very productive. I secured first place in the First Class in both the B.A. Honours and M.A. examinations and obtained the Kalinaryan Scholarship for securing the highest aggregate of marks. As a result of my academic achievements, I was under much pressure from relatives and friends to compete for the Pakistan Civil Service — the supreme attraction for all bright and ambitious young men at that time since it brought great power in the administrative hierarchy and immense prestige in society. As there was a severe shortage in the administrative services of the new nation, there were very heavy recruitments every year and competition was mild. But my father, who himself had an M.A. in English Literature from Dhaka University, who had an excellent academic record and became a member of the educational service, had other ideas. He convinced me that advanced training in one of the best universities abroad and not a powerful administrative job, however prestigious that job might be, should be my preferred objective.

In perfect timing, the government of Pakistan announced that a few scholarships were available for higher studies abroad in a very limited number of subjects all of which were to be in scientific disciplines, but included Economics. Fortunately, I was able to secure a scholarship in Economics. I had already obtained admission to the Ph.D. programme at both Harvard and Cambridge universities. After due deliberation, I chose Harvard. On the basis of extensive reading and investigation, I had come to believe that the locus of advanced training and research in economics, specially with its latest emphasis on quantitative techniques, had, by the 1950s, shifted to USA. Many well known economists and academics from Europe and elsewhere had congregated at the US universities in the post-war period. Harvard was considered to be at the forefront of modern economics and I was convinced that it would be at least on par with, if not better than, Cambridge. This was certainly true of postgraduate education, if not of education at the undergraduate level.

This judgement regarding the relative merits of US versus British Universities was also based on a very important fact: at Harvard, as at other US universities, Ph.D. students were required to go through at least two years of very rigorous course work at an advanced level in the basic branches of economics before they were considered qualified to proceed to the dissertation writing stage. In those days in a British university, one could start working on one's thesis if one had a good M.A. degree from any university abroad and could, therefore, receive a Ph.D. degree without achieving a very strong foundation in the essential branches of economics. In later years, several British universities adopted the US system in varying degrees. But in the early 1950s, I could obtain the highest academic degree from a well known university in England without obtaining a very rigorous and advanced training in economics. For these reasons, I was biased strongly in favour of Harvard.

In order to obtain the scholarship from the government, I was required to sign a contract/bond with the government of Pakistan undertaking to serve, on my return, in an institution to be approved by the government. The educational adviser to the government who was to approve my choice of the university was a B.A. in Economics from Cambridge University. He was genuinely surprised to learn, and could hardly believe, that anybody in his right mind could prefer Harvard University to Cambridge, the latter being the birthplace of modern economics and the home to Marshall, Keynes and Pigou. The educational adviser, I was sure, felt that in my youthful misconception I would be wasting away valuable opportunities, and did not readily accept my arguments. A lot of persuasion and pleading were needed before he agreed to let me make this "wrong" choice.

1.1 AT HARVARD

The four years I spent at Harvard, 1951-55, were in many ways the best years of my academic life. A *brave new world* had opened up to me and not just in economics. I revelled in the intellectual ferment around me. Harvard attracted some of the best and brightest not only from the USA but from all over the world. However, there were very few students from developing countries. Among my fellow students and contemporaries were: Henry Rosovosky, one time Dean of the Faculty of Arts and Sciences and later on a University Professor in Economics at Harvard; Alice Rivlin, who became Deputy Chairman of the Federal Reserve Board and later Director of the Office of the Budget and Management of the US government; James Henderson (deceased) and Richard Quandt, joint authors of a well known textbook in economics; others included Andrew Brimmer, probably the first African American to be appointed a Governor of the Federal Reserve Board and later an investment banker; Otto Eckstein (deceased), Professor of Economics at Harvard; James Schlesinger, former Secretary of Defense and later of Energy in the US government; Richard Caves, a well known international trade theorist and Professor at Harvard; and Ted Beza, who became Director of the Western Hemisphere Department of the IMF.

Among the students from developing countries I remember: Abdur Rahman Al Habib from Iraq who was once a Minister in the government of Iraq; Thun Thin from Burma, who later became the Director of the Asia Department at the IMF; and Oluwassami (deceased) from Nigeria who subsequently became a Professor at the University of Ibadan and a high administrative official. P.N. Dhar of the Indian Institute of Economic Growth/Delhi School of Economics, later Secretary to Indira Gandhi and an Assistant Secretary General in UN, was a visiting scholar for a year or so. So also was Kenneth Berrill from Cambridge, who later attained Knighthood and became a high Treasury official in the UK.

One of the most important features of my student days at Harvard was that we, the students, learned a great deal from each other. Whenever anyone of us had problems either with reading assignments or in following the lectures of a professor, we used to consult with each other to clarify the issues. Those of us who lived in the dormitories used the opportunities provided by common meals to discuss the unresolved questions that we faced in the course of our studies. Everyone was very helpful in this environment — though each of us wanted to excel, the atmosphere was collegial. Comprehensive examinations were held at the end of the two-year period to determine the state of our preparedness to proceed to the writing of the dissertation, and four of us formed a regular study group to prepare for these. We met regularly to review all the subjects. These sessions with my peers were immensely helpful in my final examinations and in which I did rather well and obtained the highest grade, "excellent".

I was also fortunate to have among my professors such distinguished economists as W. Leontief (later on a Nobel Laureate), the father of input-output analysis and its various applications; E.H. Chamberlin; G. Haberler; J.E. Meade, visiting from Cambridge (subsequently a Nobel Laureate); A. Gershenkron; H.J. Habakkuk, visiting from Oxford; A. Hansen; J.H. Williams; and G. Orcutt. Haberler supervised my thesis in the field of international economics, specifically on foreign direct investment. I secured the second highest grade, Excellent Minus, on the quality of the dissertation.

Leontief and Haberler were remarkable teachers, in advanced economic theory and international trade respectively, with the gift of lucid and clear exposition. They were exhaustive in their lectures with the result that the students did not have to do much additional readings to master the subjects. However, in order to achieve the maximum benefit from their lectures, we had to consult the essential reading assignments ahead of their classes and listen to them with our undivided attention in class. These two professors were, in a way, complementary. Leontief's lectures on economic theory unfolded from the theory of the firm to the theory of the market and then on to the theory of general equilibrium. Haberler expounded on economic theory's corresponding applications to international trade. He expanded upon such concepts as commodity and factor market distortions, external economies and diseconomies, social and private cost, competition and monopoly, factor mobility and price rigidity, among others.

Chamberlin explained the theory of the firm and the market in greater detail. He was well known for his theory of monopolistic competition, which he sought, assiduously and painstakingly, to distinguish from the theory of imperfect competition propounded at the same time by Joan Robinson at Cambridge. He would expound at great length the nuances of the concept of product differentiation with free entry and absence of excess profits that "differentiated" his product from that of Robinson. Both of them came up, simultaneously and independently of each other, with the concept and theory of market behaviour that lay between perfect competition and monopoly. James Duesenbery, in the early 1950s, developed the concept of the interdependence of consumer preferences or the *demonstration effect* and its implications for demand theory. We were among the first group of students to be initiated into this innovation.

Meade, visiting from Cambridge for a semester or so, had just finished writing his book *Trade and Welfare*, and tried out his exposition on us in considerable detail. He started his first day of lecture saying that he would try to teach most of the time in plain English aided by arithmetic. Occasionally, he would resort to geometry but rarely to algebra. He kept his promise at the cost of time and effort, which many of us felt could have been saved with a more frequent use of geometry and algebra. Most of us had a background in mathematics sufficient to handle its somewhat limited use in economics. It must be emphasised, however, that we had nowhere near the training in mathematics which is common fare in graduate courses in economics nowadays. I found Meade to be a good teacher but sometimes a little tedious. With hindsight, we were fortunate to have been among the early recipients of his lectures on trade theory as expounded in his *magnum opus*.

Alexander Gershenkron, a well known economic historian, was highly respected. He had developed an interesting approach for studying the stages and processes of industrialisation in Europe and its extension to other countries. In the late industrialising countries, which he defined as those that followed Britain, the state played a leading role in financing and promoting, including through direct ownership, the early stages of industrial development. At a later stage, it was the banking system that took the lead. He illustrated his approach by using the examples of Germany and France. He saw elements of this strategy in the industrialisation of Russia and Japan. He would have found the current controversy about the public sector versus the private sector redundant and counter productive since both have a role depending upon the circumstances of each country. He elaborated the role of German Junkers, on the one hand, and the British feudal lords, on the other, as well as the role of the British merchant houses in financing and supporting industrialisation. Secondly, in all cases he emphasised the role of agrarian reforms and agricultural progress as a precondition for successful industrialisation. Habakkuk expounded on the link between agrarian reforms and industrialisation in England. These propositions put forth by Gershenkron and Habakkuk provided great insights and lessons for development economists in succeeding years.

By the time I arrived at Harvard, J. Schumpeter was no longer alive. He had been a towering presence and his ideas had great influence on the study and teaching of economic history and thought at Harvard. Following Schumpeter, Gershenkron and Leontief used to elaborate how and in what respects Marx provided the most relevant and appropriate exposition of the driving forces behind the capitalist private enterprise system, with his emphasis on accumulation, innovation and the search for market power. Hansen was regarded as one of the leading Keynesian economists whereas Williams, who was actively involved in the formulation of US monetary policy as an adviser to the Federal Reserve Bank of New York, was recognised for his work on monetary policy. Orcutt introduced us to the evolving techniques of modern econometrics and its applications.

The study of the history of economic thought and economic history was accorded a high place in graduate training in economics. All the great classical and neoclassical economists had to be studied with great care and their thoughts were analysed in relation to the latest ideas in economics. Today, with the emphasis on formal and mathematical models as the most important tools of graduate training, the teaching of the ideas of classical/neoclassical economists and of the history of economic development has fallen by the wayside. This is a pity since the newly defined curricula restrict the mental horizon of graduate students by limiting the range of ideas to which they are exposed. This is of special concern for the students of economics from developing countries. Development theorists and practitioners are today preoccupied with the role of institutions and governance. Both classical and neoclassical economists paid a great deal of attention to these sets of issues.

Development economics as a separate subject had not yet appeared on the scene. Ragnar Nurkse's work on the economics of underdeveloped countries had just appeared in my last year at Harvard. John Kenneth Galbraith began a seminar on development economics which all of us from developing countries attended out of great interest and curiosity. I remember that we struggled with the concepts and implications of balanced versus unbalanced growth, cumulative causation and the why and how of deteriorating terms of trade in developing countries.

Towards the end of my sojourn, Edward Mason, well known for his work on industrial organisation and public policy, summoned me. He had just assumed responsibility for the newly established *Harvard Development Advisory Service* which eventually grew to be the Harvard Institute of International Development (HIID). It was funded by the Ford Foundation to provide advisory services to developing countries. One of its early involvements was in advising the Pakistan Planning Commission. Mason wanted me to meet David Bell, the newly appointed leader of the resident team. Bell was to proceed shortly to Pakistan and I was requested to brief him on the economy, polity and society of the country. This was my first encounter with Bell and the beginning of a period of acquaintance and interaction, which lasted over more than four decades in our various capacities.

As I completed my dissertation, Leontief, who had started a large scale project, the *Harvard Economic Research Project*, enquired whether I was interested in joining his project as a Research Fellow. I was tempted by the offer primarily because of the opportunity of working with a famous economist. At the same time, Haberler suggested that since my specialisation had been in international economics, it would be a good experience for me to join the research department of the IMF, which did very interesting work of relevance to the developing countries. He wrote a very strong letter of recommendation to the head of the IMF's research department, E.M. Bernstein. Soon I was called for an interview and was offered a job as a young professional.

During my last year at Harvard, I had received a communication from S.V. Ayer, my teacher and at that time the head of the Department of Economics at Dhaka University, urging me to return and join the department which was in great need of teachers. In any case, I told Bernstein at the IMF and Leontief at Harvard that I would like to return home and meet with my parents before I could take a final decision. In those days, we were not very eager to pursue careers abroad. Almost all my contemporaries who had gone abroad for higher studies returned home, even though good career opportunities did exist abroad for bright students and immigration was exceedingly easy.

I returned home in August 1955. Mason asked me to look up David Bell in Karachi on my return. In Karachi, Bell's preoccupation was how to build up the capacity of the Planning Commission which was severely understaffed due to the shortage of qualified economists. He had already informed Zahid Husain, the Deputy Chairman, about me. Even though I told him about alternative job opportunities, he urged me to meet Zahid Husain, which I did. The latter lost no time in trying to convince me that I had very good career prospects in the Planning Commission. After all, I would be one of their earliest recruits with good training and strong recommendations from my professors at Harvard. Since I was not ready to make a commitment, I departed on the understanding that I needed to take stock of my situation after returning home and only then would I take a decision.

At that time, trained economists were scarce in Pakistan. There was a great need for economists both in government and in the universities. I was thus in a position to choose between alternative offers. My parents were not very happy that I was considering accepting a foreign assignment, having already been away from them for so many years. After some thought, I decided to seek my professional career at home rather than abroad. Those were the days when young people felt it a challenge, if not a commitment, to serve the country. Since I decided not to go abroad, the acceptance of a job in Karachi — a foreign land as far as I was concerned — was ruled out. It had neither the advantage of my being in Dhaka nor the attraction of the IMF or of Harvard from the point of view of my professional advancement or financial rewards. Moreover, I wanted to teach the fresh young minds in Dhaka.

1.2 AT DHAKA UNIVERSITY

When I contacted Dhaka University I found that Mazharul Huq, one of my teachers, was the Head of the Department and very eager for me to join. He took me to the Vice Chancellor, W.A. Jenkins, a former member of the British Indian Educational Service, who had taught physics at Dhaka University during the British rule. Jenkins wanted me to join but there was some resistance to my appointment as a Reader/Associate Professor since I was very young and had no previous teaching experience. However, after some negotiation, the Vice Chancellor agreed. The precedents provided by earlier appointments of Readers/Associate Professors with no teaching experience strengthened my case. It is possible that competing offers of jobs in and outside the country helped to resolve the issue in my favour.

One of the first tasks I undertook was to revamp the syllabuses in order to bring them in line with the latest standards of teaching in economics. The curriculum at Dhaka University was very outdated. A second important task was the creation of a Bureau of Economic Research under the auspices of the Economics Department to carry out empirical research on economic problems and policies. We received grants from such sources as the Asia and Ford Foundations as well as the State Bank and the government of East Pakistan. A.F.A. Husain, who was by then a Professor of Commerce in the University, undertook for the first time what was then called survey research in economics i.e. empirical research based on original data collected through surveys. His study on the social impact of technological change in East Pakistan, funded by UNESCO, was the first study of its kind. It analysed the changes in attitudes and life styles resulting from urbanisation and industrialisation among the migrants from rural areas to Dhaka City and its environs. This undertaking was the first of our efforts to collect data through surveys and to analyse them for the purposes of throwing light on important economic issues of the day. We wanted to ensure that undertakings of this type would proliferate and that the efforts would be sustained over time and so we established an institutional umbrella to support them: the *Bureau of Economic Research* was born.

Under this umbrella, we conducted research on a variety of issues such as rural credit, rural unemployment and jute marketing, jointly with other colleagues, and assisted by teams of research assistants and investigators to carry out surveys. This was quite a transition for me to go from analytical and theoretical work to data intensive empirical research on rural economic problems. I learned a great deal on the rural economy as well as on the techniques of survey research. My close associate and friend in this work was Abdullah Farouk of the Department of Commerce, from whom I learned a great deal on applied survey techniques, including how to solve the problems of data inconsistency and how to improve their accuracy.

I first attempted to use quantitative techniques in economic analysis in the book, *Studies in Consumer Demand*, which estimated income and price elasticities of demand for a wide range of agricultural and manufactured goods in East Pakistan.[2] This was the first time such estimates had been made for East Pakistan. Subsequently, they were helpful in making demand projections for various commodities as a guide to investment or production programming. Based on the survey work on rural unemployment, I produced estimates of rural unemployment, both visible and disguised, published later in the *International Labour Review*.

During the course of this work, I had my first encounter with empirical verification of production decisions under uncertainty and the role of diversification. For example, a critical issue in Bangladesh's economy was: How did farmers make a choice between rice and jute, given the high volatility of jute price and income? We found that farmers chose not to specialise completely in jute, even though returns from jute production were higher. Research on jute marketing was of particular policy interest, since jute had the largest share of exports. Issues of concern were ensuring fair prices for farmers, whether jute prices were set competitively in export markets and future market prospects for jute manufactures. We confirmed that rural markets for raw jute were highly competitive. The concentration of market share and the market power of buyers increased at later stages of marketing and the highest concentration of buyers was at the last stage of export.

During this period, I continued my research on issues relevant for development, particularly in international trade and investment issues and produced a few journal articles on the subject. One such publication focused on the interwing trade in Pakistan and the terms of trade between East and West Pakistan. In an article in the *Indian Economic Journal*, I explored the concept of balanced growth and external economies in the context of underdevelopment. Around 1957-58, I started constructing a short term econometric model for Pakistan with a view to exploring the impact of various policy instruments (e.g. tax, subsidy, public expenditures, foreign trade, and exchange rate policies) on national and sectoral incomes, prices and the balance of trade. I completed this work when I visited the *Netherlands Economic*

---

[2] *Studies in Consumer Demands*, Vol. 1 and 11, Bureau of Economic Research, D.U. and Oxford University Press, 1965 and 1966.

Institute in 1959. Between 1956-60, I spent two periods of time working abroad ranging from three to six months each: at the *ECAFE*[3] in Bangkok, now known as *ESCAP*; and at the Planning Ministry in Iran. Under the former assignment, I worked on models of development planning and techniques of planning and budgeting, including foreign exchange budgeting. In Iran, I was a UN consultant advising the government on economic aspects of planning and policies for educational development i.e. how to set priorities between different levels and stages of education and how to estimate and analyse the costs and benefits of investment in education.

The Department of Economics at Dhaka University used to attract students with very good prior academic performance. Most of the best students of the Department joined the civil service of Pakistan. The latter was true of the graduates of some of the other departments as well. I tried in vain to persuade at least some of my best students to join the Department as teachers. Inducements, such as the opportunity to do advanced studies at the best universities abroad, were not enough. The result was that the teaching professions continued to languish in the absence of a regular flow of fresh entrants with bright minds. This was specially true during the years stretching from the 1950s to the late 1960s. The teaching profession suffered from the long and hard grind, first in getting a Ph.D. and then in facing the uncertain prospects of securing a reasonably good position as an Associate or full Professor. There were few jobs at such levels available at the universities. Compared to this, the alternative of a civil service job was one in which once selected, the path was relatively secure and there was some certainty of going up the ladder of increasing power, prestige and perks. Such was the manifestation of society's valuation of the differential productivity of occupations and professions. The warped system of incentives worked inexorably to the erosion of the teaching profession.

From August 1958 to December 1959, I was away on leave from the university visiting first the London School of Economics (LSE), then the Department of Applied Economics at the University of Cambridge and then the Netherlands Economic Institute at Rotterdam.

---

[3] Economic Commission for Asia and Far East (ECAFE), later named Economic and Social Commission for Asia and the Pacific (ESCAP).

The purpose was to refresh and widen my knowledge of the latest developments in economics, specially quantitative economics. I also wanted to see for myself, with my USA-oriented eyes, how economics was taught and what was the nature and state of economic research in Europe. At LSE, the technique of linear programming drawn from and heavily based on what was being done in the USA, attracted a great deal of attention. At Cambridge, the focus was on the pioneering work on national income and social accounting by Richard Stone. At Rotterdam, work focused on econometric model building and estimation techniques developed by Tinbergen and Theil.

At LSE, there was a weekly faculty seminar run by Lionel Robbins in which a faculty member would summarise and provide a critique of one of the latest works in economics. This was followed by comments and discussions by participants. The objective of the seminar was to evaluate the exact nature of the contribution and how it either advanced theoretical insight or gave policy guidance. These discussions were a very effective way to keep the faculty continuously updated on the latest developments in economics. They also stimulated research by the faculty members on ideas thrown out, or suggestions made at the seminar.

At Cambridge, there were a series of seminars for fellows and graduate students under Joan Robinson, Richard Kahn, and Pierro Sraffa. It was here that I met Amartya Sen, then a fellow at Cambridge, who had just finished his work on the choice of techniques in production, and renewed my friendship with Kenneth Berrill whom I had first met at Harvard. In addition, I continued my close relationship with Austin Robinson whom I had first met in Pakistan where he visited a few times. Our relationship continued uninterrupted for many years until his death, over the course of diverse segments of my life. He was my great supporter and helped me on numerous occasions.

In addition to these gatherings, there used to be interuniversity seminars involving Cambridge, Oxford and London. In one of these seminars, I met Jagdish Bhagwati for the first time and continued my contact with him in later years. During the early 1970s, I had the opportunity of working with him in a collaborative project on trade policy in developing countries under the auspices of NBER.[4] Upon

---

[4] National Bureau of Economic Research (NBER), USA.

invitation by Harry Johnson, I visited the University of Manchester to give a seminar on the economic development of Pakistan.[5]

In Rotterdam, I was preoccupied with completing my book on Short Term Planning Model for Pakistan. One of the reasons for my heightened interest in further developing my theoretical and quantitative skills was in order to finish this task. I greatly benefited from comments by Jan Tinbergen, a pioneer in the construction of econometric planning models for policy purposes. He was kind enough to write a foreword to the book when Oxford University Press subsequently published it.[6] The lasting memory of my days at his institute was his saintly attitude and living style. This world-renowned economist, a future Nobel Laureate, used to commute by train or bus from his home which was in The Hague. He did not own a car. He was known to donate liberally to charities. Everyday he would join the fellows of the Institute for lunch at his office over a sandwich, a fruit and a glass of milk and would often relate interesting anecdotes.

Jan Tinbergen was a master in the art of combining quantitative techniques with judgement and direct empirical observations. He enriched his research by close interaction with policymakers and economic actors. Once, he recounted to us how at the Netherlands Economic Planning Bureau he had to estimate the price elasticity of demand for Dutch exports on the basis of his econometric model. While building his model, he consulted with and sought the advice of different specialists, including private sector representatives. He presented a range of estimates for the elasticity of export demand and discussed with producers and exporters their implications for export growth. On the basis of such discussions, he chose two as the coefficient. This estimate was used in various macroeconomic models for the Netherlands economy for a number of succeeding years. It came to be known as the *Tinbergen Two*.

At the end of my visits at various research centres and universities, I was able to replenish my intellectual capital and to bring myself up to date on the latest developments in economics that I had missed out for three years in the backwaters of Dhaka University.

---

[5] Harry Johnson used to visit Pakistan Institute of Development Economics (PIDE) when I was its Director in the 1960s.

[6] *A Short-term Model for Pakistan Economy: An Econometric Analysis*, Oxford University Press, 1964.

I came back to Dhaka towards the end of 1959. By that time the military take-over staged by Ayub had run for more than a year. East-West tensions had reached a high level dominating the political arena and the economic discourse in the country. During 1956-57, the East Pakistan government established a Planning Board with M.N. Huda, A.F.A. Husain, and A. Razzak as Members of the Board and Mosharaff Hossain as the Chief Economist. This was the first attempt by the provincial government to engage in formulating a strategy for East Pakistan. Such a strategy was to be used as the basis for negotiations regarding the allocation of fiscal resources with the Pakistan government. The Planning Board did not survive after the installation of the military regime. However, a Planning Department headed by a Secretary of the provincial government continued to function to help formulate development programmes for East Pakistan. Soon after my return, I was inevitably drawn into the debate on regional economic issues in various fora, professional meetings and conferences, as well as in various consultative committees and panels convened by the government of Pakistan.

By 1960, I was appointed a Professor in the Department of Economics. This point onward marked the process of my close involvement in some of the crucial government Commissions dealing with East-West economic relations. During this period, my research publications included several journal articles, at home and abroad, on such subjects as the use of models in development planning, private versus public enterprise in development, export prospects and policies of the Asian region, and an econometric study of the import demand function in Pakistan both at the aggregate level and disaggregated for individual commodities.

1.3 ON TO PAKISTAN INSTITUTE OF DEVELOPMENT ECONOMICS

I joined the Pakistan Institute of Development Economics (PIDE) in 1964 as its Director, while on leave from Dhaka University, and continued until the beginning of 1972 when I joined the newly independent government of Bangladesh.[7] At the time, PIDE had a good complement of visiting research advisers from various universities

---

[7] The challenges I confronted at PIDE are narrated in Chapter 3.

abroad, mostly from USA, to train and guide the research work of the junior staff and to undertake collaborative research with the senior staff. The Ford Foundation provided very generous financial assistance, administered by the Yale University Growth Centre. The grant also provided a large number of overseas scholarships for PIDE staff as well as for eligible candidates from other research institutions and universities of the country; they were to be selected by PIDE for advanced studies in universities abroad.

The mandate for PIDE was not only to build up national research capacity in economics, but also to conduct empirically based policy oriented research. Its research priorities were to encompass important issues confronting policymakers. The PIDE journal, *Pakistan Development Review*, acquired international recognition and a reputation for quality during the 1960s. It was counted among the well known professional journals in development economics.

My tenure at PIDE was professionally very rewarding. It provided me with considerable opportunities for interaction with important research centres abroad. My research interests included economic growth, commercial policy and foreign assistance. At the time, the institute was one of the first research centres in the developing world to provide empirical estimates of effective protection rates. Among other things, I worked on estimates of comparative costs of industries, effective rates of export subsidy, impact of trade and exchange rate policies on export performance and industrialisation as well as international development assistance.

During this period, I spent a sabbatical year at the Yale University Economic Growth Centre and at the World Bank's Economic Development Institute (rechristened of late as the World Bank Institute). My time at Yale was spent on working on the planning experience and trade policy issues in Pakistan. At the World Bank Institute, I taught macroeconomic and trade policies as well as planning and investment programming.

A memorable event during my tenure at PIDE was the organisation of a conference in Sri Lanka of the Indian and Pakistani economists, researchers and policy advisors who until then, had very little professional contact with each other. The conference was held in the fall of 1969 under the auspices of the International Economic Association.

The two countries were faced with similar problems of development and followed in some respects similar policies diverging in others, with comparable and sometimes with widely different results. There was much to learn from each other's experience in designing a research agenda as well as in choosing between alternative policies or strategies for development. There were also possibilities for regional economic cooperation. The idea of a conference was worked out by my Indian friend, K.N. Raj, and myself when both of us were teaching at the World Bank Institute at the World Bank. Austin Robinson of Cambridge and of the International Economic Association, with which I was associated for several years, welcomed this idea and supported the organisation of the conference. The conference was held in a neutral country i.e. Sri Lanka, with the participation of a few Sri Lankan economists (Gamini Corea and Lal Jayawardena) to give the conference a South Asian cover. This was a pioneering attempt along the so-called "second or nonofficial track" to promote contact between professionals of the two countries which had been locked in adversarial relationships that were further aggravated by the war in 1965.

The range of issues discussed at the conference was large: macroeconomic issues, development strategy, sectoral priorities and policies as well as international and regional trade policies were covered. Among the Indian participants were Manmohan Singh, A.K. Sen, Jagdish Bhagwati, K.N. Raj, T.N. Srinivasan, Ashok Mitra, Gautam Mathur, and Ramaswamy (deceased). Among the Pakistani participants were A.R. Khan, S.R. Bose, S.N.H. Naqvi, Sultan Hashmi, Ziauddin Ahmed, Anisur Rahman, Wahidul Haque, Akhlaqur Rahman, and myself. The debates and discussions took place in an atmosphere of congeniality and friendliness. Unfortunately, East Pakistanis constituted most of the Pakistani contingent. We did not succeed in persuading many well known West Pakistani economists to participate. They were not enthusiastic about such a meeting even though it was a professional conference of well known researchers with no political agenda. The economists from East Pakistan, on the other hand, did not feel any adversarial relationship with India.

This is a short sketch of the evolution of my academic life until I was thrown more intensively into the vortex of the campaign for Bangladesh's political and economic rights that was taking shape.

Chapter 2

CONCEPT OF TWO ECONOMIES: FIRST ENCOUNTER WITH THE PAKISTANI ESTABLISHMENT

By the early 1950s, dissatisfaction was building up in East Pakistan[1] about slow development and inadequate investment in contrast to rapid progress in West in all areas of national life. The unhappiness was fuelled by the fact that the bulk of foreign exchange resources of East were used for the development of West. Also, there were great concerns frequently expressed in the press and on the political platform about the persistent and wide gap in the representation of East in all the branches of the policymaking machinery and administration.

2.1 A CRITIQUE OF PAKISTAN'S FIRST PLAN

It was against this background that the First Five-Year Plan (1956-1960) was formulated. At the request of the Pakistan Planning Board,[2] a conference of the East Pakistani economists was called at the end of August 1956 to elicit their views. The conference views were published in a report prepared by a group of economists, including myself. Among the members of the group were M.N. Huda, A.F.A. Husain, Mazharul Huq, M.T. Huq, A. Sadeque, M.A. Razzak, and A. Farouk (Appendix 2.1). The report forcefully put forth the concept of *two economies*, about which the East's economists had been airing

---

[1] Hereinafter referred to as East; similarly, West stands for West Pakistan.

[2] Renamed in the early 1960s as Pakistan Planning Commission.

their views for some time, as the legitimate and necessary framework for preparation of a Plan for the country. In the succeeding years, this approach towards planning and policymaking created a very serious divide between East and West. The latter apprehended that this was the driving wedge eventually to create two polities.

The concept was primarily based on the immobility of labour between East and West — two far flung parts of a country separated by more than a thousand miles — and on the high costs and the length of time needed for travel and for transport of commodities. Accordingly, interregional trade in Pakistan had the characteristics of international trade albeit with a common currency. This precluded labour in East from participating in the expanding employment and income opportunities in West that were created by high and increasing investment in West. The report concluded as follows:

> For the purposes of development planning, ... Pakistan should be conceived of as consisting of two economic units. However, for certain purposes, for example, mobilisation of internal and external financial resources, the country could be considered as a single economy.

> The primary requisite ... is a complete zonal breakdown of statistics, namely national income, balance of payments, and financial resources (internal and external). Without this, an economic plan in Pakistan does not reveal the fundamental and real issues.

The second important issue raised in the report was the impact of the nondevelopment expenditures (current expenditures of the central government) that were concentrated in West. These generated income in West through a multiplier effect, and stimulated urbanisation with the attendant external economies. This imbalance, the report insisted, needed to be corrected. This opened up an important and additional line of contention between East and West and caused considerable tension. Additional suggestions in the report were:

1. To accelerate the absorptive capacity of East for greatly expanded investment, it was necessary to establish federally managed and financed technical training institutions in East, federal financing of expanded training facilities undertaken by the provincial government in East as well as massive expansion of foreign

technical assistance to East, including training abroad on an emergency basis.

2. The central government should directly undertake development activities in an area set up separately in East under its own administrative control for this purpose. It should invest in industrial and other undertakings, including those in the field of education, health and other social sectors. This was particularly necessary in view of the effects of development and nondevelopment expenditures on economic growth ... such expenditures of the centre benefited mostly West .... A regional industrial development corporation should be set up by the federal government in East (this was done during the 1960s).

3. While the central superior service officers worked under the provincial government, their administrative and disciplinary control was vested with the central government. If the provincial government was to be primarily responsible for the formulation and the execution of development projects, the administrative and disciplinary control of the civil servants should be vested in the provincial government.[3]

4. The present deficiency of resources in East was conditioned by the past. Development expenditures and foreign exchange allocation during the past eight years had little reference to the resources, which were originating in East, or its requirements. To forget the implications of the past for the present and the future at the policymaking level would be extremely unwise and undesirable.

The reaction of the Planning Board to the report was a polite acknowledgement. It agreed that development expenditures in East needed to be increased and hoped that the East Pakistan government would be encouraged to prepare a larger portfolio of development projects. It also agreed to give due consideration to various specific suggestions. However, it was silent on the question of *two economies* or on the impact of nondevelopment expenditures.

---

[3] The senior officers in the government of East Pakistan were mostly from West Pakistan; they were members of the Pakistan superior services under the administrative control of the central government and, with exceptions, they paid scant regard to the interests of East. In the context of East-West Pakistan tension, their sympathies were with West.

The years between 1956 and 1958 were those of great political turmoil, and frequent changes in the government. The imposition of martial law in1958 dramatically changed the political context. East was effectively disenfranchised without even a semblance of its participation in the governance of the country. By this time, the legacy of the Language Movement as well as West's attempt to denigrate and discourage East's art, music, and literature as unIslamic and anti Pakistan caused growing tension between the two regions.

2.2 EAST-WEST PRICE DIFFERENCES MATTERED

In February 1960, a *Price Commission* was appointed by the central government to investigate the causes of a rapid rise in prices and to suggest remedies to stabilise the prices of essential consumer goods. The rise in prices was higher in East than in West but that was not a part of the terms of reference. Interestingly enough, the current and likely future impact of government expenditures (both development and nondevelopment) on prices was included. A veteran Muslim League politician, I.I. Chundrigar, headed the Commission. It was composed of three businessmen from West, two economists, A.I. Qureshi from West and myself from East, and one consumers' representative who happened to be a woman from East. There were three advisers to the Commission who were all officials of the central government, one of whom was from East. The Commission interviewed extensively, in both East and West, a large number of people from all walks of life specially traders, industrialists, and officials. Remarkable among the interviewees were two: the Martial Law Administrator in East and the World Bank Representative stationed in West. It was quite interesting that, as early as 1960, the government considered it important that a commission on a national economic problem should formally consult the representative of an external agency and the representative of the World Bank. This was not a policy problem that was a subject of discussion or any ongoing negotiations with the World Bank.

This was my first encounter with the civil service of West and its political Establishment, so-to-speak. Also, it was my first contact with the well known industrialists from West. The Commission provided an opportunity for an academic like myself to visit almost all the most important industrial establishments/factories in both East and West. In the course of my visits, I had discussions with owners and managers about their views on the economic situation and inflationary pressures. It provided an insight into how exchange controls, import and industrial licensing and fiscal policies worked in practice. The interviews revealed how and to what extent discretionary powers vested in the hands of bureaucrats could effectively determine the interregional and intersectoral allocation and use of resources. West's administrators and the leaders in industry, agriculture, and trade bargained in a complex variety of ways to attain their objectives i.e. profit and power. The industrialists did understand that East was a market for their surplus output as they expanded their capacity beyond the limits of the market in West. They, however, did not quite link the market in East to the need for increased investment or acceleration of income growth in East. Instead, they saw the opportunity of replacing foreign imports of East by exports from West as the driving consideration.

West's politicians and bureaucrats did not find any rationale for discussing or to be concerned with the severe inflationary pressure in East, which was much greater than that in West. They were impervious to the fact that East had a lower per capita income and the poor in East were significantly poorer than in West. The allocation of the dominant share of foreign exchange resources to finance West's imports of industrial raw materials and consumer goods exacerbated the shortage of essential imports in East. Also, the freight rates for interwing trade charged by the cartelised Pakistan shipping industry were high and were increasing over time, far out of line with comparable freight rates of international companies. This added to costs of as well as delays in imports from West. Neither would West agree that the large and continuing export surplus of East caused strong upward pressure on prices in East, strengthened by the impact of deficit financed government expenditures. Furthermore, import trade, including marketing and distribution channels in East, also concentrated in a few hands, mostly traders from West; concentration in trade at a time of supply scarcity led to speculative rise in prices.

In fact, West's representatives in the Commission were very annoyed by my insistence on a comparison of the level and the rate of increase in prices between East and West. Nor would they accept my proposal to examine the reasons for a higher rate of inflation in East and recommend special measures for its alleviation. After all, there were differences in prices of the same commodity between the various cities in West. In their view, there was no reason why price differences between East and West should not be dealt with in the same manner. The price level in any part of Pakistan or prices of a group of commodities in any city in Pakistan should be taken as the indicator of the level of prices in the entire country. After all, how could it be otherwise in one country? Any other suggestion on my part, they suspected, was a reflection of the "separatist" intention that lurks in the mind of every East Pakistani.

At one stage, I suggested that a minute of dissent from me on the issue would be in order. The chairman and the members were horrified at the suggestion. A compromise was reached that an explanatory note by me providing an analysis of the price situation, including its macro and micro aspects, in East and West, would be attached to the report as an appendix. Accordingly, the draft report along with my appendix was submitted to the government for information and use by a very few relevant ministries. It was thus meant for a very restricted circulation. When after a few months the report was finally published for wider circulation among all the government agencies and the public, the note was dropped.[4] I had naively assumed in good faith that there would be no manipulation or interference with the full contents of the report in its published version. This incident was an indication that a member from East could not trust the Chairman from West. Having failed to persuade me not to write the explanatory note, he then deviously suppressed it. The chairman and the members from West did not want any separate discussion of the problems of East, even though the note did not directly challenge or reject the findings of the main report. It was put more as a supplementary note or an addendum explaining the additional considerations that were to be taken into account in formulating policies. This was my first "brush" with the Establishment in West. Later during the 1960s when East-West issues were very much debated in the public, an explanatory note like this might not have been

---

[4] Ministry of Finance, Government of Pakistan, "Report of the Price Commission," June 1960, Karachi.

squashed. This incident, it appeared to me, was an indication of the sense of insecurity of the chairman and the members from West. The chairman was afraid that somehow a report prepared under his leadership, which carried a supplementary note, was a reflection on his ability to tame or manage a young, inexperienced and powerless academic from East.

2.3 FACE-TO-FACE WITH AYUB OF PAKISTAN

In order to add legitimacy to his usurpation of power and the introduction of an autocratic military regime, Ayub decided to accord a high priority to the task of accelerating economic development.[5] He recognised that there was the festering problem of regional income disparity and a persistent complaint of neglect or discrimination of East by the central government. As an extremely self confident general, he decided to "get to the bottom of the reason" for this complaint. He had, of course, convinced himself — as apparent from his later writings — that East's problem of underdevelopment was basically due to historical reasons, hostile natural environment, and endemic ineptitude and inefficiency. Even then it appeared to many in East that he was willing to listen and try to understand the problem and to deal with it if he could find "reasonable" ways of doing so.

Ayub had heard that Dhaka University economists were providing the economic analysis and arguments to support the complaints of East and that they had suggestions to deal with the problem of regional disparity. Therefore, they might deserve a hearing.[6] Accordingly, on 24th May 1961, a group of Dhaka University economists were invited to meet him for breakfast at the President's house in Dhaka. The group included M.N. Huda, A.F.A. Husain, Abdullah Farouk, and myself. It was a most unusual and interesting meeting. Flanked by his Secretary Q. Shahab, and Information Secretary, probably Altaf Gauhar (my memory is weak on this), he asked us to be frank and forthright in our diagnosis of the problems and our suggestions.

---

[5] Mohammad Ayub Khan assumed Presidency of Pakistan in 1968, after a short stint as Chief Martial Administrator and was finally deposed in 1968, following popular unrest and a *coup de etat*.

[6] Anwar Dil and Afia Dil, *Bangali Language Movement to Bangladesh,* Lahore: Feroz Sons, 2000, p. 363; also, Dr. A. Farouk, *Jiban Smriti,* 1988, Dhaka, pp. 101-103.

Azam Khan, the Governor of East Pakistan, was going in and out of the room when the meeting was under way. The delegation was encouraged to be uninhibited and to fearlessly express their opinions. Ayub was particularly interested in the concept of *two economies*, which, he thought, might also mean two countries.

All members of the group participated in the discussions. We explained and elaborated the comments provided earlier by the East Pakistani economists on the First Five-Year Plan. We explained to him that to decide on the location of development projects in East, for example, in industry, simply on the basis of direct cost comparisons between the two regions was misleading. It ignored the fact that past investments in West, specially in physical and social infrastructure, created a built-in cost advantage for West. The cost advantage in West due to such past investments needed to be corrected by accelerating investment, particularly infrastructural investment, in East. Unless it was done, income disparity between East and West would grow wider. Moreover, at the heart of the concept of *two economies* was the interregional immobility of labour. It followed, therefore, that investment in West did not enable the labour force in East to take advantage of the income and employment opportunities created in West. To concentrate investment now in the richer region of West, even if in many cases the short run returns were higher, and to wait until income and savings in West increased in the future significantly enough to allow a shift of resources to the poorer region of East, were not politically feasible or acceptable.[7] Various policy measures to accelerate investment in East were recommended. To suggest that the tax relief measures for private investment in East should be matched by similar measures in the less developed areas of West missed the very argument underlying the thesis of *two economies*. East was to be treated differently from West as a whole, including

---

[7] During the first decade after the creation of Pakistan, the struggle was to stop the outflow of resources, both domestic and foreign aid resources, from East. By the end of the 1960s, transfer of East's resources to West had become much less important. It was the larger share of foreign aid and the availability of captive market in East for the high cost-protected industries of West that were the driving force behind the rapid progress in West. Many thought that the rich West after it secured all the benefits of years of accumulated investment in human and physical capital, financed by resources drawn from both regions, predominantly from East, would be ready to transfer resources to East. That was not to be the case.

the underdeveloped areas of West, because of labour immobility between the two regions.

At the end, Ayub wanted each member of the group to write down his own analysis and suggestions. I felt very uneasy about it and in the light of my experience during the drafting of the report on the First Five-Year Plan, I was not sure that individual recommendations might not wander around without any order of priority or a central focus. What was needed at this early stage was to provide him with the main arguments and rationale for a change in policy.

A.F.A. Husain backed me in my perception that the submission of individual notes to Ayub would be less forceful than the united voice of a peer group. After all, some felt more strongly than others did and personal career ambitions or attitudes or commitments were different among the members. Accordingly, it was suggested by both of us that since the members of the group all had the same views overall (though not in the detail), it would be more convenient and helpful to Ayub if one consolidated statement was prepared. A short and succinct memorandum was what was necessary. Other members agreed and Ayub accepted this suggestion.

The memorandum entitled "Economic Development of East Pakistan" was drafted within a short period of time. As expected, the main burden fell upon me, the junior most and, therefore, the more enthusiastic member of the group. In preparation of the report, I sought and received enthusiastic help from other economist colleagues, some of whom were not present at the meeting (Appendix 2.2).

The memorandum elaborated on the concept of *two economies* and one polity. The main arguments were as follows:

1. As a basis for policy the concept of one economy as applied to Pakistan has been much more damaging to the welfare of the country as a whole and the majority of its citizens than the concept of two economies could have been. Location of development expenditures was not immaterial from the standpoint of the well being of the nation.

2. Disparity in income and development between the two wings had been on the rise. Higher level of development in West had been the result of past policies. It was due to higher levels of investment and nondevelopment expenditures in West, financed

by discriminatory allocation of foreign exchange, foreign aid, and liberal credit to private sector in West.[8] The indirect effects of nondevelopment expenditures such as defense, including the high level of defense related infrastructure, were significant. The multiplier effects of such expenditures generated increased income and resources in West, which in turn further fuelled private and public investment.

3. To treat the underdeveloped districts in West on a par with underdeveloped East as a whole and thus not to distinguish between interdistrict disparity from interwing disparity was tantamount to ignoring the fundamental characteristics of the bifurcated economy of Pakistan. The policy implications of the two types of disparity were radically different.

4. It was possible to reduce disparity in income and development between the two wings by appropriate policies. The criteria of income generation or employment creation should be considered for East and West Pakistan separately. Independent quantitative targets in terms of growth in income and employment for two regions should be articulated; two separate regional plans should be formulated to meet the independent targets for each wing. At the next stage, interrelationships and inconsistencies between the two sets of plans and programmes were to be sorted, dovetailed, and coordinated.[9]

5. Comparative costs of economic activities in the two wings should be analysed in their dynamic context, "taking into account the indirect effects of the future development of social overhead capital". The costs of production in East for commodities that were traded with West should be compared not with the absolute

---

[8] The central government argued that contrary to what East claimed about East transferring resources to West, it was the latter which was making transfers to East. This was attempted to be shown by straightforward comparison of the sources of collection of central revenues and the location of central expenditures. The memorandum went at great length to prove the fallacy of this reasoning and the consequent misrepresentation of facts. In fact, in a separate appendix, the memorandum suggested the appropriate framework for the analysis and the estimation of the transfer of resources.

[9] It should be noted that those were the days when the state and state sponsored private sector, rather than the free market, played a dominant role in the economy. Moreover, five-year and annual plans were the standard tools for investment decisions and programming.

costs in West, but with the landed costs of imports from West.[10] The pressing need for expanding employment opportunities in East should, wherever deemed necessary, modify cost comparisons.

6. There should be a constitutional provision, which should make the equal development of both wings of Pakistan, let us say within a period of 20 years or so, the major responsibility of the central government. The report recommended that, on certain assumptions, the proportion of total national investment in East should increase from 30 percent in 1960-65 to 60 percent in 1975-80.

Our strategy was to take Ayub at his word about accelerating development in East. Given his faith in strong central government as the *sine qua non* of a viable united Pakistan, the memorandum suggested ways in which to reduce disparity and promote a rapid development in East within his framework of a proactive central government.

The next step in our recommendations was more explosive. If, however, Ayub decided that the central government could accept no such responsibility, a satisfactory solution to the problem of regional disparity would be to separate the resources of each wing completely and to permit each to develop its own resources.[11] A complete decentralisation of resources and economic policies would involve the following:

1. The centre would only have the functions of defense, foreign affairs, and aspects of interwing communications.

---

[10]West went so far as to suggest that since the unit costs of road construction were higher in East than in West, there should be higher investment in road construction in West. The economists in West knew very well the elementary economic proposition that costs had to be compared with benefits and what mattered was cost-benefit ratio comparison. This did not deter their bureaucrats or politicians from making these false comparisons so that in discussion with the policymakers in West, we had to counter them over and over again.

[11]The entire memorandum is reproduced in the Appendix. A pertinent question has been asked as to whether there was a complete unanimity of views among the signatories to the memorandum. Only one person, because of his political views, could have questioned the suggestion in the report about weakening the Centre to such an extraordinary extent. However, in view of the rest of us being strongly in its favour, one possible voice of dissent was too weak to assert itself. It must be also noted that there were economists outside this small group, who might not have so readily accepted such a suggestion. Also, it must be said that many others had not thought through very carefully the implications of such a weak centre in 1960, but had nonetheless gone along with this suggestion.

2. While there would be a single currency for the whole country, the policies of credit control and monetary policies, including advances to provincial governments, would be decided by the local Board of Directors of the State Bank of Pakistan in the two regions.

3. All government revenues as well as domestic and foreign exchange resources would accrue to the respective regions. Regions would contribute to the expenses of the centre on the basis of ability to pay and benefits derived from central expenditures.

The suggestion for such an extreme form of regional autonomy was provided for the first time to Pakistan's supreme leadership by a group of academic economists from East without any direct coordination or consultation with the politicians in East. Significantly, this suggestion was derived from the concept of *two economies*. The demand for a diminished central government had its precedent in the election manifesto of the United Front Party, which won elections in East Pakistan in a landslide in 1954, defeating the Muslim League. It had proposed that the Constitution should provide for a federation in which the centre would only have three subjects: defense, foreign affairs, and currency.

We received no reply to our memorandum from the President or from his Secretariat. From private sources, we learned that the report was sent to the Finance Minister and the Deputy Chairman of the Planning Commission for their examination and comments. On their advice, Ayub apparently concluded that the economists in East were in cahoots with the power hungry politicians in East who would like to separate East from West. They were taking on the role of political agitators rather than that of professional economists. Accordingly, no further contact or exchange of views with them was productive or desirable for the President.

Interestingly enough, I later learned that the Finance Minister, M. Shoaib, gave a copy of the memorandum for comments to the World Bank Representative, David Gordon, who was personally and institutionally very close to him. This was the period when Pakistan was a favourite of the Western donors, specially the US and the

World Bank. Shoaib eventually became the first Vice President of the World Bank from the developing countries. Gordon wrote a set of comments on our memorandum for consideration by Shoaib.[12]

As expected, Gordon questioned the claim that there was a widening in income disparity. Moreover, West had built-in advantages unrelated to the policies pursued in the past. He doubted whether the thesis regarding the transfer of resources either way could be conclusively proven and recommended additional empirical work on the subject. Thus, he contested the very foundation of the East-West conflict since the early 1950s. He did not, however, refute and was indeed silent on (a) the framework provided by the East memorandum for estimating resource transfers, and (b) the actual estimate of transfers. This was surprising; probably, he wanted to keep his options open. He emphasised the limited absorptive capacity of East as the main hindrance to a large increase in investment. He suggested various micro policies in the field of agriculture and industry to stimulate investment in East such as tax relief, less restrictive credit facilities and a more liberal system of industrial licensing — all designed to attract private capital from West to East. Consistent with his overall approach to the East-West problem, he argued for a greater integration of East and West by reducing the cost of shipping between the two wings, which was inordinately high compared with other similar shipping routes.

Gordon was silent on the argument made by East that whatever initial advantages West had, were not being offset by special affirmative measures in favour of East. Instead, these were strengthened by discrimination against East. Investment in human capital and physical infrastructure in East continued to lag significantly behind West. He was not in favour of a policy of promoting East Pakistanis at an accelerated rate in senior bureaucratic positions in East. He did not appreciate why the dominance of the bureaucrats from West in East and in the central government contributed to discrimination against East. He could not accept that officials from West felt alien in East; that they were a product of the sociopolitical milieu which led to the estrangement between the two regions.

---

[12]David Gordon, *Economic Relations Between East and West Pakistan*, Rawalpindi, Pakistan, December 2, 1961. Gordon gave a copy of his comments to me much later.

At the end, Gordon came out with broad semi-philosophical observation and advice: "the strains inherent in the process of development
were bound to affect the relations between the two wings. Their
interests and ambitions would certainly be in conflict in some degree
for many years to come. The government should expect to confront
this problem for the indefinite future. Instead of underestimating or
suppressing it, the government should clarify the facts and identify
the real grievances and emphasise the benefits of unity."

Many of Gordon's comments confirmed what was expected of a
foreigner who lived and worked closely with West. He had only a
fleeting acquaintance with and no first-hand knowledge of the reality
on the ground in East. He naturally shared to some degree the
preconceptions and views of West. Apparently, he had inadequate
understanding of the sociopolitical forces that were bedevilling
East-West relations at the time. He was, however, in favour of
further study and analysis to examine the real grievances since the
grievances articulated by East did not seem to him acceptable.
Shoaib's policy to keep the representative of the World Bank fully
informed and involved in the East-West controversy was easy to
understand. Pakistan depended heavily on military and economic
assistance from the Western countries. The World Bank through the
"Aid to Pakistan" consortium coordinated all development assistance.
He wanted to ensure the support and understanding of the Bank and
donors in countering what West considered the "unjustified" grievances
of East. After all, the economists from East were raising issues,
which, if accepted by donors, would affect the flow of external
resources to West. It took another decade and the crisis of 1971 to
convince donors that East was right and indeed had given sufficient
early warning which donors and West had decided to ignore.

The issues raised by economists from East starting in the mid-
1950s continued to play a dominating role in East-West relations
during the next decade. To these we now turn.

Appendix 2.1

Report of the Special Conference of Economists of East Pakistan on the Draft Five-Year Plan and Connected Papers August-September 1956

Department of Economics, University of Dacca
September 1, 1956

Pakistan Economic Association

The Chief Economist, Planning Board
Government of Pakistan, Karachi

Dear Sir,

I have to inform you that in accordance with the wishes of the Planning Board a Special Conference of the Economists of East Pakistan was held in Dacca from the 24th to the 28th of August, to discuss the Draft Five-Year Plan of Pakistan. The Conference held eight sessions which were presided over by Dr. Mazharul Huq, Mr. Abdur Razzak, Mr. A.F.A. Husain, Mr. M.T. Huq, Mr. M.L. Qureshi, Dr. M.N. Huda and Dr. Nurul Islam.

By a special resolution on the 29th August 1956, the Conference requested the Chairmen of the different sessions to prepare a report generally reflecting the views of the Conference and to sign the Report on behalf of and in the name of the Conference.

A special Sub-Committee consisting of the Chairmen of the sessions and the members named below was set up by the Conference to look into the Report prepared by the Drafting Committee and to ensure that it correctly reflected the views of the Conference.

Members of the Special Sub-Committee (In addition to the Chairmen of the sessions).

1. Dr. A. Sadeque.
2. Mr. Sakhawat Husain.

3. Dr. A. Farouk.

4. Mr. A.N.M. Mahmood.

5. Mr. Safiullah.

6. Mr. Muhammad Husain.

7. Mr. Shafiqur Rahman.

The Drafting Committee held two sessions and prepared a Report. This Report was then considered by the Special Sub-Committee in two separate sessions. These sessions were attended by all members of the Sub-Committee. After careful consideration, the Report was finalised and unanimously adopted. Those who have signed the Conference Report include:

1. Dr. Mazharul Huq.

2. Dr. M.N. Huda.

3. Mr. A. Razzak.

4. Dr. Nurul Islam.

5. Dr. A. Sadeque.

6. Dr. A. Farouk.

7. Mr. A.N.M. Mahmood.

8. Mr. Safiullah.

9. Mr. Muhammad Husain.

10. Mr. Shafiqur Rahman.

Mr. A.F.A. Husain and Mr. M.T. Huq had to leave Dacca before the Report was ready for signature, but they are in full agreement with the draft of the Report.

Mr. Sakhawat Husain could not sign the Report because he had to leave the meeting earlier but before leaving he had affirmed his complete agreement with the draft of the Report.

In its concluding session, the conference unanimously adopted the following resolution in appreciation of the initiative taken by the Planning Board to consult academic opinion.

This Conference of the Economists of East Pakistan places on record its great appreciation of the opportunity provided to them by the Planning Board and the Pakistan Economic Association for discussing the Draft Five Year Plan and offering their comments and views on how the Plan can be improved upon.

Yours faithfully
(Sd.) M.N. Huda
Secretary
Pakistan Economic Association

Report of the Special Conference of Economists of East Pakistan on the Draft Five-Year Plan

The Planning Board requested the Pakistan Economic Association to convene a Special Conference of Economists of East Pakistan, so that they may discuss the Draft Five-Year Plan. It is perhaps for the first time that Government or any organ of government has sought the opinion of Economists in this province on questions of such magnitude. We are grateful to the Planning Board for giving us this opportunity of discussing the Plan in this Conference. We hope it will be possible in future to associate academic opinion at an earlier stage of the work of planning.

The Conference was held in the Assembly Hall of the Fazlul Huq Muslim Hall, University of Dacca, from the 24th to the 28th of August, 1956. It was attended by over 75 Economists from different parts of the Province, including all the senior teachers of Economics from the first grade colleges in East Pakistan, the Dacca University, the Rajshahi University and the officers of the Provincial Statistical Board.

The Conference held eight Sessions in all in the course of which a wide range of topics was discussed including (1) the problem of economic development with special reference to East Pakistan, (2) economic and social objectives of the Plan and the criteria for the determination of priorities, (3) targets for various fields such as agriculture and village AID, industry, water and power development, and transport and communications, and social services, (4) resources for development, (5) allocation of resources on a geographical basis, and (6) implementation of the Plan. The Conference expressed great concern over the slow rate of progress in the past in East Pakistan and wanted the pace of development to be accelerated to the maximum extent possible. This is the great need of the province. Many of the participants expressed disappointment with the Plan because of its deficiency from the view point of the interests of East Pakistan. Immediate steps should be taken to give effect to the desire of the Planning Board to expand the programme for East Pakistan.

In our report we have attempted an overall assessment of the Draft Plan and highlighted some of its principal features. This involves an examination of (1) the way in which the task of planning is to be approached in Pakistan in the context of the peculiar features of its economy, (2) fundamental assumptions of the Plan, (3) the suitability and the manner in which the statistical materials or information have been used in the Plan and (4) lastly, some aspects of the problem of implementation.

For purposes of development planning, particularly for the creation of employment opportunities, Pakistan should be conceived of as consisting of two economic units. However, for certain purposes, for example, mobilisation of internal and external financial resources, the country could be considered as a single economy.

The problem of planning in Pakistan is best approached by considering the basic characteristics of the two wings particularly the heavy pressure of population in East Pakistan, the comparative lack of employment opportunities, and the high degree of immobility of resources between the two wings. Due to these factors and the lack of balance between the two wings in the matter of development in the past, planning should aim at uniform rate of development for the entire country by taking into account the zonal peculiarities and deficiencies. On this basis the first exercise should be to draw up a hypothetical plan which would fulfil the basic objectives of balanced economic development and which would serve as a guide to the primary planning units in submitting plans of the right magnitude. The problem of bottlenecks, the difficulties in formulating such plans in terms of concrete development projects, should then be taken up.

The primary requisite of planning in our opinion is a complete zonal breakdown of statistics, namely national income, balance of payments, and financial resources, internal and external. Although such statistics were not made available to the Planning Board, these could surely have been prepared by the relevant statistical organisations, central and provincial. This must be done at an early date. Without this, an economic plan in Pakistan does not reveal the fundamental and real issues. In this connection we note that the zonal statistics presented in the working papers of the Planning Board require further careful examination. These are obviously administrative statistics of limited significance for economic analysis.

We are, however, aware of the difficulties in preparing such statistics but this useful task should be undertaken. A detailed report of the progress so far achieved giving zonal breakdown for that part of the plan-period which is already over, would have been very helpful.

The effect of developmental expenditure can be readily traced wherever it takes place. The geographical distribution of nondevelopment expenditure which is, at the present moment, heavily concentrated in West Pakistan, is not without economic significance. Nondevelopment public expenditures by generating income through multiplier effect and promotion of urbanisation with its attendant external economies do promote development. The possible adverse effects of an increase of nondevelopment expenditure are expected to be mitigated by the fact that such increases in East Pakistan are likely to promote a greater monetisation of the economy and also to be backed by a considerable amount of imports either from the west wing or from abroad. This aspect of the effects of nondevelopment expenditure should be reflected in the recommendations of the Planning Board to the Government of Pakistan.

One main bottleneck in planning in East Pakistan has been a shortage of technical personnel. This has been due to the large disparity in *per capita* grants to universities and training institutes as between the two wings in the past as well as the disparity in the facilities offered for training both at home and abroad. This tendency should be reversed by making far greater allocation to East Pakistan for extending the internal training facilities as emergency measures and for training facilities abroad. The establishment of federal technical institutes in East Pakistan would also be a step in the right direction. There must also be a greatly expanded programme of technical assistance to East Pakistan from foreign countries. As there is a controversy over the capacity of East Pakistan to absorb development expenditure, we feel this question should be examined and the findings be made public.

A regional planning organisation should be set up in each wing for the formulation, appraisal, and general supervision of the implementation of development projects. The Planning Board should be a permanent body with its status raised. It should function directly under the National Economic Council. The Planning Board should be responsible for submitting annual progress reports to the Parliament.

In view of the fact that provincial planning machinery has in many cases been weak, the targets fixed under the Plan should continue to be re-examined from time to time throughout the Plan-period with a view to accelerating the rate of progress.

In order to expand development in East Pakistan, an area should be set apart and placed under the administrative control of the Central Government solely for the purpose of development. In this area, the Central Government should be expected to establish a University, specialising in Technical Training. It should also establish and develop industrial and other undertakings. This is particularly necessary in view of the effects of development and nondevelopment expenditures on economic growth. Such expenditures of the Central Government in Karachi benefited only West Pakistan in the past.

In view of the fact that the progress in development in East Pakistan has been impeded because of centralisation of administrative decision in the Federal Capital in such fields as issue of import licenses and control of capital issue, it is suggested that in all such cases, where control has to be exercised by the Central Government, administration must be so decentralised that policies can be expeditiously executed at the provincial level.

A regional industrial development corporation should be set up in East Pakistan. All Pakistan organisations like the PIDC must in formulating their development projects, have as their basic aim the task of expanding activity in the less developed areas.

An examination of the cost structure of the existing industries seems to be in order. The sheltered market provided by the high level of existing import restrictions does not provide any incentive either for achieving efficiency in the cost of production or its location from the economic point of view. It is also noted that such sheltered markets provide scope for the emergence of private monopolies and consequently monopolistic price policies. In so far as import restrictions are maintained, some machinery, may be the Tariff Commission equipped with technical staff, be given the responsibility of watching over the cost situation and the price policies of these industries.

Under the present constitution, while the Central Superior Service officers work under the provincial governments, their administrative and disciplinary control vest with the Central Government. If Provincial Governments are to be primarily responsible for formulation and execution of development projects, the administrative and disciplinary control of the civil servants should vest in the respective provincial governments. The civil servants must, of course, continue to enjoy the same safeguards against arbitrary action by the Government, as they do now, but at the provincial level.

Larger employment opportunities should be provided to East Pakistanis in government service, both civil and military.

On the basis of information available we are of the opinion that external assistance will be essential for implementing development programme in either wing.

Before we conclude, it is perhaps necessary that we should remember that many of the participants in the Conference referred to what happened over the years before the Plan period. This has figured so largely because what planners should try to aim at is to undo the effects of the neglect shown to East Pakistan in the pre-Plan period and also because the recommendations of the Planning Board itself have been conditioned by the commitments of the pre-Plan period. Secondly, so far as we calculate resources today in either wing the products of past policy enter into such calculation. The present deficiency of resources in East Pakistan is conditioned by our past. The development expenditures, foreign exchange allocation, etc. during the first 8 years have had little reference to the resources which were originating in East Pakistan or its requirements. Today it is only meet and proper that our future policy should take note of the past neglects and should aim at making up the deficiency. To forget the implications of the past for the present and the future at the policymaking level would be extremely unwise and undesirable.

Dacca, August 31, 1956.

(Sd.) M.N. Huda.
(Sd.) Mazharul Huq.
(Sd.) A. Razzak.
(Sd.) Nurul Islam.
(Sd.) A. Sadeque.
(Sd.) A. Farouk.
(Sd.) A.N.M. Mahmood.
(Sd.) Safiullah.
(Sd.) Muhammad Husain.
(Sd.) Shafiqur Rahman.

Appendix 2.2

Memorandum to Ayub on Economic Development
of East Pakistan

The economy of Pakistan displays certain important characteristics which distinguish it from most other economies of the world. The country is divided into two widely separated regions between which there is very little mobility of labour and imperfect mobility of capital and of goods and services. Apart from these basic characteristic conditions in each region are widely dissimilar. East Pakistan is heavily populated and is overwhelmingly dependent on agriculture for its living while West Pakistan is sparsely populated and has considerable and growing industrial activity. West Pakistan is much more developed than East Pakistan in nearly all fields. As a result, the per capita income in West Pakistan is about 50 percent higher than that in East Pakistan.[13] Other evidences of the disparity of development between the two regions are provided by the amount of Central Government tax revenue raised in the two wings, the contribution of West Pakistan being near four times that of East Pakistan, the extent of building construction, number of persons living in urban areas, cars and telephones in use, the mileage of roads and railways, the consumption of power, iron, cement etc. in each wing of the country, West Pakistan far surpassing East Pakistan in each of these indices.[14]

Because of these regional peculiarities which mark Pakistan out as an almost unique case among the countries of the world, it has been argued by many persons that it is more appropriate to consider Pakistan as consisting of two economies instead of a single economy. In other words the country should be considered as two producing and consuming units rather than one single unit. According to this view commodities produced in one wing cannot be made available to

---

[13] This is based on the estimate of Mr. Norbye, a former Advisor to the Planning Commission, as contained in a paper (dated 31.7.59) received by the present group from the Ministry of Finance.

[14] A few important indices of regional disparities are indicated in Annex A.

people in the other wing except at a much higher cost in the vast majority of cases. The bulk of the commodities instead of being imported from the other wing can be produced in each wing more cheaply or imported more cheaply from a foreign country. More significantly, so far as employment is concerned, even considerable development in one wing will have no perceptible effect on employment in the other wing. Proponents of the two economy concept would necessarily plan economic development on the basis of each region separately.

Those who try to argue that Pakistan consists of a single economy do not seem to have tried to define the concept or spelled out its implications rigorously. They seem to identify the concept of a single economy with that of political unity. Just because Pakistan is a single state, according to them, it is of necessity a single economy. They seem to ignore or minimise the importance of the factor of immobility of labour, imperfect mobility of capital and high cost of transportation of goods. According to them, investment should be made wherever the return is higher even if it is in the more developed regions so that national income may grow at as high a rate as possible. According to them one should think in aggregate terms. Planning should be done by considering the country as a single producing and consuming unit. So long as national income and employment in the country as a whole increase, any deterioration in income and employment in any particular region or at any rate their failure to improve should not cause any concern. Further, goods should be produced wherever they are cheapest to produce irrespective of their cost of transportation to the ultimate consumer and no comparison should be made of the price the consumer has to pay with the cost to him of similar goods which could have been imported from foreign countries for that region.

As a basis for policy the concept of one economy as applied to Pakistan has been much more damaging to the welfare of the country as a whole or the largest number of its citizens than the concept of two economies could have been. Official policy in Pakistan in the past has been based on the assumption of a unified, integrated economy as is to be found in most countries of the world where imbalance in development as between regions tends to be corrected by a movement of labour from the less to the more developed regions. The concentration of investment in the past, both public and private, in the capital city and in West Pakistan appears to highlight the belief of the authorities that the location of development activities is immaterial from the standpoint of the well being of the nation. They have in fact tried to justify disparity in development as between the two major regions of the country by putting forth the analogy of other countries where similar disparities exist. All that can be stated is that while there has been and there will be natural correctives to regional disparities in the case of other countries, in the case of Pakistan these will not only persist but will in all probability widen in future. Further, while regional disparities in other countries have been generated under laissezfaire conditions and recent policy in these countries has been in the direction of minimising these disparities, it can be demonstrated that in the case of Pakistan such disparities have, in fact, been largely the result of government policy. There is also evidence that this disparity is on the increase and the Second Five-Year Plan would accentuate it further.

Reasons for the Disparity in Development as between East and West Pakistan

Economic development is at bottom the function of capital formation. Assuming that suitable projects have been drawn up, economic development would result from investment in social overheads, such as roads, railways, power generation, education, public health and also in agriculture, industry, etc. There is evidence that since independence investment, both public and private, in social overheads, as well as in other fields have been much higher in West Pakistan than in East Pakistan.[15] Central Government's development as well as other expenditure has been consistently higher in West Pakistan. Provincial Governments' expenditure has also been higher in the West because larger public and private investment has generated income which has augmented the resources available in the hands of the provincial government. Further, the bulk of foreign aid has been canalised to West Pakistan, East Pakistan being allocated only a small share of

---

[15]In the First Five-Year Plan period the development expenditure in East Pakistan has been estimated to have been half of that in West Pakistan.

the total.[16] The administrative structure of East Pakistan has been weak and its own resources poor. Besides, top civil servants in East Pakistan being not drawn from the local people until very recently have not considered the problem of economic development of the province as really important. Both the West Pakistan Government and the Central Government have directed their attention mainly to the development of West Pakistan.

It is sometimes argued that the development of West Pakistan has been due primarily to private enterprise and the lack of development in East Pakistan has been due to the inactivity of private enterprise in that wing. This, however, is not altogether true. Massive investments have been made in West Pakistan on public account and a much smaller amount on this account in East Pakistan. The import policy of the government has also been operated to the advantage of West Pakistan. Vastly more imports have been permitted in West Pakistan than in East Pakistan, enabling the trading class in West Pakistan to accumulate considerable wealth which they have subsequently invested in industry. The much larger imports of machinery in West Pakistan than in East Pakistan have also facilitated capital formation in the West. The concentration of large-scale government expenditure in West Pakistan of a nondevelopmental nature, on account of defense and central government administration, has also benefited private enterprise in West Pakistan. Apart from persons directly employed in defense and central services, many industries and services in West Pakistan have benefited from this Government expenditure. Building industry has flourished; contractors and industrialists of all descriptions providing goods and services for defense requirements have made large incomes. The creation of bank credit on an extensive scale in the private sector has added to the resources available in the private sector in West Pakistan. Even in the public sector in West Pakistan large portion of public expenditure was met by deficit financing. However, it needs to be emphasised that all the development expenditures in West Pakistan were crucially conditional upon availability

---

[16]According to data supplied by the Finance Ministry, foreign aid allocation up to 30th June, 1960, excluding project aid was $1288.4 million for East Pakistan and $2619.2 million for West Pakistan and Karachi. Foreign loans and credits to 1960-61 amounted to $519.8 million for West Pakistan, and $127.8 million for East Pakistan. The relevant tables however contain large "unallocable" sums which reduce the utility of the data.

of foreign exchange to the West from (a) East Pakistan's surplus foreign exchange earnings and (b) foreign aid. They were matched partly by deficit financing in private and public sector and partly by the reinvestment of domestic profits earned by commercial importers and later on by industrialists enjoying the highly protected domestic market, of which East Pakistan forms a significant part.

It is often tried to justify the disparity in development expenditures as between East and West Pakistan on the ground that East Pakistan contributes only 20 percent of the revenues of the Central Government while West Pakistan contributes 80 percent. It is also tried to establish on the basis of a report prepared by a panel of economists set up by the Planning Commission in 1959 that whatever development has taken place in East Pakistan has been due to a net transfer of resources from West to East Pakistan. These statements are made without qualifications so that they are quite misleading. It is necessary to examine this argument at some length.

It is necessary to emphasise that under the present system of collections of Central Government revenues the collections do not necessarily measure the actual contributions of each wing. It is well known that many firms having their principal office in Karachi pay income tax on their entire business including that earned in East Pakistan in Karachi. Even if a correction is made on this account the contribution of each wing would not indicate the real burden of taxation borne by it. For example, excise duty and sales tax paid on manufactures in West Pakistan which are exported to East Pakistan are actually borne by consumers in East Pakistan. It should also be emphasised that the amount of tax revenue raised in either wing is dependent not only on the general development of that wing but on the policy of the government. For example, as large imports have been permitted by the government in the western wing rather than in the East, collections of import duties and sales tax in that wing have automatically gone up although such imports in West Pakistan have been made possible by the diversion of East Pakistan's foreign exchange resources to West Pakistan. The position regarding collections of import duty and sales tax would have been entirely reversed if East Pakistan could have utilised her foreign exchange earnings fully for her own requirements. Concentration of Central Government nondevelopment expenditure in West Pakistan automatically means more tax collection from recipients of income in that wing either as government servants or as contractors or businessmen catering to government requirements. However, even after all corrections are made West Pakistan definitely contributes more to the revenues of the Central Government than East Pakistan. As against this, the expenditure of the Central Government incurred in East Pakistan has also been very small as compared with that incurred in West Pakistan.[17] It is quite likely that the actual current or revenue expenditure of the central government located in East Pakistan in less than the amount of tax revenue collected in that wing in the narrow sense used by the Central Finance Ministry.

The so-called thesis of transfer of resources from West to East Pakistan is dependent on the following assumptions. (i) Both West and East Pakistan should contribute equally to the nondevelopment expenditures of the Government of Pakistan in spite of the much lower per capita income in East Pakistan. (ii) Both West and East Pakistan should contribute equally to these expenditures although the bulk of these expenditures being concentrated in West Pakistan do not benefit East Pakistan directly. (iii) Inter-regional trade balance of each wing can be set off against its external balance. (iv) There is no such thing as foreign aid. It is quite obvious that points (i) and (ii) are highly debatable if not untenable assumptions. It is against all accepted canons of sound taxation that a poorer region should contribute to the exchequer to the same extent as the richer region, particularly when the poorer region gets much less benefit from Central Government expenditure than the richer region.

East Pakistan has a surplus in foreign exchange earnings which is not offset by the deficit it incurs in her inter-zonal trade. It is quite obvious that interwing trade is carried on at greatly inflated prices thanks to the high cost of transport between two wings. In order to get a correct picture import surplus should be deflated by an appropriate amount or alternatively East Pakistan's foreign exchange earnings should be valued at the market rate before deductions are made on

---

[17]Unfortunately, data supplied by the Central Finance Ministry show the greater part of the central expenditures as "unallocable." For the purpose of the analysis here the actual location of these expenditures is important.

account of import surplus and payment for services etc. from West Pakistan. It should also be noted that the goods supplied by West Pakistan to East Pakistan are of inferior quality compared to possible imports from abroad. Further, they do not in most cases serve East Pakistan's requirements for development and therefore should be regarded as substitutes for direct utilisation by East Pakistan of her foreign exchange resources for import of developmental goods.

These corrections and allowances would greatly deflate the so-called amount of net transfer of resources from West to East Pakistan even if there was no other factor involved. However, if we take into account the factor of foreign aid the entire thesis of transfer of resources from West to East Pakistan falls to the ground. It is surprising that this crucial factor escaped the attention of the panel of economists whose report has been quoted to support an altogether erroneous thesis. The fact is that the country as a whole is heavily dependent on foreign aid for economic development. The total investment in the country is substantially higher than domestic savings. In the case of West Pakistan the difference between actual investment and internal resources has been higher than in the case of East Pakistan where the total volume of investment has been much smaller. It therefore follows that so long as West Pakistan itself is heavily dependent on foreign aid for its development there cannot be any net transfer of its own resources to East Pakistan. All that could be argued is that a part of foreign resources which West Pakistan has received has been transferred to East Pakistan. A technical note on interwing transfer of resources is given in the Annex B to this paper.

Problems of Policy

It may be assumed that for the sake of national unity, disparity in development between the two regions is not desirable. So long as either wing of the country has a markedly lower rate of development than the other wing, its population will feel embittered and frustrated. We can, therefore, assume that it should be one of the major objectives of policy to promote a balanced development of both the wings of the country. The First Five-Year Plan and also the outline of the Second Five-Year Plan did in fact regard the removal of disparity as between West and East Pakistan as one of the major objectives of the plan. Unfortunately, this objective appears to have been dropped in the final version of the plan. In other words, although Central Government policy from now on will be concerned with the acceleration of development in the undeveloped regions of the country both in East and West Pakistan it will not necessarily be concerned with the narrowing of the gap in development as between East and West Pakistan. In this respect, however, the policy laid down by the government for tax holiday in which the whole of East Pakistan has been placed on the same footing as the major portion of West Pakistan with the exception of the few industrialised areas is open to serious objection. The real need is to ensure that development activities in East Pakistan are made more attractive to the private investor than development activities in West Pakistan as a whole. If a West Pakistani investor receives equal economic incentives for investing in some regions of West Pakistan as in East Pakistan, there is no reason why he should prefer to invest in East Pakistan. Although actual private investment in East Pakistan permitted by the Government as per Industrial Investment Schedule has shown some acceleration in the recent past, it appears that the schedule, even if implemented, instead of reducing disparity in private investment, is likely to enhance it since the acceleration in absolute terms in West Pakistan has been much greater.

    If balanced economic development of the two regions is to be the object of policy what prospects are there for this objective to be realised by centralising economic decisions as at present? Although it is true that central government policy since partition has more than anything else promoted the wide disparity in development between the regions, there is nothing inherent in a centralised form of government or central planning to promote such disparity. It is possible under central planning to pursue an appropriate policy which would eliminate or greatly narrow down the disparity between regions. This implies that in the matter of planning development of two wings, or in the location of economic activities a comparative cost study of existing and potential activities in their dynamic context, taking into account the indirect effects of the future development of social overhead capital, should be made and that considerations of expanding employment opportunities should, wherever deemed necessary, modify comparative cost considerations. In comparing costs of a project between East and West Pakistan the high cost of transportation and handling of the finished project involved in interwing shipment should properly be taken into account. Such comparisons will reveal that the costs of production of many commodities in East Pakistan will be less than the landed costs of similar commodities from West Pakistan which includes not only their cost of production in the West but also their cost of transportation and handling in shipment. Furthermore, in calculating comparative costs a sensible approach would be to adopt 'social pricing' of factors of production as distinguished from market pricing. If this is done, labour intensive projects would be less costly than in West Pakistan because although labour is much more abundant in East than in West Pakistan, for well known reasons, the existing wage rates in the two wings do not adequately reflect the relatively greater abundance of labour in East Pakistan.

It must also be emphasised that the criteria of 'income generation' and 'employment creation' have to be considered for East and West Pakistan separately. In other words, while planning economic development separate quantitative targets in terms of rate of growth of income and employment have to be formulated for East and West. The detailed development programme can then be formulated and executed to attain these stated objectives for the two wings separately. In other words, planning for two wings has to be separated to that extent and can be brought together as two integral parts of a National plan for Pakistan. The interrelationship between these two plans would have to be sorted out in terms of individual programmes always keeping in view stated targets to be achieved for each wing. It is most probable that conflicts or competitive schemes would emerge in the course of dovetailing and co-ordinating these two plans and in allocating resources. Here the guiding principle should be the *reduction of disparity between levels of income* which can only be attained by higher rates of growth in the East than in the West.

Judging by the performance of the Central Government in the past, the proper safeguard against one region falling behind the other in development would be to embody a constitutional provision which would make for more or less equal development of East and West

Pakistan, so as to ensure more or less equal standards of living for the citizens of the two wings in a reasonable period of time say 20 years or so, as a major responsibility of the Central Government. The Central Government will be expected to pursue appropriate policies to achieve this end, which would invariably mean in the initial years a large increase in investment in East Pakistan so that the actual investment will be much higher than in West Pakistan. For example, under various assumptions regarding capital output ratio and population growth in each region, if disparity is to be reduced in 20 years, it has been estimated that the proportion of total national investment in East Pakistan may have to increase from about 30 percent in 1960-65 to around 60 percent in 1975-80. That the application of the principal of parity in development as between regions may prove difficult in practice should not be denied. However, it should be possible to work out a formula which would keep disparities in development within reasonable limits of tolerance. A committee of economists and statisticians might well go into the problem and work out a definite principle of action.

If, however, it is felt that the Central Government can accept no such responsibility, a satisfactory solution of the problem (of regional disparity) at any rate — one which is likely to be acceptable to the population of each wing — would be to separate the resources of each of either wing completely and permit each to develop its own resources. A complete decentralisation of economic policy will involve the following things.

The Central Government will be entrusted with the functions of defense, external affairs and aspects of inter-zonal transportation. All other subjects will vest in the two provinces. Each wing will contribute to the expenses of the Central Government on the basis of the generally accepted principals of taxation, via., ability to pay and benefits received from Central Government expenditure. All resources including foreign exchange resources will be retained by the provinces and utilised for their development projects and other purposes. There will be a single State Bank and currency for the whole of the country, but policies of credit control, and advances to the provincial government etc. will be decided by the local Board of Directors of the State Bank acting under the direction of the respective Finance Department.

If the above suggestions regarding complete separation of revenues as well as responsibility for development are accepted, an expert commission could work out the details. The present group is also studying this problem and might be in a position to submit a paper on the subject as and when required.

Annex A

Regional Disparities (Indices)

		East Pakistan	West Pakistan
Area (000 Sq. miles)		54	310
Population (million)	1951	42	33.8
	1961	51	43
Density of population	1951	777	109
	1961	944	138.7
Urban population No. in million	1955	1.9	6
P.C. of total		5	18
Estimated total regional income (1957/58) million Rupees		10,000	11,500
Estimated per capita income (1957/58) (Rupees)		213	305
Estimated total development expenditure (Rs. crore, by location, 1955-60)		370	730
Tax collections (Rs. crore by location, (1959/60)		56	144
Foreign exchange earnings (1959-60 – Cr. Rs.)		129	88
Agricultural income as P.C. of total regional income (%)		60	40
Large scale industry, 1959-60, estimated contribution to national income (crores)		560	1,690
Per capita consumption of electricity, in K.W. units, 1960		12	53
Total railway tract route mileage, 1960		1,712	5,327
Railway rolling stock, 1960, locomotives		472	878
Wagons Couches	in terms of 4 wheelers	19,662 2,780	31,330 4,854
No. of personnel employed in railways 1960		55,000	104,000
No. of motor vehicles (trucks, buses, taxies, cars 1960)		12,213	76,207
No. of telephones, 1960		12,500	62,500
No. of colleges		79	130
Engineering students graduating		100	300
No. of hospital beds		7,650	20,350
No. of offices-scheduled banks		106	277
Senior civil servants, 1955 under secretary and up		51	690
Secretary		0	120

Annex B

A Note on Interwing Transfer of Resources

It follows from well known principles of economics that a comprehensive balance of payments account of East Pakistan, including all the visible, invisible, current and capital items, would record all the conceivable transfer of all possible resources between the two wings. A schematic presentation of such a balance of payments account would be as follows:

Balance of Payments of East Pakistan

Credit	Debit
1. Exports to (a) outside world. Exports to (b) West Pakistan.	1. Imports from (a) outside world. Imports from (b) West Pakistan.
2. Invisible receipts on services from abroad- (1) travel, (2) transportation and shipping charges i.e. freight and passage earnings, (3) Insurance payments, (4) Investment income, interest, dividends, and profits, (5) Miscellaneous agency services, royalties, films, rentals, educational expenses, other remittances, etc.	2. Payments abroad on these invisible accounts.
3. Invisible receipts from West Pakistan as above.	3. Invisible receipts from West Pakistan as above.
4. Central Government's expenditure in East Pakistan both for non- developmental and development purposes.[a]	4. Net Tax, nontax and capital receipts of the Centre from East Pakistan.
5. Central grants and advances in East Pakistan Government.	5. Liability of East Pakistan for a share of the Central Government expenditure in East for defense and administration.
6. West Pakistani capital investment in East Pakistan.	6. Private capital investment by East in West.
7. Foreign Aid due to East Pakistan.	

An attempt may be made to draw up an actual balance of payments table by including figures for those items for which estimates are

---

[a] Total nondevelopment expenditure:
Excluding defense = 1963 crores
Total defense expenditure = 1131 crores

available. The trade figures in the following table are based on C.S.O. returns while figures of invisible are based on State Bank of Pakistan returns for the country as a whole.

Balance of Payments of East Pakistan (1949-1960)

(in Rupees)

Credit	Debit
1. Balance of trade with overseas	+429 crores
2. Balance of trade with West Pakistan	-255 crores
Net trade balance	(169 if reduced by 1/3)[i] + 174 or 260 crores
3. Balance of invisible payments with overseas[ii]	-57 crores
Net current account	+117 or 203 crores
4. Balance on invisible payments with West Pakistan	X_1
5. Balance of Centre's total expenditure in and grants and loans to East over its total receipts from East	X_2
6. East's share of Central expenditure in West	X_3
7. Balance of West's private capital investment in the East over the latter's investment in West	X_4
8. Foreign aid and capital utilised in East Pakistan	X_5

In order that there is a net transfer of resources to the geographical area of East Pakistan, it is necessary that $(117 \text{ or } 203 \text{ crores} - X_1) < 0$.

This is on the assumption that X_1 is negative and greater than 117 or 203 crores. The magnitude of the transfer measured by this difference will be equal to [a]balance of central governments' total expenditure in and grants and loan to East (X_2), plus[b] excess of West Pakistani investment in East over that of the latter in West (X_4), plus[c] foreign aid and capital utilised in East Pakistan (X_5). This grants the contention of the central Finance Ministry that X_2 is positive i.e. expenditure of all kinds by the centre in East exceeds its receipts of all kinds from the East. If [d]is sufficient to meet the deficit, then on a net basis in real terms i.e. in terms of goods and services there can be no transfer

---

[i] This is necessary so as to allow for the higher cost of imports from West Pakistan as compared with that from foreign countries.

[ii] Total credit (all Pakistan) on invisible items + 209 crores.
Total debit (all Pakistan) on invisible items excluding government expenditure abroad on defense and foreign affairs. – 381 crores. Net debit is 172 crores.
Let invisibles be divided between East and West in the ratio of 1/3 & 2/3, so that deficit for the East 57 crores.

from West to the East. If, on the other hand, (117 or 203) > X_2 then the question of transfer of resources to the East does not arise. On the contrary, in this case East Pakistan transfers to West. However, it may then be argued that there is an obligation on the part of East to meet a part of the central expenditure in West on defense and civil administration. But then the quantitative magnitude of this share of East should be much lower than that of West considering that per capita income of West is 50% higher than that of East. In this case a transfer from outside (not necessarily from West Pakistan) to East implies that (117 or 203 – X_1 – X_3) must be negative where X_3 is East's economically justifiable share of central expenditure in West. It is worth mentioning in this connection that the popular method followed in Government documents supplied to us of dividing such central expenditure on a 50:50 basis is economically indefensible. Moreover, the method of showing a large part of central expenditure as unallocable in these documents is liable to the same criticism and is misleading. The location of central expenditure within Pakistan is certainly identifiable and only expenditure incurred abroad cannot by physically located in Pakistan. The recognised principles of Federal Finance should take care of the allocation of the latter between East and West. If foreign aid utilised in East meets the deficit, then there is no transfer from West. Moreover, what is important in this connection is not foreign aid and capital actually utilised in East but East's legitimate share of foreign aid which should be far in excess of her actual share. The question of West's transferring resources to East arises only if such a large share of foreign aid is unable to meet any probable deficit, indicated above. The same problem can be examined from another angle i.e. by examining the resources originating in each wing and expenditures (public and private) undertaken in each wing. The total domestic resources available in West Pakistan fall short of the investment (private and public) undertaken in West Pakistan. This precludes any possibility of West's transferring any of her own resources to East.

Chapter 3

ECONOMIC DISPARITY: COMMISSIONS AND PANELS

3.1 FIRST FINANCE COMMISSION: EAST-WEST SPLIT ON RESOURCE ALLOCATION CRITERIA

By the early 1960s, the Second Five-Year Plan was launched. Disparity became the predominant agenda in the economic and political discourse between East and West. It dominated the press and the platform. In October 1961, Ayub announced in a public meeting in Dhaka his intention to appoint a Finance Commission that would, among other things, examine the ways and means of removing disparity between the two regions.[1]

The most important issues to be examined were the following: (i) allocation of revenue sources between the centre and the provinces; (ii) allocation of revenues from the divisible pool of taxes,[2] collected

---

[1] The commission was composed of ten members, five from each wing. The members from East were the following: D.K. Power (Additional Chief Secretary, Development, East Pakistan government), M. Raschid (Managing Director, Industrial Development Bank of Pakistan, later on Governor, State Bank of Pakistan), S.A.F.M.A. Sobhan (Joint Secretary, Ministry of Industries, Pakistan, later on Secretary of Planning of Pakistan), Mr. S.A. Khair (Finance Secretary, East Pakistan government, later on Secretary, Government of Bangladesh), and myself. The members from West were: M.A. Majid (Finance Secretary, Pakistan), M.M. Ahmed (Additional Chief Secretary, West Pakistan, later on successively Deputy Chairman of the Pakistan Planning Commission and Adviser to Yahya during 1970-71), A.G.N. Kazi (Finance Secretary, West Pakistan and later on Deputy Chairman of the Pakistan Planning Commission), M. Zahiruddin Ahmed (Joint Secretary of the Government of Pakistan), and Dr. S.A. Meenai (Economic Adviser, State Bank of Pakistan and later on Vice President of the Islamic Development Bank in Saudi Arabia). Mr. Majid was the Chairman.

[2] The divisible pool consisted of the specific sales tax, and excise duties, the proceeds of which were divided between the centre and the provinces of East and West according to some

by the centre but shared with the provinces; and (iii) the allocation of
the surplus at the centre after deducting its expenditures from its total
receipts from (a) tax proceeds left exclusively with the centre such as
the customs duties plus (b) the centre's share of the divisible pool of
taxes, foreign aid, and domestic borrowings.

The members from West argued for reducing the share of the
centre in the sources of revenue as indicated in item (i) and (ii)
above, since it would serve two purposes. First, the fewer the central
sources of revenue under item (i), less resources it would have and
smaller would be the central surplus. Accordingly, there would be a
smaller amount to be distributed to the provinces; for example, if
sales taxes were shifted to the provinces it would reduce central
revenue and therefore the possibility of a revenue surplus to be
distributed to the provinces would be reduced. Second, the smaller
the divisible pool of taxes under (ii), less there would be to be shared
with the provinces. This would result in West getting a considerably
larger share of the total resources since taxes under (ii) collected by
West would remain with West. As a result of more than a decade of
larger investment and revenue expenditures in West, financed partly
by transfer of resources from East, income and consumption were
higher in West than in East. This naturally led to higher tax proceeds
in West, which West did not now want to share with East.

The members from East decided to proceed from a radically new
basis and argued that the proceeds of all the central tax and nontax
receipts should be put in a pool. All central expenditures should be
deducted from such a pool, with the surplus to be distributed
between the regions. In the opinion of East, the principal task facing
the Commission was to recommend the criteria for the distribution of
this surplus between the two regions. I found the distinction between
the so-called divisible or shared taxes or other taxes, an artificial one
meant for administrative purposes devoid of any economic logic or
analytical basis. Members from East readily agreed. For example, the
incidence of all taxes levied on foreign imports in West, when
reexported to East either directly or indirectly in the form of goods
produced in West using foreign imports, fell on East. Similarly, the

---

administrative formula, periodically adjusted with reference to such factors as the amount of
collections in each province, and assessment of needs, etc.

incidence of excise taxes on goods in West that was reexported to East also fell on East.

As for the allocation between the provinces, members from East suggested that the central revenue surplus should be allocated between the provinces in the ratio of populations weighted by the disparity in per capita income i.e. the excess of income of West over that of East.[3] It was a self adjusting formula so that as the disparity in per capita income was reduced over time, the weight to be given to this factor would be reduced. If the capital output ratio was higher in East, the decline in income disparity over time would be slow because the return in investment in East would not be high enough to reduce income disparity fast enough. This would provide an incentive on the part of all parties to increase the efficiency of investment in East.

This simple and very effective formula was worked out in the course of a discussion that I had with Richard Gilbert, Head of the Harvard Advisory Team in the Pakistan Planning Commission during the 1960s, when I was serving as a member of the Finance Commission. I designed alternative formulas and invited his comments on their pros and cons. Eventually, in the light of his very constructive comments, I decided to choose this particular formula and to convince my colleagues in the Commission. The issue of disparity and interregional allocation of investment resources did not escape the attention of all those, including foreign advisers, who were involved in advising on economic policies in Pakistan.[4] The traditional approach used by East in the past was to argue for an allocation on the basis of the ratio of population in the two regions. The challenge was to devise a relatively easy formula based on the population ratio plus an additional factor to take into account the need to reduce disparity in per capita

[3] The population ratio was 55 percent in East and 45 percent in West. Income disparity: West's ratio to East was 1.33. Therefore, under this assumption allocation to East would be $(1.33) \times 0.55 = 73$ percent.

[4] The Harvard Advisory Team was considered by East to be a major supporter and defender of Ayub's economic policy regime during the late 1950s and 1960s. The Team was an effective advocate in the community of donors for a substantial flow of economic assistance to Pakistan. However, at times, individual members of the team had demonstrated sympathy for and understanding of the East-West disparity issue. By the end of the 1960s, the team was beginning to appreciate the gravity of the problem and its political implications. Richard Gilbert was quite forthcoming in his discussion with me about the alternative ways in which interregional allocation of resources could be designed to provide an edge in favour of East so as to ensure a rapid acceleration of investment in East.

income. This was a straightforward formula and easily defensible in political debates.

The disparity-weighted population ratio was easy to understand and implement. The author persuaded the members from East to accept the formula. D.K. Power who as the Additional Chief Secretary of East, virtually acted as a leader of the members from East, was delighted to obtain a simple approach to determine the regional allocation of resources.[5] He took the lead in proposing the formula in the Commission meeting and argued as follows: the first component, i.e. the population ratio, reflected the current situation without reference to history; and the second component, i.e. the weighting by per capita income, took account of the underdevelopment in East for the last 14 years.

East further explained that the concentration of central nondevelopment expenditures in West, four times as large as in East, conferred on West the following benefits: (i) higher income and employment generation and consequent expansion of market demand; (ii) expansion of physical infrastructure such as roads, transportation and communication facilities; (iii) rapid urbanisation including development of cantonment towns due to concentration of defense establishments and defense related industries and services; and (iv) proximity to the central government including its licensing and regulatory institutions that stimulated and facilitated the location of private sector activities as well as a substantial flow of refugee capital (the refugees from India at partition).[6] To offset these built-in advantages enjoyed by West, there should be an additional compensatory financial allocation to East. The amount of such additional allocation should be ideally large enough to offset the cumulative effects of massive nondevelopment expenditures in West during the past two decades. At a minimum, the amount of financial compensation plus the actual amount of nondevelopment expenditures in East should be equal to half the total of central nondevelopment expenditures. In the end, East did not press the point in the interest of reaching an agreement at least on

---

[5] David Khalid Power was British and was a member of the British Indian Civil Service prior to the partition of India in 1947. He opted to serve in Pakistan after independence and served in East Pakistan. He converted to Islam.

[6] All these issues were raised in economists' reports as mentioned in Chapter 2.

the allocation of resources for development expenditures. But West was in no mood to reciprocate the gesture.

There were some less consequential items such as past debts of the provincial governments, guidelines for future borrowing from the central government and from the State Bank of Pakistan, and criteria for central *grants in aid* to the provinces. East argued that the principle of allocation of resources enunciated above should apply also to the allocation of funds derived from internal borrowing and foreign aid.

East also proposed that the Constitution of Pakistan should incorporate the following provisions: (a) the objective of eliminating disparity within a period of 25 years; (b) annual appraisal of the application of the above formula in the allocation of the centre's resources; and (c) a mechanism to review progress toward the removal of disparity, including an examination of how development resources had actually been allocated and utilised. The idea of putting a time limit was to make removal of disparity a matter of urgency and to maximise efforts to that effect in the next few years.

West opposed all the above suggestions. West did not agree with East's suggestion about the composition of the divisible pool. Instead they insisted on allocating the proceeds of individual central taxes between the provinces on the existing basis with some minor administrative adjustments. They wanted to maintain the *status quo*. They disagreed with the principle of resource allocation between the provinces on the basis of a disparity-weighted population ratio.

In fact, West went so far as to suggest that the allocations for West should be larger than for East for a multiplicity of reasons. First, West needed very massive investments for years to come on account of the Indus Replacement works[7] and projects for the prevention of water logging and salinity crucial for West's agricultural progress. Second, increased investment in less developed regions of West were necessary to bring them to the level of more developed regions. Third, higher population growth in West required a higher investment to maintain not only its past growth rate in per capita

---

[7] Construction of canals and dams to augment the flow of water in West to replace the flow that was lost to India as a result of the division of waters in the rivers common to both India and Pakistan.

income but also to increase it somewhat above the past to maintain what they called the "growth momentum".

East argued in vain that investments in flood control and irrigation in East were of paramount importance, no less if not more than similar investments in West, specially because very little was done in the past. We failed to persuade them that the problem of intraregional disparity in West was of a different nature altogether than that of East-West disparity and that it should be resolved by reallocations between subregions of West. The argument of maintaining the "growth momentum" in West was curious at a time when the Commission was expected to concentrate on generating a "growth momentum" in East for the first time. East contended that absorptive capacity is itself a function of large investment in social and economic infrastructure. This should be strengthened by a substantial use of foreign technical and consultancy services to increase the capacity of East to absorb larger investment resources, specially in the private sector.

As seen in Chapter 2, the issue of less developed regions in West was a constant refrain, whenever interwing disparity was discussed. They declined to recognise that geographical proximity and mobility of labour and capital between the subregions of West contributed to the integration of the economy of West. As for the urgency for maintaining the growth momentum in West, we explained that the suggested criterion for resource allocation was not meant to reduce the income level of West. Per capita income in West would neither decline nor remain the same under our suggested formula for resource allocation. As the population of a region increased as a result of a high population growth rate, it would receive a higher allocation. The impact of population growth would be accommodated automatically in the formula in its first component. At worst, what could happen was that the rate of growth rather than the level of per capita income would be lower than in the past.

In order to protect growth in West, East suggested that the amount of total development expenditures in West during the Third Five-Year Plan (1965-70) should not fall below that of the Second Five-Year Plan if adequate resources were available. Development expenditures in West were financed partly by the centre and partly by the provincial government in West. Therefore, the provincial government could ensure that its own resources plus central expenditures maintained the level of past development expenditures. In case the central resources available to West under the allocation criteria were not adequate to maintain the past level of expenditures, West should either raise resources on its own or should be prepared to sustain a lower growth rate. In the event of a slowdown in West's growth rate, it should be ready to accept such a slowdown in order to offset past imbalances in the interest of national harmony.

West was unwilling to accept the constitutional obligation of eliminating disparity within a definite time horizon. At best, they would agree to the objective of removing disparity but without any time frame. According to them, it was for the Planning Commission to formulate, taking into account constraints and possibilities in both the regions, a programme for accelerated growth in East. They had no objection for annual or five-yearly reviews of progress in removing disparity. In other words, they were willing to grant more of the same with some efforts to accelerate development in East without any prior commitment of resources. A commitment to allocate resources on a predetermined basis would have, *per force*, focused attention on finding all possible ways and means for increased investment in East, including efforts to greatly expand its absorptive capacity.

After a series of meetings, it was obvious that a deadlock had been reached. East proposed that under the circumstances there was no need for the Commission to meet as whole and that East would submit a separate report on the subject. Thus, for the first time in Pakistan, a high level government commission on East-West issue reached a state of serious confrontation and an impasse.

Two important features relating to the work of the Commission are worth mentioning. First, the role of the Ministers from East in the Ayub Cabinet. I kept close contact throughout with one of them, i.e. A.K. Khan, the Minister of Industries and a renowned industrialist who had known me since my student days. He was well known to Ayub when the latter was the regional head of the army in East in the early days of Pakistan. He was also a close acquaintance of the Finance Minister, Mohammed Shoaib, the principal architect of Ayub's economic policy. He encouraged me throughout to put my views and suggestions forcefully to the Commission. He felt that Ayub was genuinely interested in dealing with the issue of disparity and would therefore seriously consider our recommendations. It was essential that Ayub got a clearly articulated elaboration of the case for East and a concrete set of recommendations. Since the Cabinet would consider the Commission's report and its recommendations, he and others from East would be able to argue the case as well with the Ministers from West and the President. The other two Ministers from East interested in the Commission's deliberations were Justice M. Ibrahim, the Law Minister and a former Vice Chancellor of Dhaka University and Hafizur Rahman, the Commerce Minister. As a professor at Dhaka University I had worked under the former and known him well. I had known the latter as well. I had also kept contacts with both of them and appraised them of the progress of the Commission's work.

Justice Ibrahim was very critical of Ayub and West in general. He found their attitude toward East very unflattering and, in fact, often humiliating. He used to tell me about the various notes he had written to Ayub on different occasions protesting Ayub's views and decisions. He was very supportive of the members from East in the Commission vigorously stating their views and defending their arguments. He eventually fell out with Ayub and spent long spells in East away from Islamabad, the capital city, while he was still a member of the Cabinet.

Being a professor in those days — surprising, as it seems now — accorded a certain degree of immunity from arbitrary action even from a powerful military regime. I was at Dhaka University, the centre of intellectual ferment and in a city which was the political heartland of East. As a teacher, I was in contact with a highly politically conscious, active and organised student community that was in the vanguard of movement for the redress of East's grievances. This permitted me a certain degree of freedom of action in not only expressing my views vigorously but also in openly lobbying with the Ministers in the Ayub Cabinet as well as with the activist professionals and news media in East. Other members from East were naturally constrained by being bureaucrats; some of them were in the central government under the direct control of the military regime. All of us were, however, united in our views and recommendations that were put forward in the report.

The second important feature of our work in the Commission was the role played by Power. He was an extremely articulate, clearheaded, and confident person without any sense of insecurity. I had known him before we were both members of the Finance Commission. Earlier, in his capacity as the chief official in charge of development in East, he had requested me to undertake a study on the domestic and foreign exchange potential and development potential of East. This was intended to provide a framework for his *ad hoc* negotiations and bargaining with the central government on the size of annual and five-year development programmes in East. This was by coincidence a good starting point for me in getting involved in a detailed analysis of financial resources, both domestic and foreign, of East. I came to learn the details of various sources of central and provincial revenues, both tax and nontax, and criteria used for revenue allocation between the centre and the provinces. In this study I worked out alternative scenarios of income growth and investment requirements in East. During the preparation of this study, I had many opportunities for intensive discussions with Power on the development problems of East as well as East-West economic relations. We developed a degree of rapport and a great deal of mutual trust and confidence.

The task of the Commission members from East was organised in such a manner that each would initiate ideas and prepare notes in his area of speciality or experience. Elaboration of analytical issues such as the concept and measurement of income disparity, incidence of taxes in the two regions, effects of development and nondevelopment expenditures as well as a simple but analytically defensible formula for the allocation of resources between East and West were my responsibility. Other members had their own areas of speciality. Some were well informed about the details of individual taxes, the rationale and criteria for their division between the centre and provinces and ways of streamlining the tax structure. Some others were well versed in details of central revenue and capital expenditures, functions of central departments and agencies and the implications of their decentralisation. The arguments and possible counter arguments with reference to the issues under consideration were discussed in the meetings that we held under the leadership of Power, preparatory to the full Commission meeting. He coordinated and formulated a coherent and compelling set of arguments from the point of view of East. During the meeting of the full Commission, Power would often make the main arguments. Following him, individual members from East would intervene to supplement and elaborate upon the main argument as well as to counter the arguments from the other side, joined by Power as necessary.

It was clear to the members from West that East's entire performance was well orchestrated. The members from West did not expect this degree of cohesive performance from East. They held Power responsible for this feat in leadership. The leadership of Power gave other officials confidence, while peer pressure worked as well. The members who were employed in the central government did not want to be isolated from other members from East or exposed to their compatriots in East for not having cooperated in a common cause. Furthermore, they had known me as an academic who was an unconstrained and risk-prone activist member of the East economists' group, which was well known for its role on the issue of East-West economic relations. In the politically charged climate in East and in the light of expectations raised by Ayub's speech about the Commission, they were able to shed their fear of displeasure of or reprisal by their superiors in the central government.

The reaction of the Pakistan Establishment to the stand taken by the members from East was one of great unhappiness and annoyance. Shoaib, Finance Minister, and Ayub's economic Czar and supreme confidant decided to handle the troublesome characters first. If they would be reasonable and could be made to see the light, then it was expected that the rest on their own would not create a crisis and would avoid confrontation. After all, they were all civil servants or finance officials with their future careers under his control. He handled the two "problem cases" separately.[8] To me he laid out the prospects of a bright future that was awaiting a young economist, during a nice tête-à-tête over tea in his house. It was a very soft approach with a

---

[8] However, I had no knowledge of what pressure was brought to bear on the other members. Unlike Power, none of the others took me into confidence to tell me whether or not West also sought to manipulate them.

velvet-gloved hand. He tried to reason with me that to get involved in the political frays of the time when emotions were running high, at the cost of a sober and analytical approach, appropriate to an academic, was not an ideal role for a "well regarded" economist like me. More importantly, it was not very helpful to the cause of East. I should appreciate that the central government under Ayub was genuinely interested in taking steps to remove disparity. I should seriously concentrate on devising ways to increase the capacity of East to launch and implement a larger development programme.

Power was more crudely handled, as he related to me later on. He was told that for a very senior officer of the Pakistan Civil Service Establishment to identify so openly and in such a partisan way with the political interests of a particular region was undesirable. It did injustice to the concept of a politically neutral civil servant — an ideal to which all civil servants, in the opinion of Shoaib, should try to adhere. After all, Power had a very bright future and expected to secure a very senior and important assignment in the central government. To sacrifice such a future for short term popularity in East was foolhardy. This blandishment did not go down very well with Power. After all, he was a member of the much-vaunted British Indian Civil Service for which very few Muslims in the subcontinent had qualified. Shoaib belonged to the Pakistan Audit and Accounts Service, which was distinctly lower in rank and order in the civil service hierarchy.[9] However, Shoaib had political power and authority.

Shoaib's approaches not withstanding, we persisted in our efforts in arguing how the prevailing resource allocations were discriminatory and inadequate for achieving accelerated development of East. The members from East met independently and submitted a separate report incorporating the suggestions outlined earlier. The report of the members from East concluded as follows: *"We, for our part, feel strongly that the most crucial issue facing Pakistan today is the growing economic disparity between the two provinces, and that the present time, when a new constitution is on the anvil, is the most opportune moment for a fresh and dynamic approach to this problem, which has for so many years plagued relationships between the two provinces*

---

[9] Power was eventually transferred to a very insignificant post in the central government i.e. to the Ministry of Labour and Social Welfare.

and coloured, if not embittered, so much of the country's political and economic thinking."[10]

As a sequel to the Finance Commission and under continued pressure from the politicians and public opinion in East, the Constitution of Pakistan in 1962 contained a provision for removing disparity in per capita income between the two provinces as well as between the various areas in each of the provinces within the shortest possible time. Repeated protests from East notwithstanding, the primacy of the problem of interregional disparity was purposely diluted by putting it on an equal footing with intraregional disparity. West ignored the compelling proposition that for the purposes of policy and programmes, reducing intraregional disparity was entirely the responsibility of each region and was not within the purview of the central government. No explicit time limit for removing interregional disparity was, however, accepted. Nor was any predetermined formula for the allocation of resources, domestic and foreign, between the two regions recognised. It was argued that it was the responsibility of the Planning Commission to work out or formulate the appropriate size and composition of development programmes for East and West for realising the objective of removing disparity.

These were precisely the suggestions of the members from West in the Finance Commission, rejected by the members from East, but readily adopted by President Ayub. This was the limit of West's concessions in response to fourteen years of struggle by East. In the end, the only achievement by East at that time was the eventual constitutional recognition of the disparity problem. As the old adage goes, the devil was in the details. Actual policies and programmes for the removal of disparity were left to constant arguments as well as endless bargaining and negotiations between the two regions over the next decade.

---

[10]*Report of the Five Members of the Finance Commission.* Dhaka, Government of East Pakistan, 1962. Around this time, the Deputy Chairman of the Pakistan Planning Commission described some of the economists from East as "minions of foreign powers" in a widely publicised radio broadcast. Such was the measure of exasperation, if not desperation, of the West establishment that it stooped so low as to vilify the economists of East for their relentless espousal of the cause of economic justice for East. *Report of the East Pakistan Economists (Advisory Panel for the Fourth Five-Year Plan, 1970)* quoted the above statement and remarked as follows: It is a sad commentary on those who have led the nation that after nine years those words of the five dissident members of the Finance Commission hold only with greater force and a panel of economists sits today to repeat them. Will an impatient nation give us yet another opportunity? (p. 97).

3.2 SECOND FINANCE COMMISSION: CONTROVERSY CONTINUED

There were many ways to undermine the constitutional provision for the removal of disparity. Illustratively, the Second Finance Commission was appointed in 1964 as a follow up to the constitutional provision. The Commission was to review the progress in removing disparity during the Second Five-Year Plan period (1960-65) and to recommend how resources were to be allocated during the Third Five-Year Plan (1965-70) to make progress towards achieving this objective. The Commission had very restricted terms of reference. The first part of the terms of reference was to examine the statistical data for the past two or three years. It was not to analyse the policies and programmes affecting the disparate development of the two regions. The second part was to take note of resource allocation decisions already taken by the highest decision making body in the country i.e. the National Economic Council. Moreover, this time the composition of the Commission was so designed as to make the deliberations professionally as weak as possible. It was packed with nonprofessionals. Also, it was intended to preempt any unforeseen move on the part of East. This was done by heavily weighting the membership in favour of Ministers rather than independent technocrats and/or bureaucrats who were not directly involved in decisions on resource allocation. In other words, it was mostly the executives and the policymakers directly involved in resource allocation, who were asked to judge their own performance and decisions. Moreover, instead of an equal participation from both regions, members from West were in the majority, including the Chairman.[11]

Right at the outset of the Commission's deliberations, questions were raised about the appropriate method of measuring income disparity. This was obviously a diversionary tactic. Shoaib, assisted

---

[11] In the first Commission one of the members from West was the Chairman; this time the Chairman was Shoaib who was supported by four members from West of whom two were Ministers of the provincial government of West. The other two were M.M. Ahmad, the central Finance Secretary who was also a member of the First Finance Commission and M.L. Qureshi, Chief Economist of the Planning Commission. Members from East included Hafizur Rahman, Finance Minister of the provincial government of East; S.A.F.M.A. Sobhan, Secretary of the Pakistan Planning Commission; M. Raschid, Managing Director of the Industrial Development of Pakistan; and myself. Three of us, Sobhan, Raschid and I were also members of the First Finance Commission.

by the Chief Economist of the Planning Commission, launched a long discussion on how to measure disparity. Measurement was never the issue during the past two decades. It was the principle that was endlessly debated by economists, bureaucrats, and politicians. By consensus, disparity was measured during the past years by the absolute excess of per capita income of West over East. The percentage excess of per capita income of West over East was also used an additional measurement of disparity. West now proposed that the only reasonable way to measure disparity was the extent of variance of per capita income of either province from the national average i.e. the percentage shortfall of per capita income of East from the per capita income of Pakistan as a whole. In other words, if the percentage shortfall in East's per capita income from the national average was reduced, disparity was being removed.

West's objective was very clear because the proposed method would produce the lowest number for the measurement of disparity. When East objected to this method, West provided two additional measures i.e. percentage shortfall of East's per capita income below that of West, using West's income as the base, and the percentage excess of West's per capita income over that of East, using East's income as the base.[12] The second measure would produce a greater disparity than the first, while the third measure would produce a still higher number. The strategy was to demonstrate that there were so many ways to measure disparity that one was not quite sure about its magnitude or the exact extent of its change over time; only the direction of change could be discerned unequivocally. These gimmicks and games were played not only in order to minimise or create uncertainty about the measured extent of disparity but also to avoid the simple measurement of absolute difference in per capita income between the two regions. When members from East objected, the Chairman ruled that all the three measurements — but none based upon absolute difference in per capita income — should be used. This was to ensure that the confusion would be confounded, when several measures for income disparity were presented to the politicians.

---

[12]For example, assume West = 200, East = 100, National Average = 150. Disparity between National Average and West is 200/150 = 1.33, and for East it is 100/150 = 0.67. Each of these two measures of disparity is lower than the direct measurement of disparity: West/East = 200/100 = 2; East/West = 100/200 = 0.5.

The fact that the Commission could not agree on a single measure of per capita income disparity, kept the door open for East to go on using the absolute difference in per capita income or the percentage excess of per capita of East over that of West, as the measurement of disparity.

On the issue of whether disparity was reduced during the Second Five-Year Plan, West argued that it was not one of the objectives when the Second Plan was formulated. Therefore, the Plan should not be judged with reference to this objective enunciated at a later stage. However, even though figures were not available for the entire five-year period, the percentage disparity in per capita income for the years for which data were available, when measured by all the three methods, declined. In response to the counter argument by East that there was at the same time a small increase in the absolute disparity in per capita income, West made a concession. It agreed that since data were only available for three out of the five years and there were already bad harvests in one year, the report's observation on the decline in percentage disparity in per capita income was tentative and should be treated with caution.

Regarding forecasts for the Third Plan period, the Commission agreed that it was too early to derive any conclusions on what might happen to income disparity. The outline of the Third Plan, which was just published, allocated for the first time a larger amount of development expenditures to East than to West. Prior to the appointment of the Commission, the National Economic Council (NEC), which was a Cabinet Committee headed by the President, had already approved the outline of the Third Five-Year Plan, including regional resource allocations. Three of the Commission's members, central and provincial Ministers of Finance, were also members of the NEC and therefore, party to the NEC's preemptive decision. Consequently, it was beyond the purview of the Commission to recommend any modification of the regional allocations. The Commission's discussions on the Third Plan were superfluous and a nonevent, except to record the decisions of the NEC.

The Planning Commission was engaged in working out the detailed programmes as well as expected income growth in different sectors in order to estimate their aggregate impact on per capita income in each region and hence on disparity. Expectations were raised, however, that larger allocations to East than to West, assuming equal productivity of investment in both regions, might cause greater income growth in East. A recommendation was made that region wise statistics on the breakdown of national income should be greatly improved and expanded to facilitate future work reviewing progress in the removal of income disparity.

The attempt to treat interregional disparity at par with intraregional disparity made during the first Finance Commission was not given up. On the contrary, it was incorporated in the Constitution that the reduction in disparity, both interregional and intraregional, should be the objective of policy. The statistics in per capita income by districts in either region were difficult to come by, let alone data on their evolution over time. Therefore, very little could be said on the extent of income disparity and its development over time between the various areas or districts within each of the provinces. The Commission accordingly recommended that the provinces, in collaboration with the central government, should collect the necessary statistics in order to analyse the changes over time in district level per capita income. Under persistent pressure from East it was eventually agreed that indeed the removal of intraregional disparity was an obligation of each of the provincial governments. There was a belated recognition that it was not a matter of negotiation or resource allocation between the two provinces. Each province had the responsibility to allocate its resources in such a manner as to reduce interdistrict disparity.

By the mid-1960s, many of us realised that the East-West battle conducted by means of arguments and counter arguments in commissions/committees over a period of two decades had been inconclusive. The struggle in commissions/committees over financial allocations and associated policies and programmes was only a part of the process. But given East's lack of decision making and political power, it was an important part. It had an educative and a consciousness raising function among the population of East; it provided ammunition for the political activists and leaders to galvanise public opinion. A realisation gradually dawned that whatever allocations were made in the Plans and broad agreements on policies reached, they were not necessarily implemented. In the course of implementation, East and

Centre, dominated by West, were bogged down in endless conflicts and controversies on individual projects and specific policies. There were complaints by East about delays in the approval of projects and in the release of funds by the central government. While private investment in East was acknowledged to be deficient, preferential measures to simulate it were inadequate or slow in implementation. West resented any strong preference in favour of East as being discriminatory to its own economic interests. The mutual recrimination between the central government and East was only to be expected. In view of an absolute concentration of political power in the hands of West, the majority in East had to be a supplicant for concessions from the reluctant minority ruling class. This was a recipe for bitterness and frustration in a divided nation.

3.3 EAST PAKISTAN ECONOMISTS' PANEL ON FOURTH PLAN

One more attempt was made by economists from East to reach an agreement with their counterparts in West. This time it was not a government commission/committee but an unofficial advisory panel of economists invited by the Pakistan Planning Commission on the occasion of the preparation of the Fourth Five-Year Plan (1970-75). In this report, East Pakistani economists (Mazharul Huq, Akhlaqur Rahman, Anisur Rahman, Ghulam Rabbani, Rehman Sobhan, and myself) made a very substantial concession. We did not insist on the principle of resource allocation between the two regions on the basis of the disparity-weighted population ratio. We suggested that during the Fourth Plan we were willing to accept an allocation on the basis of the population ratio. We made a last ditch effort to reach a compromise by making concessions but West's economists rejected it. We were desperate to somehow start the process of reversal of past trends in the allocation of development expenditures by shifting it somewhat in favour of East. The Panel stated "... *earlier this process of reversal starts, the easier it is, for the greater the delay, the greater will be the extent of inflexibilities created in the more developed region and the greater the pressure generated for the maintenance of the momentum of high growth rate achieved in that region through past inequity in allocation... In doing so (proposing allocation based on population ratio) we have emphasised that this will delay the process of elimination of disparity considerably unless a bigger thrust is given in the Fifth and subsequent Plans in favour of East Pakistan. Our colleagues from West Pakistan, however, could not be persuaded to agree even to this moderate proposal. By proposing a Plan allocation between East and West Pakistan in proportion to population, we felt we were asking East Pakistan not only to forget past inequities in the allocation of resources but also to wait for a long time to reach parity.*"[13] All these arguments fell on the deaf ears of West's economists.

It was increasingly obvious that the economists' struggle for the achievement of East's economic destiny had to be carried on two fronts. First, the mobilisation of public opinion in East had to be intensified — a task primarily for politicians with the support, wherever necessary, from economists. With this end in view, cooperation and contact with politicians had to be expanded. Second, economists had to increase their efforts to educate the public and the intelligentsia in various walks of life, through professional as well as popular writings and conferences. The use of the media had to be intensified. Those among the economists who had the knack and competence in writing for the press had to resort to its use aggressively. They had to be fed and briefed by others who were involved in research as well as by those who might be working in commissions and panels and therefore had access to considerable information.[14]

The academic economists continued to work in their diverse and individual capacities on the problem of East-West relations as well as on development problems in East. In addition to Dhaka and other universities in East, a considerable amount of research was being done at the Pakistan Institute of Development Economics on the economic development problems of East, thanks to the presence of a sizeable number of economists from East as well as foreign economists with interest in regional issues. Research on many policy issues was done in their regional context i.e. for East and West separately. It was a

---

[13] Report of East Pakistan Economists — Reports of the Advisory Panels for the Fourth Five-Year Plan, 1970-75, vol. 1, p. 18.).

[14] During this period, the newsweekly, *Forum*, edited by my colleague and friend, Rehman Sobhan, was instrumental in raising awareness on East-West economic relations among the reading public.

long way from the 1950s when structural differences between East and West and the differential impacts of policies of the central government were ignored in professional analysis in the central institutions. Accordingly, a substantial amount of new statistics was collected and its analysis on a regional basis was undertaken in the Institute. For the first time, it published a very detailed comparative analysis of regional income, savings and investments in East and West based on new household expenditure surveys. Reliable and authentic regional income estimates were crucial for the analysis of income disparity, its causes and consequences. The work was done by a well recognised economist from a small Nordic country — a country with no political or economic and commercial interests in Pakistan; this fact added a considerable degree of respectability to the estimates.[15] Estimates of income disparity and its characteristics were subjects of great political sensitivity. PIDE estimates were regarded as unbiased and authentic. This was accepted as such by the international development community, which by now was getting concerned with East-West economic disparity. During the years 1965-1970, there were also a significant number of well appreciated articles on subjects ranging from agriculture to irrigation, demographic problems and industrialisation in East. Also, for the first time a regional input/output analysis for East was published.

This range of research on East-West relations and East's economic prospects was not always welcome to the officials from West who were dominant in the governing board of the institute, headed by the Deputy Chairman of the Pakistan Planning Commission. My "partisan" activities in different Commissions were well known. How did West agree to my appointment as the Director in the first place? One reason was that it was not an important enough assignment in the context of Pakistan's power structure. It was neither an executive nor a

---

[15]This was the oft-quoted article by Asbjorn Bergen, *Personal Income Distribution and Personal Savings in Pakistan*, Pakistan Development Review (Summer 1967). Other notable publications were: S.R. Bose, *Trend of Rural Wages of Rural Poor in East Pakistan*, Pakistan Development Review (Autumn 1968); A. R. Khan, *What Has Been Happening to Real Wages in Pakistan*, Pakistan Development Review (Autumn 1968); S.R. Lewis, Jr., *Pakistan's Industrialization and Trade Policies*, (Oxford University Press, 1970), S.R. Lewis was an adviser at the PIDE; *Growth and Inequality in Pakistan*, edited by K. Griffin, McMillan and Co. (1971), Griffin was an adviser at PIDE; N. Chowdhury, *Some Reflections on Income Distribution Intermediation in Pakistan*, Pakistan Development Review (Summer 1969).

policymaking position. After all, what harm could I do as the Director of a mere research Institute? How many people in Pakistan read the professional, highly technical articles and research manuscripts published by the institute? These were much less known or read than the newspaper articles or articles in popular journals, which were widely read and could inflame public opinion.[16]

An equally, if not more important, reason for my appointment was probably the pressure of the foreign economists and the Yale University Economic Growth Centre that was administering the Ford Foundation project for PIDE.[17] The Foundation provided the last foreign Director of PIDE and was anxious to replace him by a national. A candidate from amongst the well known economists from West would have been most welcome to the governing board. But there were only a very few of them. Most of them were employed in high policymaking positions in the central bank and in the government, including the Planning Commission. Teaching and research were not their preferred careers. East had most of the economists working in the academic institutions either by preference or because of lack of opportunities elsewhere in the country. West was thus in a bind and had reluctantly agreed to the choice of an economist from East. I was not very enthusiastic about an assignment in Karachi, which was for me a foreign and inhospitable land. The professors at Yale eventually persuaded me that it would be an intellectually challenging job with opportunities for frequent interaction with research centres working on economic development issues in the rest of the world.

Their judgement was accurate and my years at the Institute during 1964-71 were the most productive and professionally rewarding. At the same time, it was a period full of tensions with the governing board, which did not have much trust in me. The research output was

---

[16]In fact, technical work at PIDE, while inaccessible to the public, provided the necessary facts and analysis to the economists in East i.e. provided the grist to their mill.

[17]The Ford Foundation was also financing a large complement of foreign advisers at the Pakistan Planning Commission under the Harvard Advisory Service, who exercised significant influence on the Commission and the Finance Ministry. Until my appointment, an expatriate Director from an US university headed the institute. The Ford Foundation and the government of Pakistan decided that the time had come to appoint a Pakistani Director. The Director of the Yale Economic Growth Centre at the time, Gustav Ranis and Mark Leiserson of the Economics Department, administering the Ford grant, both had a major say as to who would replace the foreign director so that the Ford Foundation's investment was well used.

often critical of government policies and the choice of subjects, specially on East-West economic issues, was not to their liking. There was an advisory group of professional economists called *Senior Fellows* who advised on the research programme and participated in the selection of staff and candidates for overseas scholarships. The *Fellows* from West were habitually critical and obstructive. In addition, they were not very happy that most of the brighter researchers and recipients of overseas scholarship were from East.[18] They were reluctant to admit that this was partly due to a dearth of bright economists in West with interest in research. They would push me as much as possible but not so much as to make me resign for it would have been unwise in the context of the prevailing political climate of East-West tension. As a result, there was a constant tug of war.

Undoubtedly, the foreign connection of the Institute was very helpful to my effectiveness as the Director. There were two sets of helpful factors. First, there was a group of very distinguished nonresident foreign advisers — about a half dozen or so very well known economists from top universities in the world such as Jan Tinbergen (later on a Nobel Laureate), Hollis Chenery from Harvard, Austin Robinson from Cambridge, Lloyd Reynolds from Yale, Just Faaland from the Christian Michelsen Institute of Norway. They had the responsibility to appraise the quality of research and publications as well as to advise on research methodology. They visited once a year for one or two weeks; they would not only lecture on the latest developments in theory and empirical research but also held discussions with staff on their individual research projects. There were, in addition, resident foreign research advisers for longer periods of time. Second, both the Project Director and the Director of the Economic Growth Centre from Yale used to visit periodically to monitor the Institute's performance and to review the affairs of the institute with the Board

---

[18]The Ford Foundation grant for overseas scholarships was available not only for PIDE staff members but also for candidates from research institutions, universities and technical departments/agencies of the government. The objective was to augment the supply of trained economists in the country as a whole and not only in the PIDE. There was, in addition, a training programme in advanced economics for economists from other institutions in the country, organised by PIDE. The training programme was conducted by the senior researchers at the PIDE as well as by resident foreign advisers of whom there were three or four at a point of time and by short term visitors from overseas universities. A good number of economists from East were trained under the programme.

Chairman and other members of the Pakistan Establishment. These institutional arrangements involving a well known US university and a distinguished group of international economists played a key role and provided strong support to my professional leadership of the institute. They served as a much-needed buffer against the interventionist instincts of the powerful officials from West.

As we entered the second half of the decade of the 1960s, the need for political mobilisation in the country at large became increasingly crucial. It was apparent that the key to the solution of East's continued underdevelopment depended on it acquiring a decisive say in the decision making process and in the executive authority to decide its own future. The Indo-Pakistan war of 1965 was a traumatic experience for both West and East. East was kept and felt defenseless in the event of an attack by India, cut off as it was from West during the war. The economic situation deteriorated as a consequence of the war and rising defense expenditures. Development expenditures were scaled down and new projects were postponed. Rather than having a significant increase as was envisaged in the Second Plan, East suffered in the process a major reduction in development expenditures. The prospects of a turnaround in East's economy were frustrated. This was the context during the late 1960s in which East's long drawn struggle for its economic and political rights culminated into a demand for a radical, structural readjustment of political and economic relations with West.

Chapter 4

THE *SIX-POINTS PROGRAMME*: PRECURSOR TO INDEPENDENCE (1966-71)

E ast-West disparity, by the mid-1960s, was a very live issue in the political arena. It occupied an important place, albeit with different emphases, in the platforms of the dominant political parties such as the Awami League and the National Awami Party (Bhasani).[1]

Economic disparity was partly a function of disparity in political power. With the passage of time, political parties in Pakistan were organised on the basis of geographical and regional identities. Through a process of compromises, a political party could accommodate differences in language, ethnicity, customs and traditions as well as in social and economic circumstances among its members. It could then emerge as a coherent national party on the basis of power sharing, a common ideology, a shared vision and common economic interests. No political party in Pakistan was able to achieve this *raison de etre* on a national basis, and at the same time remain willing and able to deal with the overriding issue of East-West disparity. Inevitably, political configurations drifted into the formation of two major political parties representing West and East, respectively i.e. the Muslim League and the Awami League in the earlier years, and the People's Party and the Awami League in later years. Once the political parties

---

[1] The Awami League was the dominant centrist party headed by Sheikh Mujib, whereas the National Awami Party was a leftist party headed by Maulana Abdul Hamid Khan Bhasani.

became based on unalterable characteristics such as geography, ethnicity or language, there was no way in which a presidential or parliamentary democracy with a system of alternating political parties in power could function. In such a situation, there would emerge a permanent majority confronting a permanent minority.

West demanded and managed to frame a constitution, which in their view would accommodate the peculiar features of the country i.e. offset the permanent electoral majority of East if adult suffrage would come into being. This was achieved through the formation of one unit for the whole of West and parity of representation in the Parliament between East and West. There was no recompense for such contrived abdication of East's democratic rights. West continued its overpowering dominance of the executive organs, both civil and military, as well as of the economy. Predictably, the result was a period of continued political instability until 1958 when the military, overwhelmingly dominated by West, usurped political power, thus effectively disenfranchising East. Between 1958 and 1971, East had to confront the military of West in negotiations for any share in economic opportunities or in political power.

4.1 SHEIKH MUJIB'S *SIX-POINTS PROGRAMME*

East recognised the inevitable stalemate right from the mid-1950s and, therefore, suggested that the only reasonable solution under the circumstances was the granting of substantial autonomy to the two regions in both economic and political matters. Limiting the responsibilities and powers of the central government was the only feasible way to resolve the deadlock in the sharing of economic and political power. Sheikh Mujib,[2] the catalyst to articulating the accumulated frustrations and the rising expectations in East, emerged with his fabled *Six-Points Programme*. It was a clear and consolidated statement of the various strands or elements of proposals or ideas advanced by East for the past nineteen years so that both regions might live in peace and strive for prosperity. The shock effect of the *Six-Points Programme* in 1966 on the country shortly after the debacle suffered

---

[2] Sheikh Mujib, by then, was the President of the Awami League, the party that was leading the struggle for regional autonomy. He emerged as the most courageous, vocal, and relentless advocate of the economic and political rights of East Pakistan.

in the *1965 Indo-Pakistan War,* given the undercurrent of a challenge to the leadership of Ayub, was very considerable. The political landscape in Pakistan was never to be the same again.

I do not know the exact authorship of the draft of the *Six-Points Programme.* It never occurred to me to inquire about it from those who would have known, specially Tajuddin. The widely believed version was that it was Sheikh Mujib who articulated the main issues and requested Tajuddin to put them in writing in a systematic way in the form of "various points." Later on, they were reported to have been drafted in English by a senior civil servant from East who was very close to Sheikh Mujib, one of the accused in the *Agartala Conspiracy Case* and later on, Secretary General of the Bangladesh government in 1972.[3]

The main points that related to economic aspects were as follows. The federal government would deal only with the subjects of defense and foreign affairs; the residual subjects would be in the hands of the provinces. Two alternatives were presented on the subject of currency: (a) there would be two separate but freely convertible currencies for the two regions; or (b) there would be one currency but separate banking services, separate fiscal and monetary policies and constitutional provisions for stopping flight of capital from East to West; (c) power of taxation and revenue collection would be with the provinces and the centre would have a share in the proceeds of such taxes for meeting its expenditures in the form of a levy of a certain percentage on all taxes; (d) foreign exchange earnings of each region would vest in the respective region and the requirements of the centre would be met by the two regions either equally or in a ratio to be fixed; (e) indigenous products shall move free of duty between the regions; and (f) provinces would establish trade and commercial relations with foreign countries, including establishment of trade missions and enter into trade agreements. It was later amplified that each region would negotiate foreign trade and aid within the framework of the foreign policy of the centre so that there was no divergence between the two.

A few of the basic elements in the *Six-Points Programme* had past antecedents. In 1946, the British government submitted the *Cabinet Mission Plan* for resolving the constitutional problems of India upon

---

[3] Dr. Kamal Hossain, "The Making of Bangladesh," unpublished manuscript, 1998.

independence. It reserved defense, foreign affairs, and communications for the federal government. The 21-point Manifesto of the United Front in East in 1954 was similar, reserving defense, foreign affairs, and currency for the central government. The substance of these elements was also reflected in the memorandum of the Dhaka University economists in 1961 to President Ayub, as elaborated in Chapter 2. In 1962, a group of scholars in East suggested similar provisions in a pamphlet, The *Challenge of Disparity*.[4] The *Six-Points Programme* was rejected by Ayub who then unleashed a severe repression on the Awami League activists and incarcerated Sheikh Mujib and the top leaders.

My involvement in work relating to the *Six-Points Programme* started after Sheikh Mujib was released from the *Agartala Conspiracy Case* in February 1969.[5] As explained in chapter 3, by that time many in East had concluded that the traditional way of dealing with, or negotiations on, East-West relations had come to a dead end. A vigorous mass movement provided the only ray of hope. Sheikh Mujib had emerged as the only political leader who could organise and lead such a movement in the country at that stage. He had the best credentials to galvanise the masses in support of a movement for achieving the aspirations of East.

4.2 MY INVOLVEMENT WITH *SIX-POINTS*

I received a message from a friend of mine, then Governor of the State Bank of Pakistan, M. Raschid, to meet Sheikh Mujib in Dhaka as soon as possible. I had never met Sheikh Mujib before nor had I tried to do so in the past. Raschid knew my work on East-West economic relations intimately and, in particular, had shared with me the excruciating and frustrating experience of two successive Pakistan Finance Commissions as described in Chapter 3. I suspected that it was he who had suggested my name to Sheikh Mujib. When I asked him about this, Raschid's answer was that Sheikh Mujib had come to know about my work on East-West relations and was, therefore,

---

[4] Dr. Kamal Hossain, *op.cit.*

[5] Sheikh Mujib was incarcerated following his announcement of the *Six-Point Programme*, and later charged with sedition and treason against Pakistan in the *Agartala Conspiracy Case*.

anxious to meet with me to find out whether and how I could help him. The meeting was arranged at the house of a mutual friend — a non-Bengali businessman, who had migrated to Dhaka at the time of the creation of Pakistan, identified himself with the interests of East and knew Sheikh Mujib well. In the meeting, Sheikh Mujib explained that he needed experts to help him in marshalling facts, analysis, and arguments to strengthen the case for autonomy and in elaborating and defending each of the *Six-Points*. He expected to be involved in the coming months in difficult negotiations with West. Also, I should work as a member of a team on the formulation and elaboration of the economic aspects of the Awami League Election Manifesto for the forthcoming elections. I agreed to assist him to the best of my abilities.

In this task, it was understood that I would work in close collaboration with those already involved. Kamal Hossain had been for some time working closely with him during and after the *Agartala Conspiracy Case*. He emerged, in fact, as the coordinator of the team of experts who were assisting Sheikh Mujib on different tasks. These included the negotiations during and after the *Roundtable Conference in* February 1969 where Sheikh Mujib reiterated his demand for the *Six-Points Programme*. Kamal Hossain was directly involved in the drafting of the Manifesto for the 1970 election in association with party colleagues and others.[6]

It was not long before I had launched my intensive campaign to shift the location of PIDE from Karachi to Dhaka. This also required that I visited Dhaka often to make the necessary arrangements. During this period, General Yahya made a few minor conciliatory moves towards East.[7] In addition to appointing a few East Pakistani Secretaries and Ministers in the central government, he decided, in response to the persistent demands of East over many years, to move the headquarters of several central institutions to East. A few, relatively less important central institutions were thus to be shifted to Dhaka. Taking advantage of this general policy, I engaged in intensive lobbying with

---

[6] Since I was still at PIDE in Karachi, work on this assignment required frequent trips to Dhaka. The fact that there were a number of research projects of the Institute in East provided a convenient excuse for my many visits to Dhaka.

[7] General Yahya Khan, had replaced Ayub in a coup in early 1969, and introduced martial law in the country with the promise of elections on the basis of universal adult suffrage.

the Ministers and the bureaucrats from East. All of them were helpful. The fact that the Institute was not of significance in the power structure or in policymaking went in its favour. It was a research institution, though a troublesome institution and in some ways an irritant to West, but it was no threat to the regime. If shifting the Institute to Dhaka would win a "credit point" for the regime, it was a very minor sacrifice. However, even for such an unimportant issue, I had to mount an intensive campaign, eventually managing to get a sympathetic hearing from General Peerzada, Principal Secretary to General Yahya. In Yahya's Secretariat, I had another cooperative interlocutor i.e. General Karim who hailed from East and was known to me. In addition, I was able to secure the support of my friends in Dhaka in convincing the military Governor of East to support our case. With such an array of important supporters, I eventually succeeded in shifting the Institute to Dhaka towards the end of 1970.[8]

After the elections in 1970, the most important task was to draft the constitution on the basis of the *Six-Points Programme*. The political steering group for this task was headed by Sheikh Mujib and consisted of Nazrul Islam, Tajuddin, Moshtaque, Kamruzzaman, Mansoor Ali, and Kamal Hossain.[9] Kamal Hossain was in charge of drafting the constitution. The professional team consisted of Muzaffar Ahmed Chowdhury, Rehman Sobhan, Anisur Rahman, Sarwar Murshed, and myself. Sheikh Mujib was a very active and vigorous participant. We insisted that he cleared every idea and every formulation. Tajudddin was the next most active and enthusiastic interlocutor among the political leaders.

4.3 *SIX-POINTS* ELABORATED

There were different elements of the *Six-Points Programme* that required detailed scrutiny, explanation, and elaboration. Moreover, various supplementary provisions had to be introduced to ensure internal consistency and ease of implementation. As the exercise proceeded, it was apparent that the difficulties with the *Six-Points Programme* arose mainly from the need to reconcile it with the

---

[8] After independence PIDE at Dhaka was named Bangladesh Institute of Development Studies.

[9] All of them were Ministers in the government after independence.

concept of an economic union. To illustrate, if all taxes were to be in the hands of each region, the rate structure of tariffs in one region could be and would most likely be different from those of another region. If foreign imports in the region with low tariffs were reexported to the region with higher tariffs, there would be leakages in tax receipts in the latter. Also, this would undo any protection intended for domestic production against foreign imports in that region. Except for domestically produced goods, this would rule out free trade between the two regions. Even in the case of domestic goods, there were problems in free trade between regions as explained below.

To assure that such leakages as above did not occur, it would be necessary to keep close track of the origin of commodities traded between the regions. Also, it had to be ensured that goods or inputs imported in one region, after incorporating a very small addition to their value, were not reexported to the other region. If the proportion of value added in the commodity that was reexported was small, it would dilute or offset the protective margin of the tariff structure in the high tax region. This is the perennial problem of *rules of origin* of commodities that are traded within a free trade area or similar preferential trading arrangements. In order to enforce the *rules of origin*, trade in all commodities within a regional arrangement are inspected and monitored to ensure that no reexport occurred and that the *value added* component does not fall below the required minimum.

Second, domestic products from one region i.e. East exported to West could be reexported abroad and foreign exchange thus earned would accrue to West. Unless all interregional trade was settled in foreign exchange, this would negate the control of East over its own foreign exchange earnings. What would happen if East had a net export surplus with West or vice versa? How would it be financed? Exports of one region to the other were also potential exports to the rest of the world and, therefore, constitute potential foreign exchange earnings. It could be financed by the surplus region automatically lending an equivalent amount to the deficit region. Alternatively, the surplus region could be paid in foreign exchange by the deficit region. In a single currency regime, the surplus region, if not paid in foreign exchange, would be making an unrequited transfer to the deficit region. This would go against the provision in *Six-Points Programme to* prevent capital flight from East to West. This was exactly what happened in the 1950s and 1960s when the export surplus of East was absorbed in West as unrequited transfers. Also, interregional trade occurs not only in commodities but also in services i.e. travel, financial and insurance services. Thus, each region would have to keep a comprehensive balance of payments account for settling payments not only for trade in commodities but also in services to ensure that the net surplus in balance of payments was met by payment of foreign exchange or similar assets. Under this dispensation, one region would be able to regulate investment flows between regions as well as flows of funds between enterprises with branches located in different regions.

Third, in respect of East-West trade, there were two other contentious issues that were raised by East in the past. It was argued that West's high cost industries had a protected captive market in East, thus imposing significant welfare cost on East. Under the *Six-Points Programme*, East would no longer provide a protected market to West's industries. Under its own trade and exchange regime, East would be free to liberalise foreign imports so that high cost imports from West would be subject to competition from cheaper foreign imports. There was yet another problem. If there was to be free trade in domestically produced goods, how would the *infant· industries* in East face competition from the long established industries in West? This could only be done by East providing outright output or input subsidies to absorb excess costs. Under all these scenarios, compared with the past, East-West trade would become less attractive than trade with third countries. East in the interest of its own economic development would like to equalise the "playing field" for trade with West and with the rest of the world.

Fourth, if the regional Reserve Bank in East was to determine and implement its monetary policy, it would decide the interest rate policy and control the quantum of money supply (i.e. currency and deposits) in East as well. Since the quantum of money supply in East would be decided by its Reserve Bank, the power of the Central Bank of Pakistan would be restricted only to the printing of notes or minting of coins upon specific request from East. The Central Bank could serve, by the mutual agreement of the two Reserve Banks, as their clearing house or at most, as a banker's bank to provide short term credit to them, if possible, with additional resources from abroad. Any accumulation of claims by one Reserve Bank on the Central Bank would have to be settled in foreign exchange. Or else these would be unintended capital transfers between regions.

With one currency and with differential interest rates, investors in the high interest region could borrow in the low interest region for use in the high interest region, and could thus jeopardise the objective of monetary policy in the high interest region. Moreover, the region following lax fiscal and monetary policies would generate inflationary pressures in that region, which would spread to the other region through the mechanism of interregional trade. This would jeopardise the objective of tighter fiscal and monetary policies in the latter region. Similarly, under these circumstances one exchange rate would not be in the interest of both regions. An exchange rate that was appropriate in one region most probably would not be so for the other region. That the interests of two regions could significantly diverge in terms of exchange rate policies was illustrated by the historical experience of Pakistan's refusal to devalue in 1948 at a time when India did. East objected to the decision because it affected adversely East's most important foreign exchange earner i.e. jute. As a result, India gained a considerable price advantage in the world jute market, expanded its domestic production and its share in the world market. Thus, the exchange rate policy could be used to the advantage of one region and to the disadvantage of the other.

Fifth, independent fiscal and monetary policies, a separate trade and payments regime and restrictions on payments and capital transfers were not consistent with a single currency. This was the reason why the *European Union* has found it necessary, in introducing the *Euro*, to have a *stability pact* among the membership. This governs the fiscal and monetary policies of each member so that limits are imposed on national macroeconomic policies. As the experience with the *Euro* has demonstrated, a uniform exchange rate requires a very substantial integration of monetary and fiscal policies as well as trade and payments systems. The *European Central Bank* has been given functions that previously belonged to national central banks. The experiment on which we were embarking, in the context of the *Six-Points Programme*, was the reverse; instead of integrating as in the case of the *Euro*, we were engaged in disintegrating the preexisting, unified monetary, fiscal and trade policies.

Six, how could the centre meet its expenditures on defense and foreign affairs in the absence of its own independent sources of revenue? The constitution could impose an obligation on each region to contribute to financing central expenditures. The *Six-Points Programme* stated that the centre would "impose a levy of a certain percentage on all taxes." This provision was later modified to include nontax revenues as well. A predetermined percentage levy on the revenue resources of each province could not be imposed because annual expenditures on defense and foreign affairs would not remain the same over time. Neither would total revenues of each province remain the same. Therefore, the absolute amount of contribution from each province and the corresponding levy on revenue resources of each province could not be predetermined. They had to follow the finalisation of the size of the centre's annual budget. What could be predetermined, however, was the ratio of each province in the total contribution.

One suggestion was to require each province to make equal contributions. Once any ratio other than equal contribution from each region was considered, it would raise a number of issues. Should the ratio relate to the corresponding ability to pay measured, for example, by each region's per capita income? Arguably, each region's contribution could also be linked to (a) province wise location of central expenditures, and (b) employment in central services, including armed services. In both these respects, regional imbalance had been a source of friction over the past years. Should a constitutional provision to this effect be made? East was willing to consider equal contribution even though this would impose a relatively heavier burden on East in the interest of inducing West to accept the total package of the *Six-Points Programme.*

Seventh, a similar set of questions arose in the matter of regional contributions to the foreign exchange requirements of the centre. A fixed ratio or equal contributions could be considered. If foreign loans guaranteed by the centre were to be serviced by each region, how would the centre have resources to fulfil the guarantee in case any region defaults? This could be resolved by giving the centre a prior claim on the foreign exchange resources of each region for the purposes of repayment to the external lender. Alternatively, the Reserve Bank in East would agree to provide the amount to the Central Bank of Pakistan.

It was important to note that under universal adult suffrage the members from East would constitute a majority in the central Parliament. This aspect was often forgotten in the public debate in East. West, therefore, perceived a risk that East would be likely to dominate the decision making process in the central Parliament. For example, West had reasons to worry that East might attempt to reduce the overwhelming dominance of West in defense forces that it had always enjoyed in the past. Under the new dispensation, East, with its well known lack of enthusiasm for large military establishments, might seek to reduce aggregate defense expenditures or allocate them differently between the two regions.

In the *Six-Points Programme*, what we were really aiming at was a very loose form of political and economic relationship. We envisaged a confederation of economically independent and sovereign states with some common arrangements such as common defense and foreign affairs, financed by contributions from each state. It was a unique and a novel experiment in statecraft.[10]

The *Six-Points Programme* once it was elaborated in its details resembled very closely the *Cabinet Mission Plan* in 1946 for India's constitutional future which envisaged a very loose confederation between "groups of provinces" in India. The *Plan*, a response to the demand for an independent state by the Muslims of India, was more straightforward and unambiguous than the *Six-Points Programme* in terms of its specific proposals. It was a proposal to hold together a very limited political union of "three groups" of provinces in India with the centre having responsibility for defense and foreign affairs. In addition, the subject of intergroup communications, i.e. communications between the groups and not within each of the groups, was retained for the centre. This was primarily because military or defense operations in such a far-flung but physically contiguous subcontinent could not be carried out without central control over the internal communications system.

---

[10]The Commonwealth of Independent States (CIS) that was formed after the dissolution of the Soviet Union had some resemblance to what was being proposed by East. It should be noted that the CIS did not long survive.

The *Cabinet Mission Plan* did not put any of the economic powers in the hands of the centre. Currency, trade, fiscal, monetary policies, and foreign exchange resources were all in the hands of "three groups" of provinces. It envisaged correctly that these policies were linked and could not be separated easily. If one of these policies was exclusively in the hands of the regions, then the other policies could not be carried out by the centre without diluting significantly the authority of the provinces. To be sure, there could be cooperation on these subjects by common agreement from time to time like any cooperation between independent states. The only exception in the *Plan* was that the centre would have the power to raise the necessary finances to meet it expenditures. The details of how to ensure such finances were not spelled out in the *Plan*; probably it was to be done by assigning to the centre a share of the tax revenues of each group of provinces. Interestingly enough, the *Plan* also provided that any province could decide to reconsider the terms of the constitution after an initial period of 10 years and at 10 yearly intervals thereafter. In other words, it left room for them to opt out of this constitutional arrangement and to become independent.

As our work progressed, it became clear that the *Six-Points Programme* envisaging a loose confederation and a very tenuous link depended on the goodwill of the provinces. It was only a short step away from complete independence. In the course of the exhaustive deliberations that we undertook on the implementation of the *Six-Points Programme,* this implication became clear to all of us in the steering group — including Sheikh Mujib who participated fully. He realised that what was being proposed was barely a consolation prize to West. After all, given the political power and economic privileges it had enjoyed in the past, West might, after a period of time, not find it worthwhile to continue such a confederal arrangement. If that was West's decision, a peaceful separation might result. The alternative for East, to seek independence through an armed struggle in the early 1970s, was likely to be of a severe disadvantage to East since it had no military force. Moreover, the outcome of any physical confrontation, apart from inevitable bloodshed and devastation, was always uncertain. In this calculus, there was no contemplation of any arrangement with India for military assistance or intervention. In fact, as stated earlier, if the *Six-Points Programme* was to materialise, given its majority in the central Parliament, East would be able to shift over time the balance in the composition and location of military expenditures in favour of East. This would reduce the possibility of using the military to suppress East, without unleashing an internal struggle within the military itself. Equally, if not more important, the role of the para-military forces to be built up by each region as provided in the *Six-Points Programme* was critical. It would be up to East to decide how strong and well equipped such a force would be. This would further strengthen East's relative power to deal with any attempt by West to suppress her by force as and when East decided to snap the very loose link proposed under the *Six-Points Programme*.

The work by the steering group during November 1970 to March 1971, under the guidance of Sheikh Mujib and his senior political colleagues, was supposed to be done in secret. The venue of meetings was frequently shifted in the vain hope that the Pakistan intelligence services would not be aware of the ongoing exercise in constitution making. The submission of a draft constitution by Sheikh Mujib, incorporating the *Six-Points Programme* as soon as the Parliament met, was intended to keep the initiative in the hands of East. West was to be invited to debate and react to it. East with its majority was expected to get it accepted by the parliament.

During the meetings of the group, a few of us sometimes felt that Moshtaque was uncomfortable with the way we were interpreting the *Six-Points Programme* and carrying it to its logical conclusion. The questions he asked and the explanations that he sought left us with such an impression. At times I myself was unsure whether in the beginning all members of the steering group had fully appreciated how weak and limited a central government the *Six-Points Programme* had envisaged. We had laboured hard to make very clear to them the far reaching implications of the implementation of the *Six-Points Programme*. By the time the exercise was completed, it was obvious that they all understood what they were aiming at. Sheikh Mujib was the quickest to grasp it all partly because he had thought about it most and for the longest period. He was very happy that the elaboration and articulation by the experts of the summary version of the *Programme* had turned out the way it had. It met his ultimate wish to have the weakest possible link with Pakistan. The members of the steering group were happy to go along with Sheikh Mujib in whom they had full confidence. Moshtaque was the only one who seemed, to some of us, to be ambivalent.

We were surprised when we heard that the salient points of the draft constitution were published in a newspaper in Lahore in Pakistan sometime during January-February 1971. Copies of the draft were subject to a very limited distribution and, in order to ensure secrecy, all the copies were in the custody of Kamal Hossain. The individual members of the political steering group could borrow copies only for their perusal for a limited period. The most interested member to pursue this option was Moshtaque and the leak seemed to have taken place around the time when a copy of the draft was with him. A few of us suspected, but could not be sure, that Moshtaque was probably the source of this leak. In fact, a member of our group who had contacts with the press in West had first come to know about the newspaper report. We were unhappy when we came to know about this premature disclosure. West was now to get a preview of the proposals in detail and would be able to organise its response. They could plan or implement a preemptive action to undo Sheikh Mujib's strategy prior to its presentation in the Parliament. Kamal Hossain, Rehman Sobhan, and I met Sheikh Mujib in this connection and complained that one of his colleagues was most probably up to mischief. He accepted this incident as an occupational hazard and assured us that he would look into it. That was the end of the matter.

Sheikh Mujib was not sure how far all the Awami League members of the Parliament would uncompromisingly adhere to the *Six-Points Programme* in all its details. They might vacillate or waver when its full implications would be debated in the Parliament and there would be a likely confrontation with West. Members of the Parliament from West could entice away or blackmail those from East since the former had the power and resources to do so. A mammoth public meeting was held in Dhaka on 3rd January 1971 to celebrate the victory of the Awami League in the elections. All the members of Parliament were called upon to solemnly swear an oath that they would never betray the masses who had entrusted them to realise the *Six-Points Programme* and other demands of East.

Sheikh Mujib with his powerful instincts and intuition, knew very well the pulse of the nation. Between 1966 and 1969, the Awami League had been subjected to a massive repression by the military regime. Not only Sheikh Mujib but also all the prominent leaders and activist workers had been in prison. The Party was rendered rudderless and disorganised. The party structure had to be rebuilt and discipline had to be reasserted within a very short period. By 1970, there had been substantial new accretions to the membership of the Awami League. The new recruits had not gone through the crucible of struggle and suffering under the Pakistani regime. Many members of the Parliament were recent recruits. Their understanding of and commitment to the *Six-Points Programme* were uncertain. He sought through the method of public oath taking, not very flattering to the members, to do his best to minimise the risks of defection.

On the day of the public meeting for the oath taking, I happened to be at a dinner party with two newly elected Awami League members of the Parliament, one of whom was a retired colonel in the army. It was clear that they were not very conversant with the full implications of the *Six-Points Programme* in its details. As seen above, the details were too complex for non-specialists to grasp unless fully explained. They had some general idea that East under this programme would have access to and control over her financial resources, both foreign exchange and domestic resources, and would have more political power and economic decision making authority. West could no longer transfer resources from East. But they did not realise how tenuous and weak a link was being proposed between East and West and how great an opposition it would face from West. They could not quite appreciate how large a surrender of power and resources it would imply for West. That West might prefer the break up of Pakistan to the acceptance of the *Six-Points Programme* could not be contemplated. At the same time, I found them rather unhappy at having to go through a process of public oath taking. They did not appreciate being treated like school children and to be warned in a public meeting that they would face the wrath of the masses if they betrayed the cause of East.

During extended discussions with Sheikh Mujib in the course of the meetings of the steering group on the *Six-Points Programme*, there were various speculative comments on how the future scenario might evolve. Sheikh Mujib was not interested, he insisted, in becoming the Prime Minister of Pakistan. If the *Six-Points Programme* was realised, the main task would be in East. In that event he would send Nazrul Islam or Tajuddin to head the Central Government. If the *Six-Points Programme* was not realised, there was no sense in becoming the Prime Minister since he could not exercise real power for the benefit of East. The politicians in West with the help of the bureaucracy and the army would undo him or make him ineffective, as it had always happened in the past whenever there had been a Prime Minister from East. Also, members from East could not be always held together, as it happened over the last two decades. The very rationale of the *Six-Points Programme* was to reject the old pattern of constitutional arrangement. He was not interested in repeating the old arrangement.

The refusal of Yahya to summon the Parliament promptly and his successive postponements of its session led Sheikh Mujib to start a non-cooperation or civil disobedience movement from 3rd March onwards until 25th March, 1971. During this period, he effectively took over the responsibility of running the civil administration in East. Daily instructions were issued under his authority so that the economy and the administration, including essential public services continued to function smoothly.[11] During the course of the day, we received suggestions and advice from a few cooperating civil servants, bankers, and others to ensure that the directives were designed to avoid dislocations and inconvenience to the population at large. This was a period during which Bangladesh enjoyed virtual independence; the Pakistan military was confined to the cantonment. The entire population recognised Sheikh Mujib as the undisputed leader of an almost independent state.

---

[11] Instructions relating to the functioning of economic institutions were formulated and coordinated by a few of us, meeting almost continuously in my house. The responsibility for coordinating the preparation of a comprehensive set of directives over all areas of administration was in the hands of Tajuddin and Kamal Hossain. Our recommendations were finalised after discussions with them. Barrister Amirul Islam was also involved. He was a member of the Awami League and of the Parliament, and later on a Minister in the government.

4.4 NEGOTIATIONS WITH PAKISTAN'S GENERAL YAHYA AND BREAKDOWN

I was not directly involved in the negotiations that started in the second half of March 1971 between Sheikh Mujib and General Yahya. The team of negotiators under the leadership of Sheikh Mujib consisted of such senior politicians as Nazrul Islam, Tajuddin, Moshtaque, Mansoor Ali, Kamruzzaman, and Kamal Hossain. Not all of them participated continuously throughout the negotiations. Sometimes a subgroup of them met with the team from West as desired by Sheikh Mujib. If West raised any new questions on the elaboration of some aspects of the *Six-Points Programme*, I was called upon to prepare reactions or explanations in co-operation, whenever needed, with a few of my economist colleagues. However, as described above, all aspects of the *Six-Points Programme* had already been discussed threadbare ahead of time with members of the negotiating team. There was, therefore, no need for frequent consultations with us during the negotiations. The consultations with me or sometimes two or three of us, when necessary, were not prescheduled and had to be held at short notice by Tajuddin and/or Kamal Hossain.[12]

It was widely presumed or understood — and we in the economists' group were briefed by the political negotiators accordingly — that the negotiations on economic issues were going well and chances of agreement were high. The team from West, which included the veritable and omnipresent expert, M.M. Ahmed, seemed to have accepted the economic provisions of the *Six-Points Programme*, including the arrangement that external trade payments and aid would be under the control of the two regions so long as the foreign policy aspects were left with the centre. The separation of the foreign exchange account was to take place with the State Bank Office in Dhaka functioning as the Reserve Bank of East. The bifurcation of the collection of taxes was thought to be more complex and might take some time and in the interim phase, East was to submit a plan for implementation. All these arrangements were to be implemented right away and included in the draft proclamation to be issued by General Yahya transferring

---

[12] Among economists who were associated with me during this period were mostly Rehman Sobhan, Anisur Rahman, and, when necessary, a few colleagues from BIDS.

power to the elected representatives of both the regions. In other words, the *Six-Points* were to be given effect, even before the members of each region met in the Parliament. From the evening of 23rd of March, the final stage in negotiations was underway. It was decided on 24th March that the team from East would have a final meeting with their counterparts from West. That never came to pass. Instead, a bloodbath ensued the day after.

During the process of negotiations in the second half of March 1971, as a habitual cynic among the group, I remained skeptical. I claimed no credit for clairvoyance but I found the spirit of sweet reasonableness on the part of West too good to be true. I believe that a few others might have felt the same. But the contagion of optimism emanating from the negotiating team started to affect me. It lifted my spirits and raised my hopes. I thought that there might be a chance — albeit remote — that the upsurge of popular movement in East had finally persuaded West to compromise and accept the *Six-Points Programme*.

There were at least three reasons for my skepticism, which I often expressed to my colleagues. The first cause for my cynicism arose from my long frustrating experience over the years in various commissions and committees in dealing with the civilian/bureaucratic establishment of West. I remembered how West in the past had viewed East's much more modest demands than what the *Six-Points Programme* embodied. Those relatively modest demands were seen by West as examples of East's stubbornness and unwillingness to recognise the generosity of West. The nature and extent of concessions that West would be willing to make, grudgingly and under the pressure of continuous agitation in East, were evident from those that had been made by the Yahya regime in the past year or so. For example, there was to be some increase in representation in senior civil service appointments from East, few promotions in the military and some increase in the allocation of resources for development expenditures in East. There was to be no restructuring of the civilian or military establishment and the decision making power and political authority, let alone a dominant voice in the government. In this context to have a central government with no authority over economic matters or resource reallocation and in which East would exercise decisive power, as proposed in the *Six-Points Programme,* could not but have been anathema to West.

How far West was prepared to concede in economic matters was illustrated by a gesture at the height of the agitation in East during 1969-70. What West considered almost a revolutionary concession was to suggest the appointment of two Deputy Chairmen for the Pakistan Planning Commission — one for each region to be responsible for the planning of that region. Development programmes of East were to be looked after by the Deputy Chairman from East. An attempt was made to persuade me to accept this position. Ministers from East in Yahya's Cabinet and the senior-most military officer from East in his Secretariat with the support of his Chief of Staff — all of whom knew me — tried to persuade me. Ministers and others from East, who were eager to convince me, possibly believed that in the context of a total monopoly of West in economic policymaking and management, any high level participation by East anywhere in the system was progress. I had seen from close quarters, in my various encounters with West, the structure of power and authority in decision making in the central government. I had no illusion that a token appointment to a high position in a system heavily weighted against East could make a difference in substance. The entire structure of power was to be left unaltered and therefore to remain concentrated in the hands of West. Ministers from East knew in the light of their own experience how very limited their powers were in decision making and implementation. They were possibly hoping against hope. I could not be persuaded to accept the offer.

The second cause for my pessimism was that I knew at first hand from my brother-in-law, a colonel in the army and who lived in the Dhaka cantonment, that there were ongoing reinforcements of supplies, equipment and soldiers from Pakistan and their placement around the country in warlike preparations. This, of course, was no secret. Many including Sheikh Mujib and the Awami League leaders knew it. A rationale for this preparatory action by West, I was told, was that they were trying to negotiate from strength. This was an attempt to pressure East to significantly modify the *Six-Points Programme*. But there was another view that West had seen the "people power" during the noncooperation movement and had, therefore, given up its resistance to the *Six-Points Programme*. The troop movements were not to start a war but to protect the nonBengali civilians and to preserve public institutions or installations in case the masses went wild in a popular frenzy in the course of civil disobedience movement. I was inclined to find the former more convincing.

The third cause for my pessimism was the warning sounded by G.W. Chowdhury, who was, earlier in his career, a colleague at Dhaka University as a professor of political science. He was, at that time, a member of the Yahya Cabinet and was sufficiently high in the confidence of the military to be included in Yahya's exclusive advisory team called the National Security Council. Since he was on the other side of the ideological and political divide from me, we had drifted away from each other, over the last years of the military regime. During one of my visits to Islamabad shortly after the elections, I was surprised to be contacted by Chowdhury with an urgent request for a meeting with him on a matter which, he thought, was of vital interest to me. According to him, the National Security Council had met and deliberated on its strategy for meeting Sheikh Mujib's challenge that there could be no compromise on the *Six-Points Programme*. The military was aware of Sheikh Mujib's public announcements that he had received from his election victory an overwhelming mandate for his *Six-Points Programme*. The military, on the other hand, had always believed and, in fact, taken it for granted that like all election manifestos and declarations, the *Six-Points Programme* was a rhetorical declaration subject to considerable modifications and, therefore, not etched in stone. They expected that Sheikh Mujib would significantly modify his demand. If, however, Sheikh Mujib insisted on it without a compromise, as it appeared from the tenor of his post election speeches that he might do, the military would resort to force to compel him to withdraw his demands. Chowdhury confirmed that this was no empty threat. Chowdhury was aware of my close association with Sheikh Mujib and thought that I should be aware of this message of warning.

Shortly afterwards, the advice from Chowdhury was reinforced by none other than the military Governor of East, Admiral Ahsan. I was on my way from Lahore to Dhaka and I met the Governor in the plane. He knew me well in connection with my efforts to shift PIDE to Dhaka. He was a congenial and friendly person. I had no doubt that his intelligence sources had kept him fully briefed about my close association with Sheikh Mujib. In the course of a conversation on post election developments, he touched on the *Six-Points Programme*. His message was simple: Sheikh Mujib should be advised to negotiate with the army and to be flexible. It was the military that counted and any attempt by Sheikh Mujib to gain support from the politicians in the nonPunjab provinces in West for exercising any leverage on the military and the Punjab[13] would be counter productive. This was with reference to the speeches of Sheikh Mujib, which referred to the possibility of support from politicians from the minority provinces in West. Sheikh Mujib seemed to have been suggesting that as and when the Parliament met, he would be able to convince the members from the minority provinces in West that all provinces would gain from the implementation of the *Six-Points Programme*. Admiral Ahsan reiterated that any such effort by Sheikh Mujib to break the unity of the politicians in West was particularly disliked by the army, which was overwhelmingly drawn from the Punjab, the majority province in West.

The Governor reminisced about his experience in 1947 in India on the eve of independence when he was an assistant military attaché with Mountbatten, the last British Viceroy. This was when Gandhi and Jinnah were engaged in negotiations about the transfer of power from the British.[14] The future of India, i.e. whether there would be one or two countries, narrowly hung on what each side was willing to concede on their respective demands. The situation in 1971, he thought, was very comparable as the future of Pakistan hung on the outcome of negotiations between the army and Sheikh Mujib. All depended on whether there would be a peaceful transition to a viable political solution.

In fact, this message had already been carried to Sheikh Mujib by various sources, both military and civilian. Sheikh Mujib probably considered that such threats and counter threats were normal in any hard bargaining when much was at stake, as it was in 1971. How each party treated such threats was always a matter of judgement on

---

[13]Punjab was the largest and most dominant province of West, politically, economically, and militarily.

[14]Mahatma Gandhi represented the Congress Party and the majority Hindu community, and Mohammad Ali Jinnah represented the Muslim League and the Muslims of India.

its part and its expectations about the opponent's likely behaviour. In retrospect, it seemed to me he reasoned that even if there were a military crackdown, it would be a limited military action as in the past. In any case, there was no going back. The forces of nationalism that had been unleashed could not be stemmed or turned back. That was what he indicated in his speech of 7th March, 1971. It was clear that any massive military action would break up the country. Faced with this choice, the military would exercise reason and agree to live with the *Six-Points Programme* — a confederation — rather than opt for complete separation.

I was wavering between skepticism and hope about the outcome of the March 1971 negotiations. After all, a peaceful outcome was not impossible to imagine. History had many examples of the "unlikely" and the "unexpected" turning out to be possible or acceptable. Subsequent events, however, proved that the negotiations and the last minute "sweet reasonableness" were a cover for the preparations for the military crackdown.

In the end, the *Six-Points Programme* that meant an end to West's established privileges was not acceptable to West. If there was no net substantial economic gain for West from preserving one country, there were a few in the civilian/bureaucratic establishment in West who thought that it was better to let East separate. The net economic gain for West was already on the decline by that time; it was only substantial up to the early 1960s. The costs to West of preserving the unity of the country were to get increasingly high if demands of East for a significant reallocation of resources and decision making were to be met. I had often wondered during my encounters with the upper echelons of West's economic/bureaucratic establishment whether one or two officials like M.M. Ahmed and G. Ishaque Khan did not hold this view.[15] However, this was not the view of the mainstream

---

[15]Many in West believed that there were only two factors binding East to West. They were Islam and fear of India. Islam turned out very soon not to be a binding force. The 1965 war demonstrated that West couldn't defend East. Therefore, the argument that to remain united with West was in the interest of East for its defense against India proved to be illusory. The establishment in West had no doubt in their mind that the *Six-Points Programme* was virtual independence — a nominal union, which could dissolve into two independent states at any time. There were a few high level professionals and thinkers in Pakistan who right from beginning found inclusion of East in Pakistan as untenable (see Muhammed Munir, *From Jinnah to Zia*, quoted in Anwar Dil, *op cit.*).

civilian-political-military establishment of West. If there was a referendum in West on this issue, I was sure that it would have rejected the rational economic calculation of the mounting costs of keeping East and West together. They saw political and strategic gain in maintaining one country, specially in counterbalancing their archenemy, India.[16] The mainstream in West did not believe that costs of keeping East in terms of sacrifice of their entrenched power and benefits would be high because East would either compromise or with an application of force East could be made to compromise.

The Hamodoor Rahman report,[17] recently released by the Government of Pakistan, made the point that West, including Yahya and his civilian/military advisers, did not carefully study the *Six-Points Programme*. This view was incorrect. Ayub's economic experts had studied the *Six-Points Programme* and found it a cause for profound concern. Even as early as 1960, the memorandum to Ayub from us, the economists from Dhaka University, foreshadowed its principal elements. It was examined meticulously by the Finance Ministry and Planning Commission and provoked their strong adverse reaction. Moreover, it was on the basis of a thorough understanding of the *Six-Points Programme* that Ayub declared that he would meet the *Six-Points Programme* with the language of force. This was the same group of advisers who worked with Yahya and his military team. A secret study was undertaken in 1970 by the Chief Economist of the Punjab government under the direction of Yahya's Economic Adviser to work out the implications of the *Six-Points Programme* and separation of East for defense expenditures, including size and composition of the armed forces.[18]

---

[16]I recall an interesting anecdote related to me by a senior officer from East who was stranded in Pakistan after independence. He attended a meeting convened by one of Yahya's advisers immediately after independence to brief and appraise the officials from East about the latest developments and their future status. In reply to his question as to what would be the policy of West toward independent Bangladesh, the adviser confirmed that the principal focus and objective of the policy would be to ensure that that the government in Bangladesh was not friendly to but, in fact, remained in an adversarial relationship with India.

[17]Homoodur Rahman Commission of Inquiry, appointed by Bhutto in the aftermath of Pakistan's military debacle in 1971 and the independence of Bangladesh.

[18]Thirty years later, the then Chief Economist of West, who is now retired and has lived for many years abroad, referred to the study in the course of a casual conversation on the role of the army in Pakistan. He stated his finding that the armed forces of Pakistan would put an

Many in the political-civilian leadership and the military were confident that East could be forced into submission to abandon the *Six-Points Programme*. From the military's experience of dealing with these "downtrodden races" — as Ayub had characterised Bangladeshis in his book *Friends and Not Masters* — they visualised no serious difficulty if sufficient force was strategically applied. They miscalculated that the outcome of a military confrontation with a politically disaffected people was predictable and that India's intervention could be avoided even if there were substantial outflows of refugees from Bangladesh.

Why did not Sheikh Mujib compromise on *Six-Points Programme*? The overriding answer was that there was no other basis to keep a semblance of one country in name that was consistent with East's legitimate aspirations and interests. As explained above, if rational economic calculation had prevailed, 1971 was the proper moment for West to give up and accept the *Six-Points Programme*; otherwise costs to West would be too high as it would be faced in the future with a large transfer of resources to East. This would have been the most likely outcome if resource allocation remained in the hands of the central government and if East was to dominate by its large majority in the central government and all its organs. Secondly, it was also an appropriate time for East if it was to achieve the *Six-Points Programme* in its totality, which was the only viable solution. The year 1971 was the most propitious. As never before in history, East was united behind one leader in support of a set of well articulated demands. To stay a longer period with Pakistan making compromises would have brought no gain; momentum in East would have been lost. The countrywide total mobilisation of the people that was achieved would have been lost; one compromise by East would lead to another. West would be able to break the unprecedented unity that was brought about by a combination of factors and by the

---

enormous burden on Pakistan if East was to separate and would seriously constrain its economic growth potential. In fact, immediately after 1970 elections the Yahya government had the *Six-Points Programme* meticulously examined by its economic advisers and military advisers like General Peerzada. The National Security Council, as mentioned above, met to deliberate on how to meet Sheikh Mujib's demands for implementing the *Six-Points Programme*. The same group of advisers accompanied Yahya to Dhaka in March 1971 to negotiate, under false pretenses, with their counterparts.

charismatic leadership of a unique leader. The future of the movement in East would have been thrown into uncertainty. History shows that seldom the timing of a drastic realignment of economic and political power within a nation or internationally could be planned or predicted in advance. Frequently, there is a confluence of unforeseen circumstances that occur in quick succession leading to the endgame and trigger the final outcome.

Chapter 5

EXILE AND INDEPENDENCE

The night of the 25th March 1971 turned out to be the night of reckoning. There was great suspense and rumours were rife about some sort of military action by Pakistan. I had lost contact with the team involved in negotiations with Pakistan and there were rumours that negotiations with General Yahya had broken down. Curious to find out any sign of an unusual nature I went out for a drive towards the centre of the city but decided to return. It looked like the lull before a storm.

That night there was a very boisterous and largely attended party at the house of my neighbour, a First Secretary in the US Consulate. Around midnight, there was a rumble of tanks and artillery moving along the road towards the New Market and accompanying fire. All this was visible from the rooftop of my nearby house in the Dhanmondi residential area. At the crack of dawn anxious to know what had happened during the night, I tried my telephones. Finding them disconnected, I walked over to the house of my neighbour, the US First Secretary. His phones were also disconnected. When asked about the occasion for such a big assembly of so many US families in his house, he responded that it was a birthday party for one of his friends and because of the midnight commotions they had stayed overnight. I wondered what so many children of all ages, including infants, were doing at the birthday party of his middle-aged friend.

It seemed as if the Americans were forewarned by the Pakistanis about the military crackdown so that they could assemble in the designated houses that would not be in the line of fire and would be safe and out of harm's way.

Next day, a student of mine who was an activist in the National Awami Party (Muzaffar)[1] came to convince me that I was very naive to stay in my house and that I should go underground. In the course of the night, the army had killed numerous civilians including women and children, Awami League activists and students in order to quash the struggle for autonomy. My close association with and assistance to Sheikh Mujib during all these years, including active help in the civil disobedience movement, were well known to the army. They were sure to come looking for me.

I heeded the advice given and went underground that day and sure enough, the army came next day, ransacked my house and took away my domestic help for questioning. While hiding from the army, I stayed for a day in Ford Foundation's guesthouse in the company of one of the American advisers[2] to PIDE in Dhaka.

5.1 BEGINNINGS OF MY EXILE

After a few days underground, I decided to leave for India. Already streams of refugees from Bangladesh were on their way to India. My companions during my escape through the underground network, arranged by the same student of mine as mentioned earlier, were a well known Hindu painter and a Muslim businessman. The guide was a teacher of a local college who knew the route. The last leg of the journey was in the company of a professional smuggler, who knew the terrain well enough to avoid detection by the army.

Three incidents on the way are etched in my memory. First, as we moved through the villages, we received great hospitality and help from the villagers. Second, we encountered an incident which reminded me how risky was our journey. We could have been captured or killed any time by army patrols and local bands of collaborators during our

---

[1] National Awami Party (NAP) had two factions both of which were leftist in their political orientation. One was led by Muzaffar Ahmed, regarded as pro-Moscow, and the other was pro-Beijing led by the veteran leader, Maulana Abdul Hamid Khan Bhasani. Their international and national preferences were supposed to reflect the Moscow-Beijing fault lines.

[2] Professor Daniel Thorner, Directeur d'Etudes, Ecole Pratique des Hautes Etude, Sorbonne, Paris. He eventually managed to take my wife and two children out of the country on the pretext of my family responding to a long standing invitation from his wife; the American couple at that time lived in Paris. It was too early after the crackdown for the army to effectively monitor or control all visits abroad. He was helped by my close friends who had no overt political affiliations.

journey through villages and at the Indian border. The journey was particularly harrowing when we arrived in Narshingdi, a small town with a cluster of shops and warehouses, to board a river vessel. At Narshingdi, there was an outpost of the East Pakistan Rifles (armed police) who had revolted against Pakistan and were, therefore, being pounded and strafed by the Pakistan airforce. We did not anticipate this. We were exhausted from a long trek on foot and had to ride a bus for a few miles in order to reach the river port in time. But the bus after a while ran out of gas and we had to board a rickshaw. As we proceeded, we found a few planes returning from the direction of the river port. We had no idea what awaited us. We were to assemble in a warehouse to wait until midnight when our contact person would put us on a launch. On arrival, we found that the Pakistani planes had heavily bombed the shops and warehouses. The warehouse where we were to meet had been damaged beyond recognition with heavy casualties of life. But for the delay in our reaching the river port, we would have been among the victims. It was as if the Providence had wished that we survived.

The third incident occurred in the final stage of our trek. Before crossing the border, we had to stay overnight in the home of some kind of village headman i.e. a man of affluence and influence. What disturbed my peace of mind was the sight, all around his house, of a sizeable cache of lethal arms. He was a very good host, hospitable and friendly. He sympathised with us at our plight that we had to run for life to India. As a man of peace he was very unhappy at all this turmoil and violence that seriously hampered his farming and trading activities. Unfortunately, his son — a misguided fellow — had joined the local Awami League activists. He had warned his son that he would be thrown out of the house if he did not refrain from his political activities which might draw the attention of the Pakistan army and put the entire family in jeopardy. He was very anxious to know whether we would allow the Hindus, who had left the country in 1947, to come back when we got rid of the Pakistanis and achieved independence with the help of India. He wanted us to know that it would be a very unwise and unpopular step for us even to contemplate such a possibility. We assured him as firmly as we could that such a thought was the farthest from our mind.

We later learned from our guide that most of his properties, the source of his power and status, belonged to the Hindu landowners who had left Pakistan at the time of partition of India. He had acquired or occupied them without any payment. Being the illegal occupant of all the properties, he dreaded the possibility of having to surrender them once the original owners came back, specially with India's military help. We could not but be impressed as to how at that moment of crisis, when many of us were worried about our survival from one day to the next, his mind was focused on a likely postindependence scenario affecting his personal wealth.

As we crossed over to India, we faced the Indian border security forces checking the flow of refugees. There was a justifiable concern on their part that a few intelligence agents of Pakistan might be infiltrating as well. We went through some questioning before we were allowed to enter Agartala, the capital of the state of Tripura in India.

Our first worry was to find a place to stay and to arrange to fly to Kolkata as soon as possible. It was early April 1971 and a few Awami League leaders and their associates who had arrived earlier were accommodated in the hostels for the members of the State Assembly of Tripura. Among them were M.R. Siddiqui, the Awami League leader of Chittagong, and Mahbubul Alam Chashi, an official of the Pakistan Foreign Service, both of whom were well known to me. I did not succeed in getting a place at the hostel. However, thanks to the intercession by a student leader from Dhaka University who had recognised me, my fellow travellers and I were given a place to stay in the house of a local lawyer who had already been playing host to a number of refugees. This was one of the numerous instances of private individuals in India who had gone out of their way to provide help as well as to share generously their modest resources with the refugees from Bangladesh. In the same house was Taheruddin Thakur,[3] staying in relative seclusion and in visibly greater comfort and style than the rest of us. We were jealous of his privileged situation since everybody else was in a state of deprivation. He did not mix with the rest of us and was not communicative. He was generally regarded as

---

[3] During the 1990s, he was charged with the conspiracy to assassinate Sheikh Mujib in collaboration with Moshtaque.

playing an important role, even though no one seemed to be sure, in organising resistance against Pakistan.

I was anxious to get a seat on the plane to Kolkata. A number of seats were placed at the disposal of the Awami League leaders. Having failed to obtain one of those, I approached the State Minister of Education in Tripura and persuaded him to allot seats from those reserved for their officials for me and one of my companions. He appreciated that with my background I would be more useful for the cause of Bangladesh in Delhi and/or abroad rather than vegetating in Agartala.

Arriving in Kolkata, I stayed in the house of a well known Muslim barrister-at-law. He told me that the Muslims of Kolkata in general were not very sympathetic to the cause of Bangladesh. The Muslims of India believed in the cause and rationale of Pakistan. They believed that a strong and united Pakistan was a balancing factor against India and provided some constraint on India's discriminatory, if not outright hostile, treatment of the Muslims. The Muslims in East should have settled their differences with Pakistan peacefully, without destroying its integrity.

The Hindu population of India, particularly those in West Bengal, were however very supportive. In West Bengal, they felt a sense of strong concern born of a common language, a certain amount of cultural affinity and ethnicity. In the rest of India, there was also widespread public sympathy for our plight. At least in the early 1970s, there was a majority in India for whom the Bangladesh tragedy was a vindication of their belief in the concept of a secular state. The Muslims of Pakistan by waging a war on the Muslims in East Pakistan had proved them right. They were not only sympathetic to us in our agony but were willing to help in achieving our political aspirations.

The government of India, as distinct from the general trend of popular opinion in India, was more circumspect. It had to weigh many considerations, both national and international, before any overt support for Bangladesh could be provided. But the formulation of a strategy was under way.

From Kolkata, I proceeded to Delhi in the company of Amartya Sen,[4] who was then a professor at the Delhi School of Economics. He was

---

[4] Since then he has been awarded the Nobel Prize in Economics and is currently the Master of Trinity College, Cambridge University, England.

in the last stages of his preparations for taking up his appointment at London School of Economics. Later, I moved to the house of Ashok Mitra, whom I had known from earlier contacts and who had already invited one of my economist colleagues from Dhaka to stay with him. He was the Chief Economic Adviser in the Indian Ministry of Finance and was a member of the small group advising Prime Minister Indira Gandhi on the Bangladesh question, which included D.P. Dhar, P.N. Haksar, P.N. Dhar, and S. Chakravarty. There was a great need for briefing them about the background and the future of the Bangladesh freedom struggle. Tajuddin and his team were in the process of building up contacts and formulating the strategy for the liberation war. I became part of this process.

In the early days of April 1971, there was an intense debate underway in the political circles in India about the depth and intensity of the Bangladesh independence movement. India's support for the independence of Bangladesh was not yet assured. First, of particular concern was the nature and extent of support that India should provide to the Bangladesh leaders in India, and how much and how widely the latter represented the genuine aspirations of the people of Bangladesh. Second, there was a need to assess how heavy a burden such help would impose on the economy of a poor country like India. Understandably, India was very wary of any precipitate involvement. Third, its political establishment was keenly aware that for a country to readily encourage or participate in the dismemberment of another country was not accepted and was, in fact, seriously disapproved by the international community. Negotiations and settlement were always preferred by the world at large in situations which were considered internal conflicts or dissensions within sovereign states. Fourth, within the borders of India, there were dissident groups and regions that could demand independence because they were very unhappy with or were seriously aggrieved at what they considered discrimination or victimisation by dominant groups or regions. This was the case with several groups in the northeast states in India. There was a comparable case of Tamils in another neighbouring country i.e. Sri Lanka. The independence of Bangladesh might provide a precedent and incentive to intensify such separatist movements. Fifth, however much an incentive India might have to weaken the mortal enemy (i.e. Pakistan), the course and consequences of any war were always unpredictable. There were always unforeseen risks. Even if Bangladesh won independence with India's help, there was no certainty that an independent Bangladesh would not turn out to be a second Pakistan and unfriendly to India. Sixth, India was worried about the reaction of the superpowers to an active and overt help to the leaders of Bangladesh in exile. The United States and China were known to be hostile to any such help or intervention by India. The attitude of USSR was still uncertain. It was urging on Pakistan a peaceful resolution of the conflict. The rest of the world was not quite sure about the genesis or the prevailing state of the political crisis in Bangladesh. Many of them were counselling moderation and reconciliation on Pakistan.

My principal interlocutors were Ashok Mitra and P.N. Dhar whom I had known from my Harvard days. P.N. Dhar, as Secretary to Indira Gandhi, had a close relationship with her and enjoyed her trust. Among other things about the Bangladesh situation and India's possible role in it, he asked me about the relative position of Tajuddin[5] and Siddiqui in the Awami League hierarchy and whether and, if so, to what extent the government of India should accept them as representative voices of the party and its leader, Sheikh Mujib. I assumed that the intelligence and other sources of India had provided him with much more information than I probably would ever know or could tell him. But it was probably normal procedure in highly volatile situations that P.N. Dhar would collect as much information as possible from as many sources as available to crosscheck and evaluate.

I had the distinct impression, on the basis of discussions with my contacts in Delhi, that there had been no prior contact between Sheikh Mujib and Indira Gandhi before the crackdown by the Pakistan army through any high-level accredited emissary. Therefore, no contingency plan was worked out with India as to the kind of assistance that might be necessary and what would be its modalities. Tajuddin and his colleagues, on their arrival in India, had to establish their credentials as the genuine representatives of the Party as well as their capability to lead a war of liberation.

---

[5] Tajuddin Ahmed became the Prime Minister of the government in exile that was constituted in April 1971. M.R. Siddiqui accompanied Tajuddin to Delhi for discussions with the government of India.

5.2 MAKING BANGLADESH'S CASE ABROAD

After consultation with my colleagues and friends from Bangladesh present in Delhi and the Indian friends, I decided that I should be engaged in lobbying with my contacts abroad for the independence of Bangladesh. In the light of my association with Sheikh Mujib and involvement in the autonomy struggle, my comparative advantage lay in such a task. I was also anxious to go abroad to get news about my family. I had lost all touch with them since I left them in Dhaka in precarious circumstances.

I arrived in the United States around the end of April 1971 and accepted a visiting appointment at the Yale Economic Growth Centre. Even though I was engaged in research, my assignment was light enough to enable me to spend time on lobbying and mobilising support for Bangladesh. The initial reaction of the world community of nation states to Bangladesh war was not to interfere with what was called the internal affairs of a country, even if it was marked by an egregious violation of human rights or a genocide. Moreover, the powerful propaganda machine of Pakistan was vigorously misrepresenting the Bangladesh independence movement as an instigation by India to dismember Pakistan. Under the circumstances, our best efforts should be directed to educate and mobilise public opinion in the western democracies. Their governments would only act under the pressure of public opinion. This included efforts to explain to and persuade the entire range of media, think tanks and professional associations including the student community and the university faculties. The United States was the most important country and the Nixon administration was allied to Pakistan, specially in view of Pakistan's role in facilitating what was called the opening to China.[6]

---

[6] For Nixon and for Kissinger, the architect of Nixon's foreign policy, the close alliance between Pakistan and the United States was expected to balance the alliance between India and the Soviet Union. The reapproachment between China and the United States was sought by the US as a part of its global strategy in the Cold War to offset the Soviet power. China was already a close friend of Pakistan. Bringing China closer to the Pakistan-United States axis in South Asia would also contribute to the reduction of the Soviet influence in South Asia. The emergence of Bangladesh as an independent country weakened Pakistan and worse still, to have Bangladesh allied to India strengthened the influence of the Indo-Soviet alliance in South Asia. As subsequent debates and discussions on the Nixon-Kissinger policy in South Asia revealed, this line of reasoning seemed to explain, to a large extent, Nixon's unfriendly attitude towards and unhappiness with Bangladesh.

My first task was to brief the Ford Foundation in New York. My access to its highest echelon was comparatively easy in view of its long involvement in South Asia and with PIDE of which I was then the Director. Its President was McGeorge Bundy, the quintessential member of the US Establishment. He was the national security adviser in the Kennedy White House and had served President Johnson as well. He knew congressmen from both sides of the aisle, had powerful links with the Democratic Party stalwarts and also with the civil servant-technocrats in the Nixon administration. He was a close friend of McNamara at the World Bank and Pakistan was heavily dependent on the Bank.

When I met Bundy, he appeared well acquainted with the region and was well briefed on the genesis of the Bangladesh crisis. He had been told about my association with Sheikh Mujib and with the autonomy movement. He spent a long time asking me detailed questions on the political leadership including its quality, experience, and commitment. He was genuinely concerned about the atrocities committed by the Pakistan army. Given the fragile economic situation in Pakistan, he thought that the World Bank with its role in the Aid Consortium for Pakistan probably had the most effective leverage on the government in Pakistan. He thought that I should urgently call upon McNamara. While I was sitting with him, he phoned McNamara. He acquainted McNamara with my background, gave him a short account of our discussions and urged him to see me at the earliest.

I met McNamara soon after. When I met him in his office, he was ready with a long list of questions, both economic and political, relating to the genesis of the crisis. What was the origin of the inadequate or limited participation of East Pakistan in political power as well as in the civilian and military establishment? What was the nature and extent of economic deprivation in East Pakistan and what were the policies that contributed to it? What were the specific demands of East Pakistan for regional autonomy? What were the various stages of negotiations with Pakistan until the breakdown? Why Pakistan did not honour the results of election? What alternative Pakistan could have except to negotiate with Sheikh Mujib, the only representative leader of East Pakistan? And so on.

He took copious notes as we talked and following the famous McNamara method, wanted figures and quantitative evidence on the statements I was making. Fortunately, I had been immersed for the past several years in the quantitative analysis of the economic and political aspects of East and West Pakistan relations. Having been involved in the negotiation process in the immediate past, all the facts and figures were fresh in my mind. I did not have much difficulty in standing up to his relentless cross examination. As we parted, he asked me to keep in touch with him and to let him know of significant developments that might be of interest to him.

In the succeeding days and weeks, I made contacts with Peter Cargill and Greg Votaw, the Vice President and Director of the South Asia Region and other officials including Michael Wiehen, the desk officer for Pakistan dealing with Bangladesh. The Indian Executive Director at the World Bank at that time was Dr. S.R. Sen, who was originally from East Bengal, taught at Dhaka University until 1947-48 when he migrated to India. He had a good relationship with McNamara. He kept myself and other colleagues from Bangladesh informed about the events at the World Bank that affected Pakistan-Bangladesh problems. He was very helpful in our lobbying efforts at the Bank.

My next call was upon USAID, which was a more difficult task in view of the unfavourable attitude of the Nixon administration towards Bangladesh. Since I did not personally know the Administrator, I started lobbying with his ex-colleagues at the State University of Michigan whom I knew. However, I rather knew well the Deputy Administrator, Maurice Williams, and Assistant Administrator, Ernest Stern, both of whom had earlier worked in Pakistan. As I came to know later on, Williams was working very closely at that time with Kissinger for arranging his clandestine visit to China through the intermediation of Pakistan. I tried to convince both of them that aid to Pakistan, even if it was nonmilitary, spared her own resources which would otherwise have been spent on development projects but were now available at the disposal of the government to carry out atrocities in East Pakistan.

Williams provided the standard argument that by remaining closely engaged with Pakistan, the United States could exercise influence on Yahya to go slow on his repression on East Pakistan. Moreover, economic aid was meant for humanitarian relief and unavailable for other uses.[7] Stern was personally more sympathetic; his Jewish family was among the refugees from Hitler's genocide. Nevertheless, he repeated even more forcefully that aid to Pakistan was mainly of the humanitarian nature i.e. food aid and infrastructure. Stern emphasised that the use of aid would be closely monitored to prevent their diversion to the military purposes. He was too smart not to understand that resources were fungible and such monitoring was unlikely to be effective. For example, substitution of trucks and lorries between the civilian and military purposes or the use of food aid for the military could not be prevented. Stern further argued that if aid was suspended, the full force of deprivation would fall on East Pakistan because Pakistan would assign priority to its own uses of foreign aid, leaving little for East Pakistan. With a continued flow of aid, there was a likelihood that East would at least get the leftover. He grudgingly admitted that due to the prevailing state of physical insecurity as well as the disruption of transport and communication in East, there might be a problem in carrying out aid projects in East. But he was unwilling to accept the logical conclusion that as a result, whatever aid was given could only be used in West Pakistan.

An important source of lobbying with the Democratic Party and the bureaucrats in the State Department was Chester Bowles, once an Ambassador to India with links to members of the Congress. He lived near New Haven. I was an occasional visitor to his luxurious estate to discuss the latest developments on the Bangladesh crisis. He would convey such news to his friends and acquaintances in the administration and in the Congress to suggest how best to influence the attitude of the White House towards Pakistan. After liberation, he visited Bangladesh, even though he was suffering from Parkinson's disease, to find out how he could help the new nation to find its feet.

---

[7] My conversation with Williams was in April-May 1971. I was correct in my assessment that while he knew my argument to be true, he was unwilling to accept it formally. In August 1971, Williams visited Pakistan and met General Abdul Hamid Khan, Deputy Martial Law Administrator. He discussed this very subject with Hamid and recorded in his dispatches as follows: "...that gave me an opportunity to raise our concerns over reports of continued use for military purposes of boats and vehicles which were needed for transport of humanitarian relief commodities in East Pakistan. I referred to continuing problems we have had over appropriation by military of assault boats we had provided for relief work after last year's cyclone," Department of State telegram 350, quoted in *American Papers — Secret and Confidential — Indo-Pakistan-Bangladesh Documents 1965-73*, compiled and selected by Roedad Khan, Oxford University Press, Karachi, 1999, p. 639.

Chester Bowles joined hands with another powerful critic of the tilt of Nixon administration towards Pakistan, John Kenneth Galbraith, a distinguished professor of economics at Harvard. They were very vocal amongst the intelligentsia and expressed their views forcefully in the media. This was particularly true of Galbraith; with his considerable reputation, his opinions were widely publicised in the press and were as follows. Given Pakistan's brutal repression of East and, as a consequence, a large influx of millions of refugees, it was unrealistic to expect India to stand idly by. She was faced with the threat of destabilisation, both political and economic, in her eastern states. Moreover, the government of India was under the pressure of overwhelming public sympathy to support the independence of Bangladesh. Under the circumstances, the United States should prevail upon Pakistan to reach a settlement with Sheikh Mujib. In its absence, intervention by India and independence of Bangladesh were a certainty.

Their support for Bangladesh in a way was a byproduct of their analysis of what should be the appropriate policy of the United States in South Asia. In their view, the United States should aim at long run peace and stability in the region. Bowles and Galbraith held forth their view in the press and on the platform that Nixon's support for Pakistan's current policy of genocide was shortsighted and wrong. It was coloured by a particular view of the Cold War affecting South Asia. It was backing a wrong horse, a highly unstable military regime pulled apart by ethnic and religious divisions held under check only by the overwhelming might of the army. As the United States continued its policy of strengthening Pakistan with military and economic assistance, India would move closer to Soviet Union to offset the increasing might of Pakistan. The situation was getting worse with the United States drawing closer to Pakistan in order to open the door to China. The result was the creation of India-Soviet axis, on the one hand, and the US-China-Pakistan axis, on the other, and the consequent aggravation of tensions in the subcontinent. To prevent the creation of an independent Bangladesh so that the Indo-Soviet axis did not get a boost was counterproductive. It would drive India even more into the arms of the Soviet Union while the emergence of Bangladesh was inevitable. The Bowles-Galbraith school held that it was in the long run interest of the United States to be supportive of a democratic India — potentially a large economic power — not closely allied to any superpower rather than to strengthen its military alliance with Pakistan, an arch-enemy of India.

Galbraith argued that India would eventually emerge as a regional superpower in South Asia in terms of political and economic prowess, if not in military terms. Pakistan and the United States would be well advised to accept that fact. It would occupy the same status vis-à-vis its neighbouring countries as US occupied in North America in relation to Mexico and Canada. In the course of time, India and its neighbours would reach a *modus operandi* in their mutual relationships in the same way that USA and its North American neighbours had reached a viable relationship. There would be occasional tensions and frustrations, inevitable in a relationship between unequal neighbours. But these would be resolved and managed in the overall framework of peaceful cooperation. An independent Bangladesh might even help to contribute to the maintenance of a balance in the possible conflicts among the countries of the region.[8]

---

[8] It is interesting to recall here a conversation which Nancy Kissinger (spouse of Henry Kissinger, US Secretary of State) had with me and Nazrul Islam, Minister of Industries in the first Cabinet of Bangladesh. The conversation occurred at the dinner reception for Henry Kissinger during his one-day visit to Bangladesh in October 1973. I was sitting next to Nancy Kissinger with Nazrul Islam nearby. She mentioned in the course of conversation that she understood why Bangladesh might have had justifiable grievances against Pakistan but she failed to understand why we should have sought India's help and involvement in our struggle. Her query emphasised the main concern of Henry Kissinger and Nixon administration that the war had shifted the balance of power in South Asia in favour of India and the Indo-Soviet axis. It was clear that she understood that without India's help the war would have continued for a much longer period and victory was uncertain or very unlikely in the short run. That would have been an outcome which would have suited the short term interests of the United States as Kissinger perceived them. As his memoirs and other writings made it clear, Kissinger realised that in the long run the independence of Bangladesh could not have been prevented and was inevitable. But that was in the long run and after the new balance of power in favour of the China-Pakistan-USA axis was established. There would have been time enough to devise a new strategy. From the tenor of Nancy Kissinger's discussion, I could understand that she had been fully briefed about her husband's strategy.

I sought the attention of Nazrul Islam, who was the acting President of the Bangladesh government in exile and one of the architects of the Indo-Bangladesh co-operation during the war, for an appropriate reply. Nazrul Islam, who was understandably annoyed at the question, explained the enormous sacrifices the people of Bangladesh had made in the war of independence and how valiantly the Bangladesh guerilla forces had fought. He emphasised that truly enough our efforts were greatly helped by India, both logistically and by direct engagement of the Indian forces in the war. The Pakistan army had the logistics and all the war arsenal at its command. The speedy conclusion of the war required that we received India's help to overcome them. There was no reason why Bangladesh should not have sought

The most effective constituency for the cause of Bangladesh was, of course, the media. All the major US newspapers, *New York Times*, *Washington Post*, *Christian Science Monitor*, *Herald Tribune*, and others, published throughout 1971 detailed reports on the atrocities committed by Pakistan. The TV channels provided pictorial evidence of the atrocities and the gathering war.

The academic community, including the student organisations, was favourable to our cause, thanks to the lobbying and pressure exerted by many students and academics from Bangladesh. I had visited various universities, explaining the genesis of the freedom struggle and pleading for their support to influence their congressmen in favour of Bangladesh. I had made frequent visits to universities in the East Coast, where there was a very active group of students from Bangladesh. There were also a number of American academics who had spent time in the subcontinent and were closely following the events in Bangladesh with great sympathy and support. Several of the US academics who were associated with PIDE in various capacities came from such top universities as Stanford, Berkeley, Yale, and Harvard. They were a force in the academic community and were held in high esteem not only by the public but also by the government. Their opinions were taken seriously. Our contacts with the US academic community were very helpful. Professors from various universities combined together to persuade the Nobel Laureates among them to address an open letter to Nixon to change his policy towards Bangladesh. This was a very important success on the part of the Bangladesh community and its academic friends.

Several incidents are worth recounting in this context. There was a seminar on Bangladesh organised by the South Asia group at Columbia University. The South Asian experts from the university and outside including the US government, a large number of students and several Bangladeshi academics attended. A number of experts

---

help from any friendly country that was willing to help in the overthrow of our enemy. We sought India's help as she was a neighbour willing to help in order to save us from genocide.

Many years later, I related this incident to a few of my academic friends in the United States, obviously not from the Nixon administration. They felt that I should have asked Nancy Kissinger a counter question in reply to her question: "Were the North American colonies of Britain during their war of independence justified in seeking help from France?" I regret my lack of presence of mind to ask her this most appropriate question. Undoubtedly, her answer would have been most revealing.

raised a pointed question: whether in our outrage at the historical repression and current atrocities perpetrated by Pakistan we were not moving from the frying pan of the Pakistani subjugation to the fire of domination by India. We protested very strongly that this argument did not recognise the third alternative i.e. an independent Bangladesh that would hold its own against any kind of domination. The liberation struggle of 1971 and sacrifices that were being made by the people during the war were abundant evidence that we were ready to pay a very heavy price for our independence. Such questions arose partly from the legacy of the past history i.e. the Hindu-Muslim conflict and the repression of the minority Muslims in India, and partly from a perception that Bangladesh would not have adequate capacity to maintain or manage an independent economy and polity, or would not have the strength and stamina to fight, if threatened, against external domination. We had to reiterate that their perception was wrong and was based on presumptions that were not valid.

Edward Mason was in a way the doyen of the group of US academics who were involved in advising the US government and private foundations on economic development policies in the Third World. He had visited Pakistan many times over the years and had met many high officials and Ministers of Pakistan. He had, accordingly, developed a certain perception of the crisis in Pakistan. Around August/September 1971, he wanted to have a serious one-to-one discussion with me. It was his considered judgement and prediction that Bangladesh would most likely emerge as an independent country. What worried him most was whether we were ready to run an independent state. Did we have, first, the necessary quality of political leadership and second, administrative and managerial experience and competence? He had no direct acquaintance with the political leaders of Bangladesh. He had met a few civil service officers from East Pakistan, some of whom had come to Harvard for a special training programme for the civil servants. They were rather junior and had limited experience. In particular, he was concerned that Shiekh Mujib and his associates probably lacked the necessary experience in administration and policymaking. After all, they had been precluded from such positions of responsibilities by Pakistan. He admired the charismatic leadership of Sheikh Mujib, his unique capacity for mobilising and galvanising the people of Bangladesh and his indomitable courage in the face of heavy risks and grave danger. But he was not sure about his capacity to govern an independent country facing a host of accumulated problems of underdevelopment. Mason's judgement was based upon his contacts in Pakistan, which included US officials and experts who worked in Pakistan as well as the Pakistanis in the government and professions. He had close contacts with the US State Department. He was considered a South Asian expert.[9]

My approach in reply to Mason was to recognise the importance of the problems he mentioned. This is the kind of challenge which indeed faced most newly independent countries. The politicians did have a very limited experience of policymaking and administration. Sheikh Mujib was indeed aware of the problem. He would not hesitate to draw upon the required skills and experience, wherever available inside and outside the government, in order to man the new administration. He would also make use of expertise from abroad, whenever it was necessary. What was most important at an early stage was a high degree of commitment and dedication on the part of those who would be involved in building the new nation. I was not quite sure that Mason was fully convinced by my arguments but, at the same time, he recognised that there was no alternative but to proceed on the basis of my assumptions.

I realised later, when I was in the postindependent government, that the concerns and worries voiced by our well wishers abroad were genuine. However, in my judgement, there was one serious caveat.

---

[9] It is useful to quote in this context a dispatch about Sheikh Mujib from the US Consul General at Dhaka who had met Sheikh Mujib after the 1970 election in which he emerged as the undisputed leader of East Pakistan. The dispatch indicates how Sheikh Mujib appeared to the institutional eyes of the US government: "Mujib is a life long full-time politician. Since 1948, Mujib spent almost 10 years in Pakistani jails climaxed by the *Agartala Conspiracy Case* which martyrized him in the eyes of the East Pakistani people and guaranteed his rise to power. Mujib, the man, is hard to characterise. In private meetings, calm and confident, he is charming, he is well travelled and urbane, on the rostrum he is a fiery orator and he can mesmerise hundreds and thousands in pouring rain. As a Party leader, he is tough and authoritative, often arrogant, has something of a messianic complex which has been reinforced by the heady experience of mass adulation. Mujib has shown himself to be impulsive and emotional when talking of Bengali grievances." "One of Mujib's oft-quoted refrains that East Pakistan is part of South Asia and not Middle East raises the question whether accommodation between the two wings is possible or desirable." "Somehow it is hard to imagine Mujib ruling in Islamabad out of touch with and not fortified by his Bengali masses." *Ibid* Roedad Khan pp. 435-436.

It was not so much a lack of managerial or administrative experience or competence, although there were undoubtedly deficiencies on that score. More important was the lack of high degree of commitment and dedication, excepting in a few cases, that compounded our difficulties. The various segments of society were unwilling or unable to accommodate and compromise. Acute political divisions between groups and sections in the country surfaced after independence. A large section of the party in power as well as those outside had not gone through the crucible of long political training and experience. Nor did they command the wisdom and experience to contain or resolve the contradictions and divisions that emerged following independence.

While we were engaged in our lobbying efforts, Pakistan launched a powerful propaganda offensive sending emissaries to various countries, trying to influence public opinion. One such delegation consisted of a group of university professors from East collaborating with Pakistan. The delegation was sent to meet the faculties in the US university to counter the news about the atrocities committed by Pakistan against the intellectuals. Unhappily for me, there were in the delegation some who were my colleagues at Dhaka University and well known to me. The Pakistan ambassador invited a group of selected professors from the well known US universities to meet them. The delegation made the point that the military targeted only a very few intellectuals, who were actually involved in the armed struggle against Pakistan. The overwhelming majority were left alone, undisturbed to continue their professional pursuits. The educational institutions were also functioning normally.

The American academics, of course, knew differently to fall for such a canard. They were well informed by reports from nongovernmental organisations and experts working in Pakistan as well as refugees in the United States from the army action at home, adding to the extensive coverage by the media. There were also the widely circulating news at the time that a group of Foreign Service officers in the US consulate in Dhaka had protested against the White House's connivance at Pakistan's policy. They were recalled and reprimanded.

The delegation should have known better than to parrot Pakistan's propaganda line. One of the American professors with whom I had been in frequent contact asked them as to which category did I belong since I had left the country in fear of my life. The delegation emphasised that there was absolutely no danger to my life as a respected academic. I had a very nervous disposition and was unduly influenced by rumours and lies spread by the Indian propaganda. There was no reason why I could not go back and lead a normal life.

All this was said at a time when Kamal Hossain, on trial in Pakistan, was undergoing interrogation at the hands of the military tribunal as to what transpired in the regular nightly meetings he attended in my house. These meetings, according to the military, were devoted to planning for the independence of Bangladesh. Indeed, those were the days when we as advisers to Sheikh Mujib were managing the civil disobedience movement of March 1971. Also, soon after the crackdown by the military, my brother-in-law who was an army officer in the Dhaka cantonment and used to meet with me frequently, was taken away to Pakistan. He was tortured and questioned, among other things, about my seditious activities and his possible association.

The irony of it all was that the blatant propaganda by my one-time colleagues not only damaged their credibility but also did not further the objective of Pakistan. Their collaboration with Pakistan brought them little gain. When their usefulness was over, their users abandoned them. Nor did they have any place in their own country in early years, though after 1975 with a dramatic change in political circumstances some of them were brought back from oblivion and were rehabilitated.

My visiting appointment at Yale was short term and the future was highly uncertain with the possibility of a long term exile abroad. I started to explore the possibilities for a longer term appointment. In the meantime, I had visited the World Bank a few times in connection with the Bangladesh movement. Hollis Chenery had known me well because of his association with PIDE. He was on leave from Harvard, and was then the Vice President in charge of the Economics Department in the World Bank. He was in the midst of establishing a Development Research Centre at the Bank to undertake long range and basic research on economic development problems and policies. He wanted to know whether I would be interested in being its Director. In general terms, the assignment would be in line with my past experience at PIDE. But it would be on a much larger canvas and at a higher level and over a wide range of developing countries, with ample opportunities of interaction with researchers at universities and academic centres. He was aware of my close involvement in the Bangladesh independence movement. He suggested that if, in the future, our hopes were realised and I wanted to go back to an independent Bangladesh, there would be nothing to prevent me from doing so. He himself intended to return to his professorial job in the future. In fact, he did go back to Harvard in the early 1980s.

This was a very attractive offer and the rank of the job was pretty high in the hierarchy of the Bank's administration. In those days, there were very few Directors and fewer Vice Presidents. Fewer still were those from the developing world. This was thus a unique opportunity that came my way. Following my agreement to be considered for the job, McNamara interviewed me. I accepted the formal letter of appointment on the understanding that I would join only at the end of 1971.

Predictably, the Executive Director of Pakistan in the Bank vigorously objected to my appointment on the ground that I was a citizen of Pakistan who was engaged in anti state activities. Therefore, I was not eligible for appointment in the Bank that was, after all, an organisation of the member states. McNamara held his ground that he was not required by the Statutes of the Bank to obtain an approval of a member country for such a professional appointment. As far as he knew, the candidate had not been convicted for any criminal activity. In any case, I would not work on any assignment related to Pakistan. At that time Pakistan was feverishly seeking the Bank's assistance to face her dire economic circumstances. She did not consider it advisable to contest McNamara's authority on an administrative matter of professional appointment. The challenge dissipated quickly.

An important part of the mobilisation of international support for Bangladesh was to demonstrate to the world that Pakistan had lost the allegiance of the Bangladeshi officers abroad. A few of us both in the USA and Europe were in touch with the Bangladesh officers in the different embassies. The defections of the Bangladesh officers in Kolkata mission of Pakistan came in April 1971. They were contacted by the Indian military intelligence in the first week of April in order to find out whether they would join the Bangladesh government in exile.[10]

---

[10]Lt. General J.F.R. Jacob, *Surrender at Dacca: Birth of a Nation*, The University Press Limited, 1997, p. 41.

Bangladesh staff agreed if their future service, pay and allowances were provided for. After discussion with the representatives of the Indian government, the Mujibnagar government[11] agreed to the arrangement. An avalanche of defections followed in August and succeeding months. The defections were greatly facilitated by a generous provision, following the precedence in Kolkata, of financial assistance by India. By then, it was clear that, faced with the risks of destabilisation in the politically volatile Indian States bordering Bangladesh, and overwhelmed by the millions of refugees, India would take military action in favour of Bangladesh. It was also evident that in such an eventually she would have the support of the Soviet Union. The *Indo-Soviet Friendship Treaty* was formally signed around this time. Under the circumstances, we felt optimistic but not absolutely sure how soon we would emerge as an independent nation. The course of war was always very uncertain.

By the third quarter of 1971, the Mujibnagar government established a liaison office in Washington with Siddiqui[12] as its head. The Annual Bank-Fund meeting was to be held in September/October 1971 in Washington and was to be attended by the Finance Ministers and officials from all the donor countries. All of us, Bangladeshis in East Coast, had decided to mount a concerted effort to contact the donor governments in whatever way and at whatever levels we could in order to argue the case and gain their support against aid to Pakistan. Already the World Bank mission had reported in the Pakistan consortium meeting in the mid-1971 that under the highly insecure and unstable circumstances prevailing in East Pakistan, it was not possible to carry out development activities. This led them to reexamine their new aid commitment to Pakistan. Our aim was to reinforce their reexamination and convince them that any aid to Pakistan, even the disbursement of the existing commitments and even if it was limited to uses in West Pakistan, would provide additional resources to Pakistan for continuing its acts of repression. The busy officials from donor countries did not keep track of the details of atrocities carried out in East Pakistan. They had to be briefed and brought up to date.

---

[11]The government in exile was named the Mujibnagar government.

[12]M.R. Siddiqui became the Minister of Commerce in the first Cabinet.

This was an ideal occasion to exploit all the friendships and associations I had built up during my professional life until then. It was through such acquaintances that it was possible to secure access to various country delegations. The Bank officials with whom we had already established rapport over the last few months assisted by securing for us access to the delegations and introducing us, wherever necessary, to the individual delegates. The country delegations that we found specially sympathetic included the United Kingdom, France, Germany, and the Nordic countries. In fact, many donor country delegations were sympathetic but were not willing to take any initiative on their own because of a variety of bilateral commercial and political interests in Pakistan. They were, however, willing to act collectively since their public opinion in any case was supportive of Bangladesh. But they were also aware that the United States was a strong supporter of Pakistan. The World Bank as an international agency had the decisive role. If the Bank were to advise on the highly unstable situation in Pakistan and on the obstacles in the way of use of development aid, most of them were willing to join as a group in a decision to withhold aid, specially not to commit any new aid.

Japan, a very major donor to Pakistan and an important member of the Bank, was a very willing member of this group. I had visited Japan earlier in the year. My most important friend in Japan was Saburu Okita. He was a very influential economist in Japan and an adviser to the various governments in Japan on economic policy as well as on overseas economic assistance.[13] I made him fully aware of what was happening in Pakistan and he was all sympathy for Bangladesh. Japan was one of the earliest countries to recognise Bangladesh. Moreover, since a major part of Japan's assistance to Pakistan consisted of projects in East Pakistan, it was not difficult for her to delay or postpone aid in 1971. During my visit to Japan, I had met major development economists such as Shigetu Tsuru, a left-leaning economist who was a visiting professor at Harvard during the early 1960s. He and his associates were bitterly opposed to aid to military governments. To them, the Bangladesh case illustrated how military governments used foreign aid to suppress the democratic

---

[13]He was the Chief of the Overseas Assistance Agency in Japan in 1973 when Sheikh Mujib visited Japan, and later on became the Foreign Minister.

aspirations of their people. They arranged for me to be interviewed by *Ashahi Shimbum*, a renowned newspaper with great influence and very wide circulation.

It may be worth recalling here that, while all these were going on and far removed from Kolkata, I did know that there was tension — not a serious rift — between Tajuddin, the Prime Minister of the government in exile, and Moshtaque, the Foreign Minister. From time to time, I was writing to Tajuddin relating the developments in USA as well as in the World Bank and the IMF. I kept writing to Tajuddin about my various encounters and the implications thereof. These were personal letters for his eyes only and in order to make sure that they were delivered to him personally, I sent them to Mahbubul Alam Chashi, who was with Moshtaque, Minister of Foreign Affairs in the government in exile, with a request to hand them over to Tajuddin. At the same time, I wrote separately to Chashi once or twice and he wrote back to me. I took it for granted that Chashi delivered my letters to Tajuddin. But I never received any reply from Tajuddin. I assumed that he was too busy to write back. Moreover, whatever he had to say was probably contained in the messages and the letters from Chashi. I kept myself generally informed about the happenings in the government in exile. By the courtesy of friends who travelled to India and brought news from Kolkata,[14] I knew in general about disunity among the different groups in the government in exile. I did not realise that Chashi who was an important member of the Moshtaque group would go so far as to prevent or cut off my contact with Tajuddin.[15]

The start of the Indo-Pakistan war on December 3, 1971 had put us all in a state of great tension, excitement and expectations. We were glued to the media following the debates in the United Nations.

---

[14]Moshtaque, a senior member of the Awami League leadership and a few others in the Party felt that Tajuddin had out-maneuvered them in order to secure the position of the Prime Minister in the government in exile. By this act, in their opinion he had downgraded them. Accordingly, their relationship was marked by palpable tensions and became increasingly unpleasant when it became known that Moshtaque was making contacts with a Kissinger emissary in Kolkata to reach a compromise with Pakistan for preserving its unity.

[15]On my return when I met Tajuddin he asked me why I never wrote to him. It was only then that I found out how foolish and naive I was and how easily I was taken for a ride by Chashi. And I had known Chashi very well from my student days; our families had known each other and I counted him among my friends.

The Soviet Union vetoed successive resolutions on the ceasefire in the war and, in the meanwhile, the Indian army was overrunning East Pakistan, forcing the Pakistan army to surrender. We witnessed the debate between the Indian Foreign Minister, Swaran Singh, and Zulfiqar Ali Bhutto of Pakistan. Bhutto made his histrionic exit from the Security Council tearing away the piece of paper supposedly containing the UN resolution he did not approve of. His daughter, Benazir Bhutto, was an undergraduate at Harvard in those days and was following the drama as much as anyone of us. The newspapers widely covered his theatrical performance. His daughter was reported · to have been greatly perplexed and disturbed and expressed her consternation at her distinguished father's unseemly behaviour in full view of the world community. He reassured her that there were occasions when for maximum effect one had to behave in a manner which might otherwise be considered histrionic or dramatic.[16]

The Pakistan army surrendered on December 16, 1971. A new nation was born with its leader held in captivity in Pakistan. For most of us, it was the ultimate fulfilment of our hopes and a time of great excitement. Bangladesh emerged on the international scene at the height of the Cold War. The trials and tribulations that we would inevitably face in the course of time were not yet on the horizon. We were overwhelmed by the impact of what happened.

---

[16]Many years later when Benazir Bhutto, as the Prime Minister of Pakistan, was attending a UN conference in Beijing, she was asked about the Bangladesh war, including the rape of defenseless Bangladesh women by the Pakistan army. She responded that at that time she was away from Pakistan and did not know much about the details of the Bangladesh war. And this was the reply from an undergraduate at Harvard University in 1971 who was constantly suffused with reports and analyses about the Bangladesh war and the atrocities committed by Pakistan Army. She was known to be a very politically conscious and active student, and was very close to her beloved father, one of the chief architects of the repression of East Pakistan by the Pakistan army.

Part II
BUILDING A STATE

Chapter 6

PLANNING COMMISSION: ENTRY AND EXIT

6.1 INTRODUCTION

I watched the Pakistan army's surrender in Dhaka on the US television on December 16, 1971. Needless to say, I was excited and decided to return immediately to Bangladesh to see for myself the first days of the independent country and my family and friends. I arrived in Kolkata en route to Dhaka and found that the government in exile had mostly returned. But a skeleton unit of its foreign ministry, consisting mainly of Mahbubul Alam Chashi, Taheruddin Thakur and a few others, was left behind ostensibly to wind up the remnants of the establishment. I wanted a seat as soon as possible on one of . the flights to Dhaka that the government of India had placed at their disposal.

While waiting for my flight, I found that Chashi was meeting different groups of people for extended discussions. He requested me to sit in one of his brainstorming sessions with them. I was told that they were freedom fighters and the discussions related to their post liberation plans and programmes of activities. It would be most unfortunate if they were to be lost to the society when they returned home without any organisation and leadership. They were full of enthusiasm and very eager to serve in nation-building activities. His idea was to mobilise and train them as multipurpose workers/cadres for integrated development of the rural areas. However, the attitudes and methods that were useful for the guerilla war were very different from those that would be required for the agents of rural development.

They had to be trained in skills, organisation, and discipline. A great deal would depend on the leaders who would be responsible for organising and harnessing their considerable energy and enthusiasm.

When Chashi returned to Dhaka he was appointed the Secretary , of the Ministry of Rural Development. However, by that time, his alleged involvement in Moshtaque's secret negotiations with the emissaries of Kissinger in Kolkata had cast a shadow on him. He was soon transferred from the Ministry. His programme of mobilising the freedom fighters was considered to have a political agenda behind it.

After some days' wait in Kolkata, I became very impatient to return to Dhaka and decided to contact P.N. Dhar, Secretary to the Indian Prime Minister in New Delhi, for help. I was already in touch with him when I arrived in Bombay en route to Kolkata. He suggested that I should proceed to Dhaka soonest for whatever assistance the new government needed and I could provide at that time. Accordingly, he arranged for me to be flown to Dhaka on one of the helicopter flights 'run by the Indian military.

In Dhaka, the government was not yet firmly on the saddle. All the fissures in the Party and in the Cabinet that were suppressed or laid dormant during the days in exile, when the overriding need to work with the Government of India compelled some coherence, were now out in the open. Tajuddin was buffeted on all sides by conflicting pulls and pushes. Tajuddin was not his usual organised, methodical and analytical self. During my first few meetings with him, Tajuddin appeared too preoccupied to be able to respond decisively to various proposals made to him by me — sometimes jointly with Rehman Sobhan who had also returned by then — on a few urgent institutional arrangements for economic policymaking and implementation. It could also be that he did not have great interest or confidence in the quality or the nature of suggestions we made. In any case, he was pressed hard to establish law and order and manage the day-to-day administration.

As I went around calling upon the Cabinet Ministers, I found none of them in a highly receptive mood to engage in serious discussions of economic policymaking or implementation. Understandably, it was too early. They were not yet quite firmly settled in their respective Ministries. However, the Finance Minister at the time, Mansoor Ali, came out with a serious proposal for me. The currency in circulation in the country was in a chaotic state. Both Indian and Pakistani notes were in circulation. To make matters worse, there was also a large amount of counterfeit Indian notes in circulation. This encouraged smuggling, capital flight, and exacerbated inflationary pressure. There was an urgent need for remedial measures in respect of credit regulation and for printing Bangladesh currency notes to replace all the others. He wanted me to head the Bangladesh Bank as its governor and help him sort out the muddled situation. However, I was in no mood to be rushed into accepting a job at a time when the government was in such an unsettled state, yet to find a shape or a form. Its leadership was yet undecided. Sheikh Mujib's future was unknown. I suggested that he should appoint some one from amongst the bankers on an *ad hoc* basis and I and my colleagues could provide advice, if needed, to the incumbent.

By the first week of January, as I was debating how soon to return to the United States where my family was left behind, it was announced that Sheikh Mujib was due to return very soon. There was an electrifying change in the political atmosphere, attitudes and expectations in the country. It was now out of the question that I could leave without waiting for his return. I went to see him on his return. He received me with great warmth and affection. He had been deeply concerned about my whereabouts and safety. On his arrival in London from Pakistan he had enquired about me and on learning that I was in the USA, had sent messages for my immediate return to Dhaka. He wanted me to see him the next day for urgent consultations.

Next morning when I arrived, I found him in the company of several of his political associates, sworn in as Cabinet Ministers the day before: Nazrul Islam, Tajuddin Ahmed, Kamal Hossain, and a few others. Apparently, he was in the process of making high level appointments in the Ministries and related institutions. The administrative machinery had to start working at the earliest. Among the appointments announced while I was there were: Sarwar Murshid as the Vice Chancellor for Rajshahi University, A.R. Mallick for Chittagong University and Matiul Islam as the Finance Secretary. At one stage, he turned to me and announced that I was to take over as the Deputy Chairman of the Planning Commission. Of course, he would be the Chairman, oblivious to the fact that he had already appointed Tajuddin as the Minister in charge of Planning and Finance. It would take one more year to disentangle this knot. I was instructed to submit for his and the Cabinet's approval the constitution of the Commission, including its functions and composition.

My dilemma was that I had already accepted a job abroad. I consulted with my family members; they were divided in their opinions. Some were opposed to my accepting the job because they had a poor opinion of the quality of the party leadership and its commitment to and vision for the country's progress or welfare. Others were worried about the enormity of the problems I would face and the high degree of stress in such an assignment compared to a secure, well paid and highly professional job abroad. My friends and colleagues felt that this was a challenge I must accept. How could I possibly say no to Sheikh Mujib when he called upon me to help him build a new country? It was a feeling of total exhilaration at that moment which overwhelmed my misgivings. Should not those who had believed in the dream of an independent country now work for its future under the leadership of the founder of the new state?

6.2 PLANNING COMMISSION ESTABLISHED

With the help of my associates and colleagues, I worked out the functions, structure and composition of the Planning Commission. It so happened that just before the arrival of Sheikh Mujib we had prepared several proposals for discussion with Tajuddin on policymaking institutions that were to be established in the new country. The elaboration of the role and the structure of the Planning Commission figured prominently among them. Keeping in mind the lessons of experience of other countries, in particular India and Pakistan, we tried to synthesise what we considered to be their best features, adjusted to the particular circumstances of Bangladesh.

Since the structure of the government was likely to be reorganised in order to elevate it from a provincial to a national government, it was an opportune time to think logically about the structure and functions of the Planning machinery vis-à-vis the rest of the government. The basic idea was to make it the central coordinating organisation for development programmes as well as the focal point for advice on economic policies. Among the functions assigned to the Commission were the following: preparation and evaluation of Five-Year and Annual Plans; appraisal and approval of development projects; negotiation of foreign aid; formulation of policies, both macro and sectoral, in cooperation with other Ministries, including initiation of policy papers on major or new issues facing the economy; and evaluation of the performance of the economy, including that of the implementation of the Five-Year and Annual Plans.

As it subsequently turned out and as we should have known, the past traditions and attitudes of the various constituents in the government, specially the politicians and the members of the civil service, mattered a great deal. At the end of the day, they would have a great impact on what would be the role of the Commission and how effective it would be, no matter what is documented or elaborated on paper.

The composition of the Commission was dictated by the consideration that the Members were in tune with the ideology and ideas of Sheikh Mujib and of his senior advisers.[1] Moreover, they were deemed to be competent and committed. They had built up a working relationship with the political leadership during the fateful days of 1970 elections and subsequent negotiations with Pakistan. This and the confidence that they had gained in the process were also important considerations.

In addition, it was felt that in those difficult and formative days it was very essential that they were a cohesive group. They should be able to work in close harmony and trust in an environment which was likely to be plagued by divergent pulls and pressures. The team should have mutual respect and hold similar views about the role of the Planning Commission. This was important in the task of building up a new organisation in an unfamiliar terrain.

Questions were subsequently raised about the composition of the Commission. Why only economists were appointed as Members? Why there were no scientists or engineers? But once the search was extended beyond economists, the choice among the multitude of specialities in science and engineering was not easy. What criteria could be used in selecting from among various disciplines? One could have

---

[1] Professors Mosharraf Hossain, Rehman Sobhan, and Anisur Rahman joined the Planning Commission in early 1972.

chosen a water engineer, for example. After all it was a very critical sector of the economy and water development was a high priority planning and policy problem. In fact, we did not feel very badly the need for such a specialist in the capacity of a Member. It was felt that economists with a wide background would serve well as Members of the Commission dealing with policy analysis and sector programmes.[2] The inputs required from scientists, engineers, and other disciplines could be provided by technical experts in the various technical divisions of the Commission, and by outside consultants. We did take the help of consultants on numerous occasions. However, there was a political and public relations aspect that I had overlooked. The public image and political acceptability of the Commission probably would have been enhanced by the inclusion of noneconomist technical experts. I should have advised Sheikh Mujib accordingly and the omission was a mistake on my part.

Why were administrators also excluded? This was indeed an important omission but it was recognised as such right at the outset. Since civil service officials ran the rest of the government, their cooperation was essential. A search was undertaken for a senior civil servant. In fact, a retiree was needed because the rules of service required that a Member of the Commission, a political appointee with the status of a State Minister, could not continue in the civil service. Also, the candidate had to be a senior civil servant who would command the respect and cooperation of the civil service officials over the entire range of administration.

The choice was Shamsur Rahman, a prematurely retired senior civil servant well known to Sheikh Mujib. He was a co-accused with Sheikh Mujib in the *Agartala Conspiracy Case*. I persuaded Rahman with some effort and considerable pressure to accept the membership. When I approached Sheikh Mujib for his approval, he sprung on us the news that Rahman had already been nominated for ambassadorship to the Soviet Union. Rahman himself, it seemed, was taken by surprise

---

[2] Sheikh Mujib often used to remark that the Planning Commission was like "potatoes", which went well in all kinds of meals or food preparations and added flavour to them. Whenever he would appoint subcommittees or working groups, ministerial or otherwise, to examine, deliberate, and recommend policies on a wide range of issues or on programmes covering different ministries, he would invariably include a representative of the Commission in their membership.

at this announcement. In those days, seldom was Sheikh Mujib's call declined since it was deemed a patriotic act to accede to his request.

No other candidate who would meet the criteria could be easily found, i.e. a senior and retired civil servant with suitable qualifications, available and known to Sheikh Mujib. Alternatively, the candidate, if found suitable but not retired, had to be willing to retire in order to accept a temporary political appointment, thus sacrificing the career prospects of a civil servant. Most of the senior civil servants who might have been suitable were stranded in Pakistan. Thus, the Commission started with a Deputy Chairman and three Members — all economists. However, in 1974, A.K.M. Ahsan, a senior civil servant repatriated from Pakistan, was appointed a member of the Commission.

6.3 COMMISSIONS' STATUS

Why was it necessary to accord the high status of a State Minister to the Members? The Members had the function of coordinating policies and programmes which invariably cut across or had implications for multiple Ministries. The projects and policies were to be evaluated in the context of their interlinked complexities. They were to be put together within a consistent and overall framework by the Members of the Commission through a process of interministerial consultation. Their Ministerial status was deemed essential in performing such a coordination. We felt in view of the prevailing bureaucratic tradition that unless the Members had a status higher than that of the Secretaries, they would not have the authority to require the participation of Secretaries in such consultations. This was necessary to expedite the process of decision making. Junior officials would not have the requisite authority to present vigorously their viewpoints; nor would they be able to commit the Ministries to the decisions reached at these consultations. Their bosses, i.e. Secretaries, would always be able to keep their options open to the end and to decide otherwise. This was partly due to the concentration of decision making power at the higher levels of the official hierarchy with inadequate delegation of authority to the lower levels.[3] Moreover, it was the responsibility

---

[3] The system and these considerations might have changed over time and might no longer be relevant nowadays. On the other hand , the Members at present do not, if I understand correctly, enjoy the same range of functions and authority in terms of interministerial coordination.

of Members to review the results of interministerial deliberations carried out at the lower echelons of the hierarchy and subsequently to iron out at higher level any remaining disagreements. There were also occasions when it was necessary for a Member to discuss directly with Ministers to sort out issues or disagreements. The Members could thus, because of their status, directly raise interministerial deliberations from the level of Secretaries to the level of Ministers.

The question of status was also judged to be relevant for the professional staff of the Commission. The Chiefs of the technical divisions were given the status of Secretaries so that they could, first, deal with the Secretaries of other Ministries on an equal footing and, second, secure cooperation from their junior officials. If the officials in the rest of the government did not welcome the high status of the Members, then the status of Secretaries granted to the professional staff was the unkindest cut of all. This was in spite of the fact that most of them were among the best professionals in their respective fields.[4]

The Planning Commission, which by its nature could only perform its functions with the willing cooperation and assistance of the other Ministries, had right from the early days faced tensions and problems in its relationship with them.[5] Briefly, one could think of two reasons for the tensions. First, unlike in Pakistan, the leadership of the Commission did not rest with the civil servants. It was felt that a professor as a Deputy Chairman could not possibly play the role that was played by the civil service in Pakistan — the only model that the civil service of Bangladesh had known and experienced. Other models in the rest of the world, including neighbouring India, were

---

[4] The issue of status was not easily resolved and continued to hamper the Commission's work. Very soon there emerged a conflict, petty and ridiculous, between the Commission and the Establishment Division of the government, about the secretarial and related facilities including transport facilities to be provided to Division Chiefs in the Commission. It was argued that though the latter had the status of a Secretary, they were not actual Secretaries and, therefore, were not entitled to the same facilities. This issue could not be solved by negotiation at the level of the officials and had to be brought to the level of the Deputy Chairman. Since the Minister in charge of the Establishment Division was the Prime Minister, he was the only one to resolve the issue — obviously an absurd situation to be brought to such a ridiculous impasse. Indeed, the Prime Minister had to instruct his Secretary of Establishment to meet with me and resolve it.

[5] An earlier book on *Development Planning in Bangladesh* by me described the issues exhaustively. N Islam; *Development Planning in Bangladesh*, C. Hurst & Co., London, 1977; and The University Press Limited, Dhaka, 1978.

not well known. That experts from outside the government could be appointed at key decision making levels with the same status and rank as Ministers was unfamiliar. It probably seemed rather extraordinary to the civil service in Bangladesh. It was not easy to adjust so soon after independence to a new dispensation and abandon established habits.

More importantly, it was held that the role of economic policy coordination could not be entrusted to persons without administrative experience. However, the precise nature of administrative experience relevant to the work of the Members of the Commission was never spelled out. Administrative experience defined as running a district administration and supervising law and order agencies was obviously not relevant. Experience in the implementation of development projects was relevant to the Planning Commission in its task of evaluation and appraisal of projects. This kind of experience was basically gained by subject matter specialists in various Ministries and development agencies. In fact, this type of specialists manned the technical divisions in the Commission.

One could, however, argue that those experts in the Planning Commission who were drawn from outside the government agencies were unfamiliar with the rules and regulations that govern the functioning of the government departments and agencies. However, Planning Commission had taken care to ensure that administrative rules and regulations were known and followed in its work and in its relation to other Ministries. This was the defined purpose of the administrative division of the Planning Commission which looked after administrative rules and procedures. This division was run by the civil service officials who had years of experience in this kind of work in various Ministries.

In the Bangladesh context, it was ironic that the complaint about the lack of experience of the Members or Staff of the Commission was made most vigorously by those very officials who had none or very little experience in policymaking or development programming in the central government of Pakistan. Very few were senior enough to hold high level policymaking responsibilities.

The rest of the government at that time somehow was not familiar with the lessons of experience of many countries where central policymaking or planning and programming organisations were basically run and manned in the manner in which it was initiated in Bangladesh. This was the case in Korea, Indonesia, Thailand, and a host of Latin American countries. In fact, in Latin America in the absence of a tradition of a generalist civil service of the type that was prevalent in the UK and other Western European countries, even the sectoral Ministries, let alone economic planning and finance, were run by professionals at the level not only of Ministers but also of administrative and executive officials. In many countries, various economic and planning agencies and Ministries were run by subject-matter specialists and not by generalists. In cases when nonspecialists were recruited for sectoral Ministries, they made their long term career in the same or related Ministries and became specialists through further professional training and accumulated experience. This was the practice even in developed countries like the United States and Japan, for example.

In India, the functions of economic analysis and policymaking were mainly divided between the Finance Ministry and the Planning Commission, while the evaluation and approval of the development programmes and projects were left to the Planning Commission. Not just the Planning Commission, but also the Finance Ministry built up a very high level of economic expertise in the Economic Adviser's office, which also dealt with foreign aid agencies. Although initially the Finance Ministry was the exclusive domain of civil servants, their hold was eventually diluted through the appointment of an economist to the job of the Economic Secretary in the Finance Ministry.[6] In addition, highly qualified economists manned various economic Ministries as advisers.

Indian Planning Commission started with great prestige and influence because of Nehru's personal interest in its early years and was staffed and led predominantly by economists and specialists. However, foreign aid negotiations were in the hands of the Economic Secretary in the Ministry of Finance. The Deputy Chairman and the Members of the Planning Commission had the high status of Ministers and State Ministers, respectively, as was the case in Bangladesh.

In Pakistan, the organisation for economic policymaking was different. The Finance Minister for a long time during the 1960s was the dominant

---

[6] See, *Glimpses of Indian Economic Policy — An Insider's View* by I.G. Patel, Oxford University Press, Delhi, 2002.

figure in economic policymaking and he used both the Finance Ministry officials and the experts in the Planning Commission in this task. The relative influence of the Finance Minister and the Deputy Chairman of the Planning Commission depended on their political connections with the President. Even though foreign aid negotiation was formally outside the purview of the Planning Commission, the Economic Affairs Division, responsible for such negotiations, was under the Deputy Chairman of the Planning Commission who had the status of a Minister. Thus, in fact, Planning Commission was closely involved in aid negotiations because it was heavily involved in policy dialogue with the aid agencies.

The Members of the Planning Commission in Pakistan did not have the status of State Ministers but had a somewhat undefined status and enjoyed some perks greater than those enjoyed by Secretaries. Their responsibilities were, in fact, limited and were mainly of an advisory nature. They did not exercise effective supervisory or executive authority over the technical sections of the Planning Commission in the way we had envisaged it in Bangladesh. The various sections of the Planning Commission in Pakistan had more limited functions than those assigned to the Divisions of the Planning Commission in Bangladesh. At the same time, unlike in India, there were very few well qualified experts or economic advisers in the various economic Ministries.

In Pakistan, the Planning Commission was always headed by persons who belonged to one or the other branches of the administrative services. For example, the first incumbent was a member of the audit and accounts service, followed by those who came successively from the police, audit and accounts and civil services. A few of them did not have the administrative experience of the type, gained by a generalist and nonspecialist civil servant, in a wide range of government agencies and departments from the district level to the central government Ministries.

There were also Members in the Planning Commission of Pakistan who were academic economists. The Secretary of the Commission, drawn from the civil service, wielded much greater influence than the Members. It was the Deputy Chairman and the Secretary who in fact managed the Commission. The Secretary had a higher status and authority than the heads of technical divisions. However, there was a Chief Economist in the Commission who, because of his high ability and close relationship with the Finance Minister and the Deputy Chairman, wielded much greater influence than the Secretary. This led to inevitable tensions between the Secretary and the Chief Economist; in the administrative hierarchy, the former had precedence.

In Bangladesh, on the other hand, there was no Chief Economist but only a Chief of the General Economic Division equal in status and authority to the Chiefs of other divisions, including the Secretary. The Secretary was in charge of two Divisions in the Commission: Administrative and External Resources. Therefore, Members of the Commission exercised authority over the Secretary in matters related to their respective domain or jurisdiction.

It was the tradition and the practices only of Pakistan that were known to the officials in Bangladesh. Significant departures from it were not welcome. I had a taste of it early when a newly appointed Secretary wanted to follow the procedure prevalent in Pakistan i.e. to run the Commission under my supervision. In other words, it was not only that the Chiefs of other Divisions should be subservient to him but also that the Members, whatever their status might be, should serve more or less in an advisory capacity. This was a position so much at variance with the system that we had chosen that I had no choice but to ask for his reassignment.

There was yet another factor relating to the status of the Members and staff of the Commission, which introduced further complications in my task of managing the Planning Commission. There were civil servants who were senior in age to some Members of the Commission but who now considered themselves disadvantaged in status. In one or two cases, the professional staff of the Commission had lower academic attainments than civil servants when they were contemporaries at the Dhaka University. I remember an instance when two senior Secretaries complained about being requested to attend interministerial meetings presided by Commission Members who were junior to them as students in the university. Again, the Secretary of the Commission in its very early days found that one of the Commission Members was junior to him in the university and was no superior to him in academic achievement. He considered it uncomfortable to be asked to work in a position lower in status to that of the Member. He soon left and accepted a job in one of our embassies abroad.

Incidents like this reminded me of an experience I had at the Indian Planning Commission. This was an occasion when the delegations of the two Planning Commissions led by their respective Deputy Chairmen met in Delhi to discuss possible areas of economic cooperation. Secretaries of various Ministries in India participated in the meetings under the leadership of the Indian Planning Commission. During one session, in the absence of the Deputy Chairman, the Member who was heavily involved in negotiations with Bangladesh took over the leadership of the Indian delegation. He happened to be a contemporary of the youngest member of the Bangladesh Planning Commission.

Several of the Indian Secretaries were very senior and included a few from the old Civil Service of the British India. The Indian Member conducted the meeting with perfect ease and authority as he led and orchestrated the statements and replies by his team of Secretaries. The latter had no difficulty in demonstratively recognising the higher authority and leadership of a young man who was of the same age and experience as the children of some of them. The Indian civil servants had, by and large, with few exceptions — developed a tradition of working under the authority of political appointees from different walks of national life. To challenge the superior responsibility and status of the political appointees was to challenge the political leadership of the country.

6.4 DISCONTENT AND TENSIONS

There were a few other examples of frictions and discontent. However silly they might appear at present, they did detract from the congeniality of environment in the Commission. A member of the civil service sought a transfer from the Commission on the ground that one of his contemporaries in the University, an economist with a lower academic performance than his, had a higher status in the Commission. The professional economist had in the meantime acquired higher academic qualifications and research experience; he was on a temporary assignment in the Commission on leave from his parent organisation without any of the benefits of long term government employment. The "generalist" civil servant had a wide-open opportunity to move horizontally and vertically, attaining over time increasingly senior positions. He was not persuaded that the two cases were not comparable; he soon left the Commission.[7]

The resentment regarding the status and the authority enjoyed by Commission, specially its wide ranging functions and responsibilities, affected the degree of cooperation on policy matters as well. We should have known that except on issues or projects affecting their personal interests or those of their constituencies, the Ministers relied heavily on their officials for advice. We did not realise that in matters of bureaucratic infighting, we were at a grave disadvantage. We could possibly make some progress in improving the climate and in smoothing the rough edges of relationship through the exercise of personal diplomacy. For example, we could have gone out of our way to be polite and friendly rather than too formal and officious. We could have made occasional concessions, on other than strictly technical matters, on issues that appeared important to officials. After all, the human factor played a part in all interactions. We could have exploited the ties that bound us with the members of the civil service because, after all, we belonged to the same socioeconomic class.

Much later I had occasions to read about the experiences of persons who came into the government from academia.[8] I recognised that our experience was not unique; academics and professionals who came to policymaking jobs in the government usually faced difficult obstacles. They had to contend with resistance from the entrenched bureaucracy. They had to struggle constantly to make them acceptable and to establish their authority or effectiveness. Strong and unwavering

---

[7] By the end of 1975, the Planning Commission had been cut down in its status and authority. The Members and Division Chiefs of the Commission lost the status of State Ministers and Secretaries, respectively. The Secretary of the Commission was given a higher authority and status than that of the Division Chiefs. With these changes the Commission had become more like the Pakistan Planning Commission. The Division dealing with the foreign aid was shifted back and forth between the Finance and Planning Ministries and had lately settled down under the authority of the Finance Minister.

With the recent allocation of the Planning and Finance Ministries to the Finance Minister, the dichotomy had been partially ended. The integration of the Planning and Finance Ministries was long overdue. There had been frequent tensions between them in the past. In the first years of Bangladesh, tensions were kept to the minimum because of a very close personal relationship between the incumbents starting from the days of the liberation movement. Also, there were frequent consultations on all major issues between the Deputy Chairman and Members, one the one hand, and the Finance Minister, on the other.

[8] H.J. Kissinger, *The White House Years*, Little Brown & Co., Boston 1979; and I.G. Patel, *op cit.*

support provided by the political leaders openly and unambiguously was critical to their survival and success. I was not sure whether the kind of unmistakable and robust signal that was warranted in our difficult circumstances was consistently provided by the Prime Minister to the rest of the government. I felt that during the first year and half the signal was stronger than what it was in the later years.

Neither did the Commission try to develop personal relations or alliances with Ministers on matters that related to their Ministries as well as on Inter-Ministerial issues. We overestimated the power of technical arguments. We believed that concentrating on the professional work was more important than networking and making alliances. It was a mistake not to realise that both factors were important.

The Commission depended on the support of the Prime Minister and considered it more than adequate for the purpose. It was unrealistic for us to expect that the Prime Minister would undertake on all occasions the task of persuasion on our behalf or override the Ministers, whenever necessary. He expected the Commission to undertake the task of persuasion and negotiations as much as possible and to seek his intervention only on selected occasions.

As time went by, the Prime Minister felt that the Deputy Chairman, who played an important part in the making of economic policies and programmes and was responsible for steering all matters relating to the Planning Commission through the Cabinet, should also be the person to steer them through the Party meetings and the Parliament. In addition, as the Deputy Chairman, I should bear the burden of explaining and defending the overall development policies and programmes to the general public and the various interest groups as well. In this task, I should supplement and strengthen the responsibilities of the Finance Minister.

It was in the light of such considerations that he strongly urged me to contest the 1973 elections so that I should be a Member of the Parliament and a politically elected Minister. The intermediate position of a super bureaucrat cum nonpolitical Minister seemed to suffer from the worst of both the worlds. He had already discussed this idea with the Awami League party members and the parliamentarians from my home constituency. They agreed to his proposal for me to contest the elections. Rather it was most likely that it was he who persuaded them about the logic of his suggestion.

Sheikh Mujib believed that it was possible to make a politician out of a professional with support from him and the party. He realised that I was not a public speaker and, therefore, needed help. He had a simple suggestion. I should accompany him to a few public meetings at which he would do the speech making and canvassing on the candidate's behalf. I was to make suitable short statements in his presence and under his guidance. Given his authority over the party, his standing with the electorate and his personal involvement in my election, it was unlikely that he would have failed to get me elected in 1973. However, the problem was that I was not willing and ready to follow the path to a political career. I did not have "the fire in the belly" to be a politician. I did not feel that I had the necessary qualities, inclinations, and stamina. This was apart from the fact that I would not have the true credentials of a people's representative. I would be foisted from above by the *dictat* of an all-powerful political leader.

In retrospect, Sheikh Mujib was indeed right in his judgement. The job of the chief of planning and economic policymaking is as much a political job as that of a Finance Minister and could not be left to a faceless — behind the scene — technocrat without political involvement or standing. Since those early days, several professionals and civil servants went through this process and this route. They were first nominated as Ministers and then became elected politicians with the help and the patronage of the powerful leaders of the political parties. In Bangladesh, the selection of the electoral candidates had been, by and large, centralised in the hands of the Party Chief who was the head of the government as well and the process had been strictly "top-down and not bottom-up". It was not that the party members in the local constituencies selected the candidates but that the wishes of the leader mostly determined the choice. Whatever the process through which the Planning or Finance Ministers were selected, i.e. appointed by the Prime Minister with a status of a Minister or elected under his tutelage as a Minister, the effectiveness of the Minister depended on the strength of support of the Prime Minister.

An overriding factor in the tension between the Commission and the rest of the government was the Commission's exercise of wide ranging functions in approving and coordinating development projects, and in initiating and recommending policies spanning over different sectors and Ministries. Other factors, mentioned earlier, aggravated the real reason behind the resentment and the underlying tension. In the end, the basic problem was one of struggle for power and authority. It was inescapable. The Planning Commission by the nature of its functions appeared to be intervening in the domain of other Ministries. The Ministers felt that the Commission was somehow usurping their powers not in the interest of greater efficiency in policymaking and implementation, but basically in the interest of expanding its own authority and control. It was true that the National Economic Council and the Cabinet had the final say and the Commission only made recommendations and that too on the basis of extensive Interministerial consultations. However, more often than not, the Cabinet accepted the recommendations of the Commission. The Commission was, therefore, viewed as a Super Ministry. The Ministers did not either fully understand or accept the logic of the process of collective decision making by the Cabinet that was based on technical recommendations by the Commission.

This logic appeared too theoretical to most of them. Moreover, they found it difficult to accept that in their respective Ministries, once they had received the financial allocations by the collective decision of the Cabinet, they did not have the final authority on individual projects, programmes and policies. There was no reason why the examination and appraisal by the Ministry itself should not be adequate. Secondly, they did not perceive the implications of intersectoral linkages or that the viability of projects in one sector depended on policies or projects in other sectors. What was even more unpleasant from their point of view was that the Commission also had the responsibility for the evaluation of development programmes, policies and institutions in their individual Ministries. This was tantamount to passing judgement on their performance and was not welcome.

The fact that Tajuddin was the Finance Minister who was mostly in step with the Planning Commission did not help matters. His preeminent position was resented by many other Ministers who shared the legacy of intense jealousy inherited from the days of the *government in exile.*

As in all democracies, the politicians wanted their pet projects. Their preference was based on their particular experience or common sense or popular perception and not always on any serious technical or professional examination. Also, they supported projects which their particular constituencies, either geographical or sectoral, wanted in their own interests. Several controversial examples come to my mind. One was the project on the dredging of what was rhetorically called "the dead and the dying rivers" of Bangladesh. The concerned Ministry proposed this as a preferred method for the control of floods caused by the overflowing of rivers due to accumulation of silts. This conclusion was reached without any examination of the alternatives such as training of rivers, embankments or dams. Another scheme related to the establishment of an agricultural or an engineering university in every administrative division of the country, while at the same time secondary schools were underfunded and unable to get additional teachers or equipment. One Minister insisted on the construction of an international airport in his constituency, the home of a large number of the Bangladeshi workers abroad. Yet another desired the construction of surface or canal irrigation works without any consideration as to whether tubewell irrigation would not be a better alternative. In these and many other instances the Planning Commission, by insisting on the examination of alternative projects as well as on an evaluation of their costs and benefits, appeared obstructive and noncooperative to other Ministries.

How to resolve the tension between the particular interests or perceptions of individual politicians or Ministers and the collective interests is a very difficult challenge in any country. An institution like the Planning Commission which was at the crosscurrents of the decision making process could not escape the responsibility for whatever was the final decision by the Cabinet. In an open, transparent and participatory society, there was a mechanism for reaching a compromise among conflicting interest groups which might be expected to keep the inefficiencies and social losses to the minimum. A multiparty democracy with a vibrant Parliament was a primary requisite. In Bangladesh even when there was parliamentary democracy, economic policies or development projects and programmes had seldom been subjected to a process of scrutiny and examination in the Parliament and other civic forums and on a scale that was required to produce a compromise and hence compliance by all. The governance of the country was very much dominated by the Cabinet headed by the Prime Minister. There were instances when the individual Ministers or Members of Parliament sought to avoid the scrutiny of the Planning Commission and to secure the approval of their pet projects or policies. Their success in doing so depended on their relationship with or influence on the Cabinet/Prime Minister.

In the course of time, the argument that the individual Ministries should have a stronger and more decisive role in the determination of projects and policies did gain strength. This was increasingly so by mid-1974. This led over time to the erosion of the role of the Commission, specially in the task of evaluation and coordination in respect of both sectoral and economy-wide policies.

Commencing in the first quarter of 1974, the economic situation deteriorated due to the acute scarcity of resources, domestic and foreign exchange. At the same time, the law and order situation worsened with adverse consequences for the economy. The government was faced with immense sociopolitical problems characterised by a lack of cohesion and conflicts between various interest groups. In this environment, it was not easy for the politicians and the public to appreciate whether and how much the deterioration in the economic situation was due to external circumstances beyond the control of Bangladesh. Nor was it easy to determine how much of it was due to mismanagement or inefficiency in the implementation of Projects and policies or for that matter, to wrong advice or economic mismanagement by the Planning Commission.

As the economic and political situation deteriorated, day-to-day administration and *ad hoc* solutions to emergency problems, rather than careful examination of policies or programmes, became the preoccupation of the Government. It was felt that what was needed was quick execution or action rather than analysis. In order to keep the Ministers and various constituencies happy, discipline in the allocation of resources was gradually relaxed in the interest of short term expediency. Only projects above a certain size were subject to much scrutiny; over time this limit was raised to increase the independent approving authority of the Ministries. In this general environment of a decline in its influence on economic policymaking, there was one area in which the Commission's role was not much diluted i.e. its aid negotiating function. The Prime Minister seemed to believe that when it came to seeking and negotiating aid, the Commission should still be responsible. The irony was that the donors were unwilling to provide aid on the basis of *ad hoc* initiatives or proposals on projects and policies. They wanted, even when considering aid for individual projects or sector programmes, wide ranging policy reforms in both short term and long term perspectives.

This was not a very satisfactory situation. We, the Members and myself, came to the conclusion that our role was no longer very helpful to the government. We had outlived our utility, given the rapidly changing environment. If Sheikh Mujib wanted our advice on any specific matters, we could always offer it from outside the government. Overshadowing everything else were the impending constitutional changes, which were to radically alter the political, economic and administrative landscape. An all-pervasive sense of uncertainty aggravated the perception of instability around the government, including the Planning Commission.

6.5 MY DEPARTURE

At the same time, we were not willing to make any public display of our decision to go back to our academic lives. We wanted to make our departure unobtrusive and passive so as not to embarrass him publicly. Anisur Rahman had in any case decided very early on to work on a part time basis and left in 1973; he preferred to teach and enjoyed the academic independence of a professor. Mosharraf, Rehman and I struggled on. During the next two years, each of us, I suppose, had an additional reason to influence the timing of our departure linked to changes in internal and external environment. By the end of 1974, all except myself were gone. However, the more recent Member, a senior ex-civil servant did not share our thoughts. He was an insider and did not join the Commission under the same set of circumstances as the academics. He stayed on.

I decided to ease myself out slowly and in a more diplomatic manner. It was not an easy decision for me to take since I felt closer and had a sense of personal loyalty to Sheikh Mujib. I needed more time to untie the knots as painlessly as possible. I had to leave the government because I no longer had a useful role to play.

I raised the issue of my departure from the Commission on the ground that I was suffering from fatigue and exhaustion and, therefore, needed both rest and treatment abroad. In fact, I was indeed very tired and not in the best state of health. Sheikh Mujib was sympathetic. He was under no circumstances willing to consider my resignation from the Commission. He agreed to grant me leave for a period of nine months to go abroad. He was too intelligent and perceptive not to realise that I was not quite happy with my work. At the same time, he was not quite willing to close the option of my return. In fact, he might have presumed that because of the changes he was going to introduce in the political and economic system, the overall situation would take a dramatic turn for the better. Under the more congenial circumstances unfolding in the future, I should find it worthwhile to resume my responsibilities. Even though I was not sure, his approaches to me later on seemed to indicate that he might have had some such thought in mind.

By the time of my departure, Sheikh Mujib had already decided to introduce a presidential system and an autocratic rule under a one party system. The first Constitution of Bangladesh introduced a multiparty parliamentary system. He decided to discard it as not suitable to circumstances confronting the country in mid-1970s. The new party to be formed was to embrace all sections of society including the civil service and the army and was to be his supreme instrument for the governance of the country.

I was not involved in the discussions he might have had within the Awami League and with his Cabinet colleagues on the subject of the planned constitutional change. In the early years, there was no dearth of persons in various walks of life with ideas — some novel and some not so novel — about how best to organise the administrative and political structure of the country. I recall at least two examples which provide a flavour or drift of the range and type of ideas that were in the air. There was the interesting case of a civil service officer who was interned in Pakistan in 1971. I knew him from his early years as being very committed to the cause of autonomy of East Pakistan. On his return from Pakistan in 1973, he went around with a proposal that the future of Bangladesh did not lie in a chaotic multiparty democracy. In the context of our fractured society such a system was bound to be highly unstable and hence detrimental to growth and development. What was needed was a one party state under the strong leadership of Sheikh Mujib. This would ensure peace and prosperity. He was anxious to convince me of this idea and to persuade Sheikh Mujib about the merit of his proposal. He also discussed his idea with one or two Ministers in the government at that time. For a brief period he worked in the Planning Commission and then left to join the Prime Minister's Secretariat. This officer was known to have authored, along with his colleagues in that Secretariat, the well publicised White Paper following the assassination of Sheikh Mujib.

I remember one young army officer on his way to be an attaché at the Embassy in Yangoon. Through the intercession of one of my relations he came to see me and discuss what he considered a serious scheme for national development. He had fought in the liberation war and given serious thoughts to the post independence challenge of building a viable nation. He proposed compulsory military training for students in all colleges and universities. This would inculcate discipline and respect for authority — two qualities singularly lacking among the people of Bangladesh — but essential for nation building. When young men and women with such training went forward to man services and professions in the country, they would be immensely qualified to provide leadership. He did not think much of the UOTC (i.e. University Officers Training Corps) training in the universities which he termed as useless, soft training. Added to short periods of military service, his proposed system would serve as a bulwark for the defense of the country. This would also integrate the armed forces with the political and social fabric of the country and close the gap that existed between the army and the rest of the population. He thought that I, as one who was in charge of planning the future of the country, would appreciate the merit of his proposal in the prevailing circumstances of Bangladesh. In the event I agreed with his proposal, I should try and convince the Prime Minister.

In fact, I never seriously examined the proposal, nor did I take it up with the Prime Minister. I suspected in his scheme an approach towards the political system in which the army would naturally play a major role. With my background of years of army rule in Pakistan, I was not enthusiastic about it. Moreover, I assumed that I was not the only conduit he would have used for advising the Prime minister about his proposal. He would have discussed it with the upper echelons in the Army. If eventually this proposal came from them and the politicians were interested in it, I would have ample time to examine it in all its dimensions. I had often toyed with the idea that the Army should be used for developmental activities in peacetime. In view of our severe scarcity of trained manpower, productive use of the army could help our development efforts. The young officer later on became a pillar of the military government which seized power, after a brief period of confusion, following the assassination of Sheikh Mujib. I remembered this discussion with him and wondered in the light of our subsequent history how so many officers in the Bangladesh army had political inclinations and ambitions. After all, the military in Bangladesh demonstrated neither discipline nor respect for authority, civilian or otherwise, in the years that followed.

There were unconfirmed reports that Sheikh Mujib had received advice on the matter of the proposed constitutional change from various persons or groups, specially the leftist political parties in Bangladesh. They had apparently drawn his attention to the genesis and lessons of experiment with one party state and planned socialist economy in the East European countries, such as Poland and Yugoslavia. In general, these countries had imported political and economic ideas and features from the Soviet system and grafted them on their indigenous systems with modifications so as to suit their economic structure and sociocultural traditions. There were features in his proposed economic system such as multipurpose agricultural cooperatives and workers' participation in management of industries, which, it could be said, were drawn from an amalgam of experiences in a number of the East European countries. This was my guess. I had no first-hand knowledge or discussion with the leftist parties.

However, I had an occasion to raise the question of the new political system with Sheikh Mujib towards the end of 1974, during his visit to Kuwait — his last overseas visit. I accompanied him. Kamal Hossain was also in the entourage. Both of us took this opportunity of being alone with him to raise the issue of the new political system. We expressed our great disappointment and frustration that a leader who had suffered so much for so many years for political rights and democracy would now be responsible for their abrogation.

For the first time in three years that I had worked with him, I saw him very irritated and annoyed. I had asked him in the past unpleasant questions and was critical on many issues. He was never angry or irritated. He would always listen patiently and try to explain. When he was unwilling to change his course of action he would tell me why he could not do so and what his limitations were. On this occasion, he was angry at our inability or unwillingness to appreciate what he had said in his public speech about the economic crisis and the political chaos gripping the country. The situation, in his view, required drastic solution. After very serious thoughts he had decided that the proposed system was the only answer to the deep sociopolitical malaise facing the country. He made it clear to both of us that we, an economist and a barrister-at-law, did not have an adequate understanding about what was fundamentally wrong with the state of the nation and what was the solution. Therefore, we should not try to hastily judge policies that were beyond our comprehension and were the prerogative of the leader who had the ultimate responsibility to the people.

I remember the occasion when I went to say goodbye to Sheikh Mujib on the eve of my departure (for oxford) on January 8, 1975, shortly before the Parliament would decide on the new (BAKSAL) constitution. He was in a somber mood. As I offered my parting words, he started to pace up and down, in his room, and began to recite the famous Bangla lyrical poem of Tagore:

> "jodi tor dak shuney keo na ashe tobe ekla cholo re, etc." — if no one responds to your call, then proceed alone on your lonely journey. However dark and difficult the path, and no one kept you company, you should be ready to walk alone. If we call out for help and no help came, in the darkness we should become a light unto ourselves and go on.

He regretted that on the occasion of the inauguration of this bold and novel experiment I had decided not to join him in his task. He went on to say that he was engaged in a last ditch effort to save Bangladesh from economic chaos and political disintegration. Launching the new system was like a lonely ride through a thick forest in a dark stormy night marked by frequent flashes of lightning and thunder. It was a journey full of risks and uncertainties; nonetheless, it held out the hope that one would reach the other side in the morning and find a new landscape bathed in brilliant sunshine. He had no choice but to undertake this uncharted journey.

While I was in Oxford I received news from Dhaka that he wanted to hear from me about my sojourn abroad, including the state of my health. Accordingly, I wrote to him. He wrote back wishing that I would speedily regain my health and vigour so that I could resume my responsibilities as soon as possible (see Appendix 6.1).

By the end of April, the Prime Minister's Secretariat sent a message that I should meet him at the Frankfurt airport in West Germany and join his entourage to attend the Commonwealth Heads of Government Meeting in May 1975. It so happened that I had already arranged to go to Dhaka precisely during those days to bring my family to Oxford. I decided to stop over at Frankfurt where he reluctantly agreed to my request that I might not accompany him but instead should wait in Dhaka for his return. When I met the Prime Minister in Dhaka he wanted me to be sworn in immediately as a Minister to resume my responsibilities. He assured me that this time around, it would be very different. I would have complete freedom of action and would be unfettered by constraints other than what was in the best interests of the country. I would have his full commitment. The discipline of the Plan would be enforced and he would tolerate no deviations.

In my mind, my decision to leave the government was final when I left for Oxford. But at that moment I resorted to excuses and pleaded with him that I had not yet regained the mental and physical stamina to face up to such a challenge so soon. After all, more than half of my leave was still to be completed. If I was to force myself to resume my duties at this stage, it would bring nothing but stress, tension, and unhappiness all around, to the benefit of neither the government nor myself. After a few minutes of discussion, as I left, I had the feeling that Sheikh Mujib did realise that I would most probably not be joining the government even after the expiry of my leave. I was sad that I could not be of any help to him.

I never saw him again. I was still in Oxford in August 1975 when Bangladesh entered a new phase. A dishonourable chapter in its history was being written as my friends and I watched the interview of the self confessed killers — Farouq and Rashid — on the television, gloating over the assassination of Sheikh Mujib.[9]

---

[9] Cols. Farouq Rahman and Abdur Rashid have since then been charged with the assassination of Sheikh Mujib and sentenced to death, pending approval by the Supreme Court.

Letter from Sheikh Mujib

কূটনৈতিক খবরের মাধ্যম
গণভবন
ঢাকা
১২ই মার্চ, ১৯৭৫

ভাই প্রফেসার ইসলাম ,

    আপনার ৩-৩-৭৫ তারিখের চিঠিখানা পেয়ে খুশী হয়েছি । আপনি কিছুটা বিনাস্ত্য করতে পেরেছেন জেনে আনন্দিত হয়েছি ।

    নূতন পদ্ধতিতে দেশের কাজ-কর্ম ভাল চলছে যে খবর আপনি পেয়েছেন বলে মনে হয় । তবে এ সময়ে আরও বেশী কাজের লোকের প্রয়োজন । নিঃসন্দেহ, ধৈর্য ও পরীক্ষিত সুযোগ্য কর্মী ব্যতিরেকে এ দেশকে গড়ে তোলবার দায়িত্ব পালন করা সহজ নয় । তবে আমি মনে করি, আপনি দেশে ফিরে এসে দেশ গড়ার কাজ আরও সুষ্ঠুভাবে চালানো সম্ভব হবে ।

    গত দু' মাসে আপনি কিছুটা আরাম বোধ করছেন বলে আশা করি । যাবাদের সঙ্গে পুনরায় আপনার কমপ্লিট মেডিক্যাল চেক আপ প্রয়োজন । আমার অনুরোধ এ বিষয়ে কোন গাফিলতি না করে অবিলম্বে পারদর্শী চিকিৎসক দ্বারা চেক আপের কাজ সম্পূর্ণ করবেন । এরপর যদি সুস্থ্যবোধ করেন অচিরে দেশে ফিরে এসে স্বীয় কর্তব্য পুনরায় শুরু করবেন সেটাই আমার আন্তরিক কামনা । দেশের কাজ ইতিমধ্যে অনেক করেছেন, বর্তমান সময়ে দেশ ও জাতি আপনার সেবা আরও বেশী করে দাবী করছে ।

    আমি ভাল আছি , তবে কাজের চাপ অত্যন্ত বেশী তা' নিশ্চয়ই বুঝতে পারছেন । যেদিন নুরুল ইসলামের সঙ্গে দেখা হয়েছিল, তিনি ছেলে-মেয়েসহ ভাল আছেন । কবে নাগাদ দেশে আসতে পারবেন তা জানিয়ে উত্তর দিলে খুশী হব ।

    সালাম ও প্রীতি জানবেন ।

আপনার আশীর্বাদক ,

(শেখ মুজিবুর রহমান)
১২।৩।৭৫

প্রফেসার নুরুল ইসলাম,
অন্যান্যার্থ ইউনিভার্সিটি,
লন্ডনে বাংলাদেশ হাই কমিশনের মাধ্যমে ।

Chapter 7

DOWN THE MEMORY LANE: VIGNETTES OF LIFE IN GOVERNMENT

During my years in government, I had several encounters or were present during a few incidents, which throw some light on the sociopolitical environment of the country then and in the years that followed. Some of them relate to Sheikh Mujib and the way he governed the country including his relations with Ministers and officials. Some relate to my encounter with different politicians and others.

7.1 STRANGE ENCOUNTERS

As my impending departure became known I had three encounters, two with Moshtaque and one with General Zia — all related to my departure. Each encounter seemed to indicate the perspective of my interlocutors. They all seemed quite extraordinary and unexpected at the time.

Moshtaque Ahmed

The first incident with Moshtaque occurred at the end of the last Cabinet meeting in late 1974 before my departure, as we rode back to our offices in his car. At that meeting Sheikh Mujib formally announced that I was going on leave for medical reasons and he expressed the hope that I would soon come back fully recovered. Moshtaque, without any initiative on my part, began to commiserate with me as soon as we got into the car, saying that he understood the reasons why I was leaving the government. He launched a tirade against the arbitrary and whimsical way in which Sheikh Mujib was running the affairs of the nation and how he was impervious to advice and suggestions. He realised why any serious person with any commitment to the country and desire for productive work could find working in such an environment unacceptable. Therefore, he sympathised with me and shared my frustration.

It was very strange that he would speak out in such great indignation. I kept protesting that I was only going on leave for a few months in order to get some rest and treatment, and not because of any frustration. I wondered whether he was trying to find out how disaffected I was or what I was up to. He was probably disappointed at my reaction. But I could not fathom why he made such vitriolic statements in the presence of his security guard and the driver. I inferred that Moshtaque was a very desperate and unhappy man, not exercising sound judgement. By now Sheikh Mujib probably knew of his disaffection.

It is worth recalling two earlier incidents in order to put his remarks in their proper perspective. Around mid-1974, Sheikh Mujib was on a state visit to Delhi for a meeting with Indira Gandhi on a wide range of bilateral issues. Moshtaque, Kamal Hossain and I were all in the entourage. In the course of light conversations and casual banter at the state dinner, Sheikh Mujib pointed to Moshtaque and told Indira Gandhi that he wanted her to take note that he had the sweetest relationship with Moshtaque. This was because Moshtaque happened to be his brother-in-law (with emphasis, he used the Bengali word *Shala*).[1] Sheikh Mujib went on to explain how in Bangladesh one had the most affectionate relationship with one's brother-in-law.

All of us including Indira Gandhi knew that Moshtaque was no relation of Sheikh Mujib. I was sitting near by and saw all this occurring before my eyes. Moshtaque did not say a word throughout. He did not seem to treat all this as an innocent joke but rather as an embarrassment. I was puzzled and sensed that there was an undercurrent of tension between the two.

---

[1] The Indian Prime Minister had spent some time in the *Shantinekatan,* seat of Tagore's university (i.e. *Viswa Bharati*), and had some knowledge of Bengali.

On our way back from Delhi to Dhaka on the plane, there was yet another disturbing incident. While Sheikh Mujib was taking rest in his cabin, apparently with his eyes closed behind a curtain, Moshtaque and I, sitting in the same cabin were engaged in a conversation on the state of the economy. This was the time of high inflation and severe foreign exchange crisis; great worries about its consequences consumed all of us in the Commission. I emphasised that unless the government came to grips with it by adopting stringent measures there was a danger of sociopolitical turmoil. History showed that whenever the rate of inflation exceeded two digit figures the regimes usually did not survive. All on a sudden, Sheikh Mujib emerged from behind the curtain and sat next to Moshtaque. It appeared as if he was listening all the time to our conversation. He asked Moshtaque to pay careful attention to my remarks since he fully believed in and agreed with what I had to say.

Then came the climax. Sheikh Mujib went on to say that he had a very unusual dream last night. In his sleep he was asked by Almighty Allah to make a sacrifice, *a la* Prophet Ibrahim, of one who was the dearest to him. As he thought very hard about who could be his dearest one that he was asked to sacrifice, he had to conclude that the person must be Moshtaque. I was aghast and could scarcely believe my ears. Moshtaque made no comment and heard it all in silence. It would have been apparent to any observer — as it was to me — that Moshtaque looked very unhappy. Mercifully, conversation switched to some other topic.

Later in December 1974, I had yet another encounter in the course of a boat trip in honor of the visiting Australian Prime Minister Gough Whitlam. Moshtaque and Taheruddin Thakur were among the Ministers and officials accompanying the Prime Minister. As I was strolling along the deck, I ran into two of them. No sooner had I met them, they started to sympathise with me about how thankless I should have found my task in the Planning Commission and how relieved I must be to be soon out of it. Sheikh Mujib, as he was going around the boat, found the three of us together. He pointedly asked the two of them about what they were up to and why they were always huddled together and engaged in whispering campaigns? He appeared to be telling them off that they were always engaged in intrigues of some sort and that he kept watch on all their manipulations and manoeuvers. It should be recalled that by that time the country was rife with all kinds of political rumours.

I had thought about these incidents later on many times and discussed their implications with my friends. It was obvious that Moshtaque was engaged in some sort of smear campaign against Sheikh Mujib. In the light of what happened later in August 1975, when he greeted the killers of Sheikh Mujib as glorious sons of Bangladesh and took over as President, I went back in my memory and it became clear that he was indeed part of the conspiracy. Was Sheikh Mujib aware that Moshtaque was engaged in intrigue against him? Did he ever confront Moshtaque with such a query or challenge? One did not know what else was going on between him and Moshtaque at that stage. To me, it appeared that they were on a collision course. Sheikh Mujib probably wanted to tell Moshtaque, by his occasional fulminations — which appeared to me as tactless — that whatever intrigues Moshtaque was engaged in were of no avail against Sheikh Mujib's superior power and capacity to deal with him. Alas, history proved him wrong!

Ziaur Rahman

The first meeting that I had with Ziaur Rahman was in 1972 when he was the Deputy Chief of Staff in the Army and wanted to discuss additional allocations for the construction of roads in the border areas, near Cox's Bazar and Chittagong Hill Tracts.[2] Usually, the budget for the armed forces was outside the purview of the Planning Commission, decided by the Prime Minister in consultation with the Finance Minister. The allocations for the Army on account of both current and capital expenditures had already been made. Sheikh Mujib did not want to take the decision on his own nor did he involve Tajuddin. He was persuaded that such expenditures were justified as development expenditures, which were within the purview of the Commission. He sent Zia to me to justify and convince the Planning Commission to provide the additional allocations from the development

---

[2] General Ziaur Rahman emerged as the military strongman after the assassination of Sheikh Mujib and the subsequent military coup that replaced the civilian government. Eventually, he became the President of Bangladesh.

budget. Zia argued quite convincingly, with the help of maps and charts, that additional allocations outside the original provisions in the budget for the Army were justified. They would not only strengthen defense but also expand infrastructure in the underdeveloped border areas. Due to acute scarcity of resources and without any possibility of diversion from other sectors, I had to persuade him to postpone the expenditures for a later year. Zia naturally considered it a rather unsatisfactory solution.

Prior to this encounter, we had met casually at a dinner party. Zia was known to have a very active social life that extended well beyond the limited circles of the Army and included civil servants, politicians and professionals over a wide range of disciplines.

I had also met him when I was asked by Sheikh Mujib to negotiate with the visiting Yugoslav delegation about the supply of arms and defence equipment. At that time, he was a part of the team from the military services led by General Shafiullah, accompanied by the representatives of the Navy and the Air Force, to assist in the negotiations. I was engaged in negotiating the entire programme of financial assistance with the Yugoslavs. Sheikh Mujib decided that aid for the military should also be negotiated by me. There was the issue of priorities in the allocation of the total Yugoslav assistance. An allocation for the military would mean that less was available for development needs. He instructed me to consider the overall priority needs of the economy while allocating a part of the Yugoslav assistance to the military. There was yet another occasion that we met, during 1974, when the army was deployed to undertake antismuggling operations along the border with India. This incident is related in another context in Chapter 10.

The most memorable meeting, of course, took place prior to my departure from the Planning Commission. My departure was not yet officially confirmed, though widely rumoured. One of those days the late Ziaul Huq, a mutual friend, came with a request that Zia very much wanted to meet with me informally to discuss a few matters of common interest. He had heard about my strong desire to leave the Planning Commission and had requested Huq to arrange such an informal meeting as soon as possible. Even though by now Zia had come to know me well enough to call on me in my office, he followed rather an indirect route to request this meeting. I was intrigued and unsure about how to respond to his request. Huq persuaded me that I should agree to meet with him in an informal setting and that there was no harm in such a meeting. Huq was to arrange this meeting in his house where, in any case, I was a very frequent visitor. He was more aware than I about what was going on in the world of politics, both overt and covert.

I was quite curious to know what Zia had to say. It was a measure of his wide and serious interest in the political and economic affairs of the country that he kept abreast of what was happening in the Planning Commission, including the impending departure of the Deputy Chairman. It was by then widely known that he often met with professionals in different walks of life and engaged them in serious discussions on various socioeconomic and political developments. As a member of the *Pay and Services Commission* representing the armed forces, he used to meet the professionals, including economists from the Planning Commission working on that Commission. He look the opportunity to exchange opinions with them on policy issues of the day.

The meeting with Zia took place in Huq's house which was cleared of everyone including Huq himself and his family. The main theme of a rather short meeting was that he had heard about my desire to leave and was eager to persuade me not to do so. He recognised that I was not able to do my best or what was appropriate in the interest of the economy. He understood that the economy was in dire straits. There were constraints imposed by the prevailing political uncertainty, short term economic crisis and administrative weaknesses. However, he was confident that in the not too distant a future, the situation would improve and the prevailing drift and uncertainty would disappear. Bangladesh was destined to prosper and all the sacrifices for the liberation of the country would not go in vain. Therefore, I should not despair and should be able to devote my energies to the task of planning and development with full commitment and strong support from the top leadership. He strongly urged that I should reconsider my decision to depart and should stay on my job.

I was surprised by the tenor of his talk and the confidence with which he spoke about the restoration of political and economic stability.

I was particularly impressed by his confidence that in not too distant a future I would be able to devote my energies, unhindered, to my assigned task for the welfare of the country. I did not say much except repeating the formal line that I was going on leave for a few months and that I looked forward to returning to my job as soon as I recovered from my fatigue and completed my treatment.

Clearly, it was a sign of the abnormality of the times that an army General was so intensely interested in the political and economic developments as to seek out and pursue contact with people engaged in managing the economic and political life of the country. It was an expression of his deep interest that led him to engage in a serious discussion about the current state of the country with the head of the Planning Commission and to confidently predict — rather assure me — about the future political development and my prospective role in it.

7.2 THE LAST SUPPER

The state dinner for Gough Whitlam, Australian Prime Minister, was a very poignant and portentous moment for me. As we were waiting around before sitting down to dinner, I ran into Kamruzzaman and Mazumdar.[3] The former made a very unsettling remark to the effect that we three would not have another chance to meet at a dinner. This was our *"Last Supper"* together. Dire days were awaiting us. When and by the time I would come back from abroad, they would not be alive. He pointed at his throat and affirmed that his throat would be slit in the coming months. He was by then appointed as the President of the Awami League and was no longer a Cabinet Minister in the months before the introduction of the new BAKSAL constitution. It was a dismal prophecy that came true. He was not known as a very hard working person and sometimes used to doodle during the long hours of Cabinet meetings. But he was very capable, perceptive, and an intelligent person. It showed whenever he applied his mind seriously to an issue.

---

[3] A. H. M. Kamruzzaman was the Minister for Commerce in the first Cabinet of independent Bangladesh, and became the President of Awami League by the end of 1974. Phani Bhusan Majumdar was the Minister for Food in the same Cabinet.

7.3 REMEMBRANCE OF TIMES PAST: THOUGHTS ON SHEIKH MUJIB

Decision Making Process — Role of Politicians

From the beginning, there was a concentration of decision making power and authority in the hands of the Prime Minister. Some of us ventured to suggest to him that at the formative and highly unstable state of the country, there was a need for him to spend a very large part of his time and efforts in reaching out to the masses, to explain and mobilise support for his policies and programmes. He could put new life in the Party and motivate the members in the altered postindependence circumstances. There was no one but he who could provide the galvanising leadership in preparing the people in all walks of life for the uncertainties and challenges the country was faced with. In order for him to undertake this nation building task, he would have to significantly reduce the extent of his direct participation in the actual governance of the country and restrict his intervention only to decisions on major policy issues. The task of day-to-day administration could have been left in the hands of his competent colleagues such as Nazrul Islam, Tajuddin, and other senior leaders.

Unfortunately, he did not respond positively to this suggestion. He considered that the Ministers would not agree to accept the leadership of anyone else among them. We thought differently that they would accept if he would make it very clear who were the designated leaders and supported them fully. The lack of adequate delegation in decision making to the Ministers led to the unfortunate consequence that they were not able to "learn by doing" and accept responsibility for their actions. In most major matters, if not all, the Ministers would refrain from taking decisions without referring to the Prime Minister. All decisions involved some risk. They were unwilling or unable to take such risks partly, I assumed, for fear of incurring the displeasure of the Prime Minister in case the decisions proved wrong, and partly for lack of confidence and limited capacity.[4]

---

[4] It appears that after the lapse of more than two decades, the system has not changed in substance. The Government of Bangladesh, as the popular saying goes, is the Government of the Prime Minister, by the Prime Minister, and for the Prime Minister.

Ideally, Sheikh Mujib as the Prime Minister should have treated the Ministers as his chief executives to whom he should have assigned tasks and whom he should have held responsible for their execution. The Ministers in their turn should have held the Secretaries and other officials responsible. In this way, accountability was to be assigned at various stages and ensured. This was not the way in which the administration was mostly managed. There was a tendency on the part of Sheikh Mujib to deal directly with Secretaries. He expected to obtain quick action and better follow-up results by giving instructions directly to Secretaries. I had the impression that this, in turn, made Ministers feel less responsible and accountable — a vicious circle. The more they passed on to the Prime Minister all important decisions, the more they lost the habit for and confidence in their own decision making. The less he delegated to them, the less actively they were engaged in managing their responsibilities, except when their own interests or those of their constituencies were involved.

However, this pattern of decision making was not true of all the Ministers. His confidence in the capacity and judgement of individual Ministers varied. On most occasions, he would respect the authority of the senior Ministers who, as it happened, were more willing and able to take decisions on their own. Moreover, when matters were brought to the Cabinet for decision that required more thorough and detailed examination than what the full Cabinet could undertake, he would appoint subcommittees of Ministers directly concerned with the subject. They were to make recommendations to the full Cabinet after the scrutiny of all related issues. This happened quite frequently. Secondly, on matters of high policy, he relied very heavily on extensive consultations with senior political colleagues. On crucial matters, he would seldom take decisions without consulting his senior advisers among the Ministers. This group of senior advisers, as I saw and knew, consisted of Nazrul Islam, Tajuddin, Mansoor Ali, Kamruzzaman, and surprisingly, Moshtaque. On matters relating to law and foreign affairs, he relied very heavily on Kamal Hossain. The popular impression of his highly personalised decision making on important policy matters without consultation with his senior colleagues was not quite true, at least to the extent I saw him act and in matters in which I was involved or to which I was a witness.

His method seemed to have undergone a visible change by late 1974. Consultations with his Ministers and senior colleagues seemed to have declined in intensity and frequency by late 1974. He might have thought that the type of advice he received from them was no longer helpful in meeting the challenges he was facing. He seemed to have discussed very little, as I understood, the pros and cons of the one Party Presidential system, the BAKSAL system, even with his senior political colleagues and relied very little on their advice for its implementation. As a veteran politician, he had always kept in touch with the pulse of the nation through his vast network of contacts. Frequently, he used this network as his source of information and a sounding board of people's reactions to his policy decisions. There were rumours of all kinds about individuals who had grown close to him in that period. But I had no way of verifying or commenting on such rumours.

Implementation of Policies: Role of the Civil Service

He had a great deal of confidence in the civil servants for their ability in managing the affairs of the country. He did not have a comparable regard for the technical experts working in various Ministries, even when the latter had managerial experience in their respective fields. He had seen members of the Pakistan Civil Service, mostly from Pakistan in the preindependence days, wielding considerable power and performing efficiently at that. He believed that those from Bangladesh trained in the same tradition would, in general, be equally competent even though less experienced.

During 1972-73, he used to pine away for the civil service officers awaiting repatriation from Pakistan, expecting that the problems of administration would be greatly eased on their return. Visitors from countries that did not have the British-style generalist civil service, specially from the USA, wondered about this. They questioned why he could not recruit from the ranks of professionals from outside the government as well as from the private business sector to run the various Ministries and agencies. For example, the US government was run by hordes of lawyers and Bangladesh seemed to have a lot of well trained lawyers, among others. A limited experiment during that period in recruiting a few professionals from outside the government as Secretaries in such Ministries as education, health, and public works ran into opposition from the civil service. They received less than enthusiastic cooperation from their counterparts.

Many Ministers relied heavily on their officials, who did most of the thinking on the formulation of policy proposals. In Cabinet meetings they frequently called upon their officials to explain and defend Ministrys' viewpoints. At the same time, Ministers harboured an attitude of mistrust towards the civil service — an attitude they had inherited from the Pakistan days when the civil service and the army combined to exercise supreme power. This unhappy memory led them to introduce special regulations in 1972-73 to deprive the officials of the security of jobs they had traditionally enjoyed. This resulted in a great deal of uncertainty among officials and undermined their morale.[5]

I had the impression that Ministers had a very ambivalent attitude towards officials, reflecting their own sense of insecurity, on the one hand, and a grudging admiration for their ability, on the other. While they admired the officials' competence, they desired a very high degree of political control over them. Whenever there were delays or noncompliance in the execution of their decisions, a great deal of concern was expressed by Ministers that many officials did not share their economic and political views. Ministers worried that their officials were not enthusiastic in implementing policies of which they did not approve.

In this context, a discussion Sheikh Mujib had with President Tito, while on a visit to Yugoslavia, on the role of bureaucracy is worth recalling. The conversation turned to the problems that a leader faced in his attempt to build a newly independent country on the basis of a different socioeconomic philosophy. How did the officials steeped in the old traditions and ideology perform this task in Yugoslavia? Tito was emphatic that it was very essential that the bureaucrats fully shared the aspirations and ideas of the political leadership and were

---

5 Once, when I went to see the Prime Minister in his office, I found him visibly annoyed. He was exasperated with non-compliance with some of his instructions given some days back. He called one of the officials in his Secretariat to his presence and instructed him to find out the reasons. As the official was going out of the room, he exclaimed to me. ... *these officers are used to obeying very diligently the orders of smartly turned out military captains in half pants, with a baton in hand speaking cantonment English. The politicians shabbily dressed in Panjabi and Pajama, speaking simple Bangla and sometimes chewing Paan, do not evoke such obeisance or compliance. They would be happy if captains replace us.*

committed to them. Otherwise, it was not feasible to implement new policies. Accordingly, when Marshall Tito took over power in Yugoslavia, he got rid of the old guard, the experienced and senior officials of the old regime, and manned the entire government with the partisans, mostly young, who fought for independence. They were inexperienced but committed young party cadres. In his opinion, they did well because they had commitment and dedication; they were also closely guided and supervised by Tito and his senior colleagues. Many in Yugoslavia expressed apprehensions that administrative efficiency and development activities would be retarded and country's progress would be hampered. They proved to be false prophets. Tito asked Sheikh Mujib whether in the light of what he had seen during his visit of Yugoslavia and its achievements, he would consider Tito's decision to be a wrong one. Yugoslavia had done quite well on the whole on his watch.

Those of us who listened to this conversation had to recognise that the situation in Bangladesh was very different from that of Yugoslavia. We did not go through a sociopolitical revolution of the type that occurred in Yugoslavia. Our *Mukti-Bahini* was not comparable to the party cadres or the partisans of Yugoslavia, who were led by a group of dedicated leaders to overthrow the old socioeconomic order. Our war was a brief anticolonial war fought by a large amorphous group of hastily recruited youth including a few deserters from the Pakistan army — not unified in the commitment to a particular socioeconomic ideology, if at all — under the leadership of a nonrevolutionary party, which reorganised its structure and built up its strength shortly before the war. The task of securing an efficient bureaucracy with appropriate management and incentive structures, under a system of political control within a democratic framework, seemed to have escaped our grasp till today.

Political Interference in Administration

There was much talk about widespread interference by the Prime Minister and Ministers in the appointment of officials all over the government. The Planning Commission in an effort to build up a new organisation had to resort to the recruitment of a large number of staff, both professional and administrative. The Members of the

Commission and I shared the task of selecting the professional staff depending on the levels at which they were to be appointed. Similarly, the appointment of the nontechnical or administrative staff was the responsibility of the Members and the Secretary.

During the whole process of selection and appointment of the candidates, I had received no request from the Prime Minister's office. Nor did any Minister ever approach me on any candidate. I was never informed by the Members of interference from any source. I was sure that requests were made at other levels. Those requests were waived aside politely and firmly. It was possible that at the lower levels of appointment in the administration, requests were made and were met. To the best of my knowledge, it did not happen in the case of the appointment of professionals or senior administrative staff. If there was any pressure from any source that the staff of the Commission could not resist, they were instructed to refer such cases to me or to the Members. There was one rather mild exception when M.A. Wajed Miah,[6] son-in-law of the Prime Minister, requested the intercession of Tajuddin, the Finance Minister, about a candidate in a Technical Division of the Commission. Tajuddin had been very close to the family of Sheikh Mujib for many years. I listened to Wajed Miah in the presence of Tajuddin in his room where I was asked to join for a cup of tea. Wajed Miah elaborated on the qualifications of the candidate and explained how deserving he was. All that he wanted, he assured us, was to ensure that this candidate was at least given a serious consideration in view of his high qualifications. I told him that it was precisely the procedure that was being carefully followed i.e. we gave serious consideration to well qualified candidates. There was no reason why his candidate in view of his alleged qualifications would not receive our very careful consideration. That was the end of the matter. The candidate was well qualified, but there were better candidates. He was not selected. Tajuddin had absolutely no interest in this or any other appointment in the Commission. The only thing he did was to give Wajed Miah a chance to make his case — an act of social obligation that all of us had to face one time or another. I had no doubt that Wajed Miah did not bring the subject to any higher level. It was his private request on behalf of a good friend, respectfully conveyed to his "Uncle" Tajuddin.

---

[6] At the time, he was a nuclear scientist with the Bangladesh Atomic Energy Commission.

How much interference was there in the Planning Commission's approval of projects submitted by various Ministries? I do not recall Sheikh Mujib having intervened or overruled the Planning Commission in its function of the approval of projects. Whenever there were complaints by Ministers on a decision or judgement by the Commission, he would urge them to reach an understanding with the Commission; this was the pattern until the end of 1973 or early 1974. This was increasingly less so when the interministerial committee did not agree with the Planning Commission's recommendations and when the individual Ministries avoided the guidelines or decisions. Moreover, the authority of the Commission was diluted by substantially increasing the upper limit of development projects, which the individual Ministries could approve on their own.

There was the case of a project of the Works Ministry for the construction of what was called the Gonobhavan i.e. new office-cum-residence for the Prime Minister. In view of the resource shortage, we advised the Ministry to reexamine the cost estimates in the interest of economy and to provide for more modest construction. In preparing the design and quality of construction, the Ministry was overzealous hoping to please Sheikh Mujib.

We were told, of course, that the project document had already been seen and agreed to by Sheikh Mujib. We felt sure that he would not object to a reexamination of the project and its construction costs. But the Ministry was very surprised at this suggestion and informed Sheikh Mujib, no doubt with some embellishments, about the audacious behaviour of the "professors" in the Commission. Our decision evoked no reaction from the Prime Minister himself or from his office.

On the issue of Gonobhavan, his reticence as far as the Planning Commission was concerned, was understandable. While the government was publicly committed to a policy of austerity and the Commission was expected to enforce it in respect of the development projects, Sheikh Mujib decided that he could not have asked the Commission to do otherwise in his own case. The sycophants around him most probably told him how luxurious were the accommodations usually enjoyed by the heads of governments in other countries. Nonetheless, he did not want to deviate from the discipline that the Planning Commission was trying to impose on public expenditures.

This subject came up later on in a different context. During his visit to Yugoslavia, Sheikh Mujib and his delegation were taken to Brioni Island — the beautiful sea resort — where Marshall Tito had his villa and where he took his distinguished guests for a day or so of relaxation. I was in the delegation. The villa belonged to the old monarchy and was inherited and renovated by the socialist government of Tito. It was very luxurious in the tradition of palaces and villas of the European royalty of the 19th and early 20th centuries. We were all very impressed to see how the living styles of leaders in the Socialist countries contrasted so starkly with their espousal of the cause or the rights of the proletariat!

In one of his relaxed moments, Sheikh Mujib remarked to me — albeit in jest — on the great pomp and luxury in which the famous Socialist revolutionary Marshall Tito lived. On the other hand, the Prime Minister of Bangladesh was being denied by the Planning Commission a proposed accommodation for his residence and office which was very modest, not even distantly comparable to this villa or resort. Equally in jest, I pointed out that there was a very significant difference between the two cases. Tito secured these luxurious villas free from the dispossessed royals and feudals. We were very unlucky in this respect. The only palace of any sort that we had inherited was the palace of Maharaja of Santosh. This subject was dropped as casually as it was mentioned and it never came up again.

Later on the project was revised and it was built partly by renovating and expanding the existing structure, and partly by including items in current or revenue expenditures that were not part of the development budget.

Personal Style in Human Relations

Like all heads of government, he received a constant barrage of flattery and exaggerated eulogy. But it appeared to me that, in early days, he resisted more often than succumbed to it. As a veteran in human relationships, he was often quick to discern the difference between sycophancy and genuine appreciation. But then I suppose there is always a limit beyond which one cannot resist intelligent sycophancy administered constantly and carefully to exploit the weaknesses of the human spirit! In my presence, I did not find him being subjected to any unusual degree of flattery. His senior Ministers at least did not indulge in it in an obvious or transparent manner.

Sheikh Mujib was always tolerant in his dealings with me. He seldom expressed displeasure at my critical comments and protests. He would listen attentively even though no corrective action followed. Once he was sitting with his brother-in-law, Minister Sherniabat,[7] when I called upon him to discuss some urgent matter. As I entered the room, he asked the Minister to leave him alone with me with the following remarks "now that the Deputy Chairman has come to take me to task for my acts of omission and commission." This was a statement, I suspect, made in good humour and could have been interpreted as indicating either his affectionate indulgence of the simple minded, well intentioned academic or his willingness to take notice of my opinions or comments. The truth was probably as usual in between.

When Tajuddin left the government, it was reported that his movements were under constant surveillance and that it was not advisable to meet him in that highly charged atmosphere. I decided to visit him sometime in 1974 and found him very despondent. He never referred to Sheikh Mujib. We discussed various matters of common interest. I had known and worked closely with Tajuddin before and after independence. He was not only a great patriot but also in my view the most serious minded, conscientious and competent as well as the most hardworking among the Ministers. Tajuddin usually took the views of the Planning Commission seriously and, if convinced, strongly supported them during Cabinet discussions. The entire Planning Commission had great respect for him.

The split between the two closest political associates, i.e. Sheikh Mujib and Tajuddin, was a great tragedy and bode ill for the future. It was widely believed that his detractors in the Cabinet — some of whom were members of the government in exile and were no friends of his then and later on — were sowing the seeds of mistrust between him and Sheikh Mujib. It seemed to me that Tajuddin was frequently too outspoken in public. He was deeply frustrated that he had lost the full confidence of Sheikh Mujib, which he had enjoyed in the pre-1971 days. He occasionally gave expression to his frustration in public and was not very tactful.

---

[7] Abdur Rab Sherniabat was a Minister in the government.

During my next meeting with Sheikh Mujib, I informed him of my visit with Tajuddin. I let him know that in view of my past relationship with Tajuddin, I intended to keep in touch with him in the future as well. His reaction was that my relationship with Tajuddin — in whatever way I wanted to maintain it — was of no concern to him.

It appeared to me that, in general, Sheikh Mujib was kind to the politicians who were active during the Pakistan days, irrespective of their shifting party affiliations, but who did not harbour any strong personal animosity against him. He was known to have shown consideration to them when they were in personal difficulties, including providing financial assistance for their families in distress. I recall an occasion when Maulana Bhasani was agitating against the government on some issue and went on a hunger strike. Sheikh Mujib sent his Cabinet colleagues to plead with Bhasani to break his fast. I was sitting with him as his colleagues departed. Sheikh Mujib took out a letter from Bhasani, written in long hand, which addressed him in affectionate terms, and implored him for a donation to the university Bhasani had started. A donation from the Prime Minister's discretionary fund was promptly provided.

The rumours and newspaper reports about inappropriate behaviour or misdeeds of his relatives pained him. In this context, I recount an incident. Sheikh Kamal — his eldest son — participated in student politics very actively. There were critical reports in the press about his conduct in the course of clashes or tensions between rival groups. Reports about Kamal were too close to his person and were smearing his reputation. When I raised the subject with him, he agreed that Kamal's very active role in student politics was not advisable in the prevailing context of a highly volatile political milieu. This did no good either to his or his father's reputation.

I suggested that Kamal should be sent abroad for higher studies so that he could be away from this tense environment, and at the same time he could prepare for a career, perhaps a political one. Sheikh Mujib agreed that it was desirable but that he had no resources to finance such a venture. I suggested that in view of my close contact with donor agencies or foreign private foundations, I could try to arrange a scholarship from outside their regular technical assistance programmes in Bangladesh. This would not be at the cost of a qualified candidate. He argued, however, that in view of the fact that Kamal was not a very exceptional student, such an act would be a misuse of power — an obvious act of nepotism in favour of his own son, which he could not approve. This was from a man who, it was said, knowingly tolerated or indulged others to abuse public resources for private gain. I was willing to take this extraordinary action and to accept any eventual blame. In my view, it would have helped the personal reputation of Sheikh Mujib and strengthened his credibility in dealing with conflicts between rival student groups or political factions. I believed that the benefit to the country would far outweigh the damage to my integrity.

In view of his reluctance, the only alternative left to me was to find some assistance from a source other than any foreign government or donor agency or private foundation which had any association with the Bangladesh government. One obvious choice was a private university abroad. I did not inform Sheikh Mujib about my private thoughts. It was a very uncertain possibility and I was not sure whether I would succeed. On my own, I started to explore the possibilities of any assistance or scholarship that could be obtained from any foreign university. Some of my friends were running university departments and faculties as Chairmen or Deans. I wanted to choose a country, which was not in the headlines, nor had expatriate Bangladesh community of any size or a large Bangladesh embassy. This would keep Kamal as far away as possible from the Bangladesh political connections. With some effort I was able to secure his admission at Toronto University and also to arrange a stipend at least for the first year in 1973 with a promise of renewal for the next year. It was rather a modest amount but adequate. The university was advised not to publicise the identity of Kamal. It was a personal favour done for the sake of old friendship by a professor at the university. During the period of my exile in 1971, he had been very helpful lobbying in Canada for the cause of Bangladesh. In the aftermath of the war of liberation, academics in many countries were very sympathetic to Bangladesh. Friends went out of their way to do favours to help out in any way they could.

However, I did not anticipate that Kamal would be unwilling to avail of such an opportunity for higher studies abroad. Sheikh Mujib expressed his lack of success in persuading Kamal and requested that I might try to convince him. When Kamal met me, I tried to argue with him on two tracks. In a highly competitive world facing the youth of the 1970s and 1980s, whatever maybe the chosen career path, i.e. law, administration, or any of the professions, a high level of education and training would be a valuable asset. Secondly, if his ambition was to be a political leader, the days of the amateur were over; broadbased education in a well known university would be a very good preparation. It would expose him to political ideas and philosophies, both past and present. He would learn of the challenges confronting the contemporary world, political, strategic and economic, and how other countries were meeting them. In his response, Kamal was very polite but pleaded that he was not yet ready for such a step. He was extremely thankful for the efforts made on his behalf. He would like to take up such an opportunity later on. Sheikh Mujib was sorry that he could not convince Kamal. He respected his wishes and did not want to force him.

Sheikh Mujib was aware of the rumours and complaints about corruption among his Ministers.[8] Once I raised the subject with him. He responded wistfully. How could he take draconian action against his colleagues with whom he had spent years of his life in the rough and tumble of politics? With many of them he had shared deprivations and sufferings, while escaping the dragnet of the Pakistani police and the military. He had urged upon them not to damage the credibility of his government. The agony he suffered was real, all the more so because he could not be uncompromisingly strong in deterring or punishing his fellow politicians.

Yes, he also knew, he said, that rumours were circulating about a senior person in his own Secretariat who had reportedly built, with ill-gotten money, what his detractors called, a *luxury mansion*.

---

[8] In the early years, the threshold of social tolerance for corruption or perception of corruption in the government was significantly lower than it is now. Also, the scale or the incidence of corruption that was thought to be prevailing then was considerably smaller than what is now widely believed to be the case. There were rumours about corruption in high places. Fact and fiction coexisted in an uncontrolled and haphazard way. Popular expectations were very high that after the sacrifices of the war and the deprivation of the past, a new era would dawn in Bangladesh; honesty and integrity in the government would be the order of the day. There was hope, not realised, that common people would improve their condition and the rich and the powerful would share in the austerity that would accompany the post-war period.

He confirmed that serious enquiries had been made about it all. In fact, he showed me snapshots of the house in all its dimensions including the interior as well as fittings and furnishings, taken apparently by the anticorruption department, probably at his behest. But this senior officer solemnly vowed that the money his wife had inherited from her parents funded the construction. This officer was in the Pakistani prison for so-called anti state activities including his association with Sheikh Mujib and had lost his job in consequence. The matter was laid to rest.

The ability to overcome human weakness is the greatest challenge to successful statecraft. No political leader can start with a clean slate. The obligations inherited from the past act as a constraint on complete freedom of action. To shake off the burden of obligations in the interest of greater good of the country and to take stern measures against fellow-politicians/close associates require a degree of ruthlessness, which not all leaders are able to command. Sheikh Mujib showed considerable courage, made sacrifices and took risks in a relentless struggle against the Pakistani domination. His human weaknesses, however, softened his resolve to combat effectively the perception of corruption in his regime.

Gathering Storm in 1974

In the context of the deteriorating political and economic situation in late 1974, in one of his visits to my office, Ambassador A. Fomin of the Soviet Union had a very interesting conversation with me and made an intriguing suggestion. He was discussing how Bangladesh could improve the system of governance to meet the challenges of the time, both economic and political. He felt that a very strong leadership was the need of the hour. Sheikh Mujib was too kind and weak. He was often vacillating. It was imperative that a man of strong and decisive personality with firm determination and a high quality of leadership was placed at the helm of affairs of the country at that critical moment.

In his opinion, the most appropriate person who had the requisite qualities was Sheikh Moni.[9] Sheikh Mujib should, therefore, appoint

---

[9] Sheikh Fazlul Huq Moni was a nephew of Sheikh Mujib. He was very active in the Awami league in 1969-71, and later on after independence.

him in a Cabinet position and effectively anoint him as the next in command handing over major decisions and day-to-day administration to Moni. This would greatly improve the quality and decisiveness of the administration. He felt that, as a person responsible for planning and involved in economic management, I should welcome such an arrangement in the interest of improved governance in the country. He assumed that, as a non-political person, I would not be jealous or concerned that Moni should usurp such important political power at the cost of the senior leaders and the Cabinet Ministers. The Soviet Ambassador did not make this suggestion to me in great secrecy or confidence. At that time, there were widely circulating rumours about Moni's increasing political clout. The Ambassador's suggestion seemed like an endorsement of the rumours.

As the Ambassador made his case for Sheikh Moni, I remembered an occasion around mid-1974 when I was greatly intrigued by an editorial in the *Banglar Bani*, a newspaper of which Moni was the editor. While analysing the deteriorating economic situation, he referred to the mismanagement of the economy and stressed that one of the important factors was bad planning. In his view, planning was in the wrong hands i.e. the products of western universities such as Oxford-Cambridge-Harvard. The training and education that the planners had received was not very relevant or useful in the context of the circumstances of our country. It did not equip them with any close knowledge or understanding of the Bangladesh economy to deal with its myriad problems. What was needed, he added sarcastically, were *"Deshi"* or homegrown *Hekimi* or *Ayurvedic* doctors who could treat "indigenous diseases". Bangladesh did not need the western educated doctors (PhDs), like those inhabiting the Planning Commission, who were trained to treat western ailments.

It was believed that Moni was very close to Sheikh Mujib and that he had considerable influence on him. I had no direct acquaintance with him but heard of his considerable organising capacity in the service of the Awami League. It was also widely believed that Moni had fallen out with Tajuddin while in exile in India. He was reported to have contributed to the growth of mistrust between him and Sheikh Mujib. It was, so to speak, a bazaar rumour in the political circles, the *cognoscenti*. I myself never heard or received even a hint about such a possibility from Tajuddin himself. We, in the Planning Commission, were used to frequent criticisms about our policies or actions in the press, both from the left and the right. We avoided public controversy or did not counter the critics by giving public rejoinder. We used to call the newsmen to meetings with us and explained or answered questions or criticisms. In this particular instance of the *Banglar Bani* editorial, it was a strong assault on the ability and suitability of the professional leadership of the Planning Commission, rather than on specific policies. After all, Sheikh Mujib personally chose and appointed the incumbents in the Commission and was its head or Chairman. I assumed, as it turned out mistakenly, that such vitriolic attack could not have been made by his nephew, if he did not have reasons to understand that such an attack would cause Sheikh Mujib no great displeasure or evoke no serious disapproval.

It was in 1974 and our summer of discontent. I was very exasperated and took a copy of the editorial to Sheikh Mujib. I requested his reaction to this act of abuse on Moni's part. Apparently, he had not seen the editorial prior to that moment and was greatly annoyed. He advised me to pay no attention to what Moni wrote in his editorial.

Sheikh Mujib: Looking Back after Decades

After a lapse of about 30 years, how does one attempt to appraise Sheikh Mujib? Distance of time and space provides an opportunity for a balanced and wider perspective. My contact with him was for the short space of 1969-75 and in that period I had known him closely between 1972-75. It is not for me to retrace well known, much traversed history. One important way to look at his era is to distinguish between the tasks Sheikh Mujib faced in the pre-liberation (pre-1971 period) and the way he approached them, on the one hand, and on the other, the challenges he faced in the post-1971 period, the means at his disposal and the way he responded.

In the pre-1971 period, Sheikh Mujib had a long term vision for the realisation of the economic and political rights of Bangladesh. He subjugated all other objectives to this overriding goal. In the task of mobilising the country for the achievement of this goal, he ranked very high above all his contemporaries. The role of his subordinates and other leaders of his party were secondary, even though very helpful. In the postliberation period, the circumstances were radically different. The challenges were very complex, encompassing many diverse elements of social and economic transformation. To build an economically prosperous and politically stable country with widely shared economic benefits under a democratic constitution required efforts on multiple fronts. The task required much more than the charismatic leadership or mobilising capacity of one man. His single-handed efforts could not achieve the multiple objectives of postliberation Bangladesh in the way in which the sole objective of the liberation movement could reach its goal. He needed political associates who would be able to share his burden and responsibility, including the task of mobilising the masses. His colleagues needed to play a much greater and effective role in policy formulation, implementation, and administration. Unfortunately, it is history's cruel judgement that the political leadership that he had around him lacked (excepting a few) long political experience, skill, and wisdom. It could be argued that he did not do enough to build up the second tier of leadership by devolving responsibility and creating confidence among his colleagues. At the same time, it was also true that time was too short between 1969 and 1972 when the party was being reactivated and organised, and that the list of tasks was too long. But even with these limitations, more could have been done. It was a matter of high priority — much more than running the day-to-day administration.

In postliberation Bangladesh, political problems and administrative short comings were daunting and demanded a great deal of attention. As a result, they inhibited and constrained his efforts to deal adequately with economic challenges, which were no less difficult. By 1974, several contradictions and weaknesses in the system of governance, both civil and military, started to have destabilising effects. In the intervening decades since 1975, these issues have been much discussed and debated. To illustrate, one can repeat a few highlights; impatience of the highly politicised, ambitious army officials with aspirations for leadership and their apparent unhappiness with the prevailing sociopolitical system; failure to reassign them from the seat of military authority and to reward them otherwise with highly visible honours and significant civilian jobs, preferably abroad; establishment of a paramilitary force

(*Rakkhi Bahini*) that appeared to be an antidote rather than a supplement to the armed forces; insecurity of jobs among the civil servants, with a low ceiling on salary rapidly eroded by inflation;[10] blanket distinction between those officials who crossed the border and those who did not during the 1971 war,[11] perception of corruption and misuse of power not countered by visible acts of exemplary punishment; failure to convince the public that economic hurdles were severe and that the rich and the powerful were also obliged to share in deprivation. Any one of these factors by itself could not have done much harm to Sheikh Mujib's regime but all of them acting cumulatively did. The last straw on the camel's back was the establishment of the BAKSAL system.[12]

That Sheikh Mujib was not an exceptional administrator has often been mentioned. The leaders of liberation movements seldom are. As mentioned earlier, it seemed to me that he spent much time in day-to-day administration. At the same time, it would be true to say that he was very perceptive and quick to grasp critical policy issues and decisive in action. I can only base this conclusion on the basis of my own experience.

He had a fabled memory as was widely known. He remembered his instructions to or discussions with me on different subjects, weeks and months later. He had great agility of mind. On matters of policy that I had occasions to deal with, he was able to go to the heart of the

[10] To my utter amazement, the civil servants of all categories in early 1972 did not show great unhappiness and anger at the fixation of a low ceiling on salary. I could not understand whether it was a spirit of unthinking obeisance or of sacrifice, which accounted for it.

[11] It would have been possible, though with some difficulty and imperfectly, to investigate who were active collaborators. Unfortunately, the process was very haphazard and not unaffected by rumours and personal vendetta. Experience in other counties had shown that this problem did not permit of a very neat solution and false accusations were likely. With hindsight, it appears now that something like a Truth Commission *a la* South Africa or Chile would have been appropriate but in the early 1970s this idea was not born.

[12] It is most appropriate here to quote his address at the Central Committee meeting of the BAKSAL on 19th June 1975: "Ami Feresta Noi Shaitano Noi Ami Manoosh Ami Bhul Korboi Ami Bhul Korle Amar Mone Rakhte Hobe (I can rectify myself). Ami Jadi rectify Korthe Pari, Shekane Amar Bahaduri, Jadi Ami Go Dhare Bashe Thaki Je Na Ami Jeta Korechi Shetai Bhalu (that cannot be human being). Feresta Hoi Ni Je Shobe Khichu Bhalo Hobe (I am neither an angel nor a devil. I am a human being. I am liable to make mistakes. If I commit mistakes, I must remember that I can rectify myself. It all rebounds to my credit if I can rectify myself. If I obstinately insist that whatever I have done is the best, then I am not behaving like a normal human being. I am not an angel that whatever I do would be flawless and correct)."

issue presented to him, with its pros and cons. He would give his decision, sometimes after consultations with his close advisers and sometimes right in the course of discussion. I found that it was important to present to him the matter for decision in a clear-cut way — thus requiring preparation as well as clarity of thought and exposition on my part. To mention only a few instances. He quickly grasped the implications of the *Six-Points Programme* during his discussions with us in 1970-71 that independent trade, tax, foreign exchange, and currency policies for each region in Pakistan meant two separate economies in a way that would make them only nominally one country. He took the decision on the nationalisation policy in the full knowledge of its pros and cons. He accepted the logic of making the nationalised industries, independent and autonomous but he left it to the Minister of Industries to implement the policy. He understood the underlying basis of negotiations with the IMF on the devaluation of taka. He was aware of the economic costs and benefits of food and fertiliser subsidies but took decisions partly on political considerations. He understood the responsibilities of the Planning Commission vis-à-vis rest of the government and the reasons why there was friction and tension between them. In later years, he found it too heavy a political burden for him to resolve the problem. His dealing with foreign leaders was equally focused. During my tenure in the Planning Commission, I accompanied him on all his official visits abroad. I watched him in his meetings, discussions, and negotiations with the various heads of governments on wide ranging issues. He demonstrated his grasp of major issues under discussion. He established quick rapport with his warm and charismatic personality.

Sheikh Mujib was a staunch and uncompromising nationalist. His objective was to pursue friendly and cooperative relationship with all groups of countries, including superpowers. By 1975, USSR having so strongly supported us in the final hours of our independence struggle, had lost its initial enthusiasm for him as he was pursuing a more or less non-aligned policy — in fact, from their point of view, with a gradual shift towards a closer relationship with the western world. US, during the Nixon Administration, was unfavourably disposed towards Bangladesh to start with in 1971, in the context of its close bilateral relationships with Pakistan and its new China policy. Later on she was establishing a better working relations with him. The United States was concerned about Sheikh Mujib's strong negotiating stance vis-à-vis Pakistan during 1972-75 and was wary of the Indo-Bangladesh friendship in view of India's strong Soviet connection. Therefore, by 1975, because of his fiercely nationalist stand, he was not in great favour with any of the big powers. He was closely allied with none to serve anyone's global and regional interest. Any bilateral relationship, in his view, had to be consistent with Bangladesh's national interests and not in conflict with his need to maintain friendly relationships with other countries.

He was unabashedly appreciative of India's help and assistance in the war of independence, and valued her friendship. He guided with considerable skill a delicate process of negotiations on such issues as the *Farakka Barrage*, border trade, joint enterprises in industry and cooperation on jute. However, he pursued cooperation with India with scrupulous attention to and defense of Bangladesh's vital interests and avoided the appearance of subservience. Opposition groups in Bangladesh consistently propagated the view that because of her help in the war of liberation, Sheikh Mujib was always eager to accommodate India's demands or to grant concessions. This perception was far from the truth. A firm believer in the benefits of close cooperation with India on multiple fronts, he pursued specific acts of cooperation only when there were demonstrated gains to Bangladesh.

He realised that economic relations could not grow in a vacuum but had to be nurtured in the overall context of the political relationship. The Prime Minister of India, Indira Gandhi, retained a degree of friendship towards him, because of her close personal involvement in the 1971 war. However, there were those in the Indian Establishment, i.e. a few politicians and the bureaucracy, specially the foreign policy establishment, who did not adequately appreciate the internal political dynamics in Bangladesh. They had a narrow and restricted view of what Bangladesh policies should be on various individual issues in the context of their global and regional interest.[13] From that perspective, they did not always find him

---

[13]Dixit's book is a rather outspoken analysis of India's relationship with Bangladesh.

cooperative and accommodating. On the other hand, among a large section of the population in Bangladesh there was a lurking fear and suspicion about possible domination by India. His efforts to revive Islamic connections and to claim for Bangladesh the role of a large Muslim majority country in the community of the Muslim nations not only extended the scope of Bangladesh's international relationships. It was also expected to allay the popular fear of being too close to India. But this policy at the same time has unwanted side effects. It tended to make India feel uncomfortable and some groups in India even recalled pre-1971 East Pakistan.

To balance the pulls of such opposing forces, while pursuing the best interests of Bangladesh, was very challenging. It required great confidence, skill and constant vigilance on his part. This task remains a continuing challenge for the policymakers of two countries.

Chapter 8

THE FIRST FIVE-YEAR PLAN: WAS IT RELEVANT?

O ne of the first acts of the Prime Minister, as described earlier, was to establish the Planning Commission. He wanted the Planning Commission to formulate a Five-Year Plan in order to provide a framework and a perspective for development programmes and policies. I recall below: (a) the major characteristics and features of the Five-Year Plan; and (b) my perception of the way it was reviewed by the Cabinet and the essence of its comments on and reactions to the Plan.[1]

8.1 WHAT WAS THE PLAN ALL ABOUT?

The First Five-Year Plan had three parts: (a) an elaboration of the sociopolitical objectives and assumptions of the plan; (b) macroeconomic projections i.e. income growth, savings and investment, foreign trade and balance of payments; and (c) sectoral programmes, priorities, and inter-sectoral allocation of resources.

The sociopolitical objectives of the Five-Year Plan were derived from the Constitution of Bangladesh. The Plan was considered a first step towards the progressive achievement of a socialist economy in the future — an objective embodied in the Constitution and in the various policy statements of the Awami League, including its election manifesto in 1970. The Plan thus reflected the Planning Commission's understanding of the directives of the political leadership.

---

[1] Detailed discussions of the Five-Year Plan are contained in N. Islam, *Development Planning in Bangladesh, op.cit.*

It might be interesting to refresh one's memory as to how the Plan interpreted the sociopolitical objectives in the context of the mandate given. The ultimate objective, the Plan asserted, was to achieve an egalitarian society with an assurance of every citizen's right to work and with limits imposed by law on the private ownership of the means of production. The Plan recognised that the objective conditions in Bangladesh stood in the way of realisation of a socialist vision in the near future. These objective conditions were: (a) absence of political cadres who were yet to emerge; (b) alienation of the government bureaucracy from the people — an attitude inherited from colonial times; (c) exploitative forms of landownership; and (d) dominance of private enterprises in trade, construction, and distribution that created substantial scarcity premia and unearned income for a few.

The Plan proceeded to highlight some of the interim measures for the progress toward the objective of socialism .The policy of nationalisation of industry, large scale trade, and finance, already implemented by the government, was the first step in the direction of the ultimate goal. As an egalitarian society was yet to be established, material incentives would be provided to both managers and the labour force. The differences in skill and performance would be compensated by high rewards and income differentials. But at the same time the scale of unearned incomes and ostentatious consumption should be curbed.

As an important preparatory first step, efforts should be initiated to start building up party cadres, who would undergo rigorous training in the ideology and policies of socialism. The cadres, living and working with the masses, would mobilise them and transform their patterns of behaviour. They would help design development projects, remove organisational bottlenecks and constitute a pressure group on the local administration. However, the most important precondition for the progress towards socialism was a political leadership, dedicated to the ideas of socialism. It should set examples in social behaviour, share austerity under conditions of prevailing scarcity, harness the enthusiasm for sacrifice and nation building, unleashed by the war of liberation. It should motivate the bureaucracy to be efficient and people oriented.

These statements and exhortations were based upon the party's declarations and manifestos and on the Commission's understanding of their implications for progress towards declared objectives. They had drawn upon the experience in the socialist countries and were affected by the prevailing climate of thought dominant in many Third World countries. We assumed that it was the responsibility of the politicians and their constituencies to critically examine the assumptions and recommendations laid down in the Plan as guiding principles. The leaders were expected to provide unambiguous decision on this framework for the Plan. In the event, no political leader or Cabinet member appeared to have seriously examined it. As a result, the Commission ended up in assuming the two-pronged roles of a preacher and a theoretician of the party — not a viable position.

The Commission was acutely aware, even in those early days, of the importance of honesty and competence not only in running the public-owned enterprises and in the delivery of social services; these were also crucial for the effectiveness of the government's regulatory functions. To achieve growth and equity, it was essential to conquer corruption. There was at that time a public perception of the abuse of power in the government. In the early 1970s, it was unusual for a Plan document in a developing country to recognise and openly discuss the problem of corruption and the need to curb it, if not to eradicate it. It is worth recalling that, thirty years ago, the Plan had the following to say,

> To accomplish above objectives (planned development for growth and equality), it is essential that people have confidence in the integrity and the commitment of the political leadership to translate word into deeds. Economic development, in the context of acute poverty prevailing in Bangladesh, requires sacrifices all around. This is particularly true for the elite so that the burden on those at the bottom does not appear to be intolerable.

> It is specially relevant in the above context to ensure that people do not regard corruption as an endemic feature of our society. Corruption is basically an antisocial act. Those who have scant respect for society indulge in it. It tends to misallocate resources and leads to maldistribution of income. Apart from the adverse moral conse-quences of corruption, there is an economic price, which the society is required to pay. No society can make rapid progress if there is widespread belief in the prevalence of corrupt practices in the country, whether such beliefs have any foundation or not. Such a belief breeds resentment, cynicism, apathy and loss of faith in public

activities. Where there is widespread suspicion of corruption and only half hearted attempts to root it out, even honest persons show unwillingness to take initiative and exercise independent judgement because no one is immune from suspicion. Thus, everyone avoids taking personal responsibility and shares decision making to the maximum extent possible to protect himself, with resultant delay and inefficiencies. It is in this context that detection and punishment of offenders irrespective of their personal and political affiliations are necessary.[2]

The Cabinet approved the Five-Year Plan in its entirety. The Plan, its assumptions and objectives were not debated in the Cabinet, or in the Parliament, or in the meetings of the political parties, or by any of the groups in civil society. The press had, however, provided widespread coverage to the Plan but with very little examination of issues. Its comments were generally descriptive and supportive. The Commission suggested that public debates and discussions in various fora were essential if the Plan was to be realistic and acceptable to the population. Sheikh Mujib and the Cabinet responded that there was no prospect of any substantial input and, therefore, no gain from such popular participation. The debates and discussions in the Parliament and by the civil society would not have, in their opinion, contributed in any way to the improvement of the content and substance of the Plan. Therefore, time and effort involved in such a debate or a consultation process were not worth the benefit expected from it.

We failed to convince Sheikh Mujib and the Cabinet that the suggestion for public consultations and open discussions was not based upon an expectation that they would necessarily contribute profound or new ideas on either objectives or policies of the Plan. The main reason why such a process was necessary was to facilitate a wider understanding of the Plan's objectives, specially sociopolitical assumptions, investment allocations, policies and institutional reforms that were outlined in the Plan. If the consultations were well organised, they could have indicated how plausible the various sections of the population considered the recommendations on policies or institutions. A widespread public debate would have concentrated the minds of politicians, the intelligentsia and the public. They would have known

---

[2] The Five-Year Plan, May 1973, p. 80.

what the society could hope to achieve and what costs and sacrifices on their part would be required.

Two important aspects of the Plan deserved wide public participation and would have benefited from some reaction, specially from the political leadership and the party members: first, the elaboration of the sociopolitical objectives of the Plan; and second, the implications of the nationalisation of industry, trade, and financial institutions. The decision on the nationalisation policy was taken independently and prior to the formulation of the Plan in early 1972. The Plan focused on the follow up to the decision and on devising the appropriate organisational structure, incentive systems and management for the nationalised enterprises.

8.2 UNRESOLVED AMBIGUITIES AND CONTRADICTIONS

It became evident as days and months passed that the statements on the sociopolitical objectives and policies in the Plan were considered by the government and by the society at large more as pious exhortations rather than serious recommendations for action. Also, a socialist society meant many things to many people. It became increasingly clear that to Sheikh Mujib and his close political associates, socialism implied possibly no more than a limited or a populist version of *Fabian Socialism*. It visualised a kind of economy in which the government would play a significant role. It would own selected sectors of the economy i.e. the so-called commanding heights, and regulate economic activities in general in such a way as to achieve a major improvement in the living conditions of the poor.

The Cabinet did debate extensively the size and composition of the Plan outlay, in particular the sectoral and subsectoral priorities, financial allocations for specific important projects and institutional/ organisational reforms. These issues were close to the interests of particular Ministers. These aspects of the Plan could be and were discussed without reference to the sociopolitical prerequisites or the macroeconomic projections of resources. They were not too much concerned with the projection of financial resources, domestic and foreign exchange, partly because they did not have much to say.[3]

---

[3] Officials of the Ministries of Finance and Commerce had participated in the exercise along with the experts in the Planning Commission in arriving at these estimates.

In succeeding years, many observers and critics observed that the Commission should have appreciated that the political leadership not only had a limited understanding of the nature of a socialist economy but also, more importantly, had displayed an uncertain commitment to its achievement. After all, this should have been apparent to the Commission, after a year of experience of working with the regime and before the Plan was formulated in mid-1973. During this period, we had already faced major obstacles in developing the necessary institutional framework and structure of incentives for the efficient management of industries that were already nationalised in early 1972. A few of the Commission's recommendations on policies and institutions were implemented in a half hearted and halting manner. The resistance of vested interests was strong and the political will to overcome it was weak. In the light of this experience, it was said that the Commission should have realised how the experiment with a large public sector had gone awry in the face of sociopolitical constraints. Therefore, it should have advised a retreat on the policy of expanded public sector adopted in 1972. It should have advocated a progress towards a more liberal market economy with a limited role for the public sector to supplement, whenever essential, the private sector and to correct market failures — a role that was compatible with the managerial and organisational competence of the government. In other words, the Commission should have ignored the rhetoric of the politicians and advised instead a cancellation or a reversal of the ongoing policies. Instead, the Commission did not do so but left the decision in the hands of the politicians in a way that held them down to their rhetoric instead of giving them a way out of the impasse.

In the end, the political leadership did not make a choice and wandered around without a definite vision. The political environment seemed inappropriate for the reversal, so soon after independence, of policies such as the nationalisation of industries that they had advocated for so long. They were not sure about the future direction of the economy to be able so soon to go back on actions already implemented. Nor were they anxious to push ahead in building a socialist society in a comprehensive way. They let the sociopolitical assumptions of the Plan and their implications hang in the air, neither owning them nor rejecting them. The Commission did realise the ambiguities and ineffectiveness of its position. But it did not bring the matter to a head; nor I as the Deputy Chairman faced the implications of the situation. I have to acknowledge some culpability.[4]

A question was often asked why did Sheikh Mujib assign priority to the formulation of a Five-Year Plan. After all we were engaged in reviving and rehabilitating a wardamaged economy, plagued by a host of critical short term problems. In stable political and economic circumstances, a medium term plan could serve a useful purpose not so much as a concrete unalterable plan of action but as an elaboration of possibilities that could be realised if certain policies and programmes were undertaken. However, the Prime Minister felt and the Commission agreed that short term rehabilitation programmes should be put in the medium term perspective of a Five-Year Plan and should become its integral components. This was, in fact, the case. In every sector and subsector, the rehabilitation and reconstruction projects were integrated with longer term development components. The distinction between reconstruction and development was in many cases artificial; reconstruction often implied a change in the design or structure of existing projects. Also, in many cases, development programmes required the rehabilitation of existing projects before a new project could be started. The Plan had a very large component of ongoing projects and the proportion of new projects was small. The Commission produced, in fact, a Plan for Reconstruction and Rehabilitation in the first year (1972-73), which was subsequently integrated into the Five-Year Plan. One could argue that the work on medium term perspectives, policies and resource projections might have diverted a part of the time and attention, which could otherwise have been devoted to the detailed monitoring and supervision of the reconstruction efforts. However, the

---

[4] We did make an attempt to face the situation when we met with the Prime Minister around the middle of 1973. We argued that we would be more useful to him in his task of nation-building if we went back to our academic pursuits and were available to him for advice and consultation as and when needed by him. This would be preferable to our direct involvement in day-to-day policymaking, management, and implementation of policy. Moreover, we felt that in this latter task we did not have a strong political and administrative support we needed under the prevailing circumstances. The Prime Minister strongly declined even to consider any such proposal. He insisted that we must do whatever we could, even though the circumstances were not ideal, to help him in his difficult job. We were with him in the dark days of 1969-71 and we must persist now. His charisma won the day; we did not have the heart to do otherwise. We decided to do our best within the confines of all the ideological ambiguity and administrative-cum-managerial bottlenecks, hoping for the best.

Commission felt that once the Plan laid down the priorities in reconstruction and rehabilitation programmes and projects, the rest was the responsibility of the different Ministries. One could plausibly argue, on the other hand, that in view of the unusual circumstances in the country, the Commission should have been involved more heavily in the supervision and monitoring of the reconstruction programme.

Admittedly, given the time constraint, the Commission along with the rest of the Ministries/agencies engaged in project formulation, did indeed undertake an overwhelming task. The task of preparing the medium term Plan and elaborating institutional and policy reforms, combined with the formulation of reconstruction programmes and related new projects, was a very substantial and additional burden on a new government. It is arguable whether it would not have been advisable to prepare, let us say, a three-year Reconstruction Plan rather than a Five-Year Plan, which was in effect both a development and reconstruction plan. In practice, we concentrated our efforts on annual development plans. The targets and programmes were adjusted in response to changes in the availability of internal and external resources and progress in implementation.

The core of the Five-Year Plan was the delineation of sectoral priorities and the formulation of development programmes and projects that emerged out of it. Secondly, there were a set of sectoral policies and institutional arrangements which were crucial for the task of reconstruction and development. These were the two essential components, further elaborated in annual development plans, which engaged the rest of the government as well as the international development community. The estimation of resources, internal and external, available for development expenditures was, by its nature under the circumstances then prevailing, less than firm. Therefore, the size of the overall development programme and the sectoral allocation were uncertain.

It may be interesting to recall an anecdote that describes what one of the political leaders, a Minister in the Cabinet of that period, thought of the Five-Year Plan. This happened almost 30 years later. In the course of conversations on a visit to Washington, he remarked that my colleagues and I wrote a nice Five-Year Plan but it was not of much use. It seemed to me that he said it half in jest, half in earnest. He held important portfolios and participated in the Cabinet discussions on the Five-Year Plan, specially on the issues and programmes relating to sectors under his Ministry, which constituted a major important component of the Plan. We had found him at the time in agreement with the assumptions and perspectives as well as the investment allocations of the Plan. He supported the recommendations for institutional reforms which were very relevant for his sectors. To make matters even more interesting, he was known to be a member of a leftist party in his younger days. In fact, as a Minister, he led a delegation from Bangladesh, including a member of the Commission, to galvanise and mobilise economic and political support of the East European socialist countries. It appeared to me that he was a great believer in the system of planned economy within a socialist framework and, therefore, one of the few believers, I thought by extension, in the sociopolitical objectives of the Plan.

In the light of this historical background, I did not quite know how to interpret his remarks. He might have meant that the Plan, whatever merits it had in concepts and ideas, could not be implemented due to its unrealistic assumptions or recommendations. If, at all, he had such thoughts, he had kept them to himself and did not provide any such indications whatsoever during 1972-75. Alternatively, he might have meant that the Plan could not be implemented because the political leadership lacked commitment or the administrative system lacked competence. Or he could have meant that the macroeconomic assumptions of the Plan were indeed overtaken by unexpected changes in internal and external economic circumstances. He did not clarify nor did I engage in a debate with him in the presence of his officials, many of whom, he would have known, were no admirers of the first government in Bangladesh of which he was a member.[5]

---

[5] This incident was not a very isolated one in my experience in the post-1975 period. In the course of subsequent encounters with a number of politicians of that period, I often found an ambivalent attitude towards their record of economic performance. They were not ready to admit — certainly never in public in the face of a hostile and relentless opposition out to discredit them on fair or unfair grounds — their mistakes in a number of areas. Under the circumstances, it was relatively easy for them, whenever necessary, certainly in private, if not in public, to join the bandwagon to find a convenient scapegoat for the shortcomings or unpopular acts for which the government was held responsible. The chosen scapegoat, the planners, never provided a rejoinder. This was partly out of regard for Sheikh Mujib, who was at that time faced with daunting multipronged challenges that strained the capacity of his government to the utmost. After all a rejoinder would have detracted from the dignity

8.3 PLAN'S CRITICS AND CHANGES IN CIRCUMSTANCES

In the end, the performance of the Plan was affected by all of the above factors, interacting with each other. Apart from the drastic changes in circumstances in 1974, two sets of factors stood out. First, the Commission underestimated the deficiencies of *governance* to meet the challenges presented by the Plan. Secondly, the Plan was optimistic in its estimation of resources, both domestic and foreign exchange. To some extent, the shortfall in resources reflected the failure to implement required policies. In the course of 1974, two independent appraisals of the first Five-Year Plan took place: one, by a World Bank mission; and second, by the conference of the Bangladesh Economic Association on the first Five-Year Plan.[6] These appraisals were made *ex post*, more than a year after the Plan came into operation and not at the time it was formulated.

There were no important differences between the Plan and the World Bank, or for that matter, the Bangladesh Economic Association (BEA), in respect of broad sector priorities or relative investment allocations or recommended policies. However, these appraisals seriously questioned the macroeconomic projections, a portent of the economic malaise soon to overtake Bangladesh. Very soon after the unveiling of the Plan in 1973, world economy was characterised by an upheaval in commodity prices (triggered by the rise in oil and food prices), leading to a drastic deterioration in the terms of trade for Bangladesh and in the availability of foreign exchange resources. The tragic famine of 1974 completed the gloom.

The World Bank, however, questioned the sociopolitical objectives of the Plan and the relatively limited role assigned to the private sector. It also made detailed comments on specific subsector programmes and

---

of a government of which I was a part and therefore, could not escape responsibility in a broad sense.

It was one of the contradictions of the situation that politicians extolled their regime in public for its economic achievements. At the same time, they continued to find fault in private and semi-public discourse with the very Commission that, they insisted, was responsible for advice on economic policy and management. Ergo, the Commission must have contributed to the very success, which they prided themselves on.

[6] *Political Economy*, Journal of the Bangladesh Economic Association, Vol. 1, No. 1, 1974, Dhaka. Papers presented at the First Annual Conference of the BEA on the First Five-Year Plan.

the exchange rate policy.[7] The BEA conference commented on management inefficiencies and corruption in the public sector enterprises. It emphasised inequities resulting from the market imperfections and the scarcity premia accruing to those with access to power and resources.

A few of these comments had implications for the Plan's assumptions and projections. A rewriting of the Plan on the basis of changed assumptions was not considered appropriate. In any case, evolving economic circumstances could not be assessed for another Five-Year period so soon after the massive changes. The degree of uncertainty was very great. Accordingly, it was decided to concentrate on the Annual Plans, which would recast the assumptions on an annual basis, including the estimates of resource availability and its utilisation on a year-to-year basis.[8]

The accumulated experience in medium and long term planning in the developing world holds out a lesson. Any exercise in a medium or long term programming or planning, be it the public or the private sector, in a poor agricultural economy, is beset with shocks and uncertainties, at least, on three fronts. They arise from fluctuations in agricultural production (subject to climate shocks, floods/droughts), volatilities in foreign exchange earnings and uncertainties in the flow of foreign assistance. In this context, the quantitative projections of macroeconomic aggregates such as savings, investment and balance of payments are subject to revisions that are larger and more frequent than in a less open and less aid dependent economy with a large nonagricultural sector. Changes in the total resource availability in most cases also affect the intersectoral priorities and investment allocations. Too much reliance under these circumstances may not be placed on quantitative projections over the medium or long term. What is crucial is to focus on both macro and sectoral priorities and policies that affect the performance of the economy. This is a lesson which the policy planners and administrators have come to understand over the years. That is why a Five-Year Plan should be treated more as an examination of the economy's potentials, a statement of its objectives and priorities as well as a set of recommendations for policy and

---

[7] Discussed in detail in Chapter 11.

[8] N. Islam, *Ibid.*

institutional reforms. The quantitative magnitudes incorporated in a Plan should be treated more in the nature of tentative conditional projections rather than predictions. They provide a broad perspective and orders of magnitude relating to the targets that could be achieved overall as well as in the different sectors of the economy, given the exogenous factors.

Chapter 9

NATIONALISATION AND ALL THAT

9.1 GENESIS OF NATIONALISATION

The decision to nationalise industries was the most controversial one in the economic history of Bangladesh. There are two issues to be considered while appraising that decision. One is to examine it in the context of the circumstances of the time; two, what had happened since then in the realm of ideas, policy, and experience in Bangladesh with respect to the role of public enterprises.

During the early 1990s when Sheikh Hasina was the leader of the opposition in the Bangladesh Parliament, she had discussions in Washington with a group of Bangladeshi professionals on a wide range of policy issues. She asked me why did the government nationalise the Bangladeshi enterprises in 1972, apart from the abandoned enterprises owned by the Pakistanis. Even though one might agree that there was no easy choice with regard to the latter, there was an option with regard to the Bangladeshi enterprises. What were the compelling reasons for the government taking over the Bangladeshi enterprises as well?

I was surprised by this question, coming as it did from the daughter and the political legatee of the supreme architect of policies in the early years. Nationalisation featured in such programmes as the 21-point programmes of the United Front in 1954, Awami League's 11-point programme of the late 1960s as well as the Awami League Election manifesto of 1970, and the 1972 Bangladesh Constitution.[1]

---

[1] The platforms and programmes of most of the political parties in the sub-continent as well as in many Third World countries during the 1960s and 1970s contained similar policy objectives.

All these programmes asked for the nationalisation of major industries, banking, insurance, and of a large segment of internal and external trade. They went even further as to suggest that the workers were to participate not only in the management but also in the profits of industries. I took it for granted that she was aware of the historical legacy of her party and recognised the circumstances under which the Awami League programmes conceived in the 1960s and 1970s were implemented by Sheikh Mujib after independence.

Therefore, in the light of the party's heritage I found this question from the Awami League leader rather puzzling. Her question might have implied that the pledges of the 1960s and 1970s were malleable or were not to be taken seriously and, therefore, could be modified or shelved, if deemed desirable, by the party. There was no compulsion that warranted their implementation in a serious vein. Probably, this was the way it was seen by many party members in the 1970s although this was not so with Sheikh Mujib and senior leaders.

But I avoided answering her question directly. I proposed that I would like to discuss the issue privately with her rather than in a public forum. I was not sure whether I should get into a public debate with her as to the nature of the pledges her party made to the people in the past and how they were interpreted by Sheikh Mujib when he came to power as the Prime Minister. Alternatively, the discussion or arguments could have drifted to a terrain in which she might plead ignorance or lack of seriousness about very important elements of her party's and Sheikh Mujib's economic platform as of the 1960s and during the 1970 elections. I thought it would be embarrassing for both of us. At the back of my mind I suspected that she probably had believed or been told by her advisers that Sheikh Mujib was strongly advised, if not manoeuvered, by the planners into this decision. After all, he relied so much on their advice that he could not do otherwise.[2] I was not at all sure as to which way our discussion or argument would have turned. I did not know her well and did not have any opportunity in the past to have a discussion with her on policy issues either current or historical. However, by the 1990s, in the light of past experience in Bangladesh and elsewhere and the

---

[2] I discuss this issue later on in this chapter.

prevailing wave of intellectual consensus, the party abandoned socialism as an objective of economic policy in favour of market economy and private enterprise. Under today's circumstances, the change in policy was appropriate and inevitable. But the historical circumstances and intellectual consensus were different in the 1960s and 1970s.

To revert to the genesis of the nationalisation policy, it is worth recalling that there was no unanimity in the country or in the ruling party on the nature and scope of nationalisation. Also, there were many that believed in some sort of a mixed economy as it had prevailed in Pakistan in the 1960s. The public sector was to own the industries into which the private sector was unwilling or unable to venture. This could be for a wide variety of reasons such as high initial risks, technological complexity, very large capital investments, long gestation lag, and defense and munitions production requiring heavy subsidies or secrecy for security reasons. Over time, it was expected that some of these industries would be handed over to the private sector. This was also the historical pattern over a long period in such advanced countries as UK and Japan. Indeed, it is hardly remembered today that Bangladesh inherited in 1972 a sizeable number of public sector industries such as fertiliser, paper, newsprint, chemicals, pharmaceuticals, iron and steel, etc.[3] They were established under the ownership and management of East Pakistan Industrial Development Corporation (EPIDC).

During the Cabinet discussions on the nationalisation policy in 1972, the divisions between the two groups were obvious. Outside the Cabinet, the most powerful pressure groups in favour of nationalisation were the students and workers who were by then highly radicalised. Sheikh Mujib was veering mostly towards them as he felt an obligation to be true to his election pledges. He frequently proclaimed in public his commitment to socialism. It was difficult for him to compromise on the policy of nationalisation. Later on, an attempt to honour his

---

[3] Rehman Sobhan, "Nationalization of Industries in Bangladesh," in *Background and Problems in Economic Development of Bangladesh in Socialist Framework*, edited by E.A.G. Robinson and K. Griffin (London: McMillan, 1974). Upon nationalisation of industries in 1972, the total assets in the nationalised sector consisted of the following: 48 percent of assets were inherited from the EPIDC (state enterprises before 1971); 29 percent of assets belonged to the abandoned properties; and 23 percent consisted of the newly nationalised Bangladeshi enterprises.

election pledge about worker's participation in the management and profits of industries did not succeed because he could not obtain an agreement among the workers' representatives.[4] The anti-nationalisation group emphasised that the government did not have enough managerial capacity or adequate organisational structure in place to take over the Bangladeshi enterprises, in addition to the abandoned properties. Therefore, any further step towards nationalisation should wait until such capacities were built up. They argued that their disagreement was based on pragmatic reasons and not on grounds of any ideological objection. The proponents of the policy of nationalisation, however, contested that if there was a pool of managerial and entrepreneurial capacity in the country, although not within the government, the government should be able to draw upon it to manage the nationalised sector.[5] In fact, a large number of managers were recruited from the private sector to run the nationalised industries.

The antinationalisation group in the Cabinet or outside was not opposed — at least no opposition was voiced in public or private — to the government taking over the abandoned Pakistani industries. They were against the nationalisation of the industries owned by the nationals of Bangladesh. Logically, the antinationalisation group should have advocated the sale/transfer of the abandoned properties to the private sector. These properties represented a windfall gain to Bangladesh; there was no investment in them by the government. The abandoned properties could have served as an ideal vehicle to promote private enterprise. From their point of view, there should have been no predetermined dividing line which indicated that the

---

[4] I have not described in detail the decision making process and the various measures undertaken in respect of the policy of nationalisation of industries. A subcommittee of the Cabinet consisting of a few senior members was constituted to examine and recommend the appropriate policy for nationalisation. Its deliberations have been described in great detail in Rehman Sobhan and Muzaffar Ahmad, *Public Enterprise in an Intermediate Regime* (Dhaka: BIDS, 1980) and in Nurul Islam, *op.cit.* I have concentrated on a few highlights that might appear relevant in the appraisal of this episode with reference to the circumstances of today and my perceptions about this phenomenon in the early 1970s.

[5] The managers from the private sector could be enticed by offering them a system of incentives or rewards comparable to that in the private sector. The rewards of the top managers and the Board of Directors could be tied to the performance of the enterprises. It is noteworthy that the antinationalisation group formulated their objections in terms of lack of managerial and organisational competence, rather than absence of appropriate incentive structures in public enterprises, nonconforming to market driven incentives.

existing private sector was the limit beyond which private entrepreneurs were not able to extend their enterprises or that the public sector could take over only the abandoned properties and no more. They could have been sold at the minimum price to the buyers who could, in addition, have been provided with long term loans. The argument that there were few industrialists at that time able to purchase was not overwhelming. In most industrialising countries, including Pakistan in its early days, traders, indenters and landowners constituted the initial or pioneering group of industrialists. They were financed by liberal credit from the banking system and grew in size through the reinvestment of high profits and scarcity rents earned in protected markets. Bangladesh could have followed a similar policy.[6] The concern that the control of industries might have passed into the hands of a very few existing industrialists could have been partly met by broadening the net of the prospective buyers to include a wide group of rent seekers, traders, indenters, retired officials, both civil and military. After all, the thriving garment industry of today was built up by this class of entrepreneurs as well as by enterprising civil servants and military officials. What was relevant was the magnitude of incentives and prospects of windfall gains that were available to the prospective private owners/managers. Moreover, to further widen the base of private ownership the enterprises could have been sold to foreign buyers; foreign managers could have been employed to run domestic enterprises, if necessary. Inevitably, a degree of concentration of assets would have taken place as was evident in the past history of industrialisation in the developing world. Bangladesh could have followed the traditional path of capitalist development along the above lines.

It could, however, be argued that the law and order situation, political uncertainty and tensions, and inadequate infrastructure might have inhibited the success of such a policy. But these generic factors would have affected all enterprises, abandoned or Bengali owned, public or

---

[6] The initial investment in land and in a part of other fixed assets in the Adamjee Jute Mills was not only financed by the government but also largely a gift from the government to the private industrialist who had to be induced to come to Dhaka from India around the time of partition of India to start the new and eventually the largest jute enterprise in the country. This was then the accepted policy behind state sponsored capitalism that thrived in Pakistan.

private. Therefore, an attempt could have been made in good faith to promote private enterprise. In fact, this path was not followed. Why? The most likely reason was that the sociopolitical environment at that time did not favour such a step. Sheikh Mujib and his colleagues were prisoners of their rhetoric and their policy pronouncements made often enough before independence. After all, during the 1950s and 1960s there was a growing public resentment in both East and West Pakistan, fed by all shades of political parties, against few families controlling the economy and earning extraordinary profits under the patronage of the state.[7]

It was often alleged that Sheikh Mujib did not know his mind on the subject of nationalisation of industries and somehow he was pushed into it against his best judgement by a very few Ministers and the Planning Commission.[8] This reflects a gross misperception of his personality and his decision making process. He did make up his mind by examining pros and cons. His approach to the policy of nationalisation of industries had to be viewed in the context of his past commitment, his belief in some kind of populist socialism, and the heavy pressure on him by the radical elements in his party, student activists and industrial workers. He weighed the costs of meeting his past commitment and populist preferences. On nationalisation, the cost was not high; he could risk alienating the very small industrial class, as yet unorganised and without political clout. He subsequently rejected the proposal for land reform, for the same *real politic* reason. It would have affected adversely the rural power base of his party i.e. numerous medium and large farmers. Sheikh Mujib was

---

[7] These were also the unspoken reasons underlying Zia's reluctance to totally abandon or reverse Sheikh Mujib's policy as explained later in this chapter.

[8] I have encountered an even more unflattering opinion among those who should know better, about the way he decided to nationalise the Bangladeshi enterprises. This was a very important policy decision of his regime. It has been alleged that when his draft speech announcing the policy of nationalisation was sent to the Planning Commission, a member of the Commission added this provision on to the speech. Sheikh Mujib unthinkingly accepted it. This view suggests that he was "taken for a ride" by the Planning Commission. Sheikh Mujib himself would have been surprised by such an allegation, a humiliating aspersion on his decision making ability. I found it very disconcerting to find that such a view could even be considered about the way he took such a vital decision. In my experience, even on a less significant matter, he would rarely put his signature on the dotted line unless he was convinced and unless he had a final round of discussions on the pros and cons. One should note here that because of his prodigious memory, he remembered all the discussions in details, no matter how much in the past.

well aware of the differences among his Cabinet members on the issue of nationalisation. Prominent and vocal members in the pronation-alisation group were the senior party leaders like Ministers of Industries, Finance as well as the Minister of Law. The other group led by the Minister of Commerce, himself an industrialist, was weak. Many others were indifferent or did not have strong views. Also, when deciding on important issues such as the policy of nationalisation, he followed his usual practice of consulting an endless variety of persons of all possible ideological persuasions and opinions. He found that the nationalisation policy was not unpopular among the general public. Newspaper reports and public meetings and discussions following the announcement of nationalisation evidenced this. Most newspapers had welcomed the news with banner headlines and reported, often with great enthusiasm, how the first steps were being taken towards socialism. But such favourable reception should be seen in the light of public warnings by Sheikh Mujib that stern measures would be taken against those who might try to sabotage his policy. Obviously, he referred to the possible opposition — one would have suspected — by the owners and their henchmen and not certainly by the general public.

Consistent with his dislike of concentration or high inequality of incomes and preference for the middle class, Sheikh Mujib not only allowed but also was, in fact strongly in favour of encouraging small and medium scale private enterprises. The ceiling of investment for private enterprise was initially put at US$2.5 million worth of fixed assets and there was a moratorium on nationalisation for a period of 10 years.

The Planning Commission wanted to make the structure of man-agement of the public enterprises as independent and autonomous as possible, free from the interference of bureaucrats and the political pressure groups. Lessons of past experience tended to confirm that in practice the risk or the temptation of political interference in the management or the decision making process of public enterprises was ever present. Public enterprises could ideally function as profit maximising enterprises (a) by following market rules in both input and output markets, and (b) by providing performance based incentives and rewards to the public sector managers. The Commission wanted to devise a structure that would have conferred on managers the authority to run enterprises on commercial principles. It was an arduous task to convince the Ministers and the civil servants. Success was sporadic and limited.[9]

9.2 PLANNING COMMISSION AND NATIONALISATION

A question had often been posed about the role of the Planning Commission with regard to the policy of nationalisation. Clearly, the commission should have recognised that given the limited managerial or administrative competence, incentive structures in the public sector, and a low level of political motivation, successful implementation of the policy was unlikely. Just because it was called upon to work on a blueprint for the nationalisation of industries as a part of the policy of establishing socialism, it should not have gone ahead, impervious to the sociopolitical preconditions. After all, the Commission had in the Five-Year Plan emphasised the need for dedicated cadres for implementing a socialist system but decided to ignore it while working on the nationalisation policy. The Commission should have advised that the objective conditions did not exist for a socialist experiment in trade, industry and finance. Therefore, Sheikh Mujib should have pursued a policy in the old mold of a mixed economy. The fact that similar experiments were carried out in countries with widely different political and economic systems ranging from India and Pakistan to a host of post-colonial African, or Latin American countries, was no justification. If the Cabinet insisted on going ahead with the policy, the Commission could have, at least, gone on record with its contrary advice. The Commission thereby could have strengthened the antinationalisation group in the Cabinet. But in the end, the Commission supported and worked on the implementation of the policy.

I did not count myself among the more enthusiastic members of the Planning Commission in support of the nationalisation policy. I was the skeptic and did not have a great deal of enthusiasm in this regard. I knew very well the poor state of governance of the economy and the obstacles in the way of designing an efficient system of management

[9] Rehman Sobhan and Muzaffar Ahmad, *Public Enterprise in an Intermediate Regime* (Dhaka: BIDS, 1980).

and incentives for public enterprises. Nevertheless, I went along with the rest and did not feel strongly enough to voice disagreement. Looking back, I should have expressed my misgivings and doubts in the meetings of the Cabinet Subcommittee and the Cabinet even though it would not have swayed the decision either way. However, I felt that since the large-scale industrial sector constituted a very small segment of the economy — might be 5 percent or less — its less than satisfactory performance would not substantially affect one way or the other the overall economy. Moreover, the nationalisation of the abandoned Pakistani enterprises was a foregone conclusion with apparent universal approval. In retrospect, it appears that I underestimated the impact or implications of adding the Bangladeshi enterprises to the public sector for future industrial progress. The adverse impact was on the expectations of aspiring industrialists and it might have created of a sense of insecurity among them regarding the future direction of economic policy and the role of private enterprise.

As a result, the policy of nationalisation ran the risk of alienating the aspiring industrial-cum-commercial classes. In the highly volatile political situation of the time, I did not realise how important this factor might have been in strengthening the forces opposing Sheikh Mujib's regime. It was up to Sheikh Mujib and his political colleagues to evaluate its implications. Apparently, they did not consider it of any serious concern. I was not politically sensitive enough to think otherwise.

In this connection, I recall a conversation I had with a politician cum industrialist who, as late as 1991, insisted on tracing his comparative lack of success as an industrialist to the nationalisation policy of 1972. During 1991, when the Bangladesh Nationalist Party[10] was in power, I encountered him as a Minister in the government, and asked him how his industrial enterprises were faring. The textile industry of his family was nationalised in 1972. With an accusing voice he countered my question by saying that after what we (I as a member of Sheikh Mujib's regime) had done to his industrial enterprises, he could not reorganise/restart and regain his former financial strength.

---

[10]It is the party founded by Ziaur Rahman by gathering together all the political elements that were opposed to the Awami League. It was formed sometime after the assassination of Sheikh Mujib.

In his view, our policy sapped the energy and aspirations of entrepreneurs like him. But I replied that a lot had changed since those days. Many who were nondescript small traders or indenters in the 1970s had by the late 1980s and early 1990s acquired enormous riches. Some had even emerged as big industrialists. Clearly, Sheikh Mujib made enemies among the aspiring private entrepreneurs. Many of them had not forgotten or forgiven him. They persisted in their attitude — widespread among many today — to explain or justify personal inadequacies and subsequent national policy failures, by reference to what was done or left undone 30 years ago. It was as if all policy changes since the early days, all that happened in the intervening period and all the opportunities that occurred or were missed did not matter. Only the 1972-75 decisions were the overriding determinant of subsequent developments.

9.3 THE AFTERMATH

By early 1973, there were strong and rapidly growing public complaints about misappropriation of resources, corruption, and inefficiencies in public enterprises. Public opinion was emphatic on the need for determined government action to eradicate corruption and to improve the efficiency of public enterprises, but certainly not on the reversal of the policy of nationalisation.

Two lessons were to be learnt very soon in respect of the managerial-cum-entrepreneurial aspects of public enterprises. The administrators or managers, who were appointed on an urgent basis in early 1972 to run the abandoned properties, before a more permanent or long term structure could be established, were largely inexperienced. They were drawn from a wide spectrum ranging from political party workers, former managers or hastily promoted junior managers to even senior workers. Invariably, they brought financial losses to many enterprises through misappropriation of resources compounding sheer misman agement. This outcome reinforced the public perception that public enterprises were most likely to be mismanaged.

Second, in several cases, the dispossessed owners were given the task of managing the very enterprises that were nationalised without any immediate compensation for the loss of their ownership. This reflected a misunderstanding of the incentives and motivation of the owners who lost their properties. The result was that the owner-turned managers did their best to extract as much resource as they could from enterprises entrusted to them and thus, recoup their losses.

From the early days, donor agencies were not in favour of nationalisation. As time went by, they weighed heavily on the side of privatisation. While Sheikh Mujib was seen to be playing a balancing act, he faced pressure from his party leadership to permit a gradual increase in the ceiling on private investment, a further liberalisation of the economic system and a slowly expanding role for private enterprise. In response to such demands, the investment ceiling was raised to a level 12 times higher than the original ceiling, and the moratorium on the nationalisation of private enterprises was extended from 10 to 15 years.

The response of the private sector to these policy changes was insignificant partly because confidence of the private sector was yet to be restored. Probably, the more important reasons were deficiencies in the physical infrastructure and the unsatisfactory state of law and order. Due to prevailing scarcities, short run profit margins in marketing, distribution, and indenting activities were higher than in the industries. Private enterprise readily went for that option.

In early 1975, the future shape of economic policy became once again uncertain. On the occasion of the establishment of the one party (i.e. BAKSAL)[11] state, Sheikh Mujib declared a new constitution that was "to establish the economic freedom of the masses in an exploitation free society and to establish socialism and democracy of the exploited." While elaborating various ills afflicting the country that justified the change, he mentioned such factors as "bad economic condition, food insufficiency, dependence on external assistance, indiscipline in industry, and corruption, specially on the part of the opportunistic educated class who were the real bad people exploiting the masses."

The economic programme of the new regime was to be based on a more rigorous form of state control and regulation. Industries were to be run and managed by the representatives of workers and officials of Ministries of Industries and Labour. This provision obviously referred to public enterprises. There was no mention of what would

---

[11]Bangladesh Krishak Sramik Awami League.

happen to private industries in the future. The extension of the new system to the private sector was not mentioned, even though it was unlikely that once workers' participation became the norm in the public sector, the private sector could be kept outside. Large farmers who were spared so far were also brought into the net of state regulation. Even though private ownership would continue in farming, all farms were to be grouped into multipurpose cooperatives; their output would be divided in three equal parts i.e. one for the owner, one for the state, and one for the cooperative. All the landless and unemployed rural labour would become members of cooperatives and would derive equal benefits from their output. The multipurpose cooperatives would organise the purchase of inputs as well as marketing and distribution of output on behalf of farmers. They would channel various kinds of government aid to farmers. In fact, in some ways, they would replace or supplement local governments in the provision or delivery of various public sector agricultural services.

This was a far cry from the sort of economy that was perceived by many to be evolving towards the end of 1974. However, I remember Sheikh Mujib's reaction whenever, during the period of 1972-74, there were complaints by farmers about delays and interruptions in the supplies of fertilisers or about low or fluctuating prices for their output. He would often wonder aloud about the possibilities of organising farmers' cooperatives that would supply inputs to farmers and in return would buy or collect their output under a contractual arrangement. But he never pursued this idea seriously, nor was I asked to examine or study the feasibility of such a proposal. I considered such conversation as mere casual musings. With the kind of economy and polity at the village level that Bangladesh had at that time and with the past history of cooperatives in mind, I decided that it was the better part of valour not to show any interest in the idea. Little did I comprehend that his casual observations could eventually be part of a plan to radically restructure the polity and the economy? I was not privy to his intimate thoughts about BAKSAL.

In his BAKSAL declaration of January 1975, Sheikh Mujib emphasised that the kind of socialism that he was contemplating for Bangladesh was not "going to be imported one from outside, from any where in the world." It would be an "ism" of our own. Obviously, the intention was to put together in some combination several features of other socialist systems and to formulate them in a way that conformed to his own perception of what was feasible or desirable in Bangladesh. Since the proposed experiment in political and economic reorganisation collapsed after the assassination of Sheikh Mujib, it would never be known what might have happened to the structure of the Bangladesh economy or how the industrial policy would have evolved during the succeeding years.

9.4 REVERSING COURSE

Yet following Sheikh Mujib's assassination, there was no significant reversal of the policy of nationalisation, notwithstanding rising criticisms about the poor performance of the public sector industries within the country as well as from the donor community. Why did the successor regime fail to drastically reverse the past policy? After all, the interest groups adversely affected by the nationalisation policy were ardent supporters of the new regime. Fundamental changes were made in the constitution of 1972, not to speak of the constitution of 1975, through ordinances under the martial law. Changes in the industrial policy could have been made through executive ordinances as indeed was done in later years. Zia during his regime (1976-81) first with and then without the martial law, made only some incremental changes. Why more was not done? It was most unlikely that the supporters of the nationalisation policy were organised or strong enough to pose any threat or challenge, specially under the martial law if Zia had really wanted to reverse the policy. On the contrary, there was a possibility that a privatisation policy would win support among the emerging entrepreneurial class. Several hypotheses could be advanced.

First, Zia was not convinced that privatisation was essential for speeding up the industrial development of Bangladesh. There was no reason why financial discipline could not be enforced and the public enterprises could not be efficient. Did the military not run efficiently a sizeable public sector and without much corruption? Why could not the civilian public sector perform equally well? It was natural that such thoughts might have occurred to a strong willed general.

Secondly, social forces such as radical students and workers, strong advocates of nationalisation, still remained so even though they were not very vocal or active. But they were very much a part of the political landscape. The public in general continued to be suspicious of the concentration of private economic power. Therefore, reversal would not have been a very popular policy among the public. Thirdly, at the same time, Zia's public posture was one of empathy for the common man with a promise for their uplift rather than a promoter of the rich and affluent upper classes. He was known for his long walks through the villages of Bangladesh to meet the rural people and respond to their concerns. Therefore, a rapid movement towards privatisation of the Bangladeshi enterprises was not considered politically expedient or desirable. Even if there were some economic gains in privatisation — of which he was not sure — in his judgement, the gains were probably smaller than the damage to his populist image. Moreover, the public sector enterprises did provide avenues for good jobs for some of the army officers. A significant number of directors in the various Sector Corporations in charge of nationalised industries were drawn from the armed forces.

Thus, Zia proceeded very cautiously in modifying the prevailing policies. First, the provision of the constitution, which stipulated the achievement of "socialism," was replaced by "social justice." It was a very soft but a positive signal of a change in attitude of the government toward private enterprise. Second, the ceiling on private investment was raised to Tk. 100 million. This was, in a sense, a continuation of Sheikh Mujib's policy of gradual increase in investment ceiling. By undertaking not to nationalise private sector industries in the future, he tried to assuage the fears of industrialists that might deter them from investing in industries now permitted in the private sector. Eight categories of industries (including the major Bangladeshi enterprises that were nationalised in 1972 such as jute, textile, and sugar) were reserved for the public sector. Foreign participation was allowed within both private and public sectors. The list of industries open to the private sector was expanded. Ten categories of industries that were mostly in the public sector in the pre and postindependence days were now open for joint private-public enterprise but the latter was to retain a major share.

All these steps did not amount to any significant shift in policy from the rhetoric that permeated the economic scene since the late 1960s and was partly put into action in 1972. Why was the insistence on joint ownership? Why private enterprises on their own in these categories were not allowed? But most importantly, Zia did not privatise the Bangladeshi enterprises nationalised in 1972. Many aspiring industrialists came from this group. They considered the return of such enterprises to their previous owners a test of the government's commitment to the promotion of private enterprise. During the entire Zia regime (1975-81), only twenty-three industries, mostly abandoned properties, were privatised.[12] Indeed, this was a very gradualist approach to changes in industrial policy. The reason was, I believe, that it was not politically expedient nor did he believe the private sector to be necessarily economically efficient. The sociopolitical forces which drove the nationalisation policy in the 1970s were weakened but did not swing as yet to the right.

The change in industrial policy did not attract a great deal of response from the private sector. It was argued, by some, that the private sector was not quite ready to believe that the Damocles' sword of nationalisation had been removed from over their head and a reversal of policy could not occur in the future. If this perception was held, the private sector was likely to refrain from long term investment.

It was a full decade after the introduction of the nationalisation policy that a significant break with the original policy was made. In 1982, the ceiling on the size of private investment was eliminated. All but six sectors that were mainly in the nature of public utilities such as electricity, energy, air transport, communications, arms, etc., were open to private enterprise. Jute, textile, and sugar industries owned by Bangladeshi entrepreneurs — the lynchpin of the 1972 nationalisation policy — were to be privatised. All industries, excepting the six reserved for the public sector, were also thrown open to joint private and public enterprise. An important new policy was to divest the shares of public enterprises to private owners up to

---

[12]Clare Humphrey, *Privatization in Bangladesh: Economic Transition of a Poor Country*, Dhaka: The University Press Limited, 1992. See also Stanley A. Kochanek, *Patron-Client Politics and Business in Bangladesh*; Chapters 4 and 5, The University Press Limited, Dhaka, 1993.

the limit of 49 percent — a policy that drew surprisingly strong opposition from the public and had to be postponed until 1986.[13] Public opinion was not yet ready for a rapid onward march towards privatisation.

The 10-year gestation lag in reversing the nationalisation policy was due to a gradual but a slow shift in the public opinion, starting from the mid-1970s onward, away from the dominant role of the public sector in the economy. There were two factors contributing to the change in attitudes and policy. First, mounting pressure throughout this period from the donor community in favour of privatisation and the promotion of private enterprises took its toll. Second, a change in the realm of ideology, reinforced by the collapse of the Soviet Union, led to a reassessment of the role of the state in favour of the market economy. This change in policy was sweeping the developing world and Bangladesh was drawn to it as well. She responded gradually in successive stages to a general evolution of sociopolitical ideas and forces; this was not the result of a snap decision by the top leadership. The process of reversal of the old policy required, first, a slow growing change in attitudes on the part of Zia and then of Ershad during 1975-91.[14] Ershad achieved a consensus of public opinion, at least of interest groups that were deemed important. After all, some degree of acceptance and acquiescence on the part of the people to important policy changes was expedient even for the powerful military rulers.[15]

The workers in the nationalised industries were quick to oppose the reversal of policy. On privatisation, the profit seeking private owners were likely to shed the excess labour. Payment of compensation packages was fraught with uncertainty. How long will be the wait? Would the compensation package be large enough to cover the transition period? What would happen if the new job involved a change of location or a lower scale of pay and benefits? All these

---

[13]*Ibid.*

[14]General Hossain Mohammad Ershad followed General Zia first as martial law administrator and then as President of Bangladesh.

[15]The political leadership needed to be strong. They should feel secure in their hold on instruments of power and political forces in order to face any possible opposition from vested interests, and be confident and willing to take risks about managing organised protest, if necessary.

considerations and uncertainty inhibited a ready acceptance of a compensation scheme on the part of the employees. Also, implementation of a policy of privatisation required the determination of the terms of purchase by private buyers, not a very smooth process. Selling shares of state enterprises to private individuals in the stock market was only feasible, if they were profitable. This was hardly the case for most of them. The terms of purchase required an agreement on the sharing of obligations for the past debt liability as well as on the time schedule for payments by the buyers. In most cases, the valuation of an enterprise by the government, based at least partly on replacement costs, was likely to be higher than that by the purchaser based on estimates of uncertain future profitability. Should the replacement costs not be considered as *sunk costs*? Should not the *reserve price* of the government be determined by losses that are currently incurred and will be avoided if privatised? Moreover, very high rates of profits in trading, indenting for foreign suppliers, construction or other speculative activities, also depressed the offer price. These and similar considerations entered into the decision making process as the policy of privatisation was pursued at different paces in the following years.[16]

---

[16]Chapter 16 discusses the details of the various aspects of privatisation in subsequent years in Bangladesh.

Chapter 10

WHAT WAS IT ABOUT
THE 1974 FAMINE?

In the recent history of famines around the Third World, the 1974 Bangladesh famine is one of the most well known, much analysed by social scientists at home and abroad as to its cause and consequences.[1] At home, its causes have been a matter of some controversy, often subject to varying, sometimes opposing, interpretations by different analysts or people with different political affiliations. Naturally, the government of the day bore the greatest responsibility as famine always brings discredit to any government. It is considered a mark of a government's failure that in its watch people died for want of food i.e. the most basic necessity of life. As one looks back at this phenomenon, it appears that during the period of the famine itself, not all the factors that contributed to it were recognised in terms of their true significance and in proper perspective.

10.1 INFLATION, FLOODS AND SPECULATION

The proximate causes of the 1974 famine were multiple: natural disasters (floods), speculative market behaviour in response to current and expected crop failures, adverse macroeconomic external circumstances, and non-availability of food aid at the moment of crisis. All these

---

[1] A.K. Sen, *Poverty and Famine: An Essay in Entitlement and Deprivation*, Oxford (1981). M. Alamgir, *Famine in South Asia — Political Economy of Mass Starvation in Bangladesh*. Cambridge, Mass.: Oelgeschlager, Gunn and Hain, 1980; M. Ahmed, *Bangladesh: Era of Sheikh Mujibur Rahman*, Chapter 9, Food, Flood and Famine, The University Press Limited, Dhaka, 1983.

factors acted together to depress *entitlement* to food on the part of the most vulnerable groups i.e. those who depended wholly or partially on wage labour for access to food. Over the years up to the early 1970s, there had been an increase in the proportion of marginal farmers and landless labourers in the rural population. The proportion of landless households was around 40 percent.[2] There was persistent monetary expansion ranging between 70 percent in 1972 to 18 percent in 1973, resulting in a large monetary overhang up to mid-1974. This was fuelled by budgetary deficit, caused by severe short fall in revenues and increased expenditures of establishing a new government, large deficits of the bank financed public enterprises and expansion of the private sector credit for trading, construction, and commodity speculation.[3] Consumer price index rose 52 percent in 1972, 33 percent in 1973, and 21 percent in January-June 1974. Inflation led to a sharp fall in real wages of marginal farmers, agricultural workers, and urban workers.

The rise in the nominal (and real) price of rice in September-November 1974 was more than twice that in the corresponding period in 1973.[4] Why did the price of rice record such a large increase? Was rice output in 1974 smaller than that in 1973? Rice output in calendar year 1974 (consisting of *Aman* harvests 1973, *Boro* 1974, and *Aus* 1974) was higher than the corresponding output in 1973. But the floods in July-August 1974 caused not only extensive damage to jute crop, a major source of employment and cash income for the rural population, but more importantly, it adversely affected planting for the next *Aman* and created the fear of a large short fall in the next *Aman* crop. Added to this were exaggerated press reports about damage to the *Aus* crop and the impending short fall in the *Aman* crop. Both factors greatly aggravated the fears of future scarcity. The newly established crop forecasting system was not yet reliable enough to correctly estimate the crop damage by floods or possible short fall in the *Aman* crop that might be caused by the late planting. With a great deal of uncertainty among traders and public agencies regarding

---

[2] S.R. Osmani. *The Food Problem of Bangladesh*. UN WIDER Working Paper 29 (November 1987).

[3] A. Hossain, "A Second Look at the 1974 Famine: Additional Insights and Policy Implications." *Journal of Bangladesh Studies*, Vol. 1, No. 1 (1999).

[4] The real price increased by 65-80 percent between the corresponding periods.

the evolving food supply, the time was rife for speculation. Most relevant for the expectation of future prices — the critical variable that determined the accumulation of trader's stocks and speculative hoarding — was the *ex ante* expectation of a short fall in the *Aman* crop.[5] The fear of food shortage was to be judged in the background of a very fragile food situation that persisted in the years since independence. In the aftermath of six consecutive bad crops from *Aman* 1971 to *Aus* 1973, including war damaged *Boro* crop in 1972, about 1 million tons of foodgrains had to be imported during 1972-73 mostly on commercial terms. The stocks of traders and farmers were greatly depleted and badly needed to be replenished.

Prices started to rise from March 1974 onwards. Why? There was a severe reduction in public stocks starting end 1973, which fell by more than half between 1972-73 and early 1974 when it was barely 150,000 tons. A drastic reduction in public distribution, specially the modified rationing system and the relief distribution, starting January 1974[6] led to the collapse of confidence in the government's ability to stabilise the price situation in the coming months. This triggered a sharp rise in price as early as March 1974. There was an upsurge in speculative holdings of stocks by farmers, consumers, and traders (both genuine traders and the new, rich speculators) in anticipation of future scarcities.

The attempt by the government to procure food from abroad did not succeed partly because of its own limited foreign exchange resources and partly because of delays in the commitment of aid by the United States. Foreign exchange reserves in the first quarter of 1974 were less than half of that in the first quarter of 1973. Reserves in the third quarter of 1974 were about 25 percent of what it was in the third quarter of 1973. Borrowings under the IMF compensatory financing facility were also meagre — no more than US$35 million starting in the second quarter of 1974 with US$18.1 million and

---

[5] A. Hossain, *Ibid*. In the event rice output was 11.72 million tons in 1974 compared with 9.93 million tons in 1973 and 9.79 million tons in 1972. The estimates of loss due to flood and drought were 0.31 million tons and 0.25 million tons respectively in 1972 and 1973, whereas the estimate of loss was 0.65 million tons in 1974.

[6] Sobhan, R., "Politics of Food and Famine in Bangladesh," *Economic and Political Weekly* (1984). The modified rationing system was intended for the poorest segments in the rural areas, whereas relief distribution consisted of free distribution of food to destitutes and those in severe economic distress.

US$38.1 million in the succeeding quarters. The creditworthiness of Bangladesh was so low that purchases contracted under short term commercial credit were cancelled.[7] By September and October in 1974, monthly imports ranged between 29,000 and 70,000 tons compared to the monthly requirement of 250,000-300,000 tons.

10.2 HOW IMPORTANT WAS SMUGGLING?

Was smuggling to India large enough to create such a scarcity? During 1973-74 right up to the famine period, there were widespread rumours and reports in the press of smuggling of foodgrains to India. In response, the government employed the army to guard the borders against smuggling from April 1974 onwards. There was no way one could estimate smuggling of foodgrains from direct observations. From the list of goods confiscated by the army at the borders, it appeared that rice was hardly the most important item, but sixth or seventh in importance. Brian Reddaway of Cambridge University, England, visiting the Bangladesh Institute of Development Studies at that time, was requested to undertake a study of the subject. His study was based on an indirect method of comparison of rice prices in border areas with those in the interior markets that were on the direct trade route to the border areas. *Ex hypothesi*, in case there was a large scale smuggling, prices were most likely to be higher in the border areas than in the interior markets that were supplying rice for smuggling. On a study

---

[7] It is interesting to reflect on the shortness of public memory. Recently, a highly educated member of the party in power in 1974 asked me why it was not possible for the government to import rice from Thailand, a close-by country with large export surplus in order to damp down the rising prices. He had to be reminded that there was very little foreign exchange resources and that prices in the world market were sky high. Even if by some turn of luck we could get commercial credit and were able to purchase, we could not possibly ship it on time. There was a great demand on shipping space in view of many countries rushing to buy food in the face of the worldwide food crisis. In addition, shipping cost sky rocketed *pari passu*.

Even as early as the second half of 1973, in response to delays in (a) shipment of committed aid by US as well as (b) in the commitment of new US aid, the government was obliged to seek an alternative short term relief to tide over the delay. The USSR was requested to divert to Bangladesh 200,000 tons of grain she had purchased from Canada and the USA in order for Bangladesh to avert a breakdown in the public food distribution system. They were received during July-October 1973. It was expected that when the US food aid came through later on in the year, it would be possible to divert the grain shipments to the USSR to repay the debt. Subsequently, however, the US declined to accept the arrangements for "swap" and a short term deferred payment arrangement was worked out with the USSR for its wheat shipment.

of price behaviour in different markets, he came to the conclusion that smuggling was not significant enough so as to run into hundreds of thousands of tons.

Direct comparisons of prices of jute in the border market in Bangladesh with those in a neighbouring border market in India — converted at the prevailing black market rates of exchange between the Bangladesh and India currencies — did not indicate high enough profit to justify large-scale smuggling.[8] Large scale smuggling would be inconsistent with highly variable smuggling profit margin from month to month. The evidence indicated high variability. This was consistent with the hypothesis of limited smuggling.

During this period, I had an interesting encounter with Zia who was the Deputy Chief of Staff in the army and was involved in supervising the anti-smuggling operations along the borders. He at his own initiative came to see me in my capacity as the Deputy Chairman to discuss his findings or judgement that there was a very large scale smuggling ranging anywhere from half a million to a million tons. He felt that the Prime Minister was not correctly informed by his political colleagues and officials about the scale of smuggling. Under the circumstances, I should intervene to convince the Prime Minister about the gravity of the situation.

There was some discussion between us as to the evidence the army had about large scale rice smuggling. In the absence of any direct estimate of smuggling, I tried to engage him in a discussion about various indirect indicators that could help to explain or give an idea about the scale of smuggling. For example, I wanted to know how, in his opinion, hundreds of thousands of tons of rice were being smuggled in such a short time (between April-June). This discussion took place at the time of the onset of July-August 1974 floods when prices rose very sharply. If smuggling was the cause for such a spurt in prices, then it had to occur on a very large scale in the months immediately following *Aman* and *Boro* harvests. How were such large quantities transported or carried across the borders in such a short period? If rice was to be transported in such large quantities, it could not be done in small lots by individual smugglers. If that was

---

[8] W.B. Reddaway and M. Rehman, *The Scale of Smuggling Out of Bangladesh*, BIDS (February 1975).

the case, then very large numbers of people or smugglers were to be seen crossing back and forth the border continuously for a month or so. This was obviously ruled out, since the army had not confirmed a large scale continuous movement of people. Alternatively, rice had to be transported in big trucks and barges and that was possible only through a few points at the border where they could physically pass through. Therefore, if very substantial smuggling did take place, it was unlikely that such a large scale crossborder movements of trucks and barges would not have been detected by the public, the Bangladesh Rifles (BDR) and the army. However, it was the contention of the army that even if they had observed such large scale movements, they could not have seized or taken preventive action since local party workers or leaders were in league with smugglers with the connivance of local officials.[9] But then newspapers, which were full of reports and rumours on the food situation, did not report such a very large scale movement of trucks and barges within the span of such a short period.

The issue was not that there was no smuggling. In fact, there was smuggling on a regular basis since 1971 in spite of the presence of border defense forces. The relevant question was how big was this smuggling of rice (as distinguished from other commodities), and whether smuggling of rice could have taken place on a large enough scale within a very short period to cause the price of rice to skyrocket. Estimates of massive smuggling of rice that Zia conveyed appeared improbable, considering the limited time involved and the poor state of roads and transportation systems in the border and adjoining areas in the early days of Bangladesh.

Zia was unhappy about the results of our long discussion. Much later when he was the Deputy Martial Law Administrator and was, in addition, in charge of the portfolios of Planning and Finance, he had an official in his staff who had earlier worked with me. He had a long memory, recognised the officer, and recalled to him that he

---

[9] He suggested that politicians were engaged in such activities, earning huge illegal incomes in the process. There were instances when the army apprehended a few party workers or local leaders who were engaged either directly or indirectly in sponsoring or protecting such smugglers and there were interferences and interventions by the top political leadership to let them free. As against these allegations, there were counter-accusations and rumours that the party's political workers were being unduly and indiscriminately harassed by the army.

could not convince me about the scale and implications of smuggling of rice to India. At this distance of time, one remembers that those were the days when emotions ran very high and the country was passing through a great trauma. It was possible that disagreements on reasonable grounds could be considered to be a politically inspired defense of an official position.[10]

Reverting to the subject of the 1974 famine, under the circumstances depicted above, the government had three principal means at its disposal to deal with the emerging food crisis. First, it could resort to the domestic procurement of rice for building stocks to maintain the public distribution system. The circumstances were less than propitious for a successful public procurement. First, due to short falls in production in 1972 and 1973, a major effort by private traders and farmers to rebuild in 1974 their severely depleted stocks was unavoidable in any case, no matter what was the future price expectation. An attempt was launched in the early months of 1974 to intensify procurement efforts. Procurement was not a success in 1973. It was voluntary and the procurement price was lower than the market price. This was reportedly made worse by inefficiency and corruption of the government agencies. In 1974, procurement was made compulsory from all farmers according to a graduated scale. The movement of rice from surplus areas was banned in order to facilitate procurement in those areas. Local committees consisting of (a) officials, (b) representatives of local elites, and (c) political workers/leaders were constituted to facilitate procurement. The committees were ineffective and were not of much help in facilitating procurement. Already the expectation of a short fall in the next *Aman* crop had given a boost to private hoarding. The introduction of compulsory procurement had unwanted consequences;

---

[10]The alleged scale of smuggling remained a matter of casual empiricism at best. Crossborder illegal trade, in general, is a widely recognised phenomenon in response to changes in relative prices in Bangladesh and India. Unfortunately, there have been few studies done in the last 30 years on a subject of such great public concern. No comprehensive research based on a systematic collection of direct and indirect data from both sides of the border was undertaken. No attempt was made to elaborate and expand even the simple methodology of Professor Reddaway (this methodology could be improved, in fact, along the lines suggested by Professor Reddaway himself) in respect of different years and many commodities. I understand that a major study of Indo-Bangladesh trade including size and composition of illegal trade, supported by surveys and systematic data collection on both sides of the border, is underway under the auspices of the World Bank.

it aggravated the fear of future shortages and further spurred the tendency to hoard.[11] Total procurement in 1974 was no more than 130,000 tons.

The second measure available to the government was to somehow mobilise public opinion and galvanise the support of the people, including traders and hoarders, to release stocks in view of the national crisis. This required a very high degree of public confidence in the government. It was in such an environment that I ventured to approach the Prime Minister with a plea on the basis of my belief that he still had very great credibility and stature in the country. I suggested that he should go around the country to appeal to traders, hoarders, and farmers that at a time of crisis they should release their stocks, either in the market or to the public procurement agencies and share their supplies with the people at large. Under his leadership, his political colleagues should also join in the task of mobilising public opinion and organising people's participation in a common effort. After all, he had once led and mobilised the entire nation to fight for independence at great sacrifices. This was an equally great — if not a greater — challenge that he needed to face, and enthuse and lead people to overcome.[12]

As I look back, I was indeed very naïve in making such a suggestion. Appeals to collective interests or threats of penalty never did stop speculative hoarding, specially when rooted in strong price expectations. A massive countrywide mobilisation of the people at the grassroots level by highly motivated local leadership and popular organisations might theoretically achieve such a feat. Unfortunately, history does not provide such examples, not to speak of the fact that the

---

[11] J. Faaland et al. Aid and Influence (London: Macmillan, 1981).

[12] I vividly remember the occasion when I was making this plea on a monsoon day in mid 1974 darkened by heavy clouds and rain, alone in the Prime Minister's office. He was greatly worried and looked visibly concerned. He started to pace up and down in his room; soon he turned towards me and uttered in a painful voice almost as a soliloquy, "You do not know the people of Bangladesh. I have lived and worked with them at all levels for many years of my life and know them very well. They are very unforgiving. If one commits one mistake or fails them once, all your life's work goes in vain. They called me *Father of the Nation*; in no time they could turn around and call me ... *(Expletive) of the Nation.*" I realised that he did not think that he could perform the wonders that I wished him to perform. I never knew what "mistake" he was referring to in his remarks. After a few words, I left in a spirit of sadness.

socio-political circumstances in Bangladesh were a far cry from such a scenario in terms either of organisation or motivation.[13]

In the absence of the above half measures that one could suggest in a state of desperation, the real effective policy that would have averted the crisis was to substantially augment the supplies of foodgrains (rice and wheat) to break the back of rampant speculation. Building up government stocks and releasing large quantities in the market through the public distribution system could have restored confidence of traders and speculators in the ability of the government to deal with the situation. To this end, efforts were vigorously mounted to plead with all possible sources of food aid supplies. The world market was caught in a rising spiral of food prices, now known as the World Food Crisis of 1974. China and Russia made large scale purchases in the world market. The only foreign source that could provide enough food aid was the United States.

10.3 THE FOOD AID DEBACLE

Around mid-1973, we approached the USAID with a request for food aid for the fiscal year 1973-74 so as to provide a sufficient lead-time. This was not for the first time since independence that Bangladesh requested and received food aid. In both 1972 and early 1973, Bangladesh received the US food aid. In August 1973, the Bangladesh Finance Minister, Tajuddin Ahmed, made a request for food aid in a meeting with the US Secretary of State in Washington. Food import requirements estimated at 2.2 million tons were to be met by commercial imports and food aid from various sources. The United States was requested to provide about 300,000 tons of food aid. I followed it up at a high-level meeting with the USAID in Washington at the end of August 1973, and scaled down our request to 220,000 tons after consultations with the USAID officials. During the same visit, I took up the issue of food aid with the US Secretary of Agriculture since supplies were controlled by the Department of Agriculture, while the amount of aid was decided by the USAID. While the Secretary, at the time of high world prices, greatly preferred commercial sales

---

[13]At this time, there was a general lack of confidence due to widespread perception fed by press reports about corruption, poor law and order situation and violence as well as a general sense of uncertainty regarding the future.

to food aid, I tried to plead on behalf of the hungry people of Bangladesh. Consultations and discussions both in Washington and Dhaka continued at various levels between the two governments. In January 1974, the Bangladesh Ambassador in Washington again took up the matter with the Assistant Secretary of State.

While frequent contacts between the US and the Bangladesh government continued in Dhaka and Washington, an unexpected message was conveyed on 27th May 1974, by the US Ambassador. By this time price of rice was on a sustained upward trend. The US government had come to know that Bangladesh was selling jute bags to Cuba and under the US PL-480 regulations, food aid could not be provided to any country that was trading with Cuba. My response was as follows: The Jute Corporation of Bangladesh did indeed sell to Cuba 4 million gunny bags for US$5 million as a one-time transaction. There was no long term trade agreement for the sale of jute bags to Cuba and, therefore, Bangladesh was not in a regular business of selling jute bags to Cuba. Secondly, Bangladesh was desperately short of export earnings and was faced with strong competition in the world markets for jute. She was badly in need of taking advantage of any possibility for marketing its principal export i.e. jute. Thirdly, after all, the Jute Corporation was not aware of this provision of the US law. Fourthly, during the last two years, Bangladesh had received food aid and had signed several food aid agreements with the US government. They had a long list of complicated requirements to be fulfilled by the recipient country as required by the US law. But this particular provision of the PL-480 was never brought to the attention of the government. Fifthly, the request for food aid under discussion had been under negotiations for almost nine months. During this long period no mention was ever made of such a provision. If we had known it earlier, we could have refrained from the sale of jute bags to Cuba.

It was not clear whether this sudden, unexpected bottleneck was the result of an act of negligence on the part of the US bureaucracy. After all, it was well known to the US government that Bangladesh and Cuba had good diplomatic relations and the possibility of their getting into trade relations was high. I discussed this matter almost 30 years later with the concerned US official, who was then the head of the USAID office in Dhaka, now living in Washington, D.C., I asked him why we were not forewarned in 1973 when the request was first made. His reply was that neither he nor his colleagues in Dhaka office were aware of this provision. His counterparts in Washington also did not know or if they knew, did not care to inform him about such a provision of the US law. He further remarked that there were hundreds of pages of regulations in the US PL-480, all of which few USAID officials could master. This was how the lawyers made their living. Occasional lapses like this did occur. The tragedy was that it occurred in Bangladesh at a time of food crisis.

In any case, the US Ambassador in Dhaka and the US authorities in Washington pointed out that exceptions are granted only in the case of nonstrategic agricultural commodities or non-strategic raw materials for agriculture. Jute, according to them, did not fall into this category. Exceptions could also be granted if the President certified that such aid was in the US national interest and, therefore, sought a waiver from the US Congress. The USAID did not think that the US President could or would make such a case for Bangladesh in this particular instance. It was pointed out to the US government that in the recent past, the two US aid recipients such as Argentina and Brazil had exported cars to Cuba. We were told that the US citizens or the subsidiaries of the US corporations, as was the case in these two countries, could be allowed to trade with Cuba under a special license issued by the Department of Treasury. This was done under the Trading with the Enemy Act. This was unrelated to PL-480 sale, which was a government-to-government transaction in food aid. Under the circumstances, the best that the Bangladesh government could do was to provide an assurance to the US government that she would stop trading with Cuba from that moment onward so that the US could reconsider the grant of food aid.

In the meanwhile, the US Ambassador had formally conveyed its above decision to the Ministry of Foreign Affairs. After all, this involved diplomatic relations and a matter of foreign policy of the government of Bangladesh. The Prime Minister, confronted with this choice agreed to the US proposal, given the magnitude of the food crisis in the country. At the same time, he had the delicate task of conveying such an unpleasant decision to the Cuban government. After all, Cuba was one of the first countries to recognise Bangladesh in January 1972, when very few countries did so, and had sent an Ambassador to Dhaka. At that time, most small countries, both developed and developing, had their Ambassadors stationed in Delhi, concurrently accredited to Dhaka. When the Cuban government was informed by the Prime Minister of his predicament, it was both forthcoming and understanding. It assured Bangladesh that the termination of trade with Cuba by Bangladesh would not affect their relations.

In my capacity, as the Deputy Chairman, I provided the following assurance to the USAID: "The Bangladesh government is aware of the provisions of the US legislation and it does not intend to permit government agencies or government owned corporations to export to Cuba or permit vessels under Bangladesh registry to sail to Cuba ports." The written assurance from the Bangladesh government as above was provided in July 1974 but agreement for food aid was not signed until much later. Why? The US Ambassador explained that lawyers in the State Department had made the following determination. Under the US law even though the transaction for export had already been completed sometime in the past and payments had been made by the buyers, Bangladesh was regarded as "currently trading" with Cuba, so long as the jute bags were not physically shipped and had not left the Bangladesh ports. Bangladesh was not on the main shipping routes nor she had "conference lines" ships regularly calling at her ports. It took some time before arrangements for the shipment of jute bags could be made and before the shipment was physically off the dock. As shipments started, we requested that since all the requirements of the US law were now met, the food aid agreement could now be signed without further delays. We were already in the throes of a severe famine. Unfortunately, the Ambassador reported that the lawyers in Washington would like to be assured, before any agreement was signed, that the shipment was completed and the last jute bag had physically left the Bangladesh port. This seemed to us to be the harshest possible interpretation of the law. The last shipment was not completed until October 1974. Agreement was eventually signed more than a year after request for food aid was made to the US government. By that time, the worst days of famine were over and much deprivation had occurred.

Two questions were raised in subsequent years about this phenomenon of the food aid debacle. Why was the government of Bangladesh, when it embarked on the negotiations for food aid, not alert enough to learn in advance all the restrictions that were applicable to the US PL-480 food aid? After all, the Planning Commission or the Embassy in Washington should have done all the research necessary for such negotiations so that the US government was not provided with a reason for objection on any ground. As I look back on it, I wonder whether the government had any reason to be so extra careful and vigilant. As described earlier, for two years in the past, Bangladesh had negotiated with and received food aid from the United States and no hint was ever provided of such an eventuality. Numerous consultations at various levels of the US government, including US congressmen, were held and never such an issue was raised.

A second question was raised by some that even if food aid was provided on time, it was not large enough to have provided much relief in view of such a steep rise in price. The facts were as follows: By 8th November 1974, agreement was signed for a total food aid of 200,000 tons of wheat and 50,000 tons of rice under PL-480 Title I. This was in response to the original request for 1973-74. This quantity could have been delivered by late 1973 or early 1974 if there was no Cuban trade bottleneck in the way. By the middle of 1974, a new round of our requests for food aid for 1974-75 was awaiting the US government's decision. Consideration of this request was delayed because the earlier request for 1973-74 was held up due to the Cuba question. The request for additional US food aid for the year 1974-75 reached as high as 400,000 tons of wheat, bringing the total aid request to the 650,00 tons for a two-year period. If this request was acted upon earlier, i.e. middle of 1974, as it would have been the case in the course of normal circumstances, this would have created a very significant impact on the market and would have greatly dampened speculative forces. This could have effectively countered the price rise emanating from the gloomy forecast of *Aman* crop of January 1975.[14, 15] Moreover, the release of stocks as a result in the

---

[14]Brief for the visit of Mr. Parker. USAID Administrator dated 14 January 1975.

[15]Minutes of the meeting between Bangladesh Ambassador and US Undersecretary of State, December 1974. By the end of year 1974, the US government was actually considering a grant to Bangladesh ranging from 250,000 tons to 650,000 tons, additional to what was agreed in 1974. If there was any public knowledge that such quantities of additional food aid were even vaguely discussed, this could have made an electrifying impact on price expectations.

third quarter of 1974 could have, in all likelihood, moderated the impact of famine.

It should be emphasised that the role of food aid under the circumstances was not only to add to the available supplies in the public distribution system but also, much more importantly, to calm the speculative fever. To restore confidence, it was the timing of the injection of additional supplies rather than its quantum that was important. Also, food aid would have enabled the restoration of the distribution of food under the modified rationing and under relief — an avenue predominantly meant for the rural poor. This could have been focused on the areas in distress, specially in the northern districts, and would have affected speculation for the future.

One could argue why the government did not redistribute, whatever meagre supplies it had, diverting supplies to the hardest hit rural poor from the urban population, including government employees, both civil and military. The percentage of the total public distribution devoted to modified rationing and relief grants fell from 69 percent in 1972-73 to 42 percent in 1974-75. The absolute amount distributed through these two channels fell from 64,000-85,000 tons during July-September 1974 to 32,000-65,000 tons during October-November 1974, whereas the amount through urban-oriented rationing system fell from 88,000-92,000 tons to 77,000-86,000 tons.[16] It was no doubt a failure of public policy not to concentrate on the urban and rural poor at the cost of the urban middle and upper income groups. At the same time, it should not be forgotten that in the urban areas, there were also desperately poor people who were receiving food rations. If, let us say, 50000 to 60000 thousand tons were diverted to the poorest rural areas this would not have provided a great deal of help but given the dire circumstances even a small help would have mattered. I do not recall any proposal by the Ministry of Food to the Cabinet for such redistribution to the most distressed areas/people. The Food Ministry was closely monitoring the price movements as well as the levels of distress and starvation or deaths in different areas. Historically, food distribution in the rural areas was always a second order of priority, after the urban needs were met. The Food Ministry thought and acted in the traditional mode, in spite of the exceptional circumstances then

---

[16]Rehman Sobhan, *Ibid.*

prevailing. For that matter, the whole Cabinet thought in the same vein. The threat of political and social instability that could be created by the disaffected urban population might have been perceived to be much greater than what could be caused by the poor in distant, deprived areas.

Was there any other alternative way of raising the "entitlements" of the poor i.e. to add to their purchasing power to buy food in the market? In the absence of food distribution, could the government have distributed cash to the most distressed areas/people through the rural works programmes or directly to the destitutes, orphans, and widows? This was a possibility which was not even thought of or conceived at that time. The additional purchasing power of the poor would have enabled them to compete for access to food in the market place. This, no doubt, would have added to the upward pressure on local prices in distant rural areas; nonetheless it might have redistributed some amount of food available in the market towards the poor.

To revert to the case of food aid, it was intriguing to observe how the request for aid led donors to discuss, however cursorily, wider and unrelated issues of concern to them. When the Bangladesh Finance Minister called upon the US Secretary of State in August 1973, primarily to appeal for food aid, the latter spoke, first about the need for countries to develop an efficient agriculture following the example of the United States. In spite of its large production, the US agriculture was hard pressed to meet the demands from so many importing countries at a time of worldwide food shortage. Second, he gave his "occasional advice" for the speedy settlement of disputes with Pakistan. Referring to the proposal of Bangladesh for "war crimes" trials of the Pakistan army, he confirmed that humanity never learned from "war crimes" trials. He appreciated that the Nigerian government was pragmatic in not having "war crimes" trials following the Biafran war and advised that it was "not good to have such trials." The countries of the subcontinent, in his opinion, should try to work out a solution of their immediate problems and then devote all their attention to their economic and other internal difficulties.[17]

During the period that the food aid negotiations were under way, an incident was worth recalling. It illustrated how a politician could

---

[17]Minutes of meetings dated August 1973.

let his narrow electoral interests influence the provision of food aid, linking his support for aid to the recipients' compliance with his request. This was the case with Mr. Otto E. Passman, Chairman of the House Appropriation Committee on Foreign Assistance in 1974, who wanted as early as August 1974 a particular US shipping agent to be appointed by the government of Bangladesh, without resort to competitive bidding, for handling the shipment of the US food aid. The agent, he insisted, would no doubt get a "brokerage commission" from the shipping company and would, therefore, not charge a fee from the government for his services. But he conveniently forgot to mention that the shipping charges would reflect the commission that the shippers would have to pay (since there was no free lunch). This was a cost which the government of Bangladesh could have been spared if the Embassy following its standard practice was to award the contract directly to the most competitive or the cheapest shipper.[18]

Mr. Passman was from the rice growing state of Louisiana and was a vigorous promoter of rice export through food aid. He visited Bangladesh during December 1974-January 1975, following his tour of Thailand, the competing rice exporter. He supported food aid in rice rather than in wheat, even though for a given financial allocation of food aid from USAID, a smaller amount of food aid in-kind would be received in view of higher price of rice. On his arrival in Dhaka in the company of his friend — a big rice trader from the state of Louisiana — and having heard in Bangkok that Bangladesh was considering buying rice from Thailand, he met me along with the US Ambassador and his trader friend. He was unhappy that while US was providing food aid to Bangladesh, the latter instead of buying rice from its benefactor country decided to buy it from Thailand. He thought that the linking of the US food aid to Bangladesh's purchase of rice from USA was a perfectly reasonable *quid pro quo*, no matter how meagre were the financial resources of Bangladesh. This was in spite of the fact that the import price of rice from Thailand was much lower than that from USA. In fact, he proceeded to demonstrate how beneficial was such a deal for Bangladesh. After all, as an influential member of the US Congress he had supported aid to Bangladesh in the past and intended to do more in the future.

---

[18]See three attachments.

The question might be posed as to why no serious food crisis or famine conditions occurred in Bangladesh in some later years, even though there were severe floods and damage to crops. There was a great scare and fear of shortages following crop failures in 1979, 1984, 1988, and 1998. If the speculative fever in 1974, arising from flood damages and expectations of a short fall in *Aman* crop, led to such spectacular rise in price, why it was not repeated in the later years? Paradoxically, in all these years, there had been a decline in rice output compared to previous years, whereas in 1974 the reverse had happened i.e. output was larger than in previous years. The answer was that, in all these years, imports (commercial and food aid) were available to dampen speculation.

In 1979, there was a severe incidence of drought during the early months affecting all the three crops. *Ex ante* exaggerated fears of crop damage ran very high all throughout, even though crop damage was not quite so high as that in 1974. Yet increase in the price of rice was only 30 percent, as against 100-200 percent in 1974. During 1984 again, there were great fears of crop damage because of several rounds of floods, threatening to reduce four successive crops. In both years, foreign exchange reserves were adequate and food aid climate for Bangladesh was favourable. It was true of both multilateral (WFP/FAO) and bilateral food aid. In 1979, there was an specially favourable response from the most unlikely source i.e. IMF.[19] Also, the response was very prompt. There was a change in the international climate, including improved institutional arrangements for rapid response to food emergencies following the lessons of the world food crisis of 1974.

The ability to import food on commercial terms and to obtain generous food aid made it possible to extend very considerably the public distribution system, dampen rise in price as well as relieve distress through a rapid expansion of feeding and food-for-works programme.[20] All these factors convinced traders and speculators that

---

[19]There was a stand by agreement with the Fund in that year which stipulated a credit ceiling for government borrowing. Heavy government borrowing from the Central Bank to finance its commercial imports violated the ceiling but the IMF did not raise any problem even though in the next year, i.e. 1980, it did object.

[20]Osmani, *Ibid.*

the government was able to contain the impact of scarcity by releasing large stocks and expansion of the public distribution system. In none of these two years, i.e. 1979 and 1984, there was, therefore, any significant increase in prices like that in 1974. Speculative hoarding or stockholding was severely discouraged.[21] Similar experiences were repeated in 1988 and 1998. The fall in rice output in 1988 in the end was more than it was in 1983-84. There were apprehensions of a great short fall in output and high rise in price. But the rise in price was greatly moderated because of a very large increase in commercial imports, thanks to large foreign exchange reserves that were five times as high as that in 1974. Also, stocks at the beginning of the lean season in 1988 were the highest ever relative to what was usual in the late 1980s permitting a very large increase in the public distribution of food. Again, the crop short fall in 1998 was worse and it was met by a massive increase in imports and this time it was overwhelmingly private imports from India — which were easy and cheap to transport at short notice. By the 1980s and 1990s, there was a significant increase in the relative importance of the irrigated winter crop, i.e. *Boro* crop — less susceptible to the impact of weather variations. Furthermore, an expansion of wheat output added to the food availability and the diversification of sources of food supply. It reduced the impact of a fall in *Aman* or *Aus* crop.

---

[21]Osmani, *Ibid.*

Appendix 10.1

Correspondence from Bangladesh Embassy, Washington on US Congressman, Mr. Otto E. Passman

No. EC / 7 (8) / 74   August 16, 1974

My dear Secretary,

Enclosed please find a proposal from St. John Maritime, 1666 K St., Washington, DC, for handling the chartering responsibility on behalf of the Embassy for shipment of commodities under the PL-480 programme. The proposal explains in detail the mechanism through which the task is intended to be accomplished.

The present proposal from a single company is being sent at the request of Congressman Otto E. Passman, Chairman of the House Appropriate Committee on Foreign Assistance. Passman is an important and senior member of the Congress and commands considerable influence over administration in his capacity as Chairman of the said Committee. Passman personally requested me to consider this proposal and even said that his interest be conveyed to the Government of Bangladesh.

As you know, the chartering of vessels under PL-480 programme has so far been handled by the Embassy and we have been authorised to do so by the Government. It has, however, been the practice with some other Embassies like Iran, South Vietnam and others to delegate the responsibility to an agent who acts within the over all supervision of the Embassy concerned. While appointment of an agent involves no expenditure for the Embassy or the Government (because the agent receives the brokerage commission under the normal practice), the agent conversant with market conditions and the tricks of the trade, it is argued, may ensure a more competitive rate.

I told Congressman Passman that the Embassy has no discretion to decide regarding the appointment of an agent and that the Government decides upon such issues after careful consideration. I, however, promised Congressman Passman that I would send the proposal to the Government for their consideration.

You may like to discuss this proposal with the Ministers for Food and Shipping and communicate your decision early as I owe a reply to the Congressman.

Yours sincerely,
(Signed)
(M. Hossain Ali)

Encl. As stated
Mr. M. Syeduzzaman
Secretary, Planning Commission, Dacca

Ambassador
Embassy of the
People's Republic of Bangladesh
Washington, D.C.

No. EC /1 (8) / 74   December 27, 1974

My dear Foreign Minister,

Kindly refer to my cable dated December 20, 1974. On December 20 I met Congressman Passman, an influential member of the House Appropriations Committee and Chairman of the Foreign Operations Sub-Committee. Passman mentioned that he would be visiting Bangladesh from Bangkok either on the 3rd or 4th of January by a chartered plane. On his return he will be presiding over the meeting of the Foreign Operations Committee on January 15.

2.   He has been a vocal supporter of increased food allocation to Bangladesh and promised to recommend the largest possible allocation to Bangladesh in preference to other Southeast Asian countries. Congressman Passman comes from Louisiana a riverine State growing substantial quantities of rice and understandably he was interested in increased allocation of rice. I mentioned that rice being costlier we would prefer increased allocation of wheat. He, however, stated that allocation of rice would not mean any decrease in the quantity of food grain aid recommended by the Congress for Bangladesh.

3.   He was also concerned about reports of large-scale smuggling of food grain. I rectified this impression by emphasising that not only the most stringent laws have been passed by the National Assembly including provision for firing squads for smugglers, hoarders etc. but that the Government of Bangladesh also deployed the Army all along the border who had orders to shoot at sight. In fact several dozens of smugglers have been shot dead in the past few weeks. In addition the Government was procuring food grains at a reasonably attractive price after the harvest of the *Aman* crop. The procurement drive has been stepped up in every part of the country. Mr. Passman expressed satisfaction on the measures being taken by the Bangladesh Government.

4.   Passman also evinced keen interest in the Flood Control Project. I am told that the Bangladesh Government would welcome assistance

in this field in Coastal Embankments, dredging of rivers combined with embankments wherever required and irrigation projects. Congressman Passman himself suggested that coming from the land of Mississippi he could visualise the tremendous problems that the floods combined with rainwater could cause in a country like Bangladesh. He expressed his desire to fly over the terrain to obtain a first hand impression of the problems and visit one or two important places. If time permitted he might be interested in a short cruise on the river.

5. Mr. Passman has been a member of the House Appropriations Committee for several years and has grown in stature over the years. He has direct links with the President of the United States and Secretary of State Kissinger. His bio-data is enclosed. This opportunity may be utilised to bring Congressman Passman fully regarding opportunities for further assistance in the field of Works Programme, Flood Control and Rural Development.

6. Mr. Passman enquired towards the end whether it was a fact that Bangladesh have been constantly voting against the United States in the UN. I assured him that we voted in accordance with our national policy and on issues like Korea and Cambodia had not taken an anti-American line. Mr. Passman commented that this would help him in recommending more aid to Bangladesh compared to much more substantial aid given to Pakistan and other Southeast Asian countries. Mr. Passman is regarded as a conservative among the Democrats and is an ardent supporter of aid to South Vietnam.

7. I have requested in a cable to you for inviting him to Bangladesh as a State Guest. I am waiting for your approval so that I could invite him on your behalf to visit Bangladesh for a short stay of one or two days.

With kind regards,

Yours sincerely,
Sd/-
(M. Hossain Ali)

Dr. Kamal Hossain
Foreign Minister,
Ministry of Foreign Affairs
Dacca

Copy forwarded to:
1. Deputy Chairman, Planning Commission, Dacca.
2. Mr. A.K.M. Ahsan, Member, Planning Commission, Dacca.
3. Principal Secretary to the Prime Minister, Ganabhaban, Dacca.
4. Dr. A. Sattar, Secretary (Economic), Prime Minister's Secretariat, Dacca.
5. Mr. M. Syeduzzaman, Secretary, Planning Commission, Dacca.

(signed)
(M. Hossain Ali)
Ambassador

CONFIDENTIAL

Ambassador,

Embassy of the
People's Republic of Bangladesh
Washington, DC

No. EC / 7 (8) / 74

November 14, 1974.

My dear Deputy Chairman,

I wrote to the Planning Secretary on August 16, 1974, regarding a proposal for the appointment of an American Company for handling the chartering responsibility for shipment of commodities under PL-480 on behalf of this Embassy. The enclosed copy of the letter will explain the background of the proposal. I am sure the matter is under active consideration of the Government.

I met Congressman Passman at his request on the 12th November 1974, when he again pressed for a decision on this issue. I was clearly assured of Congressman Passman's continued support for our cause both in the Congress and with the administration. He said that he would try his utmost to get us more allocation under PL-480. Congressman Passman's position as a factor of influence at the policy level on matters relating to foreign assistance is conceded. To what extent his influence could be brought to bear on appropriation can only be assessed in time. One possible way to test it could be the appointment of his nominee for a period of time say a year — and to watch for a meaningful response. In any case, the appointment would not cost us anything inasmuch as the agent would earn his commission from the vessels fixed according to the normal practice of the trade.

Congressman Passman is pursuing the matter for quite sometime and he has also been calling me on telephone often on this subject. Naturally I owe him a definite reply. I shall, therefore, be grateful for a decision from the Government on the issue. I mentioned this case to the Foreign Minister also when he was here.

Congressman Passman also expressed a desire to visit Bangladesh along with other members of the Congress in the near future.

Yours sincerely,
Sd/- M. Hossain Ali

Encl: As stated above

Deputy Chairman
Planning Commission
Government of the People's Republic of Bangladesh, Dacca.

Copy forwarded to:
Mr. Fakhruddin Ahmed
Foreign Secretary,
Government of the People's Republic of Bangladesh, Dacca.

Sd/- M. Hossain Ali
Ambassador

Chapter 11

AID RELATIONS OF A NEW COUNTRY

11.1 BANGLADESH AND THE BRETTON WOODS INSTITUTIONS

The most important aid relationship in the early days of Bangladesh was with the World Bank. The World Bank as a major donor and the coordinator of the overall assistance programme from the OECD donors played an important role in slowdown of the aid commitment to Pakistan during the war. The influence of the Nixon Administration on the Bank on this issue was partly offset by the sympathy of the European governments, and by the strong support of the US public opinion for Bangladesh. Given his personal stature and reputation, McNamara as the President of the World Bank probably had some room for maneuverability and during 1971, he played a sympathetic role in favour of Bangladesh.[1]

In February 1972, while on a visit to India, McNamara wanted to visit Bangladesh even though we were not yet a member of the Bank. Since it was obvious that Bangladesh would be a member in the near future, he wanted to familiarise himself with the new leadership and administration. The Bank had maintained its resident mission in Dhaka throughout the war of liberation and continued after independence. Tajuddin Ahmed, the then Finance Minister of Bangladesh, was visiting Delhi at the same time as McNamara and the latter wanted to

---

[1] Robert S. McNamara was the President of the World Bank during the late 1960s and early 1970s, see Chapter 5.

meet him and make his acquaintance. He was rebuffed by Tajuddin under some ruse or the other. One reason could be that he did not fully accept the distinction between McNamara's role as the President of the World Bank and his previous role as one of the architects of the Vietnam war and a member of the US government. With the memory of the last crucial days of the war still fresh in his mind, Tajuddin considered McNamara, a prominent member of the US Establishment, as marginally removed or distant from the Nixon Administration that was opposed to the war of independence of Bangladesh.

In fact, he and McNamara attended on the same night the *sound and light show* on the Delhi Mogul relics and forts, sitting in the same section meant for distinguished visiting dignitaries. He declined on that occasion even to exchange formal greetings with McNamara. The World Bank representative in Dhaka related all these in graphic details to me.

In the meantime, McNamara's wish to visit Dhaka when conveyed to Sheikh Mujib, met with a positive response from him. Tajuddin, still in Delhi, was however scheduled to return to Dhaka by the time McNamara arrived. McNamara had sent a message that he wanted to have lunch with me on his arrival. Since I was well known to him in view of my contacts with him during 1971, his request for lunch with me, as the Bank representative explained it, was meant to be an informal and social affair. I, however, expected that McNamara would discuss with me, at least in general terms, the state of Bangladesh economy.

In view of what transpired in Delhi between McNamara and Tajuddin, I wanted to be forthright about the lunch with McNamara and avoid the appearance of having private negotiations with McNamara behind the back of the Finance Minister. Accordingly, I raised the matter during my discussions with Sheikh Mujib and Tajuddin about the programme for the one-day visit of McNamara. Lunch was ruled out on the insistence of Tajuddin even though Sheikh Mujib was quite agreeable. Tajuddin held that it was a visit at McNamara's own request; he had no *locus standi* in the country since Bangladesh was not yet a member of the Bank. There was no reason why McNamara should be granted the privilege of an exclusive lunch with the Deputy Chairman. Moreover, McNamara was not visiting Bangladesh as a private person and, therefore, there was no room for a private lunch. On the other hand, time had not yet come for an official lunch.

It was not quite clear why Tajuddin attached so much significance to a mere lunch. I could not understand whether it was a matter of putting McNamara in his place and snubbing him. I can only speculate on possible reasons. Alternatively, he might have been apprehensive that McNamara would manipulate me for his own ends and gain access to inside information on the economy and politics of Bangladesh. After all, I was as yet a novice in the game of international diplomacy and might inadvertently divulge information on the policies or problems of the new and fragile nation — more than what was appropriate. It was probably a measure of his nationalistic fervour and conviction that Bangladesh, having gone just a short while ago through *the baptism of fire*, was not too eager to court the club of the rich and powerful western donors. We should take time to assess the overall situation in the new context.

This was the same attitude which led to the decision that the Chief of Protocol should receive McNamara at the airport. Tajuddin obtained confirmation from the Foreign Ministry that the head of a UN agency had the status of an ambassador when visiting a member country and that the World Bank was treated like any other UN agency for the purposes of the rules of protocol. Both Sheikh Mujib and I thought that it was going too far and after some discussions, a compromise solution was found. While reception by me as the Deputy Chairman was ruled out, the Governor of the Bangladesh Bank accompanied by the Chief of Protocol was to receive him. After all, was it not quite appropriate that the head of the country's central bank should receive his counterpart who was the head of the World Bank!

The irony of the protocol decision was not lost on any one involved in these discussions. If it was only a matter of receiving an ambassador of a country or the head of a multinational bank like Chase Manhattan or CitiCorp, there was no need for the Prime Minister, the Finance Minister, and the Deputy Chairman of the Planning Commission to discuss what his programme for a one-day visit would be or who was to receive him at the airport. It would have been decided at a much lower level of the government and in a routine manner.[2]

---

[2] As subsequent experience in Bangladesh and elsewhere demonstrated, it was sometimes very costly to neglect the human factor in aid relationship. This applies to all levels of the

However, when Sheikh Mujib received McNamara, he was his natural self, exuding personal charm, politeness, and courtesy. McNamara even engaged in a brief, friendly repartee with him complaining that the latter had snatched away his Director designate, i.e. me, from the Bank. At the same time, he readily conceded that my services were needed much more at home than at the Bank.

Following the visit with Sheikh Mujib, I accompanied Tajuddin in a meeting with McNamara. We discussed the procedure and documentation that was required to expedite the membership of Bangladesh in the Bank and the Fund. The Bank was willing to extend whatever help was needed in this connection. However, subsequent discussion on Bangladesh's needs for assistance for economic reconstruction went off the rails. In response to McNamara's query about the priority requirements of Bangladesh for the rehabilitation of the economy, Tajuddin replied that the most urgent requirements were for bullocks to restart farming. He solemnly went on to explain that during the war the bullocks were either killed or dispersed all over the country as farmers fled from the marauding Pakistan army! Cattle sheds and ropes were destroyed in the process. Therefore, there was also a need for tin sheds and ropes. This kind of projects, Tajuddin volunteered, was not in the line of the Bank's business and, therefore, the Bank could not be of much help.

McNamara, not to be outsmarted, readily conceded and suggested that India, which was providing so much help, would certainly be of assistance in this as well. But what about the roads, bridges, transport, and power installations? How seriously damaged they were? What were the prospects that some of them could be temporarily repaired while more permanent reconstructions were under preparation? Tajuddin had to agree that those sectors indeed required help as the next order of priority.

Did Government of Bangladesh suffer as a consequence of the lukewarm treatment meted out to McNamara? To the best of my knowledge and judgement, it did not seem to affect his attitude in

---

donor- recipient relationship. While the broad parameters of policies and priorities are laid down by a donor agency at the highest policymaking level, the aid officials and administrators who have to make day-to-day decisions to implement such policies have the opportunity as well as the need to exercise discretion. This is where the subjective judgement of a donor official assumes importance (see, Chapter 17).

guiding aid negotiations with Bangladesh. He had held high positions in the US administration and in the private sector. Possibly, he did not suffer from a sense of insecurity and could afford to neglect slights from a person, who while leading the government in exile had reasons to feel aggrieved. The country was suffering very badly from the ravages of a war in which the government of his own country happened to befriend and support the wrong side. The unhappy first encounter did not seem to affect his relationship with Tajuddin in the following years. Subsequent discussions between them in Washington and Nairobi at the World Bank's annual meetings were business like and friendly.

11.2 APPOINTMENT OF THE RESIDENT REPRESENTATIVE

When Bangladesh became a member of the World Bank, the first step was to appoint its new Resident Representative in Dhaka. Both Michael Wiehen, in charge of Bangladesh Division at the Bank, and Peter Cargill, Vice President for South Asia Region, raised the issue and discussed what in my view should be the profile of a potential candidate. I suggested two criteria for such an appointment: one, the candidate should be familiar with the region; and, second, he should be from a small, preferably neutral country. In view of the immediate past history of the independence war when Bangladesh was caught in the crosscurrents of the cold war and big power rivalries, I conveyed our sensitivity to the presence of a big power in any form. Several possible names were mentioned; I suggested the name of Just Faaland from Norway. The Bank establishment did not generally like an outsider to represent the Bank. However, I argued that in a new country, it was in the best interests of the Bank that its representative should have good relationship with and enjoyed the trust of the member country. Michael Wiehen was very much opposed to an outsider. Thirty years later, when I recently raised the matter with Wiehen, he still remembered the incident with some unhappiness. Eventually, the Bank agreed to the suggestion.

Just Faaland was not a total stranger to the Bank. He was a member of the Harvard Advisory Service with the Pakistan Planning Commission during the late 1950s. I knew him not only when he was a member of the Harvard Group, but also later, as a member of the Advisory Board of the PIDE when I was its Director.[3]

Looking back, it was rather unusual that the Bank had succumbed to my pressure to select an outsider as its representative in Bangladesh. It so happened that the Bank soon realised that an outsider was not willing to accept unquestioningly the views of the officials in Washington. Faaland had no hesitation to argue with the Bank about their policy recommendations or programmes in Bangladesh. As the Bank's relationship with Bangladesh began to develop in the early years, sometimes through unease and stress, we found in him a sympathetic and understanding interlocutor. While he did not always agree with or even appreciated our views, he was at least willing to accept what was known in the Bank as my "argumentative and independent style" in policy dialogue and negotiations.[4]

In a recent communication to me, Michael Wiehen writes "*You were pretty hard to deal with; you were on occasion arrogant and demanding, but so were some of my colleagues on the Bank side. You were by no means unique in the development arena... I believe that it is only human that a mutually respectful manner of dealing with a professional counterpart leads to a smoother and eventually more productive relationship. Being given the benefit of doubt (that one has the interest of the member country at heart) is a high motivator. I also know that it is sometimes difficult to pinpoint the first disrespectful act, which then leads to harsh reactions from the other side.*"

11.3 INTERNATIONAL DEVELOPMENT CONFERENCE ON BANGLADESH IN 1973

In early 1973, as aid negotiations with both the Bank and the bilateral donors went into full swing, the Bank suggested convening of a Consortium of donors, following the standard practice for a major aid recipient. At the start we were less than enthusiastic. We apprehended that the Consortium would provide a forum for the exercise of collective

---

[3] Later on, he became a Director at the Christian Michelson Institute in Bergen, Norway; President of the OECD Development Centre in Paris; and Director General of the International Food Policy Research Institute in Washington, D.C., USA.

[4] Letter of the author to Michael Wiehen on 21st March, 2002 and reply from Michael Wiehen on 12th April, 2002 (see Appendix 11.2 in Chapter 11).

pressures by donors on a weak and as yet an unsettled country. Aid programmes of donors, both bilateral and multilateral, including the indicative size of their assistance for the next year, used to be discussed at different stages throughout the year not only with their resident aid missions in Dhaka but also with visiting missions from their capitals. We felt on the basis of experience of other Consortia meetings that there was no strong reason to expect a two-day meeting with all donors together to lead to an increase in the total aid commitment, beyond what had been already indicated in year long bilateral discussions. On the other hand, it could be argued that the Consortium meetings provided an occasion for the various donors to learn about each other's programmes. Moreover, they were able to obtain an overview of economic developments and policies of Bangladesh.

Donors had an opportunity to arrive at a judgement about the likely scale of their assistance in the light of their own priorities and preferences. They also formally pledged their financial contributions for the next year. At the same time, there was a downside to such a process of joint deliberations by donors. This was an occasion for them to express, with a concerted voice, their common concerns about Bangladesh's performance and to exercise collective pressure for a change in policies and programmes of which they disapprove. The meetings were usually held at the Bank's European headquarters in Paris, under the chairmanship of the Bank. There was one exception; the Consortium for Indonesia was organised under the chairmanship of the Netherlands government in The Hague.[5] The Bank explained that the reason for the exception was historical. The Netherlands in the early days was one of the most important donors to Indonesia. As a former colonial power, the Netherlands claimed great interest in the development of Indonesia, an intimate knowledge of its economy and personal contacts with members of the country's leadership.

Bangladesh wanted to take some time before deciding in favour of the traditional Consortium format. In the meanwhile, we decided to innovate and to suggest a new format, which could serve the same purpose as stated by the Bank, but would partly draw on the Indonesian model. We suggested that the meeting should be held in Dhaka under the chairmanship of the Bangladesh government. We would provide

---

[5] Later on, it started to be held in Tokyo but under the chairmanship of the Bank.

documentation on a review of the progress made and problems faced since 1972 and a memorandum on programmes for the future and requirements of external assistance. The Bank was, of course, invited to provide its own independent assessment of the situation and recommendations. We considered such a meeting to be extremely useful in that donor representatives from their capitals would obtain a first hand acquaintance with the country. They would be able to meet with a wide cross section of the country's political and economic leadership and make their own assessment of the quality of the policy-makers. If they wished, they could discuss their particular concerns about specific projects and sectors with the respective Ministers and officials. We argued that these considerations were specially relevant and carried great weight in the particular circumstances of Bangladesh, stepping for the first time on the arena of international development assistance. This format, Planning Commission argued, was much better than the traditional one in which a few selected officials from the Finance and Planning Ministries attended the Consortium meeting in Paris.

The Bank did not like this suggestion and considered this as an attempt to dislodge it from its traditional role as the leader and coordinator of external assistance. It was particularly worried that such a meeting could create a bad precedent and open the floodgate of requests for such innovations on the part of other countries. These were the Bank's private thoughts conveyed by the staff on an informal and private basis. The Bank's formal objections were different and rather feeble. The Bank argued that the donors would not be able to send a sufficiently high level delegation if it was held in Dhaka rather than in Paris, which was nearer to most donor capitals than Dhaka. Absence of high level delegations would detract from the significance or seriousness of the meeting from the point of view of Bangladesh. There would be logistic problems due to infrequent or inconvenient flight connections as well as insufficient transportation within the city of Dhaka for such a large number of people. There were not enough conference facilities, not a big enough hall for meetings and not enough microphones or photocopying machines and adequate secretarial assistance. Above all, the proceedings were likely to be leaked to the outsiders and the press, however, careful the participants might be.

This would inhibit free and frank discussion; the proceedings might embarrass the government politically as it might be accused of bowing to the pressure of donors. Bangladesh took each of these objections seriously, notwithstanding their debatable validity. In particular, the government decided to address the Bank's concerns about logistics and accordingly decided to harness the resources of all the Ministries to resolve the problems. The Bank was informed that, in the preindependence days, far bigger international meetings were held in Dhaka; various Heads of state or governments, including the Queen of England as well as the Prime Minister of China, had visited Dhaka with a large entourage and had meetings and conferences. Moreover, the United Nations Development Programme (UNDP) generously agreed to fly out from its offices in Bangkok whatever additional mechanical equipment or facilities, including secretarial assistance, were required for the meeting. In the end, help was not needed on such a scale; with some assistance for the use of mechanical equipment from UNDP's local offices, the meeting had a very smooth run. The problems of physical accommodation, transportation, and air flights, etc. were greatly exaggerated and therefore easy to solve.

The more serious obstacle was the Bank sounding a note of warning that the donors would not send high level delegations to Dhaka, which would frustrate the objectives of the meeting in facilitating discussions for the first time between top officials and Ministers of the government of Bangladesh and high level policymakers or aid administrators of the donor countries. If this was indeed the case, it seemed to us that the Bank, having opposed Dhaka as a venue, had no interest in persuading the donors to send high level delegations to Dhaka. Faced with this challenge, the Commission requested the donors' missions or embassies in Dhaka to find out from their capitals whether they would send, in response to an official invitation from the government of Bangladesh, delegations at the same level as were normally sent to Paris. All the donors replied in the affirmative. This was followed up by my sending an invitation in my capacity as the Deputy Chairman of the Commission, through the Bangladesh ambassadors abroad, to the heads of the donor agencies or aid Ministers explaining the purposes of the meeting at Dhaka and why it was important that a high level delegation was sent to participate in this meeting. The answer was always positive.

As one looks back on this issue, it was obvious that when the government, bypassing the Bank, raised the matter at the higher political level of bilateral diplomatic relations, it was unlikely for the donors not to cooperate. It would have been embarrassing for them to suggest that Dhaka was too far away or too inconvenient or unattractive a place for their high level delegations to attend a meeting to discuss a newly independent country's development prospects and aid requirements. The Bank was unprepared for this initiative on the part of the Commission and did not have enough time to launch a counteroffensive before the donors confirmed their attendance. It was palpably annoyed that Bangladesh was setting a bad precedent.[6]

Thirty years later, the attitude of the Bank and donors has undergone a dramatic change. They now seem to prefer meeting in the recipient country. How ironic it was that being a pioneer on the matter, the government of Bangladesh earned the displeasure of the Bank and donors! Also, how prescient it was for the Commission to designate the meeting of donors in 1973 as the International Conference on the Development of Bangladesh? After a lapse of three decades, these donor meetings are now called *Development Forums*. Donors are now called *development partners*. The Bangladesh policymakers in 1973, one might suggest, were ahead of time by thinking differently and for that reason caused resentment all around.

It is now understood that every alternate year the meeting of the donors is to be held in Dhaka. This is, one is told, all in the interest of greater transparency; it is a part of the process in which a wider involvement and participation in the deliberations on economic problems and policies are to be encouraged. Donors now solemnly affirm that the dialogue between them and Bangladesh is not a matter of exclusive discussion or negotiation with one or two concerned Ministries. It should be open and above board in the full knowledge

---

[6] By the end of 1973, our honeymoon period was over. When I discussed the possibility of a similar meeting in 1974 with some major donors, it was ruled out. In the meanwhile, the Bank had done its lobbying about the undesirability of setting such a precedent. The donors did not want to put down the World Bank for the second time. The Bank might have accused them of letting it down in 1973. After all, the Bank is the organisation of donors who are supposed to uphold and strengthen its status and not weaken it vis-à-vis a recipient country.

of all the stakeholders in the country's economic future. A country level meeting is expected to ensure that all sections and all elements of the civil society are made aware of how the donors appraise the challenges the country faces and the policies and institutional reforms that are required to meet them.

It is noteworthy that in 1973 it was the Bank and donors and not the government that were concerned about the leakage to the local press of the discussions in the Consortium meeting. We are told that the relative positions of the government and donors are now reversed. It is the call by donors for transparency and openness that is the order of the day. Indeed, it is now being said that while the Bank prefers donors' meeting to be held in Dhaka, the government is less enthusiastic. The main reason, one is told, is the fear of publicity in the press. In these days of globalised information technology, it is no longer feasible to keep the press in the dark by a change of location.

In the event, the donors' meeting was held in Dhaka in 1973. It was chaired and managed by the government on the basis of documentation prepared by both the Bank and the government. There was a dialogue between the government and donors; donors made comments and suggestions on the policies and programmes of the government. The Commission responded to the comments with explanations and arguments.

There were constructive exchanges on substantive matters of policy. To illustrate, there was a broad agreement on sectoral priorities. Also, both the government and the donors shared common concern about inflation and macroeconomic instability. But they expressed great worries about the ongoing heavy deficit financing and urged more stringent measures to contain it. They appreciated the priority accorded by the government to agriculture, rural development, and population problems. However, in the agricultural sector, they raised doubts about the heavy emphasis on cereals and asked questions about the desirable cropping pattern, including pricing policies.

An important set of questions related to the heavy emphasis placed by the government on the role of public enterprise. Donors stressed the need for policies to harness the resources and the enterprise of the private sector, which they considered an important tool for growth. At the same time, one Scandinavian country wanted them to respect the sociopolitical objectives of the country to build a socialist economy. In its opinion, donors should help Bangladesh achieve her objectives. Yet another Nordic country made a very revealing statement as follows: *"We, the donors, are a very dangerous crowd and we should be feared despite the gifts we bring or promise that we may convey. Too much foreign assistance has a tendency to distort priorities of the recipient country".*[7]

There was a proposal by several countries that the lending terms should be harmonised; otherwise, the lenders on soft terms ended up subsidising the lenders on hard terms, including supplier's credit as an extreme case. The food exporting countries argued that the burden of food aid should not be borne exclusively by them; other donors should provide financial assistance for the purchase of food in the world market so that the food exporting countries could sell more in the lucrative commercial market. The conflict between food aid as a surplus disposal mechanism and as a development tool or humanitarian assistance was brought out clearly in course of the discussions. The above review confirms that the policy dialogue with donors had a long history in Bangladesh; donors' preferences determined their aid commitments right from the beginning.

Apart from discussions on policy issues, there was an important distraction initiated by donors. The meeting was also an occasion for collective and heavy pressure on the issue of sharing of the external debt liability of undivided Pakistan, discussed in detail later in Chapter 12. At the same time, pledges of aid were made exactly as they used to be made under the auspices of the Consortium meetings sponsored by the Bank. The pledges, however, were made conditional on Bangladesh agreeing to accept a share of Pakistan's external debt. The government, unwilling to accept the conditional pledges, insisted that pledges linked to the issues of the pre-1971 external debt would be ignored.

11.4 WORLD BANK REPORT 1974

By late 1973, the Bank decided to undertake a comprehensive analysis of the Bangladesh economy, including developments since independence.

---

[7] Verbatim records of the Conference, Planning Commission and the World Bank's Local Offices, Dhaka, 1973.

It was to include an appraisal of the First Five-Year Plan, its strategy and objectives, both overall and sectoral, policy issues, and institutions. The resident mission of the Bank, supported by the government, suggested that the study should be undertaken in Dhaka by the mission staff, with the help of local and foreign consultants as necessary, under the overall supervision and with the participation of the headquarters staff of the Bank. The World Bank team would have obtained easy access to all the necessary information in the course of the preparation of the report. It would have facilitated consultations and discussions of the study team with the government and local experts. At the same time, participation by the headquarters staff would bring to bear on the study the accumulated wisdom of the Bank as well as the lessons of experience of similarly situated countries. The Bank rejected the suggestion and preferred to follow the traditional method of sending a team from the headquarters for a few weeks to prepare the report.

The report in its preliminary draft, (i.e. so-called *green cover*) when received by the government for comments, generated considerable tension between the government and the Bank. First, it contained very sweeping generalisations on various aspects of the economy and different policy issues a predictable result of a very superficial analysis, hurriedly put together by outsiders, including a few nonbank consultants who lacked adequate knowledge of the economy. Unlike in the older member countries, the Bank did not have a long period of association with Bangladesh at the policy making level. In addition, most members of the visiting Bank team had a very limited knowledge of the country's problems and sociopolitical circumstances. There were exceptions in respect of the report's analysis of the water and agricultural sector — a sector on which the Bank staff had worked during the Pakistan days. It demonstrated deep knowledge and awareness of the problems and prospects of the sector; it provided perceptive comments and suggestions that, though mostly critical, were nonetheless considered constructive and helpful by the government.

The Bank report disapproved of the government's socialist policies. We took it as a reflection of genuine and honest differences between the Bank's overall philosophy and the announced sociopolitical objectives of the government of the day. The report emphasised the shortcomings of a socialist system and the inefficiencies of public enterprises.

Understandably, the Bank and its shareholders were not in the business of fostering socialism. Moreover, the report questioned the overly optimistic projections regarding domestic resource mobilisation, investment, and income growth. All these were arguable points and to some extent, a matter of judgement. In fact, by the time the Bank report came to be finalised in 1974, main macroeconomic assumptions were overtaken by financial and balance of payments crisis.

What was disturbing was that the report made very denigrating and humiliating remarks on the political leadership and administration. They read mostly like reports in the local popular press — sensational reports — and consisted of half facts and half rumours. Examples were as follows: *"New men had access to political power for the first time with little conception of how to use for purposes other than self aggrandisement."* Again, *"the example is set at the political level where scarcely a foreign exchange transaction takes place, either on import or export, without some funds being deposited in the foreign bank account of a politician or businessman or some well connected private individual."* The Bank staff had no first hand or independent source of information on these allegations nor had they initiated any review of the state of corruption to assert that it was universal, widespread and pervasive at all levels of the country. To resort to such exaggerated and denigrating language and that too in a professional report intended for advice to and action by the government as well as guidance for donors was found quite extraordinary by the government.[8]

The irony was that the Plan, which the Bank team had undertaken to assess, had not only made reference to the issue of corruption right at the beginning but also explained its adverse consequences. There was no dearth of recognition of this problem by the government, as evidenced by various policy statements from time to time. What was required was not a polemical and a sensational statement but a set of thoughtful and constructive ideas for legal and institutional changes that would help reduce the incidence of corruption. If the Bank mission was seriously concerned with the problem of corruption, we would have expected them to have discussed this issue in the course

---

[8] Rehman Sobhan, *The Crisis of External Dependence,* The University Press Limited, Dhaka (1982): pp. 188-189, Development in a Rural Economy, World Bank Report (1974) (green cover).

of its consultations with the private and public sectors in Bangladesh. One had hoped, therefore, that it would identify the critical areas where reforms deserved high priority and suggest the kind of reforms which should be introduced. After all, the Bank had been working in a number of countries with a reputation for corruption. One would have liked to learn from the Bank the lessons of their experience. We were at a loss to understand the purpose the Bank wanted to serve by making sensational observations on the performance of the government and corruption. In one place, the report, for example, remarked that the government did not have the capacity to do a decent job defined in the narrowest sense i.e. *"... to organise the production of canned fruit or the importation of tallow or the pricing of razor."* By assuming such a very negative tone and making derogatory observations, the Bank seemed to ignore the possibility that constructive criticisms were likely to be taken more seriously than blanket condemnation. The report had displayed no recognition of either the achievements to date or handicaps (e.g. natural calamities and adverse external circumstances) faced by a newly independent country.

We had the impression that the Bank was angry and unhappy with the government and the report was a reflection of its unhappiness. We could not quite understand the reasons why it should be so. We speculated that we had probably underestimated the Bank's reactions to some of our actions. One could think of several. As already discussed, there was the insistence by the government that the Bank's Resident Representative should meet the criteria set by the government i.e. he should be from a small country and preferably someone whom the government knew and appreciated. Moreover, we insisted on our choice. Further, much to its unhappiness, the Consortium meeting was held in Dhaka under the chairmanship of the government and not the Bank. The government refused to permit the discussion of the sharing of Pakistan's debt liability at the meeting — an issue that the Bank had made its principal responsibility. All these might have probably added up to a critical mass to cause the Bank's deep unhappiness. The authors of the report might have thought that it was high time to send a strong message that Bangladesh was under harsh scrutiny and she had exhausted the goodwill that obtained immediately after independence. But the manner of conveying that message remains an enigma to me even after so many years. Was it noneconomic reason such as Bangladesh's estrangement with Pakistan, the staunch ally of the West? Or, could it be alleged or perceived leaning toward or friendship with the nonaligned or socialist camp in the context of the mounting tension of the cold war? Was it because we were not sufficiently obsequious in our dealings with donors or the Bank? After all, institutions are run by individuals with egos. It is not always possible to suppress subjective reactions to offended egos.

The government was perturbed because this was the first comprehensive report on Bangladesh to be presented to the international community. Accordingly, I addressed a letter to the President of the Bank with relevant quotations from the report recording various gratuitous insults. I added further that in spite of the widely held perception in the international community about a very high degree of corruption at that time in such countries as Indonesia and Kenya, to the best of my knowledge, the Bank's country reports never contained such blanket condemnation or denunciation of corruption and competence of the leadership in those countries.

Eventually, the report was edited by the Bank to omit a very few, very egregious statements or unnecessarily insulting remarks as quoted above. But the general tenor was unchanged. In course of this exchange with the Bank on its report, I had wondered whether in those days the Bank mission reports were reviewed by higher level executives/managers before they were sent to the governments or whether they were left entirely to the discretion of the team leader in charge of the report. Thirty years later, I discussed the affair of this report with the then Director as well as with the Chief of the Bangladesh Desk, long since retired from the Bank. The former claimed to remember nothing at all about the episode. In fact, he asked me whether there was indeed any corruption and mismanagement at the time in the government. If the answer was in the affirmative, he saw nothing wrong in the Bank report making such sweeping generalisations or condemnation. He also felt that, in that event, what the higher management of the Bank did in softening the strong language of condemnation was a political act of appeasement and not a professional act. The Chief of the Bangladesh Desk, on the other hand, did not remember any sweeping generalisation or disparaging remarks in the report. He remembered clearly that he had carefully read the report and cleared it without any reservation. Also, he remembered that his superior officer i.e. the Director, had also read and cleared the report. He did not remember any change made in the Green Cover version of the report by McNamara or anybody else.[9]

In the Consortium meeting, later in 1974, this Bank report and the government's comments on and reactions to it constituted the basis for discussions and dialogue between the government and donors about the policies and priorities of the government. There was a broad agreement on sectoral priorities as mentioned earlier. The Bank's recommendations for a greater emphasis on rural public works, inland water transportation, and on primary and secondary education were accepted. There were a few unresolved questions on the details of the family planning and primary education programmes. The government, however, continued to express its unhappiness with the general tone and the tenor of the report as evidenced from the final and concluding observations of the Planning Commission as follows: *"The language and style used in various places of the report greatly detracts from its usefulness. The government considers critical evaluation as constructive contribution but a negative approach is likely to be counter-productive. The sweeping generalisations made in the report while dealing with social sectors have already been mentioned. The style adopted in the report exhibits a negative approach all through." "The Bank report has expressed some disquiet about political interference and corruption... However, the government had been taking measures to reduce the incidence of abuses of power in the administration."*[10]

As one looks back at the Bank report and the rebuttal by the government, it appears that in the Bangladesh context, not much has changed in this respect 30 years later. The issue of corruption today is the staple of discussion between the development partners and Bangladesh. This is so with other recipient countries as well. But a discussion on governance, corruption in particular, in such a frank and forthright manner was very unusual in the early 1970s in the Bank

---

[9] Also, see Faaland *et al. op cit.*

[10]Memorandum for the Bangladesh Consortium 1974-75, Government of Bangladesh, Planning Commission, pp. 26-27.

reports or in the proceedings of consortium meetings. An exception was made for Bangladesh. One wonders why!

Bangladesh pioneered the "development forum" under its own initiative and chairmanship and hence, introduced the concept of *ownership* of policy dialogue with donors. Bangladesh attempted to treat the Bank and the donor community as partners, rather than a *superior — all knowing authority*. She tried to argue that recommendations on policies for development involved more uncertainties than certitude and more judgement than precise, infallible prescriptions.

The donor community considered this attitude on the part of the government as an audacious challenge by a very poor, newly born country to the established order and tradition in the donor-recipient relationship. However, in no time following drastic adverse changes in resource availability and resultant economic distress, Bangladesh had to give up these *pretensions* and followed the traditional approach, with its pride duly humbled.

11.5 POLICY DIALOGUE: AN ILLUSTRATION

As described above, consortium meeting discussed a wide range of policy issues based on the Bank Report. It concluded that the quantity and quality of aid depended above all upon the quality of performance. *"Until there is evidence that realistic and practical policies are being put into effect across a wide range of sectors, the usefulness and availability of external development assistance will be questionable."* It was agreed that another meeting should be held in early 1975 to evaluate measures Bangladesh had taken and to determine the future course of assistance to Bangladesh.[11]

The issue on which the Consortium Meeting in 1974 assigned the highest priority was the devaluation of Taka. This issue had been under discussion for some time with the Bank and the Fund. The Five-Year Plan as early as 1973 had recognised that there was a need for adjustment of the real exchange rate without suggesting an outright devaluation at that stage. It stated as follows: *"In view of a rise in*

---

[11] Report of the Bangladesh Delegation to the Consortium Meeting, October 1974. The language seems all too familiar, if one considers the conclusions of the meetings of Development Forum on Bangladesh as late as 2002.

domestic costs, wages, and prices in the last year or so, the majority of exports of Bangladesh have tended to become non-competitive in the world market. " It was particularly true of raw jute and jute manufactures, the dominant exports. At the same time, the Plan also suggested that nonjute exports had suffered even a greater fall in effective exchange rate following: (a) the withdrawal of the export bonus scheme; (b) rise in wages and raw material costs; and (c) additional selling costs to be incurred to enter new export markets.[12]

In early 1974, intensive discussions were held with the Fund when Bangladesh, faced with a large balance of payments deficit, wanted to borrow from the Fund. Bangladesh accepted the need for devaluation but disagreed with the Fund in respect of (a) timing, (b) magnitude, and (c) nature and extent of supporting measures required for the devaluation to yield its expected results.

There were successive droughts and floods in the preceding two years, and there was uncertainty regarding prospects of food production in mid-1974 (even before floods in 1974).[13] After a series of bad harvests, the food price had already started to rise and was likely to exercise an upward pressure on the general price level. In this situation, it was apprehended that devaluation would aggravate inflationary pressure; it would raise domestic prices of imports as well as domestic costs and output prices. Also, a postdevaluation rise in prices would adversely affect the vocal and politically powerful urban classes, whose real income had already suffered a decline. Secondly, rehabilitation and reconstruction of the physical infrastructure such as transport and communications, including roads, bridges, and port facilities were yet to be completed. The price incentive offered to exports through devaluation would not work effectively in the absence of their recovery. These factors suggested that due caution should be exercised as to the timing. Thirdly, in the meanwhile, it was essential that appropriate fiscal and monetary policies were adopted to achieve financial stability. This required a policy of monetary restraint, restriction of credit and higher interest rates. Improved tax collection, reduction of subsidies, and appropriate pricing policies were necessary to restore the fiscal balance. The government had already taken some

---

[12]First Five-Year Plan, pp. 63-66.

[13]Chapter 10 provides a detailed discussion.

measures in this direction during 1973-74 and intended to take additional steps to improve monetary policy, budgeting and public sector performance. The government felt that the timing of devaluation should be determined in the light of an agreement with the Fund on the necessary supporting measures and the rate of implementation of such measures. Devaluation should follow and not precede the fiscal and monetary reforms.

Donors' insistence on devaluation as an urgent, first step might have been based on the assumption that it would act as a lever to force the introduction of supportive monetary and fiscal measures. The government, on the other hand, requested an access to the fund's resources on the undertaking that it would implement the supporting measures while preparing for devaluation at an appropriate time later on. It argued that there was no universally accepted theory or formula that dictated the sequence in which various policy measures were to be implemented. The judgement of the policymakers regarding the particular circumstances of a country should be given serious consideration.

While devaluation could be undertaken by a stroke of the pen, the supporting policies needed concerted action on several fronts. Such policies had potential short term adverse effects on different entrenched interest groups, and could be thwarted in course of implementation. Unless these hard measures were implemented, devaluation by itself would result in an inflationary spiral. This, in turn, would require successive devaluations in a self-defeating process.

The government urged that the Fund should test it's resolve first in making these hard decisions since without them devaluation would not be effective. Assistance from the Fund should follow as these fiscal and monetary measures were implemented. In the meanwhile, Bangladesh would initiate an indirect adjustment of the effective exchange rate by introducing higher taxes on selected imports (except very essential imports) and by offering incentives or subsidies to exports with potentials for expansion of supply. At one stage, the case for a multiple exchange rate was discussed with the Fund. None of the proposals received any positive response from the Fund or the Bank.

Neither the Fund nor the Bank was willing even to discuss these alternatives at any level. Their attitude was one of absolute certainty about their views in favour of a predetermined percentage of devaluation. During this period, there was a visit by a Deputy Director of the Fund, whom I had known from my student days at Harvard, to consult with the government on this issue. He had long experience and expertise in a wide range of developing countries on similar issues. He was agreeable at least to consider our suggestions and not to rule them out *ab initio*. We discussed the pros and cons of these alternatives to explore whether in Bangladesh context they were suitable. He, however, argued that, while he might agree on analytical grounds that a few of these measures were worth an examination, he would not be able to convince higher authorities at the Fund. By its tradition and mandate, the Fund could not agree to the adjustment of real exchange rate through the mechanism of taxes and subsidies; it was wedded to uniform exchange rate and periodic devaluation. However, he found logic in the government's argument that there was a strong case for delaying devaluation until the next harvest when food prices were expected to be lower. With good harvests, the overall price situation would be more stable, and the inflationary impact of devaluation could be more easily managed.[14]

In the event, Bangladesh did undertake measures for monetary restraint, including demonetisation by early 1975. Food prices became stable as good crops were harvested in early 1975 and food aid was substantial and timely. In May 1975, Taka was devalued to the extent of 58 percent.

Devaluation took place in time for the Consortium meeting in June 1975. The government was congratulated on devaluation, which donors considered as an act of considerable courage, and on accompanying measures, including reduction in deficit financing and subsidies as well as credit control measures. The meeting concluded as follows: *"Considerable resolve will be needed to follow up on them rigorously and consistently. These measures are the beginning. They help to set the stage for development; they do not assure development. Having set the stage, Bangladesh must now follow through with many other measures to increase employment, to conserve resources for development*

---

[14]It should be noted that the dialogue with the Fund took place in the early 1970s. The exchange rate policies in developing countries were yet to be overwhelmed by the onward march of the unqualified "Washington Consensus". There were ongoing debates among the economists on the issues raised by Bangladesh in the negotiations with the Fund.

oriented investment, to increase output, and to distribute more broadly the benefits of higher production. "[15]

However, as was apprehended, credit expansion accelerated soon after devaluation, even though inflation was moderated by good harvests caused by good weather. In spite of devaluation, there was a need for some differential treatment of exports and imports through taxes and export incentive schemes; the gap between effective real exchange rates for exports and imports could not be immediately eliminated.[16] The postdevaluation circumstances did not materialise exactly as they were expected. There were slippages in policy implementation.

What were the lessons from the above? On most matters of economic policy reforms, there cannot be absolute certainty. There is scope for judgement in evaluating a particular situation or a policy in an individual country. *A priori* analytical knowledge can be enhanced when it is leavened by the experience of the policymakers in a recipient country, and policies/actions need adjustment as circumstances change or unforeseen events intervene.

11.6 DIVERSIFICATION OF AID RELATIONSHIPS

USA and the Socialist Countries

Aid relationships in any country were bounded by the parameters set by the considerations of its foreign policy. Bangladesh, born in the heat of a raging cold war, was not an exception. It came into being at the time of a historical shift in the evolution of the superpower relationships, with the opening of the United States to China through the intermediation of Pakistan.

In spite of the well known "tilt" of the Nixon Administration towards Pakistan during the liberation war, Sheikh Mujib decided right at the beginning that he would start out with a positive attitude towards the United States. Moreover, as an experienced politician, he knew that over time there was the opportunity to soften the attitude of the US

---

[15]Opening Statement by the Bank at the Consortium Meeting, June 4, 1975, *Report of the Bangladesh Delegation.*

[16]For a detailed discussion of the entire episode, see N. Islam, "Economic Policy Reform and the IMF: Bangladesh Experience in the Early 1970s," in *Structural Adjustment Policies in the Third World: Design and Experience*, ed. R. Sobhan. Dhaka: The University Press Limited and BIDS, 1991.

government, and that the US government, confronted with the *fait accompli* of Bangladesh, would change its negativism. He was aware of the strong support for Bangladesh among the people of the United States and among many US Congressmen during the liberation war, in spite of the negative and hostile attitude of the Nixon administration. It was well known that US State Department did not see eye to eye with the Nixon White House policy run by Kissinger on Pakistan and Bangladesh. There were officials in US Consul General's office in Dhaka and a few of their counterparts in the State Department in Washington who protested during 1971 against US policy and suffered adverse consequences for their career prospects in US Foreign Service. There was also a group of AID officials in the US Embassy in Islamabad who in early 1972 made a direct appeal to Kissinger for an immediate recognition of Bangladesh and for a quick extension of economic assistance for the rehabilitation and reconstruction of Bangladesh.[17]

As the old adage goes, there are no permanent friends or permanent enemies in international relations. Sheikh Mujib was keen to cultivate friendly relationship with the United States, partly in order to balance the perceived closeness of Bangladesh to the Soviet Union. The latter provided strong support to India when India intervened in the war of liberation of Bangladesh in 1971. But for the Soviet veto in the Security Council, the Indian forces would not have had sufficient time to bring the Pakistan army to surrender before ceasefire was enforced. This was indeed a very significant contribution to the independence of Bangladesh. In fact, during the early days when I was engaged in negotiations with the Soviet officials on various trade and aid programmes, in Dhaka and in Moscow, they often referred to this aspect of our relationship, both obliquely and directly.[18]

---

[17]This was stated to the author by the Chief of the USAID mission in Dhaka in late 1972; he was attached to the US Embassy in Islamabad in 1971. Also, see Archer K. Blood, *The Cruel Birth of Bangladesh: Memoirs of An American Diplomat*, The University Press Limited, Dhaka, 2002.

[18]The negotiations often became protracted. The Soviet counterparts were in general very rigid and formalistic in negotiations that were often interrupted by their need for clearance from the higher authorities. As I was trying to drive a hard bargain, they would sometime refer in frustration or exasperation to the fact that but for their Nyet, i.e. veto on the US and Western resolution in the Security Council, I would not be where I was at that time trying to score a point of advantage or obtain the best possible terms from such a friend in need like the

Sheikh Mujib's eagerness to develop a friendly relationship with the United States prompted his decision in January 1972 to grant full diplomatic status and facilities to the US Consul General and his staff who were stationed in Dhaka before independence and had stayed on without any official status after the birth of the new country. This was considered an extraordinary step by many in the government at the time, since USA had not yet recognised the independent state of Bangladesh.

It was not until April 1972 that the USA granted the diplomatic recognition to Bangladesh. A few US politicians, some of whom were important and influential Democrats and supporters of Bangladesh, came to visit the new country and its leadership. Sheikh Mujib received them warmly and laid his proverbial personal charm on all of them.

Sheikh Mujib used to talk frequently about his dream of making Bangladesh in the image of Switzerland — a neutral country "with friendship for all and malice towards none." As a poor country, Bangladesh needed the support and help from all powerful and big countries. He did not want to be strongly allied with one camp or the other i.e. East or West. Above all, he realised that in the search for substantial foreign assistance urgently needed for the future develop-ment of the country, he would have to rely on the major sources of foreign aid i.e. western countries led by the USA. Accordingly, right from the beginning, he decided not to be perceived as overeager to receive assistance from and cooperation of the Soviet Union at every opportunity.

Immediately after independence, there was a very urgent need to clear the two seaports of Chittagong and Chalna, which were heavily mined during the war, in order to restore them to their full operating capacity. The need was immediate and the Indian government had already helped in the partial reopening of the navigation facilities. The Soviet Union, which possessed considerable technical expertise to carry out the task of mine clearance, was very eager to help. She was able to send at short notice the necessary rescue fleet from its eastern seaport i.e. Vladivostoc. However, Sheikh Mujib did not want

---

Soviet Union. One soon came to realise in the course of dealings with the Soviet officials that they behaved as expected of any superpower but then probably had less finesse and tact in conveying their message.

to be hurried into a decision. He wanted to explore other possibilities, preferably multilateral sources that would have helped him to keep out of close association with either camp. I presumed there was a perception among his political and strategic advisers that access by the navy of a superpower to the major seaports of Bangladesh involved some risk. The Soviet Navy could, if it wished, gather detailed information on the configuration and layout of the ports as well as on their underwater characteristics. This could be used to the disadvantage of Bangladesh in case there were hostilities in the region. Sheikh Mujib probably wanted to preempt such a perception.

Notwithstanding the highly speculative nature of the risk perceived, I considered it very important that the task was completed soonest; otherwise the recovery of the economy would be delayed. It was my responsibility to negotiate such an arrangement with UN at the earliest. By coincidence, Sheikh Mujib decided at the same time to respond to an invitation from the Soviet Union for a state visit in February 1972. Those were very lonely days for Bangladesh; very few countries had recognised her independence and still fewer could be counted as friends. The visit was an important occasion for independent Bangladesh to appear for the first time on the world stage at the invitation of a superpower. There was a long list of badly needed commodity aid and project assistance that I was to negotiate with the Soviet Union. The Soviet government went out of its way to accord a rousing reception to Sheikh Mujib.[19]

In the course of the discussions on economic assistance, the Soviet offer of help for the mine clearing operations came up. Since Sheikh Mujib preferred assistance from UN and was hoping for a positive

---

[19] I remember the exhilarating and unforgettable experience of our arrival at the Moscow Airport, in a plane specially sent by the Soviet Union to bring Sheikh Mujib and his entourage from Dhaka, and to be received by the Politburo leadership (e.g. Podgorny, Brezhnev, Kosygin) to the tunes of national anthems of Bangladesh and the Soviet Union. The journey from the airport to the city through the main highway was bedecked with flags of both countries and was lined on both sides by flag-waving children. The delegation was lodged in the most luxurious state guesthouse at the Kremlin, abode of Czars and Czarinas, and reserved for visiting heads of state considered the most valuable or the most honoured by the Soviet Union. The hospitality was most lavish and extravagant, including a visit to the famous foreign exchange shop — first-hand exposure of aspiring socialists of Bangladesh to the privilege and luxury enjoyed by the "top of the pack" in a country that was the leader and pioneer of the communist world. There were visits to various republics of the Soviet Union, from Tashkent in Uzbekistan to Leningrad (now St. Petersburg) in the company of Premier Kosygin. The world famous museum, The Hermitage, was opened on a Sunday for the visiting Prime Minister.

response to our request, I was asked to delay the decision until final answer was received from UN. While in Moscow, I had to be in frequent contact with the Foreign Ministry in Dhaka and the Bangladesh mission in New York inquiring about the UN decision and urging upon it a rapid response. The government could not possibly reject the Soviet offer while the UN assistance was yet uncertain. An indefinite delay was not acceptable since Bangladesh could not go without early implementation of the mine clearing operations. The Soviets were fully aware of the Bangladesh strategy but patiently waited. In the end, no assurance came from UN and the Soviet offer was accepted for mine clearance at the Chittagong port, which was the main port and hence was of the highest priority. Eventually, UN assistance was received for the second port of Chalna.

While the mine clearing operations were under way, it was decided by the Soviet experts and their Bangladesh counterparts that the time period stipulated in the contract for the completion of the work needed an extension. This led to rumours that the Soviets were intentionally delaying the completion of the project so that they had enough time to gather sufficient data about the characteristics of the river courses and the seaport for future strategic purposes. There were even speculations that the Soviets were installing electronic surveillance equipment deep under the water. Sheikh Mujib wanted me, even though I was no expert in these matters, to lead a delegation of Bangladesh experts to visit the site of operations. I was to meet the Soviet team, to see for myself the rescue operations that were being carried out, and discuss the progress of work with the chief of the Soviet team. Since I was not only responsible for relations with the foreign donors but had also negotiated this project in Moscow, I was considered a *bona fide* person to advise whether the mine clearing operations under way required an extension of time. Our team found nothing to indicate any suspicious activity and everything seemed to be on course. Even if there was any such activity, it was beyond the technical competence of our team to find it out. Evidently, the visit was intended as a public relations exercise. It was to assure the critics that he had taken reasonable steps to ensure that nothing but legitimate mine clearing operations were being carried out by the Soviets.

The Socialist countries, in general, contrary to the expectations in some quarters at the dawn of independence, did not turn out to be the appropriate or generous sources of aid. Bangladesh urgently needed food and commodity aid — raw materials and intermediate inputs — for the rehabilitation and reactivation of economic activities. USSR and other Socialist countries were not in a position to meet the requirements. In the centrally planned Socialist economies, production of equipment, spare parts, and intermediate inputs was planned ahead of time as a part of the medium term production programme of specific industries. Given the inflexibility of the production and the planning system, the commodities could not be taken off the shelf, so to speak. They treated commodity aid as part of a barter exchange of specific commodities, sometimes facilitated by short term trade credit. They preferred to provide assistance for projects that they were able to design and build with their own equipment and technical expertise in sectors in which they had specialised skill and expertise. These sectors mainly included power, communications, transport, and other heavy industries. The period of their credit was seldom very long with repayment mostly within a 15-year period, and interest rates ranged between 2 and 5 percent. In the pre-independence period, Bangladesh had received loans in these sectors from the western donors and multilateral institutions on highly concessional terms. Accordingly, western donors supplied all project design and equipment for projects in these sectors. The executing agencies in Bangladesh, as a consequence, preferred loans from the traditional western sources. While the western donors provided very liberal terms and conditions of loans, the Socialist countries did not. But unlike the western donors, the latter were not concerned with policy or institutional reforms and did not stipulate them as conditions of aid. They considered such conditions as interference in the affairs of the borrowing countries. The Socialist countries lent to countries they found politically friendly or congenial, and preferred not to get involved in the details of their policies or institutions.

In the very early 1972, I recall to have entered into negotiations with them, particularly the Soviets, for advice and assistance in the management of the public sector enterprises in Bangladesh. I assumed that they had long experience in this respect and that therefore the lessons of their experience might be relevant. I remember the arrival of a few experts from the Soviet Union who made recommendations for a number of public sector industries. As I look back on it, it was a measure of our ignorance, regarding the poor performance of state enterprises in the centrally planned economies, that such a request was made in the first flush of our socialist experiment. In retrospect, we did not realise at the time that their assistance in management was bound to be of limited value. Besides the Soviet Union, other socialist countries that provided assistance were: Poland, Yugoslavia, Czechoslovakia, and Rumania. In each case, the amount of assistance was small and was mostly project aid.

Japan and Southeast Asia

Sheikh Mujib's dream of a neutral Bangladesh, friendly with all countries, both neighbouring and those beyond immediate borders, had multiple dimensions. One aspect was his desire to see Bangladesh as a bridge between South Asia and Southeast Asia. He wanted Bangladesh to get closer to the Southeast Asian countries, given that she was already a part of South Asia bound by history, culture and ethnicity. This would enable Bangladesh to widen her economic and political links, choices and opportunities beyond the limits of South Asia. With this end in view, a conscious effort was made to strengthen economic association with the Southeast Asian countries. I was asked to explore the possibility of Bangladesh securing membership of the Ministerial Conference on Southeast Asian Economic Development. It was an informal body under the leadership of Japan for coordinating and expanding the flow of development assistance mainly from Japan for the Southeast Asian countries. Australia and New Zealand had joined the group in 1973-74 as donors. Burma was a recipient member of the group and Bangladesh had common sea borders with this group of countries.

Since Japan was the leader of the group and the main source of development assistance to the members, I made an approach to Japan for the inclusion of Bangladesh in the group. Japan was less than enthusiastic. She felt that the group was already quite large and commitment of resources to be provided on a preferential basis was already quite substantial. To include a sizeable country like Bangladesh would put a strain and burden on the group. Moreover, if Bangladesh was included how could India be kept out since Japan's relationship with India was quite close? This would make the group unwieldy. This subject was raised also during Sheikh Mujib's state visit to Japan in 1973. Instead of saying no to a friendly country — after all Japan was one of the first few countries to recognise Bangladesh and to extend financial assistance[20] — Japan suggested that Bangladesh should discuss this question with the other member countries. If they favoured such an idea, Japan would seriously consider the proposal.

The issue was discussed with the Philippines and Malaysia, which Sheikh Mujib visited on his way back from Japan. I discussed the detailed aspects of a possible association with my counterparts in these countries. The response was not very encouraging. They did not like very much the idea of welcoming a competitor for a share in Japan's largesse. In the usual diplomatic tradition, the issue was kept open for further exploration. In the early 1970s, trade and other forms of economic cooperation among the countries in the Southeast Asia were still in their infancy and, therefore, the emphasis at that stage was on preferential access to financial and technical assistance from Japan.[21]

There were two important areas of the Bangladesh economy in which Japan took considerable interest. One of them materialised after a long time lag i.e. the *Jamuna Bridge* project. Starting in May 1972, negotiations were started with Japan for assistance in the construction of a bridge across the river *Jamuna*. It should be recalled that the idea of the project was first conceived by the East Pakistan government as early as 1960s. It did not make any progress in the preindependence days and received a serious consideration only after independence. It was accorded a high priority by the government of Bangladesh as a principal means for the economic integration of the northern and southern regions of the country. By the end of the year, the Japanese experts submitted a preliminary report on the feasibility of the bridge. They found the project technically feasible on a preliminary

[20]During 1972-1975, Japan was the third largest donor after United States and Canada.

[21]In the last 30 years, the ASEAN had made progress to include a wider range of interregional cooperation. In the meantime, in the last two decades, Bangladesh had sought to forge economic cooperation on a subregional basis with the littoral countries around the Indian Ocean. Malaysia had become an important destination for the Bangladesh workers working abroad. Also, SAARC (i.e. South Asian Association for Regional Cooperation) had come into existence since then.

basis but wanted a detailed feasibility study. It was expected that the feasibility study would take three years to complete. Japan was willing to extend a grant to finance the feasibility study.[22] The Japanese private sector was very interested in the project, because it was likely to involve substantial contracts for the Japanese industries producing equipment for such a mammoth bridge. The government of Japan became seriously interested as well. They considered it as a visible symbol of cooperation between the two countries — as a sort of centrepiece of Japan's development efforts in Bangladesh. They realised that the project would be very expensive and would take a long time to complete. These factors did not deter them from their consideration of the project as a viable one.

While Japan was considering assistance to this project, other donors, both bilateral and multilateral, raised serious doubts about its economic feasibility. For example, the costs of river training would be enormous as the river tended to change course over time. The volume of traffic would be too small to justify such a large investment. There were other cost effective methods of linking the northern and southern parts of Bangladesh. A vastly improved river transport system could be an efficient alternative.

The Japanese experts did not agree with this viewpoint. They conceded that the project might not be yielding high returns in the short term. In the long run, it would stimulate economic development in the north and promote linkages with the south of the country. In fact, they went on to suggest that if the economic feasibility of the bridge appeared less than favourable, the bridge should be assessed by the additional criterion of sociopolitical considerations and by making allowances for other wider aspects of the project.[23]

It is interesting to observe how after so many ups and downs in the consideration of the project by various donors, the project was eventually found economically feasible and financed by a combination of donors, among whom Japan was an important contributor. One could argue that in those early days, it was not possible to visualise and

---

[22]Communications from the Embassy of Japan in Dhaka to the Ministry of Foreign Affairs, Government of Bangladesh, April 9, 1973.

[23]Just Faaland, *Aid and Influence: The Case of Bangladesh* (with contributions from J. Faaland, N. Islam, and J. Parkinson), Macmillan, 1980, pp. 46-48.

estimate the full extent of the project's benefits. In the intervening years, there had been a change in the economic landscape in Northern Bangladesh stimulated by a rapid growth in agricultural and nonagricultural sectors. In the face of reluctance of other donors, Japan, in spite of her enthusiasm, could not have undertaken to finance such a large project on her own. However, the interest of Japan in the project did not flag. I continued throughout 1973-74 my dialogue on the project with the Japanese aid agency and the private sector industrialists in Tokyo and Dhaka. Japanese private sector did not relent in its pressure on the Japanese government in its favour and did not agree that it was beyond the capacity of the Japanese aid agency. While the feasibility study of the project was under way, political changes in Bangladesh were in the offing. There was a hiatus of several years before it was taken up in right earnest.

There was yet another important sector in which Japan had considerable interest. This related to the exploration of oil and gas in the offshore areas of Bangladesh. This was the period of the oil crisis, marked by a sharp increase in oil price. The oil importing countries had shown very strong interest in exploring sources of gas in various parts of the world. Japan, almost totally dependent on imported oil, had a great interest in the oil/gas explorations. She was heavily involved in Indonesia in this sector. The negotiations with Japan on this subject did not proceed as fast as it did in the case of the *Jamuna Bridge*. This was partly because Bangladesh had at that stage little experience or negotiating ability with foreign investors on various aspects of oil/gas explorations, either onshore or offshore. The government needed to organise its own institutions and technical capacity in order to make any progress in negotiations. Moreover, there were many countries around the world that had greater prospects as potential sources of oil and gas than Bangladesh. The sources, which earlier were not considered profitable, appeared to deserve serious consideration now that price had soared several fold.[24]

---

[24]During 1972-75, Bangladesh progressively widened and diversified her economic relationships and sources of aid. She received significant volume of assistance not only from the bilateral sources in the western countries, but also from the multilateral institutions, such as the World Bank and the Asian Development Bank. By end-1975, USA emerged as the largest single donor (US$ 577 million); the World Bank, the Asian Development Bank, and the EEC together constituted the second largest source (about US$560 million). The Socialist countries provided about US$390 million of which the Soviet Union provided about US$222 million.

Arab World and OPEC Countries

Shortly after independence, Sheikh Mujib devoted a considerable amount of attention to the development of diplomatic and political relationship with countries in the Arab world. During the war of liberation in 1971, the Arab countries were mostly unsympathetic to the cause of Bangladesh. They believed that we were in the process of destroying the biggest Islamic country in the world. After all, there could be disagreements and conflicts between the groups of Muslims in a country. There should be no reason why such dissensions could not be resolved by negotiations and compromises. The bond of common religion and culture should have held us together in one country.

In our lobbying with many Arab delegations at the United Nations during the war of liberation in 1971, we frequently encountered the above line of reasoning. We had to explain to them the geography, history, and politics of the subcontinent. Surprisingly, many of them did not know that there was nothing common but religion between the two parts of Pakistan; language, ethnicity, and culture were very different. We asked how was it that the Arab countries in the Middle East who had the same religion, language, and culture and in addition, were geographically contiguous, were split into so many small, tiny independent states. If religion should be the only basis of statehood, should not all of them have abundant reasons with so many common bonds to unite into one Arab State?

A patient elaboration by us of the history of how East and West Pakistan became irrevocably estranged had a slow but intended effect. Some of these countries began to see the contradictions in their positions. The Arabs had been the unthinking dupes of Pakistan's propaganda campaign. It portrayed the creation of Bangladesh as the result of a long standing Indian conspiracy to destroy the biggest Islamic Republic in the world. Moreover, Pakistan propagated that Bangladesh was a vassal state of India, which was engaged in eliminating all vestiges of the Islamic religion and culture, not to speak of economic and political subjugation. An important task for the new government was to counter this campaign and to establish normal diplomatic relationships with the Arab world.

A few countries in the Arab world recognised Bangladesh shortly after independence. The most prominent among them were Egypt,

Syria, Iraq, Algeria, Kuwait, and UAE. As relations developed with several of them, the responsibility fell upon me to start negotiations for possible economic assistance. Arab countries in the Gulf region had become very rich within a very short period. Bangladesh suffered heavily due to a very great increase in her import bill caused by world inflation and rising oil price set in motion by the action of the OPEC.

The United Arab Emirates (UAE) was forthcoming in the early years, and so also were Kuwait and Iraq. Sheikh Mujib visited a number of these countries where I had accompanied him. Among the visits, the memorable ones were to Kuwait, Iraq, Egypt, and Algeria. Anwar Sadaat of Egypt extended the warmest welcome and treated him like a personal friend.[25] There was not much assistance to be provided by Egypt, being one of the biggest recipients of foreign aid, but she did provide a few second-hand tanks for the army. Egypt had also helped to ease our relations with the other Arab countries that were lukewarm in their attitude towards Bangladesh.

Oil rich Iraq, on the other hand, provided economic assistance, including oil. This was the time when the military had assumed power in Iraq after a coup. Surprising though it might seem, a young army officer named Saddam Hussein, reported to be the cousin of the strong man who had staged the coup, was the Vice President with responsibility for external economic relations. He presided over the negotiations for economic assistance to Bangladesh. He did not say very much. His ministers conducted the discussions but he had the final say. We received some assistance in terms of the supply of oil and finance for the import of commodities.

I visited the Iraqi Planning and Finance Ministries and was quite impressed with the quality of their senior economists/officials. The Ministers were highly trained economists from well known foreign universities. The Planning Ministry was using standard planning and programming techniques in vogue in those days. The Ministry and the statistical office had computing equipments, known at the time only in the relatively advanced developing countries.

---

[25]Sadaat was sick on the day we arrived and invited Sheikh Mujib along with two or three of us to visit him in his home. While Sheikh Mujib was taken to his bedroom to speak with him, the rest of us were received in the living room where Mrs. Jehan Sadaat engaged us in pleasant conversation.

Besides the supply of oil under credit and financing of untied commodity aid, we had discussed various other ways in which the countries such as UAE and Kuwait could assist Bangladesh. One was for them to deposit a part of their foreign exchange resources in our banks, principally in the Bangladesh Bank, thus augmenting the foreign exchange reserves on a short term basis. This would tantamount to a short or medium term loan. An additional way for them was to invest in joint enterprises with Bangladesh for petrochemicals and construction materials like cement. We argued that an ideal foreign investment for them was to invest in developing countries. They faced less potential risks in such investments than those in developed countries where, in case of potential conflicts, their assets were in danger of confiscation. In the light of what happened subsequently, this was not a bad projection. A number of delegations visited Bangladesh investigating such possibilities.[26]

Nothing much materialised. At the time, OPEC's hike in oil price had began to cause inflation and severe shortage in foreign exchange resources among the oil importing developing countries, specially the poorer ones among them. OPEC, on the whole, did extend assistance to developing countries and the *International Fund for Agricultural Development* (IFAD) was born as a part of their attempt to participate in international development assistance. However, they found the western developed countries a more attractive and safer place for their investments. They invested heavily in the purchase of government securities in USA, Europe, and Japan and in the equities of the OECD private sector. Thus, the OPEC countries recycled the resources that they had siphoned off through a rise in oil price from the developed countries, back to the very same countries.

The visit to Algeria was on the occasion of the meeting of the Non-Aligned Heads of the Government/State in September 1973. President Boumediene of Algeria had already visited Bangladesh and become a very good friend of Sheikh Mujib.[27] He had been apparently trying to convince China to grant diplomatic recognition to Bangladesh.

---

[26]During 1972-75, aid from the OPEC countries amounted to no more than US$166.2 million; the major donors among them were UAE, Kuwait, and Iraq.

[27]The current President of Algeria, Abdul Aziz Bouteflika, was then a very youthful foreign minister.

This was Sheikh Mujib's maiden appearance on the international scene and in a gathering of the leaders of the entire Third World. With his charismatic and warm personality, he quickly developed personal relationships with several Heads of State. He could easily absorb and remember "the briefs" that were prepared for him, about the issues and individuals he was likely to encounter in the conference.

Bangladesh was elected the chairman of one of the economic committees in which I was involved; the Algerian counterpart was Idriss Jazairy who later on became the President of IFAD in the late 1980s. This was the venue where Sheikh Mujib for the first time met and discussed with King Faisal of Saudi Arabia the prospects of Saudi Arabia's recognition and bilateral relationship. This was a very unusual meeting. After the preliminary pleasantries, Faisal expressed his concern that the Bangladesh war had resulted in the break up of a great Islamic country i.e. Pakistan. As a leader in the Islamic world, Faisal considered it his obligation to help the Muslims and to protect the cause of Islam. Therefore, he felt unhappy at this loss to the Islamic world. Moreover, Bangladesh had become a secular state with a constitutional provision to that effect. This was also a matter of some concern.

Sheikh Mujib appreciated Faisal's concern for the Muslims and for the cause of Islam in the world. He explained the history of Pakistan's policy for over two decades, which consisted of suppression and exploitation of fellow Muslims. Moreover, over a period of nine months, Pakistan had unleashed a reign of terror in Bangladesh killing innocent Muslims — men, women, and children — not to speak of raping young girls and women. He wished that the King in his role as a protector or a guardian of Islam was greatly concerned at this and had intervened to stop Pakistan from perpetrating such atrocities against fellow Muslims. Faisal had not expected such bold statements from Sheikh Mujib and had nothing to say in response, except faintly expressing his sorrow at such unfortunate happenings.

On the question of a secular state, Sheikh Mujib explained that it was a decision by the peoples' representatives and did not at all imply that the state was antireligion. In fact, the Muslims of Bangladesh were deeply religious and devout. Secularism in this context was meant to ensure that there was no discrimination on the basis of religion in respect of political, economic, and social rights and opportunities.

A very significant visit that I had to undertake during 1973 was to Iran, which until then had not granted diplomatic recognition to Bangladesh. Iran, however, was willing, as was conveyed through a third-country intermediary, to receive a delegation from Bangladesh to explore the possibility of economic cooperation ahead or independently of a formal recognition. Accordingly, I accompanied Kamal Hossain, the Foreign Minister, conveying a letter from Sheikh Mujib to the Shah of Iran. We very much wanted to call upon the Shah to personally convey the message of Sheikh Mujib but were told that such a meeting was unlikely. However, discussions were held not only with the Iranian Foreign Minister but also with the Commerce, Economic, and Oil Ministers. Iran agreed to supply crude oil on soft loan terms. This was an important gesture because not all types of crude oil were ideally suitable for the refinery at Chittagong and the Iranian crude was very compatible.

While we were about to leave Tehran, an urgent message was received that the Shah had finally agreed to grant an audience. It was a remarkable meeting in that a formal courtesy call not only lasted a long time but also included an unexpected lunch with the Shah as well.[28] The Shah made two points: one was related to his views about and attitude towards the Iran-Bangladesh relationship, and second was his vision for Iran and the future of Asia.

He confirmed that he had received several personal messages from Sheikh Mujib during and immediately before March 1971 through his consul general in Dhaka, requesting his help in the mounting crisis with Pakistan. His consul general was friendly with Sheikh Mujib while the Shah was known to be close to General Yahya of Pakistan. He had seriously tried to persuade Yahya for reaching a political settlement with Sheikh Mujib and had intervened with Yahya to save Sheikh Mujib's life. He continued pleading with Yahya during the 1971 celebration in Persepolis, commemorating the thousand years of the Iranian monarchy. He did this in the presence

---

[28] He was a short man but was seated on a raised dais so that he attained a height suitably taller than that of his visitors. In the author's experience, another Head of State had the same habit. That was Ferdinand Marcos of the Philippines.

of a few world leaders assembled there at the time. He had the friendliest attitude towards Bangladesh. He was happy to deal and cooperate with Bangladesh even without the benefit of formal recognition and had instructed his Ministers to explore various ways in which Iran could assist Bangladesh. However, he could not grant formal recognition to Bangladesh as yet because he had given his word of honour to Bhutto, the then President of Pakistan.[29] Iran would follow only after Pakistan had granted a formal recognition. He very much expected that Pakistan would come around soon.

At lunch he was in an expansive mood and expounded his vision for the future of the whole of Asia. For the first time, the oil producing developing countries were able to obtain their legitimate share in revenues from the exploitation of their scarce and nonrenewable resource. It was known that Iran played a leading role in uniting the OPEC countries to act as a cartel for the first time in its history and to initiate a rise in oil price. With their considerable financial resources, they should now undertake massive modernisation and development efforts. They would greatly accelerate their economic progress if they acted in cooperation through trade, investment, and transfer of technology, and if they also extended their cooperation and joint efforts to other Third World countries.

His vision was to promote a common market ranging from the Pacific and the Southeast Asia region to West Asia, including the countries in North Africa bordering on the Atlantic. With this grand vision in view, Iran was, of course, very eager to play a leading role in stimulating and goading the countries to enter into an economic alliance. This vast region had abundant, diversified agricultural and mineral resources, huge manpower, and potential for technological breakthrough and industrialisation. The global scene was propitious for such a development if only the leaders of this region would seize the opportunity. He also foresaw a bright economic future for Iran as a partner in this great enterprise. He was trying his best to overcome the social and institutional constraints limiting Iran's rapid development.

He was well acquainted not only with the various aspects of the world economy, in particular the oil industry, but also with the

---

[29]Z.A. Bhutto, President of Pakistan from December 1971 to July 1977.

problems and potentials of the Iranian economy. He explained in considerable details the prospects of various sectors down to an individual industry or an agricultural crop in Iran. He appeared to have seriously thought about particular solutions to specific problems. He displayed broad knowledge about the economies of the region and beyond, and spoke about the world economic trends and prospects.

The reason why his performance appeared to me impressive was that I had not expected the Head of the State of a Third World country to have such a wide ranging acquaintance with and awareness of regional and international issues. In particular, I had not expected this from a luxury loving autocrat and a playboy, as he was reputed to be. Obviously, he was not very profound or always right in his analysis and conclusions. But given the range and complexity of the issues, it was only to be expected. It was true that he had delusions of grandeur regarding the role of his country and of himself. Also, there was a major contradiction. In spite of his detailed knowledge and information about the Iranian economy, he knew so very little, as it turned out, about the scale and intensity of the sociopolitical discontent in his country and the extent of popular opposition to his regime. It had been simmering and gathering momentum to rapidly devour his regime within a few years. We were surprised at the very rapid pace of subsequent developments. Very few, if any, of the Ministers and officials, Kamal Hossain and I had met survived the revolution.

Appendix 11.1

Correspondence with the World Bank Official
Mr. Michael Wiehen

3/21/02

Dear Michael Wiehen

I hope you would remember me, from the early 1970s when you were dealing with Bangladesh in the World Bank and I was running the Planning Commission. I am trying to write up some of the historical things about me and the Bank. I very much hope that you will help me in this task. I have the following queries.

1. Cargill visited Pakistan in the middle of the war to report on the economy. His report was unfavourable to Pakistan and helpful to Bangladesh. Later on, the Bank decided not to commit new loans but why did it decide to continue disbursements on existing loans? What were the arguments? If the conditions were not suitable for normal economic activity in East then obviously existing loans or projects could not be carried out either. Was the motive to let West Pakistan carry on normal activities — no matter what happened in East? Did all the bilateral donors follow the same policy? Was it the result of pressure from the powerful member country?

2. On the question of Pakistan debt liability, why did Cargill write to me that he was sorry that donors behaved unexpectedly at the Dhaka conference while all the time he was co-ordinating, meeting with, and briefing them about the tactics before and after the conference sessions? Was it because McNamara, when informed by us and Executive Director Sen about his activities, thought that Cargill had overplayed his hand? He even told us at that time that he kept McNamara informed and

took his advice. McNamara totally denied in his meeting with Sen any prior knowledge about the happenings at Dhaka.

3. World Bank Economic Report 1974 (Kavalsky report). As you recall there were very damaging sweeping generalisations about the political leadership and corruption? What was the purpose he had in mind? Was it cleared by you, Diamond, or Cargill? What did you think and what were there internal comments and review of the report? Was it not normal procedure to show it to the relevant division staff for comments? Why did not he discuss his comments with the officials of the government or the Resident Representative in Dhaka? History should be set right. Was the report not eventually modified to expunge some of those remarks when I wrote to McNamara directly rebutting the various points?

4. Why was the consortium meeting in Paris not attended by Cargill? He usually led the world Bank delegation? This was the first consortium meeting of a new country. This was crucial for setting the tone for the future.

It is very crucial that you be kind enough to be totally honest. I have tried in the above as straight as I can be. I would like to be told how I mishandled the situation and how I could have done it differently and in the best interest of all of us.

Please let me know next time you visit Washington.

Best regards
Nurul Islam

Excerpts from Letter of Michael Wiehen

Munich, 12 April 2002

Dear Nurul Islam,

1. "No new loans" was clear. Stopping disbursements under old loans would primarily have hurt foreign suppliers and contractors who had already supplied the goods and services and now should be paid for that. Disbursements slowed down anyway very quickly because no new activities leading to subsequent disbursements took place in the East. In the West, some implementation continued — again the suppliers etc. were to be protected, not the GoP. No — this was not due to pressure from anybody. After considering the options this seemed the most sensible course. Whether the bilaterals did the same — I believe so but cannot be sure.

2. I remember little as to the Dhaka conference. Cargill (and I) would have much preferred to have the meeting in Paris (or elsewhere outside of Bangladesh) — simply to assure the donors would send high level representatives and to have acceptable logistics at the meeting), and so Cargill was quite unhappy to start with. I know nothing about McNamara-Cargill relations at the time. But I would think that Cargill dealt with this issue pretty much on his own — as being clearly within the realm of a Vice President.

3. Re the Kavalsky report — of course, it was cleared by Diamond, myself, and Cargill (whether Peter actually read it I do not know though). I do not remember what you call "damaging sweeping generalisations" — after all it goes back more than 30 years. The report was considered good, appropriate and refreshing. I do not remember that the report was altered on instructions from

RSM [Robert Strange McNamara] after you "set the record straight." I may not have been around when it happened. Or I may have not considered the changes very significant. I do not know.

4. You were pretty hard to deal with, you were on occasion arrogant and demanding, but so were some of my colleagues on the Bank side, and you were by no means unique in the development arena. Bank staff (with exceptions, as among normal human beings) were (I can only speak about that time) very keen to do an entirely professional job and the majority were very sympathetic to this new country that had suffered badly. We were assigned to do business with Bangladesh (I for one had been given the option, when the two Divisions were split, to chose between East and West, and chose East), we saw a professional challenge (which usually includes some personnel challenges as well) and dealt with it as best we could.

5. To give you one example of where you created bad feelings with some of us: When I met you in Dhaka, just before you joined the government, I asked for your ideas who might best represent the Bank in Dhaka. You made it quite clear that you would accept (!) only one person — Just Faaland. Faaland is/was (?) a very competent economist, but he knew little about the Bank, and making him the Bank's ResRep had high risk attached to it. I took your choice to Cargill and RSM and against my better judgement supported it. The rest is history. But my unhappiness with your choice of ResRep did not for one moment influence my professional judgement about Bangladesh, or my total commitment to doing the best possible for your country. And that is how most of my colleagues acted.

6. I believe it is only human that a mutually respectful manner of dealing with a professional counterpart leads to a smoother and eventually more productive relationship. Being given the benefit of the doubt (that one has the interest of the other-country-at heart) is a high motivator. I also know that it is sometimes difficult to pinpoint the first disrespectful act, which then leads to harsh reactions from the other side.

Best regards
Michael Wiehen

Chapter 12

SHARING PAKISTAN'S EXTERNAL DEBT LIABILITY: AN EXAMPLE OF DONOR PRESSURE

12.1 NEGOTIATIONS WITH DONORS

The saga of the resolution of Pakistan's external debt liability incurred prior to 1971 provided an interesting illustration of the issues underlying the settlement of past debts. It also constituted a precedent for other similarly placed countries. First, how one was to allocate the external debt liabilities of a country that was subsequently split into independent states? Second, how and to what extent the creditors could and did exercise pressure at a time considered most inappropriate by Bangladesh for the resolution of the issue of debt liability? To what extent were such pressures exercised primarily in the light of their own overall economic and political interests? Third, how far a poor country, having marshalled sufficient arguments and evidence, was able to extract some concessions? To what extent she could take the risk of collective displeasure of donors by resisting what she believed to be unjustified pressure?

The primary responsibility for the resolution of the debt problem fell on the Planning Commission in cooperation with the Finance and Foreign Ministries. A Debt Committee consisting of the two Ministers and the Deputy Chairman was constituted to deal with the policy issues.

Bangladesh applied for membership in the World Bank and the International Monetary Fund around the middle of 1972 and was admitted to their membership in August 1972. Around the time of discussions on membership, the issue of the sharing of Pakistan's external debt liability was raised by the Bank. The government of the United States, Germany, and France, being the three largest bilateral donors, also added their voice to that of the Bank. In the meanwhile, eager to start the process of economic recovery, Bangladesh began to negotiate with donors for the reactivation of the ongoing projects in Bangladesh inherited from the Pakistan period and, accordingly, accepted the liability for these projects. However, she did not accept automatically the obligation to reactivate all the ongoing projects; donors were informed that it was up to Bangladesh to decide which of the ongoing projects to reactivate and on what terms. In most cases, the old terms were renegotiated and in some cases, they were converted into grants. At the same time, it was made clear that the assumption of liability for ongoing projects in Bangladesh was not related in any way to or provided no precedent for the overall question of the assumption of the liability for past debts of Pakistan. We made two simple points: one, since Pakistan did not recognise the independent state of Bangladesh and, in fact, considered (this was in 1972) Bangladesh legally as a part of its territory, Pakistan's debt could not be shared by Bangladesh; two, as and when Pakistan recognised Bangladesh, we would enter into negotiations with Pakistan on the whole range of assets and liabilities (both external and internal) on the basis of sovereign equality. The assumption by Bangladesh of liability for any part of the external debt of Pakistan should be a part of an overall and comprehensive settlement with Pakistan. Therefore, until then the liability for the pre-1971 debt should be placed squarely and fairly on Pakistan.

Bangladesh had, in the meanwhile, consulted famous international legal experts in the field and was assured that Bangladesh had no obligation whatsoever to share Pakistan's external debt liability. The creditors had a clear option and an obligation to ask Pakistan to accept its legal liability. Pakistan was in need of substantial foreign assistance and would have accepted the liability rather than default. The creditors could have renegotiated with Pakistan the terms of the past debt on generous terms, if they so desired. Also, the creditors could have insisted on Pakistan to negotiate a settlement of the debt issue with Bangladesh. While they encouraged both countries to negotiate the apportionment of Pakistan's pre-1971 debt liability, they made it clear that, in bilateral negotiations, the introduction of such factors as flow of resources or transfer of assets between the two parts of Pakistan before 1971 would be regarded by them as "extraneous factors".[1] Thus, as far as the creditors were concerned, Bangladesh should share the debt liability of Pakistan, if possible through negotiations with Pakistan but without any reference to the division of total assets and liabilities of Pakistan.

Bangladesh, on the other hand, had always argued that the external debt liability could not be shared with Pakistan without any reference to assets created by the liability; secondly, equally if not more important, Bangladesh had transferred on a net basis resources to Pakistan, which must be offset against the flow of foreign assistance during the pre-1971 period.

The creditors, by delinking the two issues, were, in fact, doing a great favour to Pakistan by letting off the latter from an obligation to negotiate with Bangladesh. If the creditors had not reinterpreted sovereign liability and foreswore pressure on Bangladesh, Pakistan would have either accepted the liability or would have entered into negotiations with Bangladesh for the settlement of all assets and liabilities. In either case, Bangladesh would have greatly benefited, given the difficult economic circumstances facing her at that time.

There was another fundamental reason why Pakistan should have assumed the burden. Pakistan had inflicted severe losses of income and destruction of capital assets on Bangladesh during the war, which had weakened the latter's capacity to repay. The burden on Pakistan of the repayment of whatever was Bangladesh's share would have been very small compared to the losses inflicted on Bangladesh. The donors were fully aware of the war damages; they were, in fact, engaged in assisting the rehabilitation and reconstruction efforts in Bangladesh. A tentative estimate made in 1974 of the share of Bangladesh in Pakistan's total assets was US$4,000 million; if war damages to the order of US$1,000-US$1,500 million were added,

---

[1] Just Faaland, *Aid and Influence*, p. 133. They went so far as to say that if the introduction by a country of such extraneous factors substantively delayed or jeopardised the outcome of negotiations, the creditors would consider that as an unreasonable attitude on the part of the country concerned. This was, in fact, a warning to Bangladesh not to insist on the question of overall assets and liabilities.

the share would be US$5,000-US$5,500 million in 1971-72 prices (Appendix 12.1). Arguably, Bangladesh was in a net creditor position with respect to Pakistan.[2]

12.2 WORLD BANK AND DEBT

Under the World Bank's leadership, donors chose to ignore all these considerations and went ahead to make the case that the debt burden should not be carried by Pakistan alone because its "territory and population no longer enjoy the benefits of loan given for East Pakistan..." ... "Pakistan received the loans for a larger economy which is no longer hers."

One could not but think that geopolitical considerations rather than economic reasoning or legal obligations weighed heavily with donors. Pakistan was, after all, an important strategic ally in the cold war confrontation. Donors were treating Pakistan with great sympathy, as if it was a wronged country, weakened by the loss of her territory in a war with India. Pakistan should not be weakened beyond what she had already suffered for the loss of East Pakistan, as if the pre-1971 economic gains of Pakistan from East Pakistan and losses inflicted on East Pakistan during 1971 were of no account. Therefore, they were not willing to lean upon Pakistan as the legal borrower to settle the issue with Bangladesh. Instead, they pressed upon Bangladesh to accept a share. Pakistan was a richer country than Bangladesh. Compared with Bangladesh, Pakistan after rescheduling, if she had accepted the full liability, would have borne a smaller burden in relation to her capacity to pay.

In the meanwhile, Pakistan unilaterally imposed a moratorium on debt service payments due on her outstanding external debt between March and December 1971. In May 1972, the creditors agreed for the second time to reschedule her debt for a further period up to June 1973. To settle the issue before that date, pressure was mounted on Bangladesh during the March 1973 Conference that Bangladesh had

[2] A recent estimate of the economic costs of war puts the amount at US$21-23 billion of which the destruction of physical capital accounted to US$20 billion and human capital lost amounted to US$1-3 billion. S.A. Chowdhury and S.A. Basher, "The Enduring Significance of Bangladesh's War of Independence: An Analysis of Economic Costs and Consequences," Trent University, Canada (unpublished paper), 2001.

convened to seek assistance for reconstruction and development.[3] When donors made pledges of future assistance, conditional upon Bangladesh accepting a share of Pakistan's debt liability, Bangladesh declined unequivocally to recognise such conditional pledges. This was in spite of the fact that in a separate meeting held during the Conference between donors and the Ministerial Committee on Debt, we reiterated our arguments. The creditors, who adopted a united and common stand with the advice and under the leadership of the Bank, did not expect the strong stand taken by Bangladesh against their pressure i.e. the threat of nonavailability of aid.

Donors knew on the basis of consultations with their legal experts that Pakistan was legally responsible for such liability (Appendix 12.2). Therefore, the only way to make Bangladesh accept the liability was to hold back any assistance from Bangladesh, which Bangladesh could ill afford to forego. They thought that Sheikh Mujib was not fully acquainted with the adverse consequences of the strong stand taken by the Debt Committee. Therefore, the Vice President of the World Bank, as the leader of the creditors, wanted a meeting with the Prime Minister to explain personally to him the need for sharing Pakistan's debt liability. Sheikh Mujib was by this time fully briefed by us about the state of negotiations. To the surprise and chagrin of the Bank Vice President, he reiterated even more emphatically why Bangladesh could not accept the liability for a share in Pakistan's debt. In fact, he went on to add that Bangladesh had suffered so much and shed so much blood to gain its independence from Pakistan that she would be ready, if needed, to make further sacrifices for the defense of her legitimate rights i.e. full settlement of all assets and liabilities of Pakistan. He was not willing to submit to such unjustified pressure and the threat of no offer of aid by the donors. In his view, donors were exercising pressure on Bangladesh on behalf of, and in order to provide relief to, Pakistan. Pakistan had continued to challenge until then the nationhood of Bangladesh and was, in addition, engaged in a vigorous campaign to prevent her various allies from recognising Bangladesh as an independent country.

As I watched his forceful defense of the case for Bangladesh, I was overwhelmed by the strength and vehemence of his assertion

---

[3] The details of the Conference are discussed in Chapter 11.

of national self respect and dignity. This event remained deeply etched in my memory. The strategy of the creditors for forcing an immediate concession by Bangladesh failed. Maximum pressure had been applied by them and now there was no way forward any more except to reverse the tactics, but not the ultimate objective. They were not too far wrong in assuming that Bangladesh being a desperately aid dependent country would eventually succumb, but the matter should be handled more carefully and in measured steps. In the short run, the performance of the officials of the Bank and of the bilateral donors at the Dhaka Conference was recognised by their superiors at home as overzealous and impervious to the prevailing political mood in the country. It was counterproductive as well as prejudicial to the long term relationship with Bangladesh. In the meanwhile, we decided to mount a campaign to bring the incident at the Dhaka Conference to the attention of the political authorities of the donor countries.

By May 1973, a change occurred in the tone and approach of the donors led by the Bank. The Bank Vice President, who had orchestrated the entire process from the beginning to the end, wrote to me about the Dhaka Conference as follows: *"It seems likely to me that the briefs from which the donor country representatives spoke were drafted with two narrow a perspective and ignoring the longer run economic and political implications"* (Appendix 12.3). In a separate letter to the Finance Minister, he added, *"Bangladesh has shown itself willing to take on the responsibility of foreign debt, but the timing of certain decisions must be appropriate with the total context and your government feels that only it can determine the opportune moment"*.[4]

The message from the Bank Vice President and the President was quite fascinating. It seemed to indicate that the strategy followed by donors at Dhaka was without the Vice President's prior knowledge or clearance (quite the opposite was true as seen below), and that they were concerned at the loss of the Bank's credibility. The President seemed not to have been kept fully informed about the details of the steps taken by the Vice President to resolve the debt issue (Appendix 12.4).

---

[4] Letter May 3, 1973, from Cargill to Tajuddin.

In point of fact, the Bank was advising, orchestrating, and coordinating the formulation of a common strategy on Pakistan's debt issue with the various donors during the successive Pakistan consortium meetings in 1972, 1973, and 1974. Even during the Dhaka meeting, the Bank was briefing donors and orchestrated how they should adopt a common approach. For example, on the eve of the Dhaka meeting, the Bank advised them that on the first day of the meeting, all of them should make discreet reference to the debt issue. After the encounter with the Debt Committee, they again met under the chairmanship of the Bank and decided to make "conditional pledges" next day (Appendix 12.5). Also, the Vice President gave me to understand that McNamara knew about the problems at Dhaka and was being kept duly informed. But this was not so clear from the discussions McNamara had with the Bangladesh Executive Director at the Bank. One suspected that the Vice President had invoked the higher authority of the President in order to impress and weaken the government's resolve.

Donors again rescheduled Pakistan's debt and allowed a moratorium on her debt service payments up to June 1974. In the meanwhile, the pledges made in Dhaka were made unconditional, but assistance beyond 1974 June, it was made clear, would be dependent on Bangladesh achieving a satisfactory solution of the debt problem. Even though conditions on the aid flow for 1973 were removed, in practice significant delays continued to occur in negotiations for the commitment of aid. The delays, one suspected, were partly intentional.

During the second half of 1974, Bangladesh made an agonising reappraisal and eventually agreed to accept a share of debt and reach an agreement with the creditors. By mid-1974, Bangladesh was in the throes of an acute foreign exchange crisis and a serious food crisis. She urgently needed foreign assistance on the most concessional terms. Faced with the financial crisis, the government requested the Bank to convene an emergency meeting of donors to secure assistance for Bangladesh. It was obvious that unless some kind of agreement was reached with donors, Bangladesh was unlikely to receive the required assistance. Donors offered to renegotiate the terms of credit on most generous terms. Also, it appeared that they might agree to a compromise solution if Bangladesh decided to accept the liability for projects that were "visibly located in Bangladesh." This would be an extension of the principle that Bangladesh had already accepted the liability for "ongoing projects" in Bangladesh even though only on a case-to-case basis. As for commodity and food aid, Bangladesh argued that the determination of the location of its use was very difficult and could not be done without a great deal of ambiguity and complexity. To the extent that commodity/food aid was paid for by the agencies that utilised such aid, it was already paid for in domestic currency to the Pakistan government. To ask for repayment from Bangladesh would impose a double burden on the users of such assistance in Bangladesh. Bangladesh's decision on "visibly located projects," was eventually accepted by donors. The Pakistan Consortium Meeting in 1974 absolved Pakistan of the liability for such projects.

In the course of detailed negotiations on the "visibly located" projects, donors also agreed at our insistence to exclude (a) repayment for consultancy and technical assistance services, and (b) losses incurred by the projects during the war. The United Kingdom, West Germany, and the Netherlands converted loans to grants. Several Scandinavian countries had done so already; United States, Japan, and the World Bank renegotiated them on the IDA terms.

The eventual liability accepted by Bangladesh was US$356.6 million.[5] It was small — less than one-third of the original figure quoted by the Bank at around US$1,200 million. This was partly due to the strong negotiating position adopted by the government, supported by very painstaking work on marshalling all the detailed information on project assistance, including the location of projects in East Pakistan and the amount disbursed for each project. The exercise consumed a great deal of time and effort on the part of the Planning Commission, the Finance Ministry, and the various government agencies and departments.

12.3 UNSETTLED QUESTION

There was an unfavourable legacy of the circumstances under which Pakistan's pre-1971 external debt liability was settled. Bangladesh's acceptance of a share of Pakistan's debt liability under the relentless pressure of donors deprived Bangladesh of its leverage in negotiations

---

[5] Rahman, *Ibid*, p. 185.

with Pakistan. Nevertheless, Bangladesh persisted to raise the issue of overall assets and liabilities in all the bilateral meetings with Pakistan during the period that followed the mutual recognition of the two countries in 1974. It was a matter of friction and tension during the visit of Bhutto, President of Pakistan, to Bangladesh in June 1974. In fact, prior to Bhutto's visit to Dhaka in June 1974, it was suggested by us that a delegation of the Bangladesh officials should visit Islamabad to discuss the outstanding issues in detail and to explore the possible ways in which they could be resolved. The final decision could then be taken when Bhutto met Sheikh Mujib at Dhaka. Pakistan, on the other hand, suggested that there was no need for consultations in advance in Islamabad and provided an assurance that exhaustive discussions could be held and a settlement could be reached in Dhaka during Bhutto's visit. Bangladesh put forward the following proposals during his visit: (a) Pakistan should agree in principle that assets and liabilities should be shared equally; (b) a joint commission should examine the details; and (c) in the meanwhile, Pakistan should make a token payment within two months. The initial payment should consist of Bangladesh's share of the easily quantifiable assets such as gold and foreign exchange reserves, civil aircraft, and ships. The amount of this token payment was estimated between US$200 and US$300 million, a very small percent of the total assets that were to be split between the two countries. After all, Bangladesh had already accepted a share of Pakistan's external liability. The token payment was expected to be the confirmation of Pakistan's commitment in principle to share the preliberation assets. This would lend credibility to subsequent negotiations. Bangladesh went so far as to suggest that if Pakistan was unable to find the necessary foreign exchange resources for the token payment, friendly oil producing countries (who had already shown an interest, in the course of consultations with Bangladesh, to facilitate reconciliation between the two countries) would be willing to extend assistance to Pakistan.

In the event, however, Bhutto declined to enter into any discussions or negotiations on the issue of sharing assets, let alone accept the proposal. He argued that he had brought no experts, even though he had confirmed beforehand that he would be ready to have substantive discussions and negotiations during his visit. As a result, no joint communiqué was issued after his visit on the normalisation of relations between the two countries.[6]

During the regime of Sheikh Mujib, this was a festering issue, which stood in the way of complete normalisation and establishment of full diplomatic relations with Pakistan. This issue was raised by Bangladesh in all possible international forums until mid-1975. Sheikh Mujib raised it in his statement at the UN General Assembly in October 1974, with reference to the full normalisation of relations with Pakistan (with a suggestion that a Bangladesh delegation should and was ready to visit Islamabad to negotiate). He took it up again at the conference of Commonwealth Heads of Government in April 1975; it was also raised in July 1975 at the Islamic Foreign Ministers' Conference.[7]

The Commonwealth Conference communiqué in April 1975 urged that the outstanding issues such as the sharing of assets that were impeding the normalisation of relations should be solved through mutual discussions. At the Islamic Foreign Ministers' Conference in July 1975, Kamal Hossain suggested mediation by three Arab states (Saudi Arabia, Kuwait, and the United Arab Emirates); as far as Bangladesh was concerned, all three or one of them could act as a "mediator". They could, after examining the relevant arguments on both sides, propose the "elements" of a solution. Bangladesh was agreeable to commit itself in advance that it would accept the proposal of the mediator. Bangladesh had suggested earlier that the United Arab Emirates, a close friend of Pakistan, might be requested to act as a mediator. The Pakistan delegation at the conference was not willing to discuss the proposal and hence did not respond to the most generous gesture by Bangladesh. At best, it agreed to convey the response of the Pakistan government only after its return to Islamabad. The response never came.

On August 1975, a new government in Bangladesh took over after a military coup. It forthwith announced its intention to establish full diplomatic relations with Pakistan without any preconditions relating

---

[6] The issue of repatriation of non-Bangladesh refugees to Pakistan was also one of the issues in these negotiations. This issue was also not resolved by Bhutto or even discussed in any great length. Therefore, it remained a point of disagreement and tension.

[7] Kamal Hossain, "The Making of Bangladesh, Chapter X — Bangladesh and Relations with Pakistan," unpublished manuscript, Dhaka.

to the settlement of the outstanding issues.[8] Pakistan until today has shown no interest in discussing, let alone resolving, the issue of the division of assets and liabilities with Bangladesh. This issue has effectively disappeared from the agenda for serious negotiations with Pakistan, as it has been caught in the maze of political changes at home and geopolitical developments abroad.

---

[8] Kamal Hossain, *Ibid.*

Appendix 12.1

Note on Sharing of Assets and Liabilities between Bangladesh and Pakistan

An equitable "divorce" settlement may be determined either from a study of resource creation and resource flows (inter-wing and with foreign countries) or from an assessment of assets and liabilities as of the date of separation. Most of the discussion in the past has concentrated on resource flows. This short note ignores implications of uneven resource flows and deals exclusively with the balance sheet of assets and liabilities as of 1971.

The location of this asset creation was a result of Government policy with respect to use of export proceeds, foreign assistance, taxes, licensing, defense, administration, etc. This note seeks to establish the balance sheet of the resource flows for the volume and location of assets created.

Physical asset creation can, in principle, be determined by an inventory; for some physical assets that may be the only course open. However, as far as economic assets are concerned, those that constitute productive capital contributing to the current production of goods and services, it is possible to determine the orders of magnitude by an indirect, and a generally acceptable approach. This method would concentrate on the determination of the increase in current output that has occurred over the period, introduce an estimate of how much additional capital is required to obtain the volume of current output, given the Incremental Capital Output Ratio (ICOR), and then estimate of the addition to the capital stock that has occurred. This exercise is reproduced in Table 1.[9]

---

[9] Note that more accurate figures of GNP per capita, population, and ICOR could no doubt be found. For the purpose of establishing orders of magnitude, however, the figures in the table might serve well enough. The note with few modifications was published since then in

Table 1: Calculation of Increase in Current GNP, 1947-1971

	1971	1960	1947	Increase 1947 to 1971
GNP per Capita (in US$ at 1971 prices)				
Bangladesh	70	65	60	10
Pakistan (West)	130	90	65	65
Population (in millions)				
Bangladesh	72.5	54.0	41.0	31.5
Pakistan (West)	62.5	45.5	34.5	28.0
Total GNP (in US$ million at 1971 prices)				
Bangladesh	5075	3510	2460	2615
Pakistan (West)	8125	4095	2240	5885
Total for both countries	**13200**	**7605**	**4700**	**8500**

The efficiency of capital accumulation in terms of current output for whole economies is a most complicated and controversial concept. Rarely is this ICOR estimated at less than two, much more often is it around three. For the purpose of this illustrative exercise — and in order not to overstate Bangladesh' case — an ICOR of 2.5 is used for both countries.

On the basis of the above, the value of net productive capital assets created in the 24-year period are of the order of US$6,500 million in Bangladesh and US$14,700 million in Pakistan.

Before proceeding with the argument, one should take note (a) that Pakistan also had assets abroad, physical and financial, private and public; (b) it also had liabilities abroad, public and private (and for both assets and liabilities this includes foreign ownership or share of ownership in capital assets in Pakistan and vice versa); (c) that there was also an assets and liabilities balance (public and private) between Bangladesh and Pakistan.

It is suggested that with respect to (a) and (b) only *public financial* assets and liabilities be considered; with respect to (c) all assets and liabilities are ignored, partly because they have been "nationalised" anyhow, partly because it is the "equitable" net balance in this category which is being estimated.

Faaland and Parkinson, *Bangladesh: A Test Case of Development* (C. Hurst and Company, London, 1976).

Foreign creditors of the old Pakistan have pressed for a division of Pakistan's debts to them as between the two countries. The principle that formal, legal liability of Pakistan for all debts contracted up to 1971 remains with Pakistan until and unless another party (Bangladesh) actually assumes liability, appears to be generally accepted. Nevertheless, Bangladesh has, in fact, assumed such liability for some categories of debts and is currently negotiating with creditors about others. Nothing similar has yet taken place with respect to the old Pakistan's public financial assets abroad.

With respect to public financial liabilities of Pakistan to foreign countries, the total in 1971 was of the order of US$4,000 million equivalent. A possible outcome of completed and current debt negotiations may be that, say three-quarters is written off by creditors (a good deal of this write-off has in a sense already occurred in that the original loan agreements included grant elements. A further grant element is bound to be added now to both countries.) As a result, Bangladesh may end with a financial debt burden in real terms of between say US$150 to US$300 million equivalent, Pakistan with say between US$700-US$850 million.

With respect to public financial assets of Pakistan in foreign countries, data are not readily available. These assets include foreign exchange reserves (as of December 1971), contributions to international agencies, etc. Besides the need to establish what amounts are involved, the respective claims of Pakistan and Bangladesh on these assets may be the subject of heated and difficult debate. Since we do not now have the basic information, this item is included for illustrative purposes only with a figure of US$500. All of this is presently held by Pakistan, no division of such assets has been initiated. It could be much more. Now, it is necessary to establish whether the net value of assets should be divided equally or on a population basis between the two countries. Again in order not to overstate the Bangladesh case, it is here assumed that Bangladesh agrees to divide on the basis of equal shares to each country. A settlement in 1971 on the above basis would then come out as shown in Table 2.

As shown in Table 2, on the assumptions made above, including assumptions with respect to internal capital creation, external debt settlement and retention of Pakistan of external financial assets,

Table 2: Balance Sheet as of 1971 (in Million US$)

	Pakistan	Bangladesh	Total
Value of domestic productive capital assets	14,700	6,500	21,200
Public liabilities abroad	850	150	1,000
Public financial assets held abroad	500	–	500
Net Assets before "divorce" settlement	14,350	6,350	20,700
Equitable (equal) division of net assets	10,350	10,350	20,700
Net liability of Pakistan to Bangladesh	-4,000	+4,000	–

Bangladesh has a claim on Pakistan of the order of US$4,000 million equivalent. With some adjustments in the above assumptions (which may not be in themselves unreasonable), the case could be made for an even higher claim.

Finally, in making this estimate of a *net* claim on Pakistan of US$4,000 million, no account is taken of any claim Bangladesh may raise with respect to war damages. That might well add another US$1,000-US$1,500 million or more to Bangladesh's total net claim on Pakistan.

Appendix 12.2

Memoranda and Miscellaneous Correspondence on Sharing of Pakistan's External Debt

World Bank: Office Memorandum

DATE: March 23, 1973

TO: Mr. A. Broches — Vice President and General Counsel
FROM: Piero Sella — Assistant General Counsel
SUBJECT: East Pakistan Debt

(Relevant paragraphs)

4. Pakistan became a member of the Bank in 1950, some three years after India had been partitioned into the Dominions of India and Pakistan in 1947. India retained the original membership in the Bank of pre-partition India, without reduction in its capital subscription. Bangladesh became a member of the Bank in 1972, after it declared its independence from Pakistan and Pakistan has retained its own membership in the Bank Group without reduction in its capital subscription. Both with regard to membership in the Bank and other international organisations and in its relations with other states, Pakistan, after the loss of its East wing and the majority of its population, seems to consider itself and is considered by others as still continuing the identity of the original Islamic Republic of Pakistan to which, or with whose guarantee, the amounts in question were loaned by the Bank and IDA.

5. Under the terms of the relevant loan, credit or guarantee agreements with Pakistan, no legal grounds exist for a disclaimer of liability by Pakistan for the amounts in question.

6. The question, however, may be asked whether under customary international law the liability of Pakistan for the amounts in question has ceased or has been transferred to Bangladesh because these amounts were disbursed for the benefit of that clearly identified part of the original Pakistan which is now controlled by the Government of Bangladesh.

7. State practice in this field offers no helpful guide, since almost invariably the question of succession in respect of debts has been settled sooner or later by agreement, sometimes imposed by outsiders (e.g. in peace treaties). However, a review of the leading legal writers in this field, as well as of the practice of the Bank itself in similar cases, shows that no rule of international law that would exonerate Pakistan exists ... the State that has lost even a substantial portion of its territory remains liable for all debt it had contracted prior to that loss.

9. Most cases of debt succession in the past having been settled by agreement between the States concerned (including debt succession as a result of the partition of Pakistan and India), no clear customary rule has emerged.

10. They (creditors) can, of course, as a matter of policy, insist on obtaining the agreement of Bangladesh that the latter assume liability for those debts before they provide additional financing — as IDA has done in respect of credits for ongoing projects.

11. Failure by Pakistan to service on time Bank loans or IDA credits for East Pakistan projects would constitute a default.

13. The case of Jordan, which continues to service Credit No. 43 JO, although parts of the project are in the territory now under Israeli occupation; the case of Malaysia which remains the guarantor for a loan to the Public Utilities Board in Singapore (Loan No. 405 MA), in spite of the fact that the separation agreement between Malaysia and Singapore provides expressly for the assumption by Singapore of such liabilities and the release of Malaysia ...

Appendix 12.3

Memoranda and Miscellaneous Correspondence on Sharing of Pakistan's External Debt (Continued)

May 3, 1973

Dr. Nurul Islam
Deputy Chairman, Planning Commission
Eden Building, Dacca, Bangladesh

Dear Nurul:

After my discussions with you and the Prime Minister on April 2 I became increasingly concerned about the outcome of the meeting in Dacca. The discussions we had both before and after the meeting served to put the problem in a longer perspective and I regret very much that it had not been possible for me to have had fuller and less hurried exchanges of views with the donor countries.

The cause of my concern is this. It must clearly be the objective of all those countries who have so far generously provided aid to the countries of the Indian sub-continent, and specially in the past 15 months to Bangladesh, to do all that they can to bring about economic and political stability in the sub-continent. Given the circumstances in which these problems have to be considered, it seems clear to me that no action should be taken which would impede a resolution of the problems with which everyone has to be concerned and I have particularly in mind the problems of the relationships between Bangladesh and Pakistan. It seems to me that any diminution of aid to either country at this time might indeed cause difficulties that could make it more difficult rather than easier to achieve these results.

Since my return I have had a number of discussions with representatives of the donor countries and on April 25 I wrote formally to the heads of delegates to the Dacca meeting setting out my views and inviting them to attend a meeting on May 30 in Paris to discuss proposals I am making which would I believe relieve the situation. I am sure that these invitations will be accepted but, of course, I cannot undertake that the proposals I am making will be acceptable.

I think possibly too much importance can be attached to the statements of the donors at the Dacca meeting. There is no doubt that the possibility of a default on debt owed to the donor countries presents them with considerable problems, but it seems likely to me that the briefs from which the donor country representatives spoke were drafted with too narrow a perspective and ignoring the longer range economic and political implications. In retrospect, I am sorry that the Dacca meeting came so soon after the Pakistan Consortium meeting in Paris as a result of which it was not possible for me or anyone else to make the proper soundings in the various capitals. I was, of course, somewhat surprised, after the statement that you made and after the meeting on the afternoon of March 31 with the Foreign Minister, the Finance Minister and yourself, that the donor country representatives persisted in making conditional pledges. However, I hope that all of us will put the events of the past in their proper place so that we can all face up to the difficult challenges that confront us.

I hope that Just Faaland will be able to attend the meeting on May 30 and will then be in a position to give you a first-hand account of it. The timing of the meeting is, of course, awkward from the point of view of your planning but I am afraid it was not practical to set it earlier. I am writing separately to the Foreign Minister and the Finance Minister.

With warm personal regards.

Sincerely yours,

I.P.M. Cargill
Vice President, Asia

Memoranda and Miscellaneous Correspondence on Sharing of Pakistan's External Debt (Continued)

	No. I-132
	SECRET
Place: Bangladoot New York	
To: Pararashtra Dacca	DTO – 27-4-73
No.: 27	DTD – 299345
Dated 27th (received 28th) April, 1973.	DTD – 291115

Secret, Director General Abul Ahsan from Muhith. Kindly convey following message to Professor Nurul Islam, Deputy Chairman, Planning Commission.

"From S.R. Sen, Executive Director. Spoken in detail to McNamara and Cargill Thursday regarding point raised by you. Cargill put entire blame for Dacca conference happenings on MacDonald (a bilateral donor – USA). He is trying best to repair damage and is appealing to all donor Governments to pledge unconditionally by May. Held discussions already with high-level British authorities. Cargill has agreed with me that you can prepare plan on the basis of pledges already made. He will shortly write in detail which, when shown to Prime Minister, would allay his misgivings. McNamara reacted positively to my approach and said he did not receive any telephone call regarding debt sharing. He further said that Bank was not a party to Dacca happenings. He is concerned at loss of credibility by Bank because of Dacca events. He accords top priority to Bangladesh programme and is happy that Faaland is well received in Dacca. I advised that Bank's Dacca office should have some status and power as those of Jakarta office. He thinks there might be problems but he would give careful consideration. He requested me to assure you on his behalf and through you Prime Minister that he would do everything possible for assisting Bangladesh and that it is better to forget Dacca happenings. He is looking forward to see you in August."

Distribution:

1. Prime Minister.
2. Foreign Minister.
3. Foreign Secretary.
4. Deputy Chairman, Planning Commission.
5. Addl. Foreign Secretary.
6. Director ...

Memoranda and Miscellaneous Correspondence on Sharing of Pakistan's External Debt (Continued)

BD / DEBT
SECRET
6

OFFICE MEMORANDUM

TO: Files

FROM: Michael H. Wiehen (signed)

SUBJECT: BANGLADESH — International Conference in Dacca

(Relevant paragraphs)

4. One issue which is not specifically referred to in the Press Release but which was discussed in various fora, and at great length, was that of the responsibility of Bangladesh for a portion of the external debt incurred by Pakistan prior to 1971. About one week before the date of the Conference, the Prime Minister of Bangladesh had established a committee to deal with this subject. Members of this Debt Committee are the Foreign Minister (Dr. Kamal Hossain), the Finance Minister (Mr. Tajuddin Ahmed), and the Deputy Chairman of the Planning Commission (Dr. Nurul Islam). Two days before the Conference opened, Mr. Cargill met with the Committee, apprised it of the position of the creditor countries as it had emerged at a Heads of Delegations meeting in Paris on March 23 (held there on the occasion of the Pakistan Consortium meeting), and arranged for a meeting of the Heads of Delegations of the creditor countries with the Committee during the Conference.

5. On the eve of the Conference, Mr. Cargill met with the Heads of Delegations of the creditor countries and advised them of his earlier discussions with the Debt Committee. It was agreed that all creditor delegations in their first statements at the Conference would discreetly refer to the debt problem as an issue to be resolved, and would then wait for the outcome of the meeting with the Debt Committee. Consequently, all creditor delegations (including the Bank) made more or less oblique references to this issue on the first day of the Conference.

6. In the late afternoon of the first day, the Heads of Delegations of the creditor countries met with the Debt Committee and a rather open exchange of views took place. It became apparent quickly that the committee, having been informed of the urgency of the issue (the presently existing arrangements ending on June 30) only two days earlier, had not had a chance for a full internal review of the Government's previous position, and consequently was just reiterating the former position: that (i) there was no legal basis for Pakistan to renounce its debt obligations, particularly since the new Constitution of Pakistan still refers to "East Pakistan" as an integral part of Pakistan; and (ii) any responsibility of Bangladesh could be established only after the entire financial relationship between the two former wings of Pakistan had been fully considered.

7. In the light of this meeting with the Debt Committee, the creditor countries agreed at another Heads of Delegations meeting late the same evening, that the situation called for a position exactly as had been taken at the Pakistan Consortium meeting in Paris, namely that they would make conditional pledges the next day.

8. On the second day of the Conference, the Chairman's statement on the balance of payments position was followed first by two brief statements of the head of the IMF delegation and of Mr. Cargill (copy attached as Annex 6). Before giving the floor to the first country delegation, the Chairman stated that, since he knew that some delegations could not make unconditional pledges, he did not wish any pledges to be made at all. Despite this opening statement, the first country delegation called upon

(the US) did pledge food, commodity and project assistance for FY73/74, and added that any assistance other than humanitarian was "subject to a satisfactory solution of the debt solution". This statement, in just about the same terms, was repeated by every other creditor country delegation (except for Sweden which had advised Bangladesh of its pledge for FY73/74 prior to the Conference). However, most delegations also expressed their hope that there would soon be further discussions among the Government and the creditor countries on this issue.

9. After the round of pledges, the Chairman stated that, since he had specifically requested delegates not to make pledges, he and his government would not take note of either the pledges or the conditions placed on them.

10. The total amount pledged at the Conference fell considerably short of the US$825 million requested by the Government of Bangladesh. Some pledges were unclear, others had to be translated from kind into cash, and this process of clarification was not complete by the time I left Dacca. I have requested our Dacca Office to send us a detailed analysis as soon as available and will give it the same distribution as this memorandum.

Attachments

cc (Annex 1 only):   Messrs. McNamara
                     Knapp
                     Broches
                     Cargill
                     Diamond
                     Weiner

Chapter 13

INDO-BANGLADESH ECONOMIC COOPERATION

13.1 INTRODUCTION

Indo-Bangladesh economic relations during 1972-75 could not be separated from the context of the overall relationship between the two countries. It was a period during which a broader relationship was evolving over a very wide range of often closely interdependent issues. Successful relations or negotiations in some areas helped in other areas and the same was true with failures. A close interdependence between political and economic relationships was widely recognised.

Indo-Bangladesh relations, in general, remained throughout a complex one, fluctuating between being very close and intimate at certain times or in certain respects and not so close at certain other times or on some other issues. This complexity had an added dimension. The mainstream in India viewed Bangladesh as not very appreciative, if not ungrateful, for all the help provided and sacrifices made by India during the war of independence. In the changed circumstances, there were exaggerated expectations in India that Bangladesh would make concessions or generous accommodation on bilateral issues that had remained unresolved and contentious during the Pakistan times. A large majority in Bangladesh acknowledged strong and genuine sympathy of the people and the government of India for the cause of Bangladesh in 1971. At the same time, there were those who considered that India's help in the war of liberation was motivated by her strategic interests in the subcontinent, specially in relation to her ongoing conflict with Pakistan. These strands of thought have not totally disappeared until today in either country and in some ways they seem to influence, albeit subconsciously, the relations between the two countries.

The development of Indo-Bangladesh relations during 1972-75 could not be completely free of the historical legacy of the Hindu-Muslim tensions and conflicts in the subcontinent. There were some in Bangladesh who opposed or many who were apprehensive about independence from Pakistan. In their view, it weakened the relative strength of the Muslims in the sub-continent vis-à-vis the Hindus by helping to establish the pre-eminence of India in South Asia. As a result, Bangladesh was now exposed to the risk of domination by India. They presumed that India wanted to dominate or exercise influence on Bangladesh's domestic and foreign policy in order to suit India's interests. This perception was strengthened and spread among the public by rumours, by the press and by the political opposition as well as by interest groups of different affiliations/persuasions, who for varying reasons were opposed to close cooperation with India.[1]

Similarly, the Indian policymakers — specially the officials, including in particular, the foreign policy establishment — could not completely shed the attitudes and suspicions that guided their relationships with Pakistan. After all, to many of them Bangladesh almost resembled erstwhile East Pakistan. Some of the actions and misjudgements of the Indian armed forces and their civilian counterparts, in the days and weeks immediately following independence, seemed to lend support to this viewpoint. The ambivalence on the part of the policymakers

---

[1] A few of the wildest rumours circulating at the time which I had to encounter or deal with in my discussions with supposedly well informed individuals are described as follows. There was a secret treaty with India, which granted India extraordinary powers to control Bangladesh's domestic and foreign policy, both economic and political. Most of these comments were often by those who had never seen or read the *Indo-Bangladesh Treaty of Friendship*, even though it was in the public domain. When confronted with the actual treaty, critics would retreat and suggest that there was a secret second treaty which, by its nature, could not be in the public domain. Only Indira Gandhi and Sheikh Mujib knew about it and it was kept in his personal custody. When one asked how was it that the secret treaty could not be made public, after the assassination of Sheikh Mujib, one was told that it was not kept in Bangladesh but in a secret safe deposit in India. Again, there were strange rumours about *Rakkhi Bahini*, a para-military force Sheikh Mujib built up outside the purview of the regular armed forces, to aid civil authorities in the maintenance of law and order. It was said that this force was manned by the Indian recruits, mostly from South India. This was the way India kept physical control over Bangladesh. It was, however, true that in the training of the paramilitary force, the Indian military officers did help.

in India might have been fed by what they considered as anxious efforts by Bangladesh to normalise relations with Pakistan, so soon after the events of the 1971 war, as well as to assert her role as a Muslim majority country in the community of Muslim nations. There could be some elements of truth in these diverse perceptions. Like all distortions and exaggerated perceptions, they tended to hamper the uninterrupted evolution of smooth and harmonious bilateral relationships.[2]

It was in this emerging environment that economic relationships between India and Bangladesh had to be forged. At the highest political level in both countries, there was a conviction that considerable potentials existed for developing mutually beneficial economic relationships. The Prime Ministers of both countries understood that the potentials could only be realised if constraints were also acknowledged and dealt with tact and patience. India should recognise and act in such a manner as to respect the sensitivity of a newly independent country which would resent any indication or hint of a big brotherly behaviour. Bangladesh had to demonstrate that she was a friendly neighbour to a big country which did have other regional and global interests. Both the leaders were cognisant of these factors in their dealings with each other. They realised that to maintain a delicate balance between these considerations required a high level of diplomatic skill and sophistication.

An interesting anecdote in this context would indicate how delicate and complex was the environment affecting the overall relationship and how easily wrong perceptions might develop. A senior Indian academic-turned official, who was a member of Indira Gandhi's core team of advisers to coordinate Indo-Bangladesh relations, once remarked to me that this relationship was, from the Indian point of view, a no-win situation. India, according to him, was accused either of patronising and throwing her weight around like a big brother or ignoring and even discriminating against Bangladesh. He gave an

---

[2] This is not the place nor do I make any effort to analyse or examine these views and perceptions. Much has been written about them in both countries. See Dixit's analysis of events in the early years and mistakes made by India as well as the reasons thereof, J.N. Dixit, *Liberation and Beyond — Indo-Bangladesh Relations*, Dhaka: The University Press Limited, 1999. It is a very revealing and interesting analysis from the point of view of India. Even though it is written from the perspective of the foreign policy establishment of India, it has a wider perspective. It does, for example, describe what is now generally perceived as missteps by India in early years which affected subsequent attitudes of Bangladesh.

example of the Nepalese students at the Institute of Economic Growth at Delhi University. At the outset, the Nepalese students used to go around wearing the same type of trousers and shirts as were used by the average Indian students and appeared indistinguishable from them. They complained that their fellow Indian students treated them as "locals", did not recognise their separateness and showed no respect for their distinctive cultures, habits, and traditions. As a reaction against what they considered the patronising behaviour of the Indian students, they started wearing their traditional dresses with their distinctive headdress. Thereafter, they felt that the fellow students were treating them with distant formality and did not socialise with them as intimately and as frequently as before. This they considered unfair and discriminatory. The narrator of the anecdote wondered aloud whether this example did not bear some similarity with the Indo-Bangladesh relationship.

This story revealed how even for the perceptive elements in India it was not easy to fully comprehend the complexity of the Indo-Bangladesh relations. In the Nepalese example, it was not readily apparent to my interlocutor that what they wanted was a middle of the way approach between the two extremes. The Nepalese students desired respect for and recognition of their separate identity and did not want to be treated as a subgroup of the Indian society, but at the same time they did not want to be denied a friendly and cooperative association. However, the Indo-Bangladesh relationship was not quite comparable. It had a very different dimension; it was a relationship between two sovereign states and not a case of relationship between two groups of individuals. The relationship was also multifaceted.

13.2 MEETINGS OF THE PLANNING COMMISSIONS

As one involved in dealing with economic relationship with India right from the beginning, I discuss the evolution of this relationship in a few selected areas in the early years. My experience has a few aspects which bear some relevance to the problems and prospects of forging bilateral economic cooperation now and in the future, though the economic environment and policy framework have changed in both countries.

As early as February 1972, during the meetings of the Prime Ministers of India and Bangladesh in Kolkata, India, it was agreed that the two Planning Commissions would meet periodically to identify areas of mutual cooperation and to exchange views on the immediate, short term and long term development strategies of the two countries.[3] This was further confirmed in the joint declaration of the two Prime Ministers in Dhaka in March 1972 that regular consultations, at least once every six months, shall be held between the officials of the two Planning Commissions to strengthen cooperation.[4] The principal areas of economic cooperation between the two countries identified by the Indo-Bangladesh Friendship Treaty of 1972 were as follows:

> Mutual cooperation would be developed in the fields of trade, transport, and communications on the basis of the principles of equality, mutual benefit, and most favoured nation treatment. Joint studies would be made and joint action taken in the fields of flood control, river basin development, and development of hydroelectric power and irrigation.

The first meeting of the two Planning Commissions was held in early 1972 with the Indian team consisting, among others, of the Deputy Chairman and a member of the Indian Planning Commission, who was specially designated to deal with matters of economic cooperation with Bangladesh. A broad range of possibilities of economic cooperation were discussed; the Indian delegation left the initiative for articulating the requirements of Bangladesh in the hands of the Bangladesh team.[5]

---

[3] Minutes of the meeting between the two Prime Ministers, dated February 9, 1972, M.M. Islam, Finance Secretary, Government of Bangladesh.

[4] The Planning Commission right from the beginning was designed as the main co-ordinating agency for initiating and managing policies for economic cooperation with India. Therefore, the Commission could not escape the taint of being locked in an "unequal relationship" with India. To illustrate, early in 1973, I accompanied by a member of the Commission visited Delhi for discussions with Indian Planning Commission regarding a few areas of trade and investment cooperation. This was the time when the Five-Year Plan was being finalised. As we returned from Delhi, there were headlines in a Dhaka newspaper reporting that the Bangladesh Planning Commission visited Delhi to seek blessings and approval of the Indian government on the Five-Year Plan.

[5] There was one slight distraction though. The Indian delegation had an impression that Bangladesh in those early days was greatly deficient, not only in administrative capacity but also in expertise in economic programming and planning. This led the economist member from India to suggest in good faith that the Indian Planning Commission would be glad to extend technical assistance in this field. The latter happened to be a very young but well regarded

The main emphasis in the meeting was, on the short term, urgent requirements of Bangladesh for the rehabilitation of its economy. During the period i.e. 1972-73, India provided generous assistance not only for the supply of food and consumer goods, but also for the repair and rehabilitation of transport and communications as well as for the supply of essential raw materials for industry. A much needed help was the supply of crude oil for the Bangladesh refinery, even though India herself was an importer of crude oil. India supplied civilian aircraft and ships. The most vital need for the new nation was the supply of food; Bangladesh was hit by two consecutive bad harvests in early 1972 as well as by the dislocation caused by war. India not only supplied 800,000 tons of food as outright grant but also helped in the transportation of food. Foodgrains supplied by India contributed 74 percent of all the food aid distributed in the first six months. Between December 1971 and June 1972, India supplied about US$200 million in grants and US$42 million in highly concessional loans for commodity imports and projects. It was only later that Indian assistance started to be on commercial terms. Between 1971 and 1974-75, India provided assistance to the tune of US$304.3 million, being the second largest among the donors, next to the United States (US$577 million). [6]

Attempts were made to formalise trade relations and to regulate smuggling. Geographic proximity and low cost of transport made it easier to establish trade relations, which were disrupted during the Pakistan years. On the other hand, Bangladesh suffered until recently from the domination of the Pakistani traders in her domestic and foreign trade. She was very sensitive and averse to the possibility of a highly visible or a prominent role of the Indian nationals in the field of trade. Therefore, it was decided that trade between two countries was to be conducted on a state-to-state basis. This was to preempt a role

economist with family roots in Bangladesh and was known to us. I had professionally interacted closely with many Indian economists, both in and outside the Indian government over many years. I thought it was presumptuous for the Indian economist to assume that we somehow lacked ability to perform our primary task and needed help. With a wounded ego, I was about to react rather harshly in a rebuttal when the Deputy Chairman, D.P. Dhar, the diplomat-negotiator, ever attentive to the sensitivity of the newly born nation, was too quick not to notice or anticipate my likely reaction. He stopped his member short in course of his remarks and changed immediately the subject of discussion.

[6] Rehman, *Ibid.*

for the Indian private traders, who were liable to exploit their monopoly position under conditions of acute scarcity. Moreover, Bangladesh had already decided through its policy of nationalisation that the State, not the private sector, would play the dominant role in industry and trade, foreign and domestic.[7]

The meeting in May 1973 between the two Planning Commissions in Dhaka identified a wide ranging agenda covering the programmes of economic cooperation between the two countries. The Indian delegation stated its basic objective as "the emergence of a viable, self reliant and prosperous Bangladesh economy. For this purpose, India was prepared to render such assistance as may be desired by the Bangladesh government subject to the constraints of her own economic capabilities." Prominent among the areas identified for assistance (grants or loans on variable terms) by India were as follows: reconstruction of railways, road repair and bridge building, power transmission and distribution as well as supply of clothing such as *sarees*, *lungi*, cotton cloth to relieve immediate and acute shortage.[8] Until Bangladesh was

---

[7] A high level Indian official, who was an economist and visited Bangladesh with the Indian Prime Minister in March 1972, made an interesting, friendly comment on Bangladesh's economic policy. He was not involved in any of the negotiations or discussions with Bangladesh on economic cooperation. In India, he was known not to be enthusiastic about the pursuit of the "socialist pattern of economy" and was very pragmatic in his policy recommendations. He wondered in a strictly private and informal conversation with me whether Bangladesh was not moving rather too fast towards a socialist economy. He was not at all happy with the results of socialist experiments in India with the state playing a leading role in terms of ownership and regulation of many economic activities. He pointed out the less than commendable performance of the Indian economy since independence. He thought it might be worthwhile to examine India's experience for possible lessons.

[8] An interesting episode occurred at this time regarding the import of clothing from India. It highlighted the perception that economic relations with India might sometimes turn out to be exploitative and to the disadvantage of Bangladesh. It was widely reported in the press that *sarees* imported from India were too short and were not customary or suitable for women in Bangladesh to wear, not to speak of its inferior quality. This, it was alleged, was an attempt on the part of the Indian traders to exploit Bangladesh through a fraudulent deal. In reality, these purchases were made by a team of the Bangladesh Trading Corporation i.e. a state agency, which visited India to ensure that items supplied by or under the auspices of their counterpart in India i.e. Indian State Trading Agency, met the specifications and requirements of the customers of Bangladesh. Also, the Bangladesh team was expected to ensure the required quality. Any mistake in the specification of appropriate size and quality could have been due to negligence or inefficiency on the part of the Bangladesh team.

Another interesting — I should say — an amusing incident occurred in connection with the decision to import uniforms or cloth for uniforms, required by the Bangladesh armed forces. If the purchase was to be made in the United Kingdom which was the armed forces' preferred source, the price would have been much higher than in India and could be procured

able to produce (or procure) sufficient quantities of raw cotton, the government of India agreed to export reasonable quantities of raw cotton to Bangladesh for meeting the urgent needs of the handloom weavers.

Two important areas for long term cooperation were agreed upon at the May 1973 meeting: first, establishment of joint industrial ventures; and second, cooperation in respect of flood control and irrigation. In respect of joint ventures, three projects were identified: a fertiliser plant in Bangladesh for export of its output to India on a long term basis; expansion of cement production in Bangladesh with limestones supplied by India; and gas-based production of sponge iron in Bangladesh using ore imported from India. Already during 1973, preliminary discussions had started on possible joint enterprises and the May 1973 meeting confirmed and provided the seal of approval to these projects so that joint feasibility studies could be carried out.

To promote cooperation in the area of flood control and irrigation, a Joint Rivers Commission (JRC) was established in 1972 in which the Planning Commission was represented. It was the responsibility of the two Planning Commissions to jointly review the progress of its work. The review in 1973 decided to urge the quick implementation of several short term and medium term measures. Also, JRC was requested to undertake special studies and surveys on the upper reaches of common rivers with a view to formulating a comprehensive basin development plan. JRC reached no agreement on the consequences of the completion of the *Farakka Barrage* in India and the related matter of sharing of the waters of the *Ganges* River.[9] Further work in finding a solution to the problem was to continue.

---

under the existing bilateral trade or loan agreements. The disagreement between the Finance and the Defense Ministries was so strong on this issue that General Osmani, who was Minister in charge of shipping, and not defense (defense portfolio was with the Prime Minister), but who considered himself a protector of the interests of the armed forces, raised the issue in the Cabinet. It was argued that cloth or uniform for the military, if procured from India, would be inferior to what the armed forces were used to wearing in the past. This would adversely affect their morale. That the Indian armed forces, in spite of wearing home-made uniform, were not known to have suffered from low morale or inferior performance, as Pakistan's armed forces could vouch did not win the argument. Eventually, a compromise was reached to split the purchases between India and overseas sources, depending upon the particular items of purchase and their relative quality.

[9] Joint Statement by the Indian and Bangladesh Planning Commission at the conclusion of the meeting, 21-25 May 1973, Bangladesh Planning Commission, Dhaka.

13.3 INDO-BANGLADESH JOINT VENTURES

The history of attempts to develop joint industrial ventures with India in the early years of Bangladesh illustrates how, given a determined leadership, backed by concerted professional work at technical and administrative levels, significant progress could be made within a short period of time. It also demonstrates how once the interest of the leadership waned and political relations started to cool off, economic cooperation stalled.

The two Commissions undertook to coordinate efforts, both technical and administrative, by the agencies/Ministries in the two countries, for detailed formulation of joint venture projects that were agreed upon during May 1973. On May 16, 1974, the Prime Ministers of both countries in their Joint Declaration supported these ongoing efforts and confirmed their decision to establish four joint ventures (expanding the original three mentioned above, by another) as follows:

> As a further step towards greater economic cooperation between the two countries, the two governments will establish the following four industrial projects based on the supply of raw materials and products from one country to the other with a guaranteed off-take of the exportable surplus of these projects on mutually acceptable terms and conditions: (a) cement plant at Chatak in Bangladesh based on limestone from Meghalaya in India; (b) a clinker plant in Meghalaya for supplying clinker to Bangladesh; (c) a fertiliser plant in Bangladesh for the supply of urea to India; and (d) a sponge iron plant in Bangladesh based on the supply of iron ore from India.[10]

Joint teams of experts from both countries continued their work throughout 1973-74 in preparing the feasibility studies relating to these projects. The work programmes of the study team were periodically reviewed and monitored by the two Planning Commissions. By the time of the meeting of the two Prime Ministers in mid-1974, the plans for the cement factory — work on which was started in 1973 — were finalised. The plant was to be owned by the government of Bangladesh with India providing credit to cover costs of goods and services, including limestone and other inputs. The amount of credit initially estimated at Rs. 50 million was revised upwards to Rs. 160 million.

---

[10]Minutes of Meetings of Planning Commissions on Joint Ventures, 1973-74.

India offered to convert her credit subsequently into equity ownership wholly or in part if Bangladesh so wished. However, regarding the supply of clinker on a long term basis to the cement plant in Bangladesh, it was decided to explore more favourable sources of supply in India other than Meghalaya. Investigation of the alternative sources within India was to be continued in the following months.

The sponge iron project was to be based on the long term supply of iron ore from India — one of the largest producers of iron ore in the world. This was to be utilised in the manufacture of sponge iron, using natural gas in Bangladesh. India would purchase the surplus sponge iron from Bangladesh under a long term contractual agreement. Bangladesh would hold equity ownership while credit from India would finance the supply of inputs and services. The export of surplus sponge iron from Bangladesh would substitute for scrap in India's mini-steel plants. The feasibility study was to be completed by December 1974.

Preparation of the feasibility study on the fertiliser plant progressed rapidly during 1974. It was the biggest joint venture under consideration. The entire output of the fertiliser plant was to be exported to India under a long term contract — at least for a period of 10 years, if not more. The government of Bangladesh was to hold 100 percent (with a contribution of about Rs. 980 million) of the equity with a credit from India varying between Rs 300 and 600 million (depending upon the final cost estimates and the contribution that India would make in terms of goods and services); the remainder (i.e. Rs. 1,100 million) was to be financed from third countries. The Indian contribution was intended to be paid back out of the proceeds of exports to India. The sales of fertiliser to India would be on the basis of international prices and be paid in foreign exchange when the repayment of the Indian credit was completed.

It should be observed that in respect of the two joint projects, even though there was the alternative of joint equity participation (usually the standard pattern for a joint venture), Bangladesh preferred exclusive equity ownership. Secondly, the proposed Indian credit for the fertiliser plant was much less than what was to be obtained from the third countries. This was mainly a reflection of India's limited capacity to provide finance and also suited the desire of Bangladesh to diversify, if possible, sources of investment.

By late 1974, the negotiations for the fertiliser project reached a very advanced stage. Specific details of the project were to be approved by the Bangladesh Cabinet before final project preparations, including engineering specifications, were to be undertaken. The Planning Commission, which was coordinating and monitoring the negotiations, sent the detailed proposals to the Minister of Industries for his approval and submission to the Cabinet. To my surprise, the project proposal was referred back to the Commission by the Minister of Industries with a confidential note, seeking my reaction to the comments by his own Secretary. The Secretary considered the joint venture in a very vital field such as fertiliser to be a very serious step, specially since it was based on the utilisation of a scarce natural resource of Bangladesh i.e. natural gas. Therefore, in his view the project required serious reexamination. He raised two questions. The first set of arguments was as follows: a long term binding contract for the supply of the entire output to India was undesirable since it deprived Bangladesh of the freedom to sell in alternative markets, including within Bangladesh to meet rising domestic requirements in the future. This objection was already considered carefully by the joint study teams in which the representatives of the Ministry and of the Sector Corporation in charge of the fertiliser industry were represented.

India was one of the two largest importers of fertiliser in the world, along with China, and was expected to increase her imports to meet rapidly rising demand. The proposed project would enable Bangladesh to obtain a foothold in this expanding market through an assured share. Second, at that time the oil producing countries were aggressively expanding their production of gas/oil-based petrochemical industries, including fertiliser. Their cost of production was likely to be lower and to obtain a market share they were willing to offer concessional price. Bangladesh as a new entrant was not likely to find a ready international market in competition with the other established and new suppliers in the world market. Therefore, the guaranteed market share, under the proposed project, was very important for Bangladesh. Third, Bangladesh had, at the time, a large adverse balance of trade with India. The export of fertiliser was an important way of partially redressing that balance. Fourth, in view of the projected expansion of fertiliser production in Bangladesh, in addition to the joint venture with India, there was no likelihood of shortage in the country that would require a diversion of sales from this venture. Moreover, if in the meantime projections of domestic demand were revised upward, Bangladesh would be able to expand production from the existing plants or through an expansion of their capacity or if need be, from new plants. Fifth, since the sale price to India was to be based on the international price of fertiliser, there was no possibility for Bangladesh sustaining a loss by not being able to sell to third countries in case such possibilities ever arose.

The second set of arguments advanced by the Secretary centred on political and strategic considerations. He speculated on the outcome of an interruption of supplies from Bangladesh due to labour indiscipline, political disturbances or violence, leading to disruption of production or of transportation/shipment to India. In such an eventuality, there was every possibility of tension or strain in relationship with India. Under the worst of circumstances, there was a risk of intervention by India to ensure supply from the jointly financed project.

The risk mentioned by the Secretary was highly exaggerated, if not disingenuous. India's imports of fertiliser from the proposed joint venture project would have been a small share of her total fertiliser imports from the rest of the world, and a much smaller proportion of her domestic supply. India's dependence on fertiliser export from Bangladesh would be too small, a far cry from being a vital lifeline for India to cause serious impact, if interruption of supplies was to occur. Moreover, as was customary in such bilateral supply arrangements, there would be a provision in the long term contract for unforeseen emergencies that might affect supplies. But the Secretary was apparently concerned that the written agreements could always be interpreted by a more powerful partner in its favour. There was an underlying lack of confidence about how India would behave and whether Bangladesh would be able to deal with such an eventuality. In any case, this argument basically belonged to the realm of political judgement and it was a matter for decision by the political leadership in the light of overall relationship with India. It was surprising that a political argument was raised by the Secretary, who had the responsibility for administrative and technical aspects of the project.

These arguments were gone through, *ad nauseum*, over the preceding negotiations. The Secretary was fully conversant with all the arguments and conclusions. While he was not a participant in the discussions and arguments and was not directly involved in the final recommendation in favour of the project, his officials and experts were involved all throughout. Yet he had kept his personal opinions and judgement to himself for so long and sprung it on his Minister at the last moment. It is remarkable that he decided to raise such basic objections only at the last stage when the main elements of the project were already incorporated in the joint declaration of the two Prime Ministers. In other words, he took it upon himself to question the wisdom of the decision of the highest political authority. The Secretary's arguments were also familiar to the Minister of Industries. The Planning Commission had intensively briefed him on them and he was a party to the decision by the Cabinet and by the Prime Minister. Even then the Minister was so concerned about the comments that rather than dealing directly with his Secretary, he wanted me, as the Deputy Chairman, to counter the arguments.

It was possible that the Minister was trying to play safe in the prevailing political climate in which the opponents of the government were spreading rumours about India's undue influence on Bangladesh and the government's inability or unwillingness to counter it. The Secretary's comments were in line with the viewpoints of the increasingly vocal opponents of the government. Most probably, the Minister did not want to be known as having ignored and overruled the concerns expressed by his Secretary. He did not want to be identified as an advocate of very close cooperation with India, even though in the Cabinet discussions he had enthusiastically supported the project. It was well known that the Planning Commission was driving the process of negotiations on joint ventures. Therefore, the Minister might have wanted the Commission and its Deputy Chairman to confront and deal with his Secretary.

Both myself and the member of the Commission responsible for the project were rather exasperated at the Minister's indecisiveness. Being in no mood to let him play safe, I suggested that if the Minister had reservations about the proposal, he should discuss them with the Prime Minister. There was no reason for sending the project proposal back to me for resolving the issues raised by his Secretary. The Minister had second thoughts and sent the project with his approval to the Prime Minister.

Negotiations with India and the work of the technical experts/ consultants on the elaboration of the joint projects were in varying stages of progress when there was a change in the government of Bangladesh through a military coup. Further progress on these projects stalled due to the changed environment in Indo-Bangladesh relations.

13.4 COOPERATION IN JUTE

Another area of economic cooperation with India during 1972-74 related to trade in raw jute and jute manufacturers in which both countries were partly complementary and partly competitive. During the period of stand-off between India and Pakistan, marked by· very limited cooperation in trade and economic matters, import of raw jute from Bangladesh was substituted by increased production in West Bengal. This was promoted by means of financial incentives/subsidies as well as by intensive research and development efforts for the improvement of productivity. The Indian jute manufactures were dominant in the export markets, but Pakistan, through export incentives, made substantial inroads.

As suggested by the joint study team appointed by both governments, the starting point of bilateral collaboration in the changed environment was to make joint efforts to hold and expand the world market for jute manufactures in the face of competition from synthetic substitutes, through an assured and stable supply of jute manufactures at competitive prices. A reduction in the cost of manufactures was linked to the availability of raw jute at low cost. Given its cost advantage, Bangladesh argued that the production of raw jute in West Bengal should be gradually reduced. Correspondingly, production in Bangladesh should be expanded to provide an assured supply of raw jute to India. At the same time, Bangladesh should strive to reduce the cost of raw jute production. The incentives structure (i.e. prices and subsidies) for raw jute and for jute manufactures should be modified in both countries to advance these shared objectives. For example, Bangladesh would withdraw export incentives designed to cut into the export market of India for jute manufactures. Given an appropriate exchange rate policy, at the margin Bangladesh was expected to gain more by expanding raw jute export to India than by exporting jute manufactures at steadily declining export prices in the world market. With rapidly increasing demand for jute manufactures in the domestic market of India, Bangladesh would have an assured, expanding market for raw jute. In view of her comparative advantage in the production of raw jute, increasing export would help offset Bangladesh's trade deficit with India. At the same time, such a mutually beneficial result would require Bangladesh to improve the efficiency of raw jute production.

The joint Indo-Bangladesh study team on jute emphasised two important measures in order that both countries could maximise their benefits from such a collaborative effort. First, Bangladesh should be able to supply raw jute to India at internationally competitive prices, in competition with the new producers of raw jute such as China, Thailand, and some African countries. Second, both countries would undertake not to further expand capacity in the production of jute manufactures beyond what was already in the pipeline. Any additional capacity should be linked to an increase in world demand; each country's share in the world market would depend on its ability to guarantee continuity and stability of supplies and low cost. There was also a possibility of two countries specialising in different categories of jute manufactures. To ensure stable and uninterrupted supplies in the world market, both countries should cooperate in the fulfilment of overseas contracts and in shipping; they should consider the possibility of buffer stocks to iron out fluctuations in export supply.

The study team recommended the establishment of an international jute body (i.e. *Jute International*) to promote overall world market demand for jute and jute goods, and to undertake cooperative efforts in technological research and sales promotion. It was considered advantageous to pursue such activities under the auspices of an international body rather than in a bilateral, cartel-like setting so as to avoid opposition from consuming countries as well as small producers. Further, India and Bangladesh were to explore the possibilities of establishing jute manufacturing industries abroad in the large consuming countries, based on the export of raw jute from Bangladesh and of jute manufacturing machinery from India.

I discussed the recommendations of the joint study team with the Indian Planning Minister in 1973. He was generally agreeable to the study team's recommendations and bilateral action in this regard. He was reluctant to support the establishment of the *Jute International* right at the initial stage of the Indo-Bangladesh cooperative activities. He wanted its establishment to be a gradual process while bilateral cooperation should be started forthwith. Other countries could be invited to join in stages. In the meantime, Nepal had agreed to become a full member and Thailand was willing to join initially as an observer, and full membership was to be considered later on. He, however, strongly supported that bilateral action should begin in right earnest, keeping in abeyance for the time being the idea of a broader membership. He felt that the task of readjustment of production of jute and jute goods in the two countries would be a complex and difficult enough exercise; there was no need to complicate it further with the involvement of third parties i.e. the broader membership of the *Jute International.*

I made an additional suggestion that the *Jute International* in its task of research, development and market promotion would benefit from the assistance of international agencies. The World Bank was willing to undertake a feasibility study of the proposed international organisation while other UN agencies had offered to provide technical assistance for the promotion of its activities. He disapproved of the external agencies participating in either the feasibility study or in its financing, even partially. He doubted their *bona fide* and competence in the matter and argued that the financial and technical resources of India and Bangladesh were quite adequate for the purpose. He stipulated that, "it is unsatisfactory to barter away the freedom of pursuing bilateral action in favour of aid from international agencies."[11]

Even though the Planning Commission was promoting and monitoring the progress of the work on bilateral collaboration in respect of jute, the detailed negotiations as a member of the study team were conducted by the responsible Ministry i.e. the Commerce Ministry. Subsequently, the negotiations for collaboration on jute were raised to a higher political level for follow up and implementation. The Commerce Ministers of both countries in May 1974 decided to

---

[11] Minutes of meeting with Mr. D.P. Dhar, Indian Planning Minister, September 29, 1973, Delhi.

establish a joint Ministerial Commission to review and recommend comprehensive measures for cooperation. The measures to be considered by the proposed Commission were to include the following: to export agreed quantities of raw jute from Bangladesh to India at mutually acceptable prices both on annual and long term basis; to determine whether incremental demand for raw jute in India could be procured from Bangladesh keeping in view their comparative costs and the corresponding production adjustment; to undertake cooperative efforts for reduction in the cost of production of raw jute and jute manufactures in both countries; to forecast world demand for jute manufactures in relation to their substitutes; to expand the production capacity of jute manufactures in both countries keeping in view the world demand; coordinated price policy for the export of jute manufactures; to make institutional arrangements for effective implementation of the coordinated jute policy; and to improve shipping facilities for exports.

The joint declaration was exhaustive in covering all the issues relating to trade and production of raw jute and jute manufactures. The political process for decision making on the complex and interrelated issues was set in motion. Some preliminary discussions were held in the succeeding months but the initiative lost its momentum, caught as it was like many other issues, in the vortex of political and economic changes that occurred in Bangladesh in 1975.

It was several years later in the 1980s that the United Nations Food and Agriculture Organisation (FAO), where I was the Assistant Director General and was in charge of international policies for major agricultural commodities, sponsored the establishment of International Jute Organisation (IJO). It was assigned broadly the same set of objectives and responsibilities as *Jute International*, but without any reference to any coordinated adjustment of production and exports in India and Bangladesh. The membership of IJO was to comprise the major producing and consuming countries; it was to be established with financial assistance from international institutions, including UNDP, FAO and bilateral donors. After a series of preparatory meetings and intensive lobbying with the FAO-member countries, FAO was able to sponsor the establishment of IJO in Dhaka. However, the organisation, established with so much effort, could not be ultimately sustained in the long run. This was the outcome, among other factors, of its lacklustre performance, absence of strong cooperation among the producing and consuming countries, and a decline in the interest of donors — all reinforcing each other. IJO was subsequently closed down in early 2002 and was substituted by some type of an intergovernmental committee on jute.

13.5 COOPERATION IN FLOOD CONTROL AND IRRIGATION

The rivers of India and Bangladesh criscross each other's territories. The upper reaches of most of the rivers lie in India. What happens to the river system in one-country, specially in India which is the upper riparian country, affects Bangladesh in respect of flood control, irrigation, and navigation. It was recognised early in 1972 that cooperation in the development of the *Ganges-Brahmaputra* and *Meghna* river basin would greatly benefit both countries. In 1972, they established Joint Rivers Commission (JRC) to undertake cooperative activities in respect of the common river systems. The areas of cooperation were to include river development, flood control and irrigation. The objective was to utilise water resources of the region on an equitable basis for mutual benefits.

The Planning Commission was not directly involved in JRC's work, except placing one of its experts as a JRC member. Detailed negotiations with India and the actual implementation of the programme of work were the responsibility of the Ministry of Irrigation and Flood Control. However, the Planning Commission had the responsibility to review its work as well as support and encourage its progress. Between early 1972 and mid-1973, there was not much progress; JRC only undertook an examination of the on-going and projected projects and programmes of each country in the border or nearby areas, with implications for both or either. It made suggestions for modifications in projects, wherever necessary, in order to enhance the beneficial impact of such projects. No exercise was undertaken on the long term and medium term planning for flood control and irrigation or for the long run development of the river basin. Nor any exercise was done to initiate or propose any preparatory work needed to identify joint projects.

The composition of JRC contributed much to its lack of progress. There were difficult and inconclusive negotiations on common rivers during the Pakistan days, specially on the *Farakka Barrage* in India which affected water supply in the Bangladesh rivers. A few Commission members from both countries were involved in those unsuccessful negotiations. They had both inherited the attitudes and the mindset of a period when the overall economic and political relationships between the two countries were marked by antagonism and adversarial confrontation. Their inherited baggage was not congenial to a fresh and cooperative approach in the new environment. The implications of the change in the political relations, however, did not adequately percolate to the technical experts. Secondly, the problem of the *Farakka Barrage so* dominated the atmosphere that discussions on additional flood control or irrigation projects were always held in the shadow of the unresolved issue of the *Barrage*.[12] Thirdly, the two Irrigation Ministers decided that the problem of the *Farakka Barrage*, almost completed and to be commissioned by 1974, would not fall within the competence of JRC.[13]

In May 1973, the two Planning Commissions discussed the slow progress of work of JRC and decided to provide a push. JRC was requested to undertake special studies and surveys in the upper reaches of common rivers. Along with a review of the planned projects for river control in both countries, the additional surveys and studies were to be so designed as to lay the foundations in the course of time for a comprehensive basin wide development plan. JRC was urged to

[12]The rapid and intensive expansion of irrigation, both surface and ground water, during the 1950s and 1960s along the upper reaches of the *Ganges* in Bihar and Uttar Pradesh in India, contributed to the reduction of water flow of the *Ganges* towards the *Hoogly* River and the *Kolkata* port. To offset the effect of such a reduction in water flow, India built the *Farakka Barrage* to regulate water flow to the Eastern part i.e. Bangladesh, in order to ensure adequate supply to the *Hoogly* River. Thus, the primary cause leading to the construction of the *Farakka Barrage* appeared to be a lack of coordination between the states of India where the upper riparian states obtained water supply without regard for long term consequences for water supply for irrigation, navigation, transportation or environment in the lower riparian Indian states as well as Bangladesh. Specially critical were the consequences for Bangladesh of the diversion of water supplies by the *Barrage* to meet the needs of the lower riparian Indian state during the low-flow winter season. Bangladesh being a lower riparian country was to be adversely affected if water was withdrawn by the *Barrage* during the lean season resulting in a decline in water flow to Bangladesh and the rivers in Bangladesh drying up.

[13]During 1972-73, the Bangladesh Minister in charge of Flood Control and Irrigation was Khandker Moshtaque Ahmed who could not, through negotiations with his Indian counterpart, reach an agreement on *Farakka*. The two Ministers agreed to put the issue outside the scope of the Joint Rivers Commission. Further, they decided that the matter should be resolved at the level of the Prime Ministers instead.

ensure a quick implementation of short and medium term measures for flood control and irrigation that were identified for joint action.

In September 1973, in a meeting with the Indian Planning Minister, I suggested that JRC's task should be expanded to explore seriously in right earnest — rather than in the distant future — the possibility of an integrated project approach to the development of water resources in the *Ganges-Brahmaputra-Meghna* river basin. Earlier in the year, the President of the World Bank had expressed a great deal of interest in (a) the provision of technical assistance for a feasibility study of such an integrated river basin development project, and (b) possible financial assistance by the Bank in the implementation of such a project. The Indian Planning Minister was agreeable to expand JRC's work in this respect, but he was opposed to technical assistance from the World Bank for any such project. He considered that the two countries were quite capable of undertaking the feasibility study for an integrated river basin development project. The question of possible sources of financing for the implementation of such a project should be kept open for the time being.

I was, however, convinced that Bangladesh did not have enough technical competence to participate in such a feasibility study and that external technical assistance was essential in order for Bangladesh to play an effective role in the study. Since JRC could not receive technical assistance without the concurrence of both countries, I urged on the Bangladesh Minister of Flood Control and Irrigation, directly responsible for JRC, to make best efforts to convince his Indian counterpart to agree to such a proposal. Bangladesh could not attach external experts/advisers to its team without causing a breakdown in JRC's work. There was no progress on this issue.

Thwarted in my efforts to provide technical assistance to JRC, I decided that it was necessary to strengthen the capacity of the Bangladesh experts so that they could effectively participate in JRC's deliberations if it was to be engaged in the development of a comprehensive plan for the river basin. This could be done independently and outside the purview of JRC. In this task, we sought the assistance of the World Bank. It was decided that a review should be undertaken to identify the steps needed to prepare a long term water resource development plan for Bangladesh and within the confines of Bangladesh.

An intensive, multidisciplinary review of the already available studies and plans relevant to the subject should be undertaken. It would draw upon a major study by the World Bank during the 1960s on the development of water resources in Bangladesh. Moreover, it would identify additional studies as well as surveys for the collection of data that might be necessary to prepare a long term development plan. The review would be done by an *ad hoc* group of Bangladeshi experts, with the assistance of external experts provided by the World Bank. The findings from such studies and plans within Bangladesh could be subsequently used by the Bangladesh experts in JRC, if and when the latter undertook to prepare a plan for integrated development of the river basin encompassing the territories of both countries. Accordingly, a team of experts in Bangladesh was appointed and it did identify, with some assistance from the World Bank, the studies and surveys to be undertaken in the first stage by Bangladesh.

A question may be raised as to why India was opposed to technical assistance from the World Bank to JRC for the feasibility study and was also lukewarm to the idea of eventual financing of a collaborative project by the Bank. Admittedly, difficult and hard bilateral negotiations involving adjustments and modifications of the individual country plans would be required, if an integral plan for the whole basin was to be prepared. Moreover, these questions would also be raised in the course of the preparation of the detailed feasibility study. It appeared that India did not want any external agency to be involved at that stage and, in fact, imputed that it might create misunderstanding or friction between the two parties. One could only speculate on the various reasons for India's reluctance. Clearly, it was a constant refrain in respect of the whole range of bilateral economic cooperation. As far as possible, India preferred not to have any assistance from or involvement of a third party.

One reason could be that India felt that major western countries, which dominated the international donor institutions, were generally unhappy with India during that period. India had flouted the wishes of one super power and its allies when she intervened in the Bangladesh war of independence. She had caused a shift in the balance of power in the subcontinent in her favour with the break-up and consequent weakening of Pakistan, a committed western ally. Therefore, in the aftermath of the 1971 war, India had formed an attitude of distrust and suspicion towards them. India might have thought, therefore, that the external donors would have some interest in creating suspicion and distrust or ill will between the two countries. It would be easy to exploit the grievances of the smaller country, real or imagined, to the disadvantage of India, the big neighbour.

Earlier, India had eagerly accepted the World Bank's assistance and intervention in the negotiations with Pakistan, an adversary, on the *Indus Replacement Works*. Furthermore, it had accepted that the Bank not only provided technical and financial assistance for the preparation of the Indus project but also coordinated a large volume of assistance from other donors for its implementation. To explain the change in her attitude between the two periods, one could hypothesise that during the 1950s and 1960s, India had a good relationship with the western countries. Except for her neutral stand in the Cold War tension between the Soviets Union and the United States, there was no major direct friction with India. Moreover, she was very popular in the development assistance community and was a very eager and significant recipient of assistance from the western donors. This was the period when the *Indus project* was negotiated and finalised.

More importantly, this project was successfully negotiated at a time when the bilateral relationship with Pakistan was adversarial and confrontational. There are two probable reasons. First, in the case of the *Indus Replacement Works*, both India and Pakistan would have suffered seriously in the absence of an agreement in the sharing of water, critical for agricultural development in both countries. The need for a settlement was very urgent and immediate. Second, the project, which was the essential component of the agreement, could not under any circumstances have been undertaken within the limits of the technical and financial competence of either India or of Pakistan.

The situation was not comparable to the case of India-Bangladesh cooperation with respect to the sharing of the waters of the *Ganges* or for that matter, jute. The absence of an agreement with Bangladesh did not involve heavy economic costs to India. Since 1947, India had proceeded to prepare her policies and projects on the assumption of noncooperation with Pakistan. Undoubtedly, now that a new chapter in the Indo-Bangladesh relationship had opened up, cooperative activities with Bangladesh would have brought additional advantages to India. But there was no sense of great urgency about it. India could wait and see how the overall relationship with Bangladesh, political, strategic and otherwise, developed over time.

Moreover, there was a matter of special concern for India at that time. India, at time, was involved in negotiations with Bangladesh on this issue with all the bargaining advantages of an upper riparian country. An involvement by an external agency in any joint water resource planning, impinging even indirectly on the *Farakka* issue, might dilute her bargaining advantage and add to whatever tension that was in any case bound to arise in the course of negotiations on the *Barrage*.

There was yet another issue pending settlement related to the *Farakka* issue, which related to the longer run perspective. Water supply available during lean season at the *Farakka Barrage* would never be adequate to meet future requirements of both countries. A long term solution would require an augmentation of the water flows in the *Ganges* during the lean season. This would require an agreement on the optimum way of augmenting water supplies by channelling waters from other rivers passing through both countries like *Brahmaputra* or from upper reaches of the *Ganges* in Nepal. India and Bangladesh had so far indicated different or divergent approaches not only in respect of the sources but also of the manner of augmentation of water supplies. The involvement of an external agency would have "muddied the waters," so to speak, from the point of view of India.

However, India was very agreeable that JRC should undertake the study of long term water resource development. Accordingly, in March 1974, JRC was asked to take up studies and investigation of the river basins of the *Ganges*, *Brahmaputra*, and *Meghna*. In addition to an analysis of the investigations and surveys already available, JRC was to undertake additional surveys in order to formulate a programme of water utilisation to optimise the benefits of irrigation, flood control, drainage, and navigation for both countries.

The two Prime Ministers reaffirmed in May 1974 that since the minimum flow of the *Ganges* would not be enough to meet the needs of both, water flow in the lean months needed to be augmented to meet their requirements. JRC was enjoined to study the best measures for augmenting the water flow and to make recommendations. At the same time, both governments agreed that before the *Farakka Barrage* was commissioned, they would arrive at a mutually acceptable sharing of water during the lean period when the water supply dropped to a low level. Such an agreement was reached in early 1975 on the sharing of water on an interim basis. The 1975 agreement went through a few extensions. The last agreement was reached in 1996.[14]

As difficult negotiations on the *Farakka Barrage* and discussions on the common water resources proceeded, there were the idealists in both countries who occasionally expressed private thoughts about their long term vision. They harboured a wild vision about an ideal solution to the problems of long run development of the common water resources. They asked whether it was possible to learn from the efforts that were being made for the integrated development of the Mekong Delta Basin in Southeast Asia or the Colombian Basin in Latin America?[15] Ideally, there should be an independent Authority comprising representatives of both countries, with adequate supporting staff and expertise, jurisdiction and financial resources, to prepare and to implement an unified river basin plan for the common water resources. This *authority* should also assist and coordinate the efforts

---

[14]Negotiations on the *Farakka Barrage* during the meeting of the two Prime Ministers were quite intensive and productive. It was the culmination of a series of negotiations at different levels, including at the level of the Ministers. The Bangladesh Minister involved in the negotiations from the beginning was Moshtaque Ahmed whose relationship with India dating from the days of the *government in exile* was strained. He was known as a hardliner on the issue of negotiations with India. He drew natural sympathy from the political groups opposed to co-operation with India. By the time of the Prime Minister's visit to India, he was relieved of the Ministry of Flood Control and Irrigation and was put in charge of the Ministry of Commerce. The new Minister of Flood Control and Irrigation was not, however, included in the Prime Minister's delegation. As a negotiator on the *Farakka Barrage*, it was believed that Moshtaque Ahmed wanted to create a posture in the public view as the valiant protector of and fighter for the interests of Bangladesh. His inclusion in the Prime Ministers' delegation for negotiation on the *Farakka*, in lieu of the new Minister in charge, could have been designed, as far as I could speculate, to ensure that he would be seen to be a party to whatever agreement was reached with India by the Prime Minister assisted by his technical team. This would pre-empt any possibility for him to distance himself from the agreement. Moreover, he would not have the courage to go public with his reservations, even if he had any, and challenge Sheikh Mujib. After all, no bilateral agreement was possible without concessions on both sides. This way, with Moshtaque's participation, it was not possible to argue that concession by one party (in this case, Bangladesh) was greater than India's and therefore, was a sacrifice of national interest.

[15]It is true that those projects and plans, though they made some progress, did not fulfil the high expectations they raised. Efforts are believed to be continuing towards the achievement of modest goals.

of member countries in drawing up their national components of a joint river basin development plan. Such a unified development plan could be, at the final stage, integrated with other projects in both countries not directly related to the common rivers. The *authority* could draw upon or negotiate whatever external technical and financial assistance it considered necessary for the implementation of such a project. As years went by, such dreams assumed the character of pipe dreams and were washed away in the whirlpool of multifaceted relationships between the two countries.

Part III
POSTSCRIPT: A VIEW FROM AFAR.

Chapter 14

SOJOURN ABROAD: NEW PERSPECTIVES

14.1 AT OXFORD

The three years that I spent in the government of Bangladesh were full of new insights and rich in experience. Nevertheless, I returned to academic life in Oxford in early 1975. From January 1975 to mid-1977, I was a Fellow at St. Anthony's College and Queen Elizabeth House at Oxford. I embraced this opportunity to refresh myself with the knowledge of the latest developments in economic thinking and research. While at Oxford, I completed two books drawing upon my experience: *Development Planning in Bangladesh* and *A Development Strategy of Bangladesh*.

This was the period when a rethinking was under way on the limits of state intervention in correcting market failures. A large number of empirical studies on the inefficiencies of the prevailing system of state control and regulation of trade, foreign exchange, and domestic investment in developing countries were coming to the fore. In the international arena, the most important issue concerned the equity of international economic relations and the distribution of gains and losses among developed and developing countries. There was a great deal of research and debates on the ways in which developing countries could enhance their gains from international trade and investment. Establishment of new international economic relations was the talk of the day, following the UN resolution on the New International Economic Order (NIEO). I participated in the ensuing discussion as a member of the Commonwealth Expert Group on the

New International Economic Order. Experts from both developed and developing country members of the Commonwealth constituted the Group. During this period, I was also a member of the UN Committee for Development Planning, debating and producing reports on the international economic development issues and policies for consideration by the UN General Assembly. The committee consisted of nongovernmental experts from both developed and developing countries, appointed by the UN Secretary General. It had the responsibility of determining which of the developing countries should be considered as the least developed on the basis of a set of agreed-upon criteria. Among other things, Bangladesh came to be included in the category of the Least Developed Countries (LDCs) during my tenure in the committee.[1]

When I left Dhaka for Oxford, my immediate plan was to be away for a year. I was uncertain about my plans beyond that period. I did not rule out my return to the country. But with the change in government and the dramatically altered political circumstances in the country from 1975 onwards, I was increasingly unsure of the desirability of my return to the country. A few of my friends and colleagues joined me at Oxford in late 1975. Several others who were associated with me in Bangladesh drifted away to various assignments abroad at different times following August 1975.

What would I do if I went back to Dhaka? Various thoughts crossed my mind. I would not have enjoyed teaching the traditional courses in economics, which were the standard fare in universities in Bangladesh. I felt that I had outgrown that stage in my academic career. The alternative was to go back to BIDS, where I still had my lien. To go back to BIDS raised different sets of considerations. After all, in many countries, professionals do go back and forth between academic life and political appointments in the government. Why should I have problems in a readjustment to my former career? However, the cultural and bureaucratic traditions in Bangladesh were different. In Bangladesh, a research institution like BIDS was not really autonomous, with the governing body chaired by a Minister of the government of the day, in which, in addition, officials played a

---

[1] The entire episode of the inclusion of Bangladesh in the category of the least developed countries is described in Appendix 14.1 of this chapter.

major role. Because of its dependence on the government of the day for budgetary resources on an annual basis, the head of the institute was obliged to cultivate and be in the good "books" of the government, so to speak. I was the Chairman of the BIDS Board during 1972-75. I felt it awkward to go back after a lapse of only two years, reversing my role and seeking help from and cultivating relationships with a set of new incumbents in the government.

14.2 AT UN/FAO

In any case, while I was debating these questions and was keeping my options open, the opportunity came up for a job as the Assistant Director General of the Economic and Social Policy Department in FAO. The job was challenging and interesting. I joined FAO in mid-1977. From being a Professor at Dhaka University, the Director of PIDE/BIDS, the Deputy Chairman of the Bangladesh Planning Commission, and then a Fellow at Oxford, I entered a new arena in a United Nations organisation. It was a very new world compared to what I had been involved in so far. The Economic and Social Policy Department of FAO, which I headed, undertook analytical studies on national and international food and agricultural policies, including nutrition, agricultural trade, price and subsidies, food aid, agrarian systems, and rural people's organisations. A number of intergovernmental committees on food security, food aid, and commodity trade provided opportunities for the exchange of ideas and experience among member countries as well as for reaching a consensus on policy issues, with a view to promoting world food security. The department was also involved in providing experts/consultants and training facilities to developing countries.

We had a number of technical assistance projects in Bangladesh, specially in the food and agriculture related ministries. A few studies on Bangladesh were undertaken in cooperation with BIDS. A fair number of my professional colleagues from Bangladesh served as consultants at FAO headquarters as well as in other developing countries.

Intergovernmental organisations are by their nature representative of the strengths and weaknesses of national governments. Bureaucratic tensions and coordination remain as much of a problem for them as for national governments. They are, in fact, run by people who have been involved in national governments and who carry over to the international organisations the same traditions, attitudes, and methods of work to which they have been used. Representatives of the various member governments constitute the intergovernmental committees that decide the rules and procedures of the UN agencies. In the light of these facts, it has always appeared to me strange that critics of the UN organisations, specially in the developed countries, expect them to be very different from national governments. This view is unrealistic and destined to create undue expectations that are likely to be frustrated. The decision making process in the international organisations suffers from an additional handicap. The Cabinet in a national government headed by a Prime Minister or a President exercises a degree of authority, coordination and leadership in the decision making process which does not exist in international organisations. The executive head of the latter does not have the same degree of constitutional authority or power as that of the head of a national government. In policy matters, it is the member countries which determine the agenda and take decisions. However, in administrative matters, the latter has a greater functional authority. The oversight function exercised on a regular basis by a national legislature cannot be performed by one or two meetings a year of a large number of governments with wide and diverse political and economic interests. Under the circumstances, the head of the organisation has a degree of leeway in internal administrative matters. The member countries can only counteract it by a degree of micro management, which is likely to be too complex to be operationally feasible.

FAO, like other UN agencies, has a large technical assistance pro- gramme. In many cases, it has an interest in launching and implementing a large programme. This is considered an evidence of its effectiveness and usefulness to the member countries in responding to their needs and requests. In the absence of well articulated and felt needs in many developing countries, it has often turned out to be the case of "supply creating its own demand." That is, countries basically respond to the offer of assistance from FAO. There is often no institutional arrangement in the developing countries for the use of assistance; suitable national counterparts are seldom in place to be trained and long term capacity building frequently does not take place. All this and more about technical assistance that is discussed in Chapter 17 a applicable, *mutatis mutandis*, to FAO.[2]

At FAO, I was involved in two international and two Bangladesh-oriented regional projects. These illustrate the possibilities and limits of a UN agency in raising consciousness about development issues and in stimulating action at national and regional levels. On an international level, the first priority task assigned to me was the organisation of World Conference on Agrarian Reform and Rural Development (WCARRD) in 1979. This was a wide-ranging conference to discuss national and international measures for achieving food security, promoting rural development, and reducing poverty and undernutrition. The concept of "agrarian reforms" in the conference had much wider connotations than is traditionally meant by land reforms or land redistribution. The assessment of alternative land tenure systems, ranging from communal landholdings to different forms of private ownership, including common property rights, and their impact on poverty, constituted the core of deliberations. Among the major issues debated at the conference were the access of small farmers to inputs, technology, credit, and markets as well as rural nonfarm employment and safety net measures for the rural poor.

The outcome of the conference was the adoption of a Declaration of Principles and a Programme of Action for Agrarian Reform and Rural Development. It was followed every two years by a review by FAO and member countries of the progress in the implementation of the agreed measures and in the achievement of the objectives. The process of preparation for the conference and the follow up reviews of its achievements greatly enhanced my knowledge and understanding of agricultural policy and rural development issues. As I look back on it, I feel this was a unique experience.

The conference was held in the aftermath of the ILO Employment Conference in the early 1970s in which the emphasis was on the fulfilment of basic needs for all as the primary objective of development strategy. Maximisation of income was dislodged from its place as the sole end of development. Questions were asked whether achieving

---

[2] In Chapter 17, experience of Bangladesh with technical assistance from FAO and IFPRI to the Ministries of Food and Agriculture is analysed.

growth was a sufficient condition for the satisfaction of basic needs. Was it not necessary to combine income redistribution with rural and agricultural growth and to promote public action to meet the needs of the poor that market would not provide? Coming in the wake of such rethinking in the development community, the Conference was an important occasion for debates on these and similar issues.

Several relatively new or inadequately appreciated issues came to the fore in the programme of action of the conference. First, the concept of poverty was broadened to include its multiple dimensions, moving away from the exclusive focus on income to such aspects as nutrition, health, and education. Second, the poor were no longer treated as a homogenous entity but as a differentiated class, among whom women constituted a disadvantaged group with special concerns and problems requiring special attention. The broad and wide ranging impact of women's advancement on socioeconomic development was recognised and policies were to be designed to promote their progress. Third, the concept of participation of the poor or the beneficiaries of rural development projects was a prominent issue of the day. The beneficiaries were to participate in the formulation, monitoring, and evaluation of development projects. Fourth, decentralisation of the decision making and implementation process was essential if the people were to participate in the process. For a rural development strategy to be effectively implemented and to yield the expected impact on growth and poverty alleviation, rural self-governing institutions, such as democratically elected local governments were to be established. Along with these, it was necessary to promote people's associations and organisations such as those of farmers and agricultural workers to facilitate their participation in the various aspects of the decision making process.

Admittedly, all these concepts and ideas were in their very early stages of analysis and empirical verification. They were just beginning to be recognised among the policymaking circles and were gradually and slowly aired in various international fora and conferences. WCARRD was one such occasion but not the only one. In subsequent years, these ideas have been refined, tested, empirically verified, further developed, and elaborated. Increasingly, these have become elements of mainstream development thinking, as finally reflected in the formal

Poverty Reduction Strategy Paper (PRSP) exercises currently under way in developing countries under the auspices of the Bretton Woods Institutions. A few elements of the follow up to the Conference are noteworthy.

The developing countries were to formulate national and rural development strategies in the light of guidelines provided by WCARRD. FAO and other multilateral and bilateral institutions — all of whom were party to the recommendations of the Conference — were to assist them in this task. Second, each country was to constitute a national committee to participate in and assist governments in the preparation of the strategy. Since rural development was a multisectoral activity, each government was to designate a lead ministry to coordinate the preparation of the strategy. This committee was to include, in addition to the various government ministries and agencies, other nongovernment institutions such as research groups and rural development specialists to assist and cooperate with the relevant ministries in the task. Third, the national committee was to monitor and periodically review the implementation of the strategy.

As a fourth measure, there was to be, at the regional level, similar review and appraisal of the national strategies where each country would present its national reports on the progress achieved and problems faced in course of implementation of the programme of action. This would occur in each of the regions as designated in the United Nations i.e. Africa, Asia and Pacific, Latin America and the Caribbean, etc. The countries would exchange experiences and were expected to learn from each other in the implementation of the strategy. These reviews were to take place every two years at the regional level. Fifth, there was to be periodic review at the world level at FAO where the secretariat would report on its own review and appraisal of the implementation of the programme, and at the same time the national governments would present their national implementation reports.

The above was indeed an impressive follow up arrangement. This was to avoid the past experiences of international/UN conferences, which produced agreed resolutions, declaration and proposals for action which would dissipate without follow up and implementation. By making detailed arrangements for follow up action, it was hoped that pressure would be kept alive at all levels — national, regional, and international — so that commitments made would not be forgotten. Regional and international review and appraisal were expected to exercise peer pressure on countries. There was no sanction on countries for their nonimplementation of commitments made in international fora, except moral suasion and peer pressure. As history and my experience with this and other conferences demonstrate, these two factors work, if at all, very slowly and very inadequately. But arguably, the growing strength of civil society organisations constitutes an additional instrument or weapon for advocacy in an uphill struggle for generating pressure for change in policies and actions in respective countries.

We, in FAO, spent a considerable amount of time in the follow up activities. We persuaded and assisted member states in formulating their national programme of action. We stimulated the formation of national WCARRD committees. In some instances, we sent consultants to assist in the preparation of national strategies. We assisted governments in preparing the review and appraisal papers and participated in their national review meetings. We had to secure extra budgetary resources for such technical assistance from a few enthusiastic donors and, through the exercise of peer pressure from some other reluctant donors. Over the years, the enthusiasm of members waned and issues other than WCARRD follow up came to dominate the subsequent agenda.[3] There was no strong and lasting commitment on the part of the countries to embark seriously on the formulation of rural development strategy following the guidelines laid down by WCARRD.

The WCARRD strategy formulation is, in some respects, comparable to the ongoing exercise on PRSPs under the auspices of the World Bank. The PRSP process encompasses the economy as a whole and is not limited to one sector such as the agricultural and rural sector as was the case with the WCARRD strategy. But countries themselves initiated neither of them. They were both prodded and stimulated by the international community. Secondly, PRSP is intended to be a much more inclusive exercise involving consultations with the widest possible

---

[3] Food emergencies and the ways to prevent and to combat them, once they occurred, became the focus of attention and action. This was greatly spurred by the food crisis in Africa and famines in countries like Ethiopia. FAO launched a major study on the food and agricultural problems of Africa and formulated a programme of action to meet them.

spectrum of public opinion at al levels all over the country. The WCARRD exercise was more exclusive. It was basically a document produced by the government with some consultation with the national advisory committee. The large scale participation of NGOs and civil society organisations that is expected — at least in theory — to be a part of the preparation of PRSP, was not required for the formulation of the country strategy or a follow up of WCARRD. In any case, civil society organisations did not occupy then such an important place in polity and society as they do today. Third, the most fundamental difference is that PRSP is used by donors as a basis of, or a framework for the provision of development assistance. The WCARRD document was not directly related to dialogue with donors or the provision of external assistance. The developing countries have more of an incentive to engage in the PRSP exercise than they had for the WCARRD follow up. Even then, PRSP is not born out of a felt need on the part of a country; it is mainly viewed as a necessary instrument for the negotiation of assistance.[4]

A question has often been asked about the cost and benefit of conferences and meetings held in the UN fora where endless discussions and debates on national and international issues are held and various consensus, agreements are reached. UN organisations, unlike the Bretton Woods Institutions, are not financing entities and hence have no authority or the sanctioning power available to a financier. However, they serve two important purposes. They facilitate an exchange of views on international issues of common concern, specially between the rich and poor nations. Each group of countries is exposed to the concerns and interests of the other group without the pressure to negotiate and reach an agreement as happens in a negotiating forum, such as the WTO or environmental conventions. In the endless drafting sessions on the various nonbinding resolutions incorporating exhortations, there is an intense exchange of views. There is no other forum in which the governments of all groups of countries could hear each other out on important issues of national and international concern. For developing country officials and policymakers, this is a unique opportunity and an educative experience. Second, this also constitutes a forum for the exchange of experience among countries on various

---

[4] For detailed discussion on PRSP, see Chapter 16.

aspects of national policies. FAO and other UN agencies frequently produce documents and reports analysing experience on important policy issues around a wide range of countries and seek to derive lessons from them.

The second project in which I was involved at FAO was a research and analytical study on the future state of world agriculture and food security in the year 2000. The study I was enjoined to undertake in the mid-1980s was called *Agriculture: Towards 2000*. Ten years had already elapsed after the world food crisis and the World Food Conference of the early 1970s. Most of the targets and action programmes, solemnly agreed to by the international community at the conference, were far from achieved or implemented. Meanwhile, several studies, following the pioneering study by the Club of Rome, on the limits of growth set by technology and scarcity of resources, raised concerns that the food needs of an expanding world population would not be adequately met by prospective increases in food production. Two issues were emphasised: one, the rapidly increasing population in the developing countries; second, the degradation of the environment and depletion of agricultural resources caused by intensive and extensive cultivation on the basis of existing and known technology.

This study was coordinated by my office; it drew upon inhouse expertise and also relied on the help of a core group of external specialists and modelling experts. The study analysed the supply and demand prospects of agricultural commodities in various regions of the world; it examined the impact of income and population growth on demand as well as that of resource constraints (land, water, and labour) and technological progress on supply. FAO had a comparative advantage in the assessment of technological prospects. It had a large number of agricultural specialists who had the requisite knowledge and practical experience related to the application of technology in farmer's fields. The study also assessed the evolving pattern of poverty and undernutrition in the developing world and measures to combat it. Among the country studies undertaken to supplement the global and regional studies, there was one on the supply and demand prospects for food in Bangladesh.

What was the objective of this study? First, it was expected to stimulate international and national measures in support of increase in agricultural research expenditures at the national and international levels. Investment in water resource development and the production and supply of agricultural inputs also had to be greatly increased. Second, incentives and institutions for agricultural development had to be strengthened. These were not earthshaking conclusions. But they were intended to remind policymakers, convince them, and stimulate them to action by providing them with new evidence of success and failures in the development of the food and agriculture sector. Also, it was to demonstrate how inadequate was the rate of investment in the sector as compared to what was required to meet future world food needs. It indicated that for individual countries to formulate long term agricultural development programmes, it was necessary to take into account future prospects in world markets of supplies and prices of commodities of interest to their agricultural economy.

The two important projects for the Asian region that occupied a great deal of my attention were: the International Jute Organisation (IJO) and the establishment of the Centre for Integrated Rural Development for Asia and the Pacific (CIRDAP). Both projects required consensus building among the member countries, developed and developing, first, on the need for such institutions; and second, on the provision of financial and technical assistance.

Our efforts for the establishment of the International Jute Organisation (IJO) to promote research and development on raw jute and jute manufactures are partly described in Chapter 13. It was to be a cooperative effort by consumers and producers and not a producers' cartel. To secure the cooperation of the consuming countries, specially the EU, required considerable persuasion. The second issue related to its location and to the nationality of the head of the organisation. The member countries had to be persuaded that to locate it in Bangladesh, the largest producer of raw jute, was justified. Bangladesh as a host country was willing to provide physical facilities. At the same time, the government wanted a Bangladeshi official to head the organisation as well.

In my view, Bangladesh was unreasonable in wanting the location of IJO as well as its directorship. We, at FAO, thought that this would create a situation whereby countries would cooperate less than enthusiastically in its effective operation. Our preference was for someone from one of the consumer countries in the developed world. The developed countries were to be the main source of technical and financial assistance, and it was important that they should acquire a stake in the organisation. Eventually, however, we went along and pleaded with other countries to accede to the request of Bangladesh. Bangladesh mounted a vigorous campaign for mobilising support and succeeded in selecting a Bangladeshi as the first Director.

CIRDAP was intended as a regional organisation for Asia; hence, no developed country except Japan was involved. FAO Regional Conference in Asia in the early 1980s, as a follow up to WCARRD, urged FAO to help establish it. CIRDAP was to undertake research and studies on the analytical and methodological aspects of rural development strategies. It was to promote national institutions to undertake cooperative studies, implement pilot programmes at the country level, and help formulate national strategies as well as organise the exchange of experience among member countries. The location of CIRDAP in Bangladesh was advocated by the government and FAO on the ground that it had wide ranging experience in rural development institutions, such as the Comilla Academy for Rural Development. Moreover, as one of the poorest countries in the region with a very large rural sector, Bangladesh was in paramount need of a well designed rural development strategy. Once its location in Bangladesh was accepted, the government of Bangladesh strongly wished that the head of CIRDAP should be from Bangladesh. Again, by a process of intensive canvassing and campaigning undertaken jointly by the government and FAO, countries in the region agreed to have a Director from Bangladesh. FAO had a very crucial role and interest in CIRDAP; it had to provide resources in the initial stage for its operation and convince the donors to provide financial resources on a sustained basis. The government of Bangladesh made a generous contribution not only for its physical facilities but also for its operating expenses. This strengthened her case for its location and directorship. Bangladesh held the post for several years. Unlike IJO, CIRDAP was able to survive well, drawing upon the support of member countries and donors.[5]

---

[5] These two instances illustrate how the process of establishing regional or international institutions is seldom determined solely by the merits of their case. Political considerations,

After 10 years at FAO, the challenge of the assignment wore out. A large part of the work became repetitious; it was a matter of consolidation rather than exploration of new issues. More importantly, the administrative responsibility for a large staff was very heavy. Management of the intergovernmental committees with meetings throughout the year and endless sessions often until midnight were exhausting. These meetings were not very stimulating as we spent hours in negotiating resolutions, which I eventually realised, were seldom pursued or implemented even though they did serve a useful educative role for the officials from the developing countries. My interest in the system had reached the stage of diminishing returns. There was not much of a challenge any more to my negotiating or expository skill, enmeshed increasingly as I was, in managing the "store." By the end of 10 years, I yearned for something less hectic and less physically demanding. I wanted to go back to a more sedate life where I could pursue my own research interests. I wanted to go back to a life of academic and research pursuits. Accordingly, I moved to IFPRI in 1987.

At IFPRI, my major research interests covered mainly two broad areas: international trade and food security, and domestic food security policies. The impact of multilateral trade liberalisation on the food security of developing countries engaged my interest. Among my research publications were some on nontraditional agricultural exports and intradeveloping country trade. On national measures for food security, I worked on domestic food price stabilisation policies, nonfarm rural employment, and microcredit and safety net measures for the rural poor. I was involved in a number of research projects on

---

both intracountry and intercountry, play an important role. In these particular instances, canvassing for the support of other member countries and negotiating with them on the basis of a *quid pro quo* were some of the elements in the process. To have a national of Bangladesh in an important decision making position in order to lobby for his country certainly helps. Strong support by the Bangladesh government delegates to the head of FAO in his administrative or political manoeuvers with member countries, in return for his support for the appointment of a Bangladeshi Director, added up to the arsenal of bargaining. It was no less important who was the Minister or the Secretary at that time and how close was his relationship with the head of the government to ensure the provision of generous physical facilities and financial contributions for the regional centres. In both the cases, it was either the Minister or the Secretary who ended up being the head of the centre. It was, therefore, a combination of factors — some fortuitous and unforeseen — that produced the intended result.

food policies in Bangladesh. IFPRI had maintained a local office in Dhaka manned by expatriate and local researchers. While at IFPRI, I continued with my research work and publications before I retired in early 1994.

As I come to the conclusion of my reflections on my experience in Bangladesh and abroad, I felt that I should venture into discussions of a few current problems facing Bangladesh. I make such an attempt in the following chapters. There are several important policy issues that I could discuss. I have chosen those issues which, on the basis of my experience depicted in earlier chapters, seem relevant to the present and to the future of Bangladesh in the light of unfolding circumstances. It was Keynes who said that an economist must "study the present in the light of the past for the purposes of the future."

Successful policymaking as well as its quality and content depends not only on the competence of policymakers but also equally, if not more, on enabling institutions that facilitate the formulation, scrutiny, and coordination of diverse policies. Furthermore, it depends on the ways in which programmes linked to policies are evaluated and monitored. In the early days, Bangladesh tried to build a institution of planning and policymaking. When its role and influence waned in a few years, no substitute institution replaced it to perform essential policy analysis and coordination functions. The baby was thrown out with the bath water. After more than two decades, it is all the more clear how important is the need for such a mechanism or institution. My reflections on this subject are provided in Chapter 15.

Bangladesh has embarked on a policy of market liberalisation and privatisation, and integration with the world economy. While attempting to combine incentives with appropriate regulation to govern the market and compensate for its limitations, Bangladesh is also going through a process of democratic transition with severe teething problems. Managing the process of liberalisation in two spheres has posed the challenge of governance, which so far has escaped an effective response. Chapter 16 contains my observations on the unfolding process and its ramifications. An important issue related to the international integration of Bangladesh is the management of development assistance. Bangladesh has a long history of aid relations. The aid strategy of donors has evolved over the years and donors are now heavily involved in domestic policy reforms. New ways of dealing with old and emerging problems in the realm of development assistance are needed. I had to deal with foreign aid in different capacities at home and abroad at different times from both the receiving and giving ends. In this light, I find that donors and Bangladesh are suffering from "aid fatigue" from their respective viewpoints. But they are also caught in an uneasy but inseparable embrace. A few comments on the aid dialogue and relations are offered in Chapter 17. In Bangladesh's regional economic relations, because of the unalterable facts of geography, India looms very large. The issue of a harmonious and cooperative Indo-Bangladesh relationship will always remain with us. I concentrate only on selected economic aspects of this wider relationship in Chapter 18.

Appendix 14.1

Bangladesh — A Least Developed Country

The Committee for Development Planning (CDP), now rechristened as the Committee for Development Policy, consists of independent, nongovernmental experts, mostly economists, nominated by the Secretary General of the United Nations. It has the responsibility to deliberate on and analyse development issues and problems of the world and submit a report once a year to UN Economic and Social Council (ECOSOC). It draws attention to the important current issues in the world economy and recommends action by national governments and the international community.

In addition, it has a specific obligation to determine the criteria for defining the least developed among the developing countries; and secondly, to identify the countries which should be included in this special category. The basic idea is to identify countries in the developing world, which suffer from special handicaps and obstacles in the way of achieving economic growth and, therefore, need special measures of assistance from the developed countries and international community.

It was, in 1971, that ECOSOC decided for the first time to designate a special group of poor countries in the context of the formulation of the International Development Strategy. It requested the committee to undertake this task. The CDP was given this responsibility because of its strictly, nonpolitical independent status. ECOSOC does not want to overrule or act contrary to its recommendation. Under exceptional circumstances, ECOSOC has sometimes requested CDP to review its recommendations in the light of additional considerations or particularly adverse circumstances facing a country. CDP so far has strictly adhered to its impartial character. ECOSOC realises that, once it overrules CDP, it would open the floodgate for political manoeuvering.

After all, ECOSOC is an intergovernmental political body. Therefore, the best policy for them has been to accept the recommendation of CDP and to take shelter under the cover of its technical and professional integrity.

CDP decided in 1971 that the Least Developed Countries (LDCs) were to be defined as those low-income countries that suffered from long term handicaps to growth, in particular low levels of human resource development and/or severe structural weakness. Three criteria were selected to define the category of least developed countries. They were: per capita income and share of manufacturing in total output and literacy ratio. The developing countries were ranked in order from the highest to lowest values in respect of each of the three criteria and the threshold value for each of the criteria, usually relating to the lowest 20% to 25% of the countries in ranking order, was decided. Countries falling below the threshold values in respect of each of the three criteria were defined as the LDCs.

As of 1971, twenty-five countries were included in this category of which eighteen were from Africa, four from Asia (Bhutan, Afghanistan, Sikkim, and Nepal), one from the Pacific, one from the Caribbean, and one from Near East. After every few years CDP reviewed whether new countries would qualify to be included and whether any one from the existing members needed to be graduated out of this category. A review was undertaken in 1975. Among the twenty-four members of CDP in 1975 were John P. Lewis, I.M.D. Little, Jean Ripert, Janos Kornai, H.C. Bos, Saburo Okita, Ester Boserup, Widjojo Nitisastro, J.H. Mensah, H.M.A. Onitiri, K.N. Raj, Leopoldo Solis, Alister McIntrye, and myself.[6]

In that year, the Committee took up the question of the possible inclusion of Bangladesh in the list. Bangladesh met all the three criteria and, therefore, on the basis of strict, mechanical application of the criteria she was to be considered eligible for inclusion. The Committee, however, was required to exercise judgement while applying the criteria. In general, it was to examine closely the various constraints to development and the extent to which in specific cases obstacles to their growth prospects were aggravated or partially relieved by other factors. Two additional factors made such a wider examination and

---

[6] UN Report of the Committee for Development Planning, 1971 and 1975.

exercise of judgement necessary in specific cases. First, data on the various variables bearing on the criteria relating to many of these countries were not very reliable. Frequently best guesses had to be made. Secondly, judgement and guess estimates were specially necessary when countries were on the borderline.

Implicit in much of the discussion was the notion that the classification was meant to designate countries of small size. In 1975, all the member countries in the group were small countries. Nineteen of the twenty-five countries had population size below 10 million and six had below 20 million. Three other countries that were found to satisfy the three criteria and were qualified along with Bangladesh to be included in the list had each very small population i.e. below 2 million.

Bangladesh in the mid-1970s had a population of the size of about 78 million i.e. several times larger than most of the members of the group. Her potentials for future growth were considered to be better than most of the other members. A big country had advantages, which tended to offset the disabilities indicated by the three criteria. For one thing, its large market size provided the scope of economies of scale, division of labour, and opportunities of specialisation. Similarly, a large, densely populated country had the added advantage of providing low cost of physical infrastructure per head of the population. Also, it was argued that with her huge population, presence of Bangladesh in the group would be incongruent and she would be out of their league. Moreover, in any negotiations with the developed world, Bangladesh and her concerns were likely to dominate the negotiating agenda or strategy vis-à-vis the developed countries. What was more relevant was that the developed countries while considering concessions in trade or aid to the LDCs would be constrained by the big size of Bangladesh. The impact of trade preferences, for example, granted to the rest of the LDCs, on the import trade or the domestic economy of the preference giving country would not be very significant. But it was likely to be large in the case of Bangladesh because in absolute volume the export of Bangladesh would be larger than most of the LDCs or even a combination of them. After all, such concessions had to be extracted from not so generous or willing developed donor countries. Similarly, the cost to the developed countries from the grant of greater aid concessionality to the rest of the LDCs would be small in absolute amount but it would be large if Bangladesh was also to receive such concessions.[7]

Most of the CDP members opposed the inclusion of Bangladesh. The rest were non-committal or neutral. I was the only one to disagree. It turned out to be a debate between me and those who opposed. My arguments were twofold. First, there was no explicit recognition of size in all the discussions that took place since 1971 in CDP and in ECOSOC about the criteria and various supplementary considerations for defining the status of a least developed country. Unlike the other criteria, the influence of size on development potential of a country was not easy to determine. Not much analytical and particularly, empirical verification of this problem were available. The Committee would be required to undertake the necessary research and empirical work on the subject before it could take a decision on the subject. By proposing to introduce size as a main criterion to exclude Bangladesh, the Committee was exceeding the authority given to it by ECOSOC. This was specially so because Bangladesh met all the criteria fully and she was much below the threshold values. She was not a border line case. The Committee did not have the authority to change the criteria at its discretion and on an *ad hoc* basis. As it stood in 1975, CDP was asked to apply the existing criteria and identify the eligible countries. If it wanted to expand or modify the criteria, it should seek the approval of ECOSOC. It had to convene a session to reconsider and decide on the additional criteria. All the economic and practical

---

[7] In fact, many years later during the mid-1990s when the liberalisation of restrictions on exports of garments and related textiles was seriously considered by the developed countries, this issue became relevant for them. For many of them, Bangladesh was a major supplier in their domestic market so that the relaxation of restrictions on her exports would have a significant impact on their domestic industry. The rest of the LDCs were very minor exporters and their capacity to supply the export market was limited. Therefore, the impact on the domestic competing industry in the developed countries would be limited. In fact, in 1997, when I was for the second time a member of CDP and its Chairman for the term 1996-98, the Committee discussed the nature and extent of special measures that the developed countries had so far taken in favour of the LDCs. The UNCTAD secretariat which was reporting on the subject referred to this issue verbally when pressed by the members to know why the developed countries were dragging their feet in spite of the repeated commitments they made not only at the Paris conference on the least developed countries but also during the WTO negotiations. The same was true for the United States, which had liberalised garments virtually from all the least developed countries under a different trade initiative i.e. for Africa and the Caribbean. EU eventually extended unrestricted access to its market for all the exports from the LDCs under the "All but Arms" trade initiative.

considerations, raised by the other members, against the inclusion of Bangladesh had to be taken up for extensive debates in a separate session of the Committee.

Even if GDP wanted to consider size as a criterion, the difficult question would have been how to decide the cut-off point for the appropriate size above which a country should be ineligible for inclusion in the list of LDCs. It was thus confronted with a legal and procedural question, which it could not possibly resolve without considering the matter in a separate meeting. But I was also raising an analytical argument, which they could not brush aside without further thought on and discussion about the pros and cons of country size as a criterion.

Second, apart from the fact that Bangladesh fully satisfied currently accepted criteria for LDCs, there were additional constraints on Bangladesh's development, which should receive serious consideration. From the vantage point of the 1970s, there were two specific, widely recognised adverse or unfavourable factors inhibiting Bangladesh's development. One, floods frequently afflicted Bangladesh resulting in considerable losses in assets, lives, and crops, and long term debilitating effects on health of the poor through waterborne and other diseases as well as fall in food consumption. Moreover, the spread of high yielding technology in agriculture had been severely restricted in the flood-prone areas. This hindered efforts to significantly increase food production to meet the needs of an increasing population. The second constraint was the heavy pressure of population. While a very small size of population limited the size of market, for Bangladesh, which had among the poor countries probably the highest density of population, its size was a significant negative factor. The demand for aggregate current consumption needs both for public services and private consumption was so high that it left very little surplus for capital accumulation and income growth. It would take time to bring down its high population growth rate. Until then Bangladesh would continue to suffer from severe constraints on per capita income growth.

After a long discussion, the opposition group gave up and agreed to include Bangladesh. I was able to win the argument single handedly, primarily because I was dealing with a group of highly sophisticated independent professional economists with no agenda and no political interests. We had a great deal of respect for each other and they had an open mind and were amenable to analytical arguments. Secondly, it was an established tradition of CDP that decisions were taken by consensus and not by majority votes. If one individual member felt very strongly and he could not be persuaded by professional arguments to accept the view of the rest, the majority would not overrule him. Those were the early days for CDP, which was established in the 1960s under the inspiration of that great internationalist among the economists i.e. J. Tinbergen, not yet the Nobel Laureate. Since there was no consensus, the committee had to accept my argument and agree to include Bangladesh. The tradition of decision by consensus continues till today.

The Committee did not feel comfortable about the conclusion of the debate that I had forced on them. However, its membership changed every three years. Even then not all the members are replaced every three year. Only a certain number is replaced in order to maintain continuity. I had left the Committee when I joined FAO. I was no longer an independent expert. Periodically, the Committee was asked to review the methodology and the criteria for defining the LDCs as well as to recommend whether, in the light of change in circumstances, new countries became eligible. It was also to examine whether anyone of the existing members was to be graduated from the list due to improvement in socio-economic circumstances.

By the late 1980s, the Committee, after considering various factors, decided and ECOSOC agreed that not only in the border-line cases as was customary hitherto but also in general, it should be "flexible and pragmatic" in deciding on the list of LDCs. For example, a set of countries could be geographically isolated, being islands or landlocked or could be subject to frequent climatic disasters. Also, the small size of a country did create special set of disadvantages for a poor country. In 1991, it decided that population size should be taken into account explicitly and countries with a population of larger than 75 million should not be considered for inclusion in the list. It so happened that in 1975 Bangladesh were already bigger than the stipulated minimum. By this criterion, Bangladesh would not have ever qualified. By 1991, she had a population of a size of 110 million or more. Since Bangladesh was already included in the list before the new criterion was added, it was decided to put her under the "grandfather" clause and thus was exempted from the axe. Bangladesh "happily" went on enjoying the status of the least developed country.

The diplomats at the Bangladesh UN Mission in 1975 were aware of the debate in the Committee. They were anxious that Bangladesh might not qualify for inclusion. They had no way to intervene or to resort to any lobbying. The Committee was not amenable to such approaches. It all depended on twenty-five argumentative professionals who prided themselves on their independence. I did not discuss with them the details of the debates. A few of them who eventually came to know the details were relieved and had a few words of appreciation for my efforts.

It was a sheer accident that due to my persistence and the Committe's tradition of decisions by consensus, Bangladesh became a least developed country. This was for the first time and probably the last time that this type of incident ever took place in the history of CDP. I am indulging in this self promotion because I never achieved single handedly anything like this in all my meandering around Bangladesh and the world in multiple jobs.

I am not sure, as I look back on it at this distance of time, whether I did the right thing for Bangladesh. I wonder whether this status has not aggravated the propensity of Bangladesh to engage in aggressive pursuit of special treatment in external economic relations and foreign assistance. In other words, Bangladesh believes — and it has coloured all her external negotiations — that as a poor country she not only has a claim on the generosity and charity of donors but, as the poorest of them, has, in fact, a prior claim. It is as if among the supplicants standing in the receiving line for assistance she has a right to be at the front of the line, be that for a large amount of aid or for the most concessional terms of aid.

Did it encourage a certain amount of complacency about national shortcomings? Did such a frame of mind detract from vigorous domestic efforts to improve economic performance and was it a detriment to progress? After all, given that some development assistance would always be there, Bangladesh by pleading dire poverty would always end up getting a reasonable share. Is this kind of psychology or dependence syndrome honourable for a nation? I often wondered and still do not know the right answer. Was the Finance Minister of Bangladesh giving vent to this tension that might exist in the mind of the policymakers when in early 2002 he exclaimed in public that he did not want Bangladesh anymore to be in the front line of the poorest countries pleading for help from the rich nations?

In a perverse sense, Bangladesh could even be proud of her status. Being the biggest LDC, she could take the leadership role for the group in international organisations. This gives her a prominent role to play in a particular segment of international conferences and negotiations under the UN system. Bangladesh delegations and diplomats have a degree of visibility in the international development fora, which otherwise would not have been available.

In 1991, the three criteria for the identification of the least developed countries were refined in the light of further study and analysis and availability of additional data. The refined criteria were: per capita income, Augmented Physical Quality of Life Index (APQLI), and Economic Diversification Index (EDI). APQLI was a composite index consisting of life expectancy, per capita calorie consumption, primary and secondary school enrolment, and adult literacy. EDI was a combined index comprising share of manufacturing in GDP, share of labour in industry, per capita electricity consumption and export concentration ratio. Bangladesh continued to meet the newly formulated criteria. In 1997, for per capita income, she was below one-third, for APQLI below fourth-fifth, and for EDI slightly below the threshold values of the three criteria, respectively. In order to graduate out of the list, she had to be above the threshold values of at least two criteria.[8]

Every few years in the light of new knowledge and advances in development thinking and in empirical research, CDP had been engaged at the request of ECOSOC to refine and improve the criteria so that they reflect more accurately the constraints facing the poorest countries. For example, there had been considerable discussion as to whether the relative risks posed to a country's development by exogenous shocks were to be considered an important factor in determining the least developed status of a country. The relative risks

---

[8] Committee for Development Planning, 1997, 2000, and 2001.

or vulnerability to shocks depended not only on the magnitude of shocks but also on the structural characteristics of a country. Two kinds of shocks had been considered: weather related shocks were reflected in the instability of agricultural production; external shocks were to be indicated by instability of exports of goods and services and export concentration ratio. Structural characteristics that determined the severity of exposure of a country to shocks were considered to be the share of manufacturing and services in GDP and population. These five characteristics were combined into what was called Vulnerability Index. The diversification index used earlier had been partly subsumed under the new index, Economic Vulnerability Index (EVI). There had been some modifications in the components of the APQLI index. Per capita calorie consumption had been replaced by per capita calorie consumption as a proportion of per capita calorie requirements and life expectancy had been replaced by under five child mortality rate.

In 2000, new threshold values were calculated for the three redefined indices. The rule for inclusion in the list of LDCs was the same as before i.e. a country in order to be eligible had to be ranked below the threshold values for all the three indices; the rule for graduation was that a country had attained a level which was 15 percent above the threshold values of any two of the criteria. In 2000, Bangladesh had less than 30 percent and about 60 percent of the threshold values of GDP and APQLI respectively whereas she had 25 percent below the threshold value of vulnerability index. Therefore, she had graduated in respect of only one of the criteria. She had much longer distance to travel towards the threshold value in GDP i.e. to increase her income three-fold to cross the threshold whereas she had a shorter distance to go before she would be able to cross the APQLI threshold. In other words, she might cross the latter barrier before she exceeded income criteria. In any case, on the basis of past trends in respect of these criteria, she might continue to enjoy the status of LDC for many years to come. I leave it to more sophisticated projections to estimate how soon she would cross one of the remaining thresholds.

In the early 1990s, Ghana was found to meet all the criteria for inclusion. When its UN representative came to know that the Committee was about to recommend its inclusion in the list of LDCs, he earnestly requested ECOSOC that Ghana did not want to be. considered a least developed country. The CDP had freedom to identify the eligible countries but neither the CDP nor ECOSOC could compel a country to accept such a status. No country has the right to demand inclusion. That was the prerogative of the CDP but a country had the right not to accept the honor and the privilege! Ghana thought that the advantages of being included among the LDCs were more than offset by the indignity of being considered as the poorest country — to be relegated to the company of countries deemed unfortunate and hopeless. She thought that somehow a stigma was attached to it.

In fact, the concessions that the LDCs receive currently in terms of development assistance are the same as those that all low income developing countries receive i.e. very long term low interest bearing loans. These are the standard terms that are granted by the International Development Association (IDA) of the World Bank. These are also the terms which are granted by the soft loan windows of the Regional Banks as well as most bilateral lenders. The total amount of assistance received by individual LDC is not determined entirely by her low income or least developed status even though this is an important factor. There are other considerations, which are of varying importance such as policies and economic performance. For bilateral donors, the criteria often included such factors as political and strategic considerations.

It is only in respect of the obligations under the WTO that the LDCs receive special treatment by an international treaty agreement that is not available to any other group of countries. The developing countries, in general, are treated less generously than the least developed countries. The latter are allowed a longer period for meeting commitments under the WTO as well as less stringent obligations than the rest of the developing countries.

Chapter 15

INSTITUTIONS FOR POLICYMAKING FOR DEVELOPMENT

15.1 THE CASE FOR ECONOMIC COORDINATION

The concepts and institutions of planning were historically associated with a socialist economic order under which the state directed and owned the dominant, if not all, sectors of economy. With the establishment of market economies and the march towards liberalisation, planning is now considered a relic of the past order, and has fallen out of fashion in the contemporary discourse on economic development.[1] However, the major underlying idea remains valid even in a market economy so long as there is a public sector or, for that matter, a government budget which lays down measures for the mobilisation of resources through tax and nontax revenues and which allocates public expenditures among competing demands of various Ministries and public agencies. Whatever is the size of the public sector, resources for the public sector have to be mobilised and expenditures have to be allocated.[2] Given the aggregate amount of

---

[1] An interesting episode in international response to this change in thinking is worth a mention here. The UN Committee which has been an existence since the 1960s to deliberate and report on development issues and policies was called *Committee for Development Planning* until the late 1990s, when its name was changed to *Committee for Development Policy.* Planning was considered inappropriate and replaced by policy. I chaired the Committee during 1996-98 (see Appendix 14.1).

[2] In the industrialised countries as a whole, currently central government expenditures constitute about 30 percent of GDP. In fact, in the ten OECD countries during the late 1990s, public expenditures constituted around 40 percent of GDP with USA having the lowest percentage at 20 percent. In developing countries, the corresponding percentage was around 20 percent, varying between 12-23 percent *(World Development Report 2001).* In Bangladesh, the

public expenditures, there is a question not only of their allocation between competing uses or sectors; there is also a need to ensure that intersectoral linkages are recognised. The sectors/subsectors not only compete with each other but also in some areas, they reinforce or complement each other. There is, therefore, a need for a central agency, which can play a determining role for expenditure composition and its internal consistency. Even if guidelines and detailed instructions are provided to the sectoral ministries to evaluate their particular expenditure programmes, there is always a need to have a second look at them. They need to be examined/evaluated in the light of the stated criteria and within the overall perspective of the aggregate expenditure programmes. The central agency, however, as a part of its own evaluation of the particular expenditure programmes can associate others in the process through the mechanism of intersectoral/interministerial consultations. Even in a free enterprise market economy like the United States, programming of expenditure programmes and allocation of resources between different sectors/departments are undertaken by a central agency called the Office of Management and Budget (OMB) in the White House.

The second task after the programming of public expenditures is that of policy analysis — macro, micro, and sectoral. Policies are required not only for the public sector but also for the markets i.e. for managing the markets. There are policy issues relating to each sector of the economy, the analysis of which can be undertaken by the sectoral Ministries. Examples of sectoral policies are competition policies, regulation of the financial sector, market intelligence and information, price, subsidy, and safety net policies. There are also economy wide policies which affect all sectors as well as the economy as a whole. They cover such macro policy issues as fiscal, monetary, exchange rate, and trade policies. Also, there is the additional task of examining the economy-wise implications of sectoral policies. For example, food or fertiliser pricing policies have implications for sectors other than agriculture and for macroeconomic balance. The

___

percentage of public expenditures to GDP during 1995-2000 was about 18 percent, split between current expenditures at about 9.30 percent and development expenditures at around 8.25 percent (Raisuddin Ahmed, "Public Expenditure and Rural Development in Bangladesh," unpublished report for ADB/IFPRI, November 2001).

sectoral Ministries can seldom take the wider view effectively and examine the interconnectedness of policies in different sectors.

Therefore, there is a need for a focal point for economic policy analysis that will not only analyse economy wide issues, but also synthesise and integrate views and analyses of different agencies or Ministries. It may undertake additional analytical work to supplement their analysis. For example, in respect of the trade policy analysis, there are some specific policy issues or aspects which can be analysed without placing them in the economy-wide framework. But there are also broader aspects to be analysed taking into account their implications for other sectors. Trade liberalisation by means of a reduction in import tariffs may affect adversely fiscal balance by reducing tax revenues. Trade Ministry has the comparative advantage in commodity, country and sector specific trade issues as well as in conducting trade negotiations. However, the central agency needs to analyse trade policy issues in the context of fiscal, monetary, and exchange rate policies and economy-wide consequences of trade policy. The overall analysis has to be done in an integrated way. For example, the analytical work of the Central Bank on macro issues needs to be integrated with the research and analytical work done in other Ministries such as Finance or Planning Ministries.

The central coordinating function of policy analysis and programming includes the evaluation of the past and ongoing policies. Also needed is the evaluation of the impact of various sectoral programmes. The implementing Ministries and agencies are not the appropriate institutions to undertake an evaluation of their own policies and programmes. Evaluation of the performance of the economy and the different sectors should be done by an independent Ministry or agency. This will include an overview and appraisal of the entire range of government policies and programmes as well as of their impact on economic growth, structural change, and social development.

In addition to budgeting and programming of public sector expenditures, and coordinating policy analysis and impact evaluation of development programmes, there is yet a third category of central coordinating function. This relates to the analysis of the future perspectives of the economy. This is closely related to the review of the past performance and progress of the economy but goes beyond and looks towards the future. It looks forward to medium and long term prospects. It identifies future challenges to the economy and examines the strategic ways in which such challenges can be met. The task is in the nature of forecasting and projections — based partly on trends and partly on an analysis of the factors that modify the past trends. The degree of sophistication of analysis and techniques for forecasting depend on the professional quality of the institution. The conclusions and findings of the exercise on the future outlook should be subject to examination, debate, and discussion by agencies/Ministries of the government as well as by outside experts and institutions. This analysis provides the basis of decision making by private and public sectors in programming their expenditures and investments in the medium or long term. To illustrate, forecasts of population growth, its age and sex composition and their implications for the size and composition of the labour force constitute the broad framework for policies designed to meet the needs of future population. Similarly, future resource availability and prospects of technical change have to be assessed and appropriate incentive and investment policies have to be formulated.

Most countries, both developed and developing, undertake such futuristic exercise on the outlook of the economy for the medium or the long term. Markets do not provide future perspectives; current market signals through price movements do not incorporate long term future possibilities. Perspective analyses or studies on the future prospects of the economy can be done by a government agency or by outside experts and institutions. But it is essential that the government provides a perspective of its own; it does not preclude a close interaction between the work of nongovernmental experts or think tanks and the government.

Given the foregoing description of the essential tasks in policymaking for developing countries, the relevant question is where in the structure of the government of Bangladesh these functions and tasks should be performed. Should the three sets of functions be split into different Ministries or should they be in the same Ministry? There is no unique model; institutional arrangements in different countries are determined by history, traditions, administrative structure as well as system of government, such as parliamentary, presidential, autocratic, and democratic. In the United States, for example, these functions are divided between Treasury, Office of Management and Budget, and Council of Economic Advisers as well as other economic units in the President's office engaged in coordinating economic policy. In recent times, an Economic Council in the White House along the lines of the National Security Council was established to oversee and coordinate a few of the economic policy functions. In some developing countries such as Indonesia, there is a Minister for Economic Coordination or similar nomenclature for coordinating different Economic Ministers (e.g. commerce, trade, industry, finance, and planning).

In the light of past experience, what should be the institutional arrangement in Bangladesh that will be efficient and at the same time can be built into the existing structure of the government? Three decades ago, an attempt was made to locate these functions in the Planning Commission. It was not successful partly because it was ahead of its time. It was too much of a change in the prevailing machinery of administration that was struggling to graduate from the status of a provincial to that of a national government. Times have changed; one hopes that there has been a great advance since then in thinking about and understanding of the issues raised above. The first step in the process is to integrate the Planning and Finance Ministries but not merely in terms of putting them under one Minister, while keeping the structure of the two Ministries unchanged.[3] The functions have to be integrated so that there is no possibility of duplication and friction. There may be a need in the process to change the structure of the two Ministries, specially the Planning Ministry. A senior Secretary supervising a number of Secretaries in the two Ministries could be useful. This would require a consolidation of the work of the various units in the two Ministries. The economic and analytical work of both Ministries needs to be streamlined and greatly expanded in size and in quality. Moreover, this requires recognition that the

---

[3] The integration of Finance and Planning Ministries would enable development and nondevelopment expenditures to be considered together. Also, capital and current expenditures would be programmed in an integrated fashion. This would ensure that maintenance and working expenditures are provided ahead of time or programmed in advance of the completion of a development project. Both development and nondevelopment expenditures would be matched with resource availability, domestic and foreign, right from the beginning of the budgeting process. It is, of course, possible to undertake these exercises jointly even if the units and divisions are located in different Ministries. However, the spirit of cooperation and the task of coordination are facilitated if they are in the same ministry.

tasks involved are very technical in nature and require more than generalists and "informal" economists to perform them adequately. It is this reorganised Ministry of Finance and Planning that could be an appropriate location for the central policy analysis, programming and coordinating functions.

The newly organised Ministry, which can be called Ministry for Economic Affairs or Coordination, may, however, contract out some medium or long term policy analytical work, including the work on future perspectives and outlook of the economy to nongovernmental research organisations. Evaluation and programming of projects and sectors and formulation of a consistent and integrated development programme cannot, however, be contracted out to organisations outside the government.[4] The resource allocation function of the Planning and Finance Ministries needs to be done inhouse on the basis of priorities set by the Cabinet. Nor short term, policy oriented research and analytical work to respond to specific day-to-day policymaking functions can be subcontracted to outside agencies. It has been argued that, given the current scales of salary and benefits for government employees, it will be difficult to attract highly trained professionals of requisite quality and experience envisaged for the new Ministry. High level professionals in these days of globalisation, with access to research contracts at internationally competitive rates and jobs abroad, would demand commensurate salary and related compensations. This is a challenge, which the government has to meet if it is committed to building up a high level of professional expertise in the government.[5]

If this new Ministry has to perform its role effectively, its overriding responsibility has to be understood and accepted by the rest of the

---

[4] There is currently a division that is responsible for the evaluation and monitoring of the implementation of programmes and projects. It is concerned less with costs and benefits of the programmes or their overall impact than with their physical implementation and utilisation of resources. The task of evaluation of the sectoral programmes or the performance of the overall economy can also be undertaken by institutions or "think tanks" outside the government. However, assessment and appraisal by independent nongovernmental institutions should not substitute the government's own self appraisal.

[5] As has been explained in Chapter 17, this is all the more imperative if the government is to claim ownership of policies and programmes in course of its negotiations for foreign economic assistance. In its absence, the task of policy analysis and the choice of policies and priorities for development will necessarily rest with the donor agencies. The government's role would be mainly to react to donor's policy prescription on an *ad hoc* basis and accept them, albeit grudgingly, as conditions of aid, it so anxiously covets.

government, including other ministries, and their subordinate agencies/ departments. The task of economic coordination in policy and programming will necessarily confer on this Ministry a position of superior authority and status above other Ministries. At the same time, the Coordinating Ministry would work together with them, through the mechanism of interministerial committees and consultations, so as to ensure participation and cooperation of other Ministries. Also, at the level of the Cabinet, the National Economic Council/Executive Committee of the National Economic Council needs to be made more effective in policy deliberations and decision making so that the active participation of all the Ministers is ensured. They must perceive that they jointly and collectively make the policy decisions, while the analyses and recommendations originate from the Coordinating Ministry.

The Coordinating Minister would not only be the *First Among Equals* but also would have the *de facto* authority of a Deputy Prime Minister. In view of the sensitivity of other Ministries, it may be better part of discretion based on past experience to make the situation transparent and designate the Coordinating Minister as the Deputy Prime Minister. Alternatively, the Prime Minister assumes the role of the Coordinating Minister but in view of multifarious political and administrative responsibilities of the Prime Minister, the *de facto* power will be assumed by a civil servant looking after economic matters in the Prime Minister's office. That would be a considerably inferior solution; because of lack of transparency, the conflicts and tensions between the Coordinating Ministry and the rest of the government would, in fact, be aggravated.

15.2 INFORMATION, TRANSPARENCY AND PARTICIPATION

Adequate, high quality, and reliable information and statistical data constitute the foundation of good economic analysis and policymaking. Lack of adequate data is frequently lamented by all concerned, including the policymakers. Not much is done, partly because programmes for improving the quality and expanding the quantity of statistical information do not have high political visibility. By now, it is widely known what kind of data is needed for purposes of economic analysis and policymaking. There is no shortage of expertise in the country in this regard, greatly dispersed though they are among various institutions, including private organisations.

Bangladesh Bureau of Statistics (BBS), currently under the Ministry of Planning, should be converted into an autonomous organisation with a considerable degree of flexibility and freedom of action. It should have a governing board of its own. This should represent various users of statistical data in the government, including Ministries collecting data of their own — sometimes duplicating rather than supplementing — as well as independent experts and researchers. BBS is a servicing organisation; it needs emphasis that it should service not only Ministries but also the private sector, universities, research organisations, independent scholars, and nongovernmental organisations. It should be led by those with expertise in the field and manned by specialists in various branches of national statistics. The leadership of the organisation should have a high status and an autonomy — not less than that of the Auditor General or the Governor of the Bangladesh Bank and not subject to frequent changes. Once appointed, he should be for a fixed term of office, not subject to the whims of the political party in power. The leadership must be stable and secure; it must ensure the primary role of the experience and expertise in the organisation.

Independence of BBS from interference by political authorities is essential. There has been a tendency in the past for an incumbent government to influence or misrepresent the statistical information on the economy in order to present its performance in a favourable light. This temptation is understandable and, therefore, has to be neutralised by an institutional guarantee of its independence. Once the users of the data perceive that there is the possibility of manipulation for political purposes, BBS will lose its credibility among not only the public but also the rest of the world. This would defeat the very purpose for which the misrepresentation of data is attempted in the first place. Furthermore, this will adversely affect the credibility of the government itself in international economic negotiations.

It will help improve the quality and credibility of data collection and statistical analysis if BBS subcontracts sectoral or issue oriented surveys to nongovernment research organisations, with expertise and experience in techniques of sample surveys. It is unlikely that

BBS would have staff with expertise in all the necessary fields. Indian Statistical Institute played a pioneering role along with other nongovernmental research organisations in carrying out important surveys on vital aspects or sectors of the Indian economy.

It is important to realise that the work of data collection of high quality and reliability is expensive. But to economise on such expenditures is highly counterproductive. Policymaking without reliable and adequate information runs serious risks. Returns on investment in information that improves the efficiency of markets and government policies are widely recognised to be very high. This is all the more so as Bangladesh seeks greater integration in the world economy. The absence of adequate information on the economy hinders trade and investment transactions with the rest of the world.

Bangladesh Bank should also serve as an important source of data and analysis on subjects relating to its responsibilities. Data relating to monetary developments and foreign exchange/balance of payments that lie within the province of the Central Bank should be coordinated with the statistical data collected by BBS and other Ministries. Again, as in the case of BBS, the independence of Bangladesh Bank from political interference is important if its data or analysis or its supervisory authority over the banking system has to achieve any credibility. Most recently, there have been tentative signs of progress in this direction.

In a democracy, wide public participation in debates on economic policy issues is important. This requires that independent centres of research and analysis should be encouraged and promoted. In recent years, several private "think tanks" have been established in the country, which carry out research on public policy issues and organise debates and discussions on public policies. They suffer from a limitation; they are overwhelmingly dependent on financial support from donors who have their own perspectives and priorities in terms of research questions and findings. It is true that it is possible for a think tank to include in its research programme a few of its own research priorities along with those of donors. It depends on the quality of its leadership, its bargaining strength, and how strong is the competition among donors to buy its services. It is preferable not to let the research priorities to be left to the process of negotiation between donors and think tanks, and to their relative bargaining strength. In the absence of domestic private donors or foundations as in developed or more advanced developing countries, there is no alternative to financing by the government in Bangladesh.

Such financing should not be limited to designated research projects-cum-consulting as at present. It should promote a wider participation in policy research. The project tied research/consulting grants to "think tanks" are designed to help answer questions relevant to the government's short term policymaking. Frequently, they assist the government in its negotiations with donors. But its focus remains narrowly utilitarian and restrictive. Therefore, the government should provide grants on the basis of an overall research programme of a "think tank" and an evaluation of its quality. One way to do this is for the government to establish a foundation or a council consisting of independent researchers and academics to channel resources to the "think tanks". The council or foundation should be run by independent nongovernmental experts of known integrity and experience.

In order to guarantee the integrity and independence of a few selected "think tanks", an additional method of funding may be explored. The government might provide an endowment so that their core research programme and overhead expenses are met from income from the endowments rather than from uncertain annual grants.

How does one ensure that the research results and findings of "think tanks" on important policy issues are considered seriously by the government in the course of its own policy deliberations? The risk of such "think tanks" suffering from benign neglect cannot be ruled out. Apart from the fact that research findings of the "think tanks" should be in the public domain through publications, seminars, workshops, and the media, as they are at present, it might be useful to devise a regular mechanism through which their policy conclusions and findings are brought to the attention of the policymakers. This can be done if various Ministries have regular arrangements for consulting with private "think tanks".

Economic policymaking in a democracy requires that the parliamentarians actively participate in the debates on policy issues. This should take place on the basis of information and analysis provided by the executive Ministries/Departments as well as by outside experts.

The importance of providing specialised staff as well as research support and facilities to the parliamentarians has been discussed in the past but not much has been done. Participatory democracy, if it is to function efficiently, is neither without risks and tension for the government of the day, nor it inexpensive. In fact, the costs of running a pluralistic democracy are quite high. One hopes that, in the long run, the benefits of achieving a stable and progressive society are correspondingly very high.

The Standing Committees of the Parliament should deal with (a) important economic issues/subjects, as well as (b) programmes and policies of the individual sectors/Ministries. They should also be able to constitute *ad hoc* committees on new issues that may be identified from time to time. The committee debates, if open to the public and media, can contribute to a wider public awareness and education. The Ministries/Departments should prepare policy briefs for consideration by the committees. They should be able to call upon the Ministers and officials to explain policy issues and answer specific queries from the members of the committees. Experts from universities and research institutions, various interest groups as well as nongovernmental organisations and members of civil society should be invited to provide testimony to the committees on issues in which they have either interest or competence. At the same time, they should have the opportunities, if they so desired, to present their views on their own initiative to the committees. What is equally important is that these submissions and testimonies should be published and available to the wider public.

The first step in this direction is to "declassify" to the maximum extent possible policy analyses undertaken and documents prepared by the government. The policy proposals under consideration by the government should be published for eliciting public opinion. This would promote public understanding of policy issues and of the manner in which the government functions. The right to information about the government's deliberation on its policies and actions may be deemed to be one of the fundamental rights of the citizens of a democratic society. This is an important way of mobilising support of the public for government policies and improving the quality, content and effectiveness of policies. Second, public understanding and support for policies and programmes of the government can also be promoted by an exchange of ideas and experience between the members of civil society and policymakers. This is important not only at the stage of formulation and review of economic policies but also during their implementation. One way to accomplish this is to set up Advisory Councils/Committees attached to different Ministries/ Departments. Such advisory groups, if they are designed to function effectively and not as a mere public relations exercise, would serve two purposes: One is to solicit and secure reactions from affected groups and from experts to proposed policies as well as their suggestions for dealing with any anticipated problems; second is to secure a feedback on the effects of policies already under implementation so that corrections and amendments may be made in the light of experience. It is rare that at the stage of formulation the whole range of consequences of policies or problems of their implementation can be foreseen.

The various suggestions for strengthening and improving institutional arrangements for policymaking made above are not new and have been made before. To some, they may seem even common place. Some of these institutions do now exist. For example, there are Parliamentary Committees and *ad hoc* Advisory Committees for some individual Ministries. The critical question is whether there is motivation and interest on the part of the political leadership to make them effective. History to date indicates no such strong willingness or interest on their part, no matter which political party is in power. Yet these suggestions are made on the assumption that a repetition of valid and worthwhile propositions may at some stage convince the policymakers to act.

Chapter 16

LIBERALISING AND MANAGING THE MARKET

16.1 INTRODUCTION

At independence, Bangladesh inherited a large number of regulations and restrictions constraining the operations of the market, in particular, in industry, trade, and finance. Also, it had a sizeable public sector inherited from the Pakistan days in agricultural marketing, manufacturing industry, financial sector, trade, transport, communications, and energy. After independence, during the 1970s, she extended the range and scope of public ownership as explained in earlier chapters.

Beginning with the 1980s, Bangladesh started to reduce state control and regulations and proceeded on the path of privatisation. This was in conformity with new trends in development thinking. The wave of socialist thinking and practice that swept the developing world during the 1960s and 1970s, subsided by the 1980s, greatly influenced by the economic collapse of the Soviet Union and of the rest of the socialist world. Free market, privatisation, and liberalisation constituted the new development consensus. Bangladesh followed suit partly as a result of its own rethinking and reassessment of its experience and partly as a result of the pressure of the donor community. It is difficult to identify the relative importance of these two factors i.e. conviction and reappraisal of past experience, on the one hand, and donor pressure, on the other. One does not know how far the growing private sector has exercised any influence on the change in policy. Also, it is difficult to totally reject the impression that Bangladesh has been a reluctant liberaliser. This could be partly due to uncertainty about the consequences of liberalisation as perceived by the policymakers.

The process of liberalisation has not been carried out in a predetermined, planned, and systemic way, after thinking through the rationale of the pace and sequencing of the reforms. It has neither been strategic or planned gradualism nor shock therapy. It has fallen between the cracks. Planned gradualism implies (a) a clear definition of goals and (b) a deliberate choice of a plan of action, indicating a time path to reach the goals in such a way as to reduce the pain of transition. Reforms have taken place at varying paces in different sectors and at different times. As a result, the interlinkages between reforms in different sectors have not always been considered and integrated. For example, loan default or nonrepayment of loans in the nationalised commercial banks is linked with persistent and accumulated losses in the nationalised industries. Reforms, in general, have taken place on an *ad hoc* basis in response to a combination of circumstances such as budgetary crunch or impending balance of payments crisis. This has required an urgent access to resources from the Bank and the Fund, which in turn have imposed conditionality regarding policy changes. This is the way liberalisation has happened in many developing countries and Bangladesh is not unique in this respect.

There has not been much debate prior to reforms, and hardly any analysis and public information to enable constructive debates. The situation has improved over time but then debate in the later years has been mostly *ex post* as in SAPRI debates.[1] Advance notice to the affected sectors and their participation in the timing and sequencing of reforms have to be carefully managed. Policymakers face a dilemma. The attempt to reach a consensus on *ad hoc* basis with the affected groups can lead to delays and, if the process is slow, there might be backsliding or retreat from reforms. To preempt such a possibility, the government has to be firm in its convictions and give clear signals, not marred by vacillation and uncertainty, about the

---

[1] D. Bhattacharya and R.A.M. Titumir (ed.), "Stakeholders' Perceptions, Reforms, and Consequences," Structural Adjustment Participatory Review Initiative (SAPRI), Shraban Prokashoni, Dhaka, 2001.

basic components and direction of reforms. The reformers in the government have to convince and persuade the gainers from reforms and mobilise their support. Effective and skillful leadership of the reform process is the most important precondition for success. Many macroeconomic reforms in Bangladesh did not face as much resistance as sectoral reforms such as in agriculture or privatisation. The consequences of the former such as devaluation were diffused. The impact of elimination of import quotas was cushioned by the imposition of equivalent tariffs. In the case of trade liberalisation, the import competing sectors were not given much previous warning and it was undertaken speedily. It was over time that resistance developed to further liberalisation as the affected sectors or groups managed to organise some lobbying power. In the case of sectoral reforms, there were clearly identified groups which were adversely affected and they were well organised as in the case of workers or managers in, and politicians indirectly benefiting from, public enterprises.

Economic reforms to liberalise the market do not mean the end of all regulations. The state cannot retreat altogether if a market economy has to function successfully. But markets to function well need government oversight as the free market in developed countries amply demonstrate. Economic theory expounds on the need for government intervention in case of market failures i.e. to achieve its avowed objectives of efficient allocation and utilisation of resources. The most critical requirement for a functioning market is the availability of necessary information. Market left to itself does not generate the full range of information needed by market participants i.e. users and suppliers of goods and services. Furthermore, market failures include absence of competition, externalities, divergence between private and social costs or benefits, risks and uncertainties, fluctuations in income and prices and unemployment.[2]

Three questions are raised regarding the rationale, extent, and the type of state intervention in the market to achieve efficiency and

---

[2] One can stretch the concept of market failure to include unequal distribution of income — not considered as such as by traditional economic analysis excepting in so far as it is caused by market imperfections. Efficient market does not necessarily produce or promote stakeholders' and peoples' empowerment and participation in decision making in the private or the public sector. State intervention is now also advocated to empower the powerless in the decision making process.

equity. First, it is not always easy to identify and quantify the incidence of a particular market failure and the losses it inflicts. In real life, what is considered a market failure is sometimes the result of lack of institutions which are the precondition for a market economy to work well: security and enforcement of law, property rights, enforcement of contracts, and lack of corruption. Moreover, it could itself be the consequence of current state intervention, which turns out to be inefficient or ineffective. Second, market failures cannot always be corrected by public intervention because what is nowadays called government failures i.e. inefficiency and capture of the state power by interest groups, impede competitive forces. Intervention to correct market failures is only justified when it can be ensured that government failures do not make the situation worse than before either in terms of efficiency or equity. Similarly, intervention should be eschewed if it does not correct market failures since in that case there is a potential net loss since resources of the public sector because of ineffective policy instruments could be wasted. Third, there is the question of the choice among an array of policy measures, which can be potentially used to correct market failures. It is more efficient to use indirect controls and regulations. In general, the government should eschew large scale micro and direct interventions by a heavy discretionary exercise of its bureaucratic power.

The task of formulation and implementation of rules and regulations for the market economy, in fact, require, a sizeable public service with a high level of competence and sophistication. It does not mean less government; it involves different kinds of functions. Regulations, instead of dealing with specific actions or transactions, should provide incentives and general guidelines. It is important that regulations are not too complicated. The more complex are the regulations, the greater is the scope for discretionary exercise of power by the regulators. This, in turn, provides an opportunity for misuse of power for private gain. Secondly, regulations should be widely known and publicised so that all economic actors know and understand their implications. Legal procedures should be transparent and predictable without a scope for arbitrary action. The greater is the transparency and openness of the government's policies and regulations, the smaller is the chance of their being misused.

16.2 MARKET REFORMS AND REGULATION: ILLUSTRATIONS

Agriculture

Liberalisation of agricultural markets, both for inputs and outputs, is one of the earlier cases of market opening in Bangladesh. It provides an interesting case study of the process of liberalisation, its time path, forces propelling it, as well as its extent and sequencing. Furthermore, it illustrates that, in order to correct market failures and make it function efficiently, liberalisation is not enough. Regulations need to be put in place.

Agricultural market liberalisation happened gradually over a period of time as a result of long drawn out discussions and debates, mainly inspired and initiated by donors. Reforming and reducing direct public participation in the marketing and distribution of foodgrain and in the provision of fertiliser and irrigation water had been under discussion and debate among policymakers as well as researchers since the late 1960s and 1970s. This debate was supported by numerous empirical studies. More important was the consistent dialogue with and pressure from donors. Assistance for imports of agricultural inputs such as fertiliser and irrigation equipment was accompanied by pressure for reforms in the markets for agricultural inputs; provision of food aid was linked with changes in the system of food subsidy and rationing. Generally speaking, the timing and extent of liberalisation in each case were to some extent determined by a build up of cumulative pressure of donors. At the same time, there were other enabling factors. The abolition of rural rationing was facilitated by the findings of various research studies about the very significant leakage of benefits to the non-target groups i.e. the nonpoor. The timing of the abolition of urban food rationing, which covered both the poor and nonpoor in the urban areas, was facilitated by two factors: first, considerable improvement in the food availability due to increase in food production; second, greatly expanded and improved private food marketing and distribution throughout the country. This reduced the gap between the open market and rationed prices so that the impact of the abolition of rationing on the consumers was not significant, given the leakage and inefficiency of the system. However, the subsidised food distribution to a significant nonpoor group i.e. the army and security forces, was retained.

While the government had withdrawn from direct participation in the pricing and distribution of foodgrains, it devised other measures of protecting access to food by the poor. First, distribution of food to poor families was linked to school enrolment of their children. Very recently, it has been replaced by making transfer of monetary income to the target group, withdrawing from government's direct participation in the distribution of food. It is yet to be seen whether this measure is more efficient and equitable in actual implementation. Second, the targeted food distribution programmes such as the feeding programme for vulnerable and destitute women, and an expanded food-for-works programme for the poor or unemployed have continued.

There is another area in which the government retains its responsibility, that is, for moderating the fluctuations in food prices. A minimum level of public stocks remain an important policy instrument to provide food security and to meet unforeseen emergencies caused, for example, by floods or droughts. The market takes time to adjust supply shortfalls through imports; private food imports, which were previously banned, are now permitted and help the process of adjustment. Speculation caused by anticipated shortfalls leads to withholding of stocks from the market by traders and farmers. As discussed in an earlier chapter, such market behaviour contributed to the upward spiralling of prices of rice in 1974. Imports and public stocks can quickly restore market stability. Thus, the government's role in targeted food distribution or in monitoring markets, supplies, and prices for cereals and essential inputs remains crucial. The above illustrates how government needs to combine its policy of liberalisation of agricultural markets with supplementary measures to manage the markets in order to promote stability and equity.

A similar case was that of public distribution of the urea fertiliser at subsidised prices. This measure was originally designed first, to induce the introduction of a new untried input and to cover farmers' risks in using a new input by increasing prospects of substantial gains to compensate for additional cost; second, by cheapening its cost, the subsidy provided access to poor farmers with limited resources or credit to finance an additional input. The twin aspects of market failure, i.e. inability of the market to compensate for the risks of investing in a new technology and failure to ensure access to the poor, led to state intervention. After a number of years when farmers got used to the use of urea, measures to cover risks from new technology were no longer needed. With the improvement in the supply situation and a fall in relative price, the poor now had easier access to the urea fertiliser at a lower price. In the past, in a situation of scarcity, the nonpoor could exercise influence to get a large share of the public distribution and the poor was left with recourse to the black market at a higher price.

The process of liberalisation of the fertiliser market took a longer time than that of foodgrain market. Evidence accumulated on two fronts: (a) that there was significant leakage of fertiliser distribution to the nonpoor; and (b) that incentive to farmers was no longer needed, as gains from its use were perceived to be high and its use greatly increased among farmers. But it was the pressure of donors that clinched the issue, supported by the evidence. Even though high cost domestic urea produced in the public sector continued to receive some indirect subsidy, the liberalisation of the market and private fertiliser trade did not rule out the government playing a role in other ways.

Has liberalisation of agricultural input markets unequivocally improved efficiency? Reference is often made to an incident immediately following the privatisation of the distribution of fertiliser, when there was a sudden spurt in the price of urea, the most important category of fertiliser, accompanied by shortage in the market. There was a failure of market information about the projected supply; unexpected export by the publicly owned fertiliser enterprise created expectations of scarcity. This caused a few wholesalers to hoard supplies, which in turn led to a rise in price. Even though marketing of fertilisers was privatised, production, pricing, and export of urea (in case of excess supply) were in the public sector and under the control of the government. While the ex-factory sales price of urea was determined by the government, the wholesale and retail prices were left free to be determined by the market. The government failed to provide the required market intelligence on production, demand forecasts, and exports. The traders did not have adequate information on which to base their price expectations. Their speculative behaviour in response to exports led to hoarding and rise in price. The supply did not respond to a rise in price since, in the short run, response would have been possible only through an increase in imports but private imports were not allowed.

The government's failure in monitoring supply, demand, and price led to yet another unfortunate incident. At one stage, private traders sold an inappropriate type of fertiliser to the farmers through recourse to misinformation. The government did not monitor the variety and quality of fertiliser that was supplied by private traders. Subsequently, the government strengthened its monitoring system and banned the import of the inappropriate types of fertiliser.

The two examples above indicate that private markets do not necessarily provide appropriate and objective information; there is an asymmetry in respect of the available information between traders and farmers. Therefore, the provision of information on the safety and quality as well as market intelligence on supply, demand, and prices of crucial outputs and inputs has to be regulated or directly undertaken by the government. This is all the more important if one segment of the market, as is the case with fertiliser production, is dominated by public enterprise or if market conditions are not competitive as in the case of oligopoly.

The provision of irrigation water is yet another area where the market does not offer an efficient solution to all types of irrigation. In the case of surface water or gravity flow irrigation, private ownership and market mechanism do not work efficiently. It is a field for both the public sector and collective action among farmers through whose lands water flows. While large scale investment in water development is beyond the capacity of private farmers and requires public action, the characteristics of common property resources necessitate the participation of both government and farmers in water management and related functions. There is room for water users' associations in distributing irrigation water as well as in the repair and maintenance of irrigation works. In Bangladesh, the surface water or canal irrigation system is run by the public sector without any significant participation of users. This leaves considerable room for improvement by means of organisational and administrative decentralisation and participation by users. The installation of shallow tubewell for the use of underground water has been entirely in the private sector.

Investment by individual farmers has been facilitated by free private trade in tubewells, accompanied by liberalisation of their imports. The former could not work efficiently without the latter. In fact, in the case of both fertiliser and food, foreign trade liberalisation has followed internal market liberalisation.

16.3 TRADE AND FINANCIAL REFORMS

During the 1980s, the main thrust of liberalisation was in the field of agriculture, described above. In addition, there were the beginnings of liberalisation in industry, financial sector, and foreign trade. Quantitative restrictions on trade were significantly reduced during the 1980s. During the 1990s, the emphasis in trade liberalisation has been on tariff reduction, current account convertibility, and elimination of virtually all restrictions on foreign investment. There has been occasional backsliding on trade liberalisation mainly in response to fluctuations in foreign exchange reserves. Should the government continue to control the market for foreign exchange as it does now by a combination of periodic small doses of devaluation, changes in margin requirements for imports and in tariffs? Or should it let the exchange rate float rather than periodically adjusting at its discretion in response to changes in the balance of payments and in reserves? The present policy has two important limitations: one, it is difficult to decide on the right amount of devaluation to be undertaken periodically in small doses; second, because of the traditional public perception that an act of devaluation reflects unfavourably on the quality of economic management, it becomes a political decision resistant to frequent changes. In fact, in exchange rate adjustment, Bangladesh lagged behind countries which are her competitors in trade. Most of them have been floating their exchange rates or have undertaken a greater degree of adjustment in response to movements in trade and payments.

Is it inherent in foreign trade and payments structure that its response to frequent market driven variations in a floating exchange rate is likely to be weak or slow leading to large swings in the short run? Does not the present state of physical infrastructure dampen the supply response in production and trade? How would Bangladesh manage excessive fluctuations in the exchange rate caused by speculative expectations and sudden movements in the current account balance of payments, including fluctuations in worker's remittances? In other words, complete liberalisation of the exchange market would require the Bangladesh Bank to develop tools for managing the exchange market. The traditional macroeconomic tools for managing the demand and supply of foreign exchange i.e. instruments of monetary and fiscal policy, are yet undeveloped. Should exchange liberalisation wait until financial sector reforms have progressed far enough, the instruments of monetary control are developed, supporting fiscal policy is agreed upon and experience in monetary management accumulates? All these questions and more are relevant in deciding the timing of the introduction of the floating exchange rate system. An active market in government securities such as treasury bills of different maturities, for example, is one important element in helping to develop open market type operations to regulate money supply, influence interest rates and hence demand for foreign exchange. At present, treasury bills are of relatively short duration and predominantly held by the Bangladesh Bank. Access to foreign exchange reserves, for example, by standby arrangements with the Fund to meet short term fluctuations in the exchange market is yet another tool for managing a floating exchange rate. A complete liberalisation of the foreign exchange market, as the above illustrates, requires that not only the tools for managing the market have to be developed, but also related markets such as financial and money markets have to be reformed and managed at the same time. No less important is the role of prudent fiscal policy since fiscal deficits and variations in inflationary pressures destabilise the exchange market.

Reforms in the financial sector initiated in the 1980s allowed private banks to compete with nationalised banks which dominated the banking system. The entry of foreign banks offered additional competition. The banks are now allowed to freely decide their interest rates for both deposits and lending. Instead of quantitative targets directed to priority sectors, ceilings are placed on lending rates to the priority sectors. The financial market is fragmented into three segments i.e. nationalised banks, the largest segment, followed by private domestic banks and foreign owned banks. Each has its specialised clientele, though some competition exists. The customers who are very risk averse to bank failures dominate the first category. The foreign banks do not undertake all types of business, are not present all over the country, and prefer industry and trade in major urban centres, specially foreign trade. Interest rate differences are only one instrument of competition between them and other considerations such as customer service and perception of security are important as well. The nationalised banks act as the leaders in the oligopolistic market structure and rates decided by them are followed by other banks. The trend towards increased competition is likely to continue. Foreign banks are more efficient and with lower costs are more profitable. Private domestic banks are more efficient than nationalised banks and are responding to the competitive pressure from foreign banks, hopefully learning from their best practices.

Freeing the competitive forces in the banking system is not enough. Freedom to set interest rates, or set lending limits or freedom to choose whom to lend to and for what, does not eliminate the risk of misallocation and waste of resources. The market for loanable funds is characterised by asymmetry of information between lenders and borrowers, and between shareholders/depositors and managers. In the context of asymmetry of information in the market, an exclusive reliance on the interest rate mechanism to allocate credit among the prospective borrowers and to balance supply and demand of credit does not ensure market efficiency and stability. For example, the higher the lending rate, the riskier will be the borrowers — who will be forthcoming to bear the burden of higher rates. As a result, the risk of nonrepayment of loans is greater and so also is the danger to the solvency of the banks. In this context, the discretion of the bank officials in the choice of projects and borrowers plays a critical role. Therefore, financial institutions require regulations.[3] They encompass such aspects of banking operations as capital ratios, reserves, liquidity requirements, risk management and enforcement of repayments.[4]

---

[3] Among the reasons for regulation are also increased systemic consequences of banking crises, and tendency of the government to bail them out as a result of systemic worries.

[4] How to develop adequate banking regulatory standards and how to supervise and monitor them have baffled the regulators of the developed countries for years. The episodes of banking crises in developed financial markets confirm the difficulty of devising a regulatory system. It has taken years in many countries to train and put in place an adequate supervising system. S. Stigliz: *State Versus Market*, The University Press Limited, Dhaka, 1999.

The case for an efficient regulatory framework is best illustrated by the experience of the financial sector in Bangladesh, where reforms are underway in tentative and *ad hoc* steps. It is important, among other things, to ensure that bank officials have no interest, direct or indirect, in the businesses they finance, and that directors/owners do not borrow excessively from their own banks or, through an inter-locking of directorates, do not lend to each other's owners/directors. In Bangladesh, currently the owner-directors are allowed to borrow from their banks. There is a legal limit to the extent of the directors' participation in capital and of borrowing from their own banks. The enforcement of these regulations is reputed to be lax. The competence of the banking staff and their capacity for appraisal and supervision of loans are limited. The incentive structure and the internal management of the banks, specially the public sector banks, leave much to be desired. Above all, supervision of the banking system as a whole is weak. There is a need for transparency in lending operations and their supervision by an independent and competent authority such as the central bank. Default of loan repayments in Bangladesh — a chronic phenomenon — is due to a weak regulatory system and an inadequate enforcement mechanism. Interference by political authorities and by government officials compounds the problem of default.

In order to formulate and enforce necessary regulations, it is necessary to have a regulator, i.e. a central bank, with the capacity, independence and authority to govern the financial market and its participants. Bangladesh Bank also suffers from limitations in respect of the required level of skill and authority. Recommendations to improve the governance of the financial market and to strengthen the authority of the Bangladesh Bank have been made many times over by national experts and donors. Implementation faces obstacles from vested interests and the government officials who fear the loss of their discretionary power.

There are three aspects of the autonomy of the Bangladesh Bank. First, the authority over internal administration, finance and personnel should obviously rest exclusively with the bank management and its Board of Directors. Second, the Bangladesh Bank should have the sole responsibility for the supervision of the banking system and enforcement of regulations. This is an area in which independence from political influence and interference is essential for the maintenance of the health of the banking system. Third is the realm of monetary and exchange rate policy in which the Finance and other Economic Ministries have a role to play. Exchange rate policy has to be consistent with monetary and fiscal policies. A flexible or floating rate, if it is to avoid wide fluctuations or large and frequent depreciations, would imply more disciplined monetary and fiscal policy. A relevant question in the prevailing context is whether the government has the authority to borrow from the Bangladesh Bank or the commercial banks at its will. If the Bank has responsibility for monetary management and inflation control, then the government's unrestricted authority to borrow from the banking system and to resort to deficit financing would jeopardise the objective. On such crucial policy questions, there is room for wider participation in the decision making process in a democracy. For example, there should be a parliamentary committee on monetary and banking issues for debates and discussions on policy issues. Admittedly, at the current level of background, experience and training of the Parliament members, the contribution of their deliberations to the substance of policymaking would be limited. However, it would certainly, over time, build up awareness among them of relevant policy issues. Recent strengthing of the authority of the Bangladesh Bank may have already included some of the above changes.

The role of the Parliament as an educative forum should not be underestimated. Also, it should be emphasised that to govern an economy in modern times is no longer the domain of the amateur. There should be an advisory committee consisting of people with expertise and experience. It should include representatives from relevant Ministries involved with macroeconomic policies as well as financial market institutions. The Bangladesh Bank would service such a committee with the Finance Minister as its Chairman and the Governor of the Bank as its Vice Chairman. Such an advisory committee widens the scope of consultations and facilitates the decision making process. The final decisions on objectives and, in some cases, on the modality of monetary and exchange rate policy could be the responsibility of a smaller executive committee consisting of the Finance Ministry and all or selected members of the Board of the Bank. This is one possible outline of a framework for reconciling independence in operational and supervisory functions of the Bank, on the one hand, with the ultimate political responsibility of the Finance Minister for macroeconomic policy, on the other.

16.4 PRIVATISATION

As the economy has moved into the process of liberalisation, privatisation has been the second plank of policy. The first plank, as illustrated above, has been the movement towards the substitution of widespread discretionary control and micro regulations by selective non-discretionary, macro rules and regulations to manage the market.

The issue of privatisation in any sector, be it the financial sector, trade, or industry, should be seen in the broader context of the role of the state versus the market. It is generally accepted that private enterprise should replace public enterprise, if the former is more efficient by the test of the market. The evidence in Bangladesh that several industrial units after being transferred to private owners continue to run at losses is no argument against privatisation. The accounting losses of such enterprises might be misleading. They are often a cover for the avoidance of income and corporate taxes, and profits are hidden in falsified accounts. Secondly, losses of public enterprises are a burden on the taxpayers on a continuing basis. This is not the case in respect of losses incurred by private enterprises. Thirdly, if indeed the private enterprises suffer losses due to inefficiency and inability to compete, they will eventually close down. A competitive market economy is characterised by the closure of inefficient firms and emergence of new efficient firms.

There are additional arguments in favour of privatisation. Even if public and private enterprises are equally efficient in any sector, private enterprise should be preferred. This will leave the public sector free to concentrate on the provision of goods and services, which are unlikely to be provided by the private sector. Activities with significant external effects in which social benefits exceed private benefits and private profitability is low, fall into this category. They include property rights and contracts enforcement, on the one hand, and the provision of social services, such as health, education, and infrastructure, and research and development, on the other. Efficient provision of such public goods is necessary for markets to function and for a stable social and political order. This argument applies with some force in Bangladesh. The provision of essential public services already seems to constrain the capacity of the public sector to the limit or even to be beyond its capacity. While propagating liberalisation and privatisation, it should be kept in mind that there would remain in any case a significant public sector, even though its character and composition would change. Therefore, sustained efforts to improve the efficiency of the public sector, whatever its size and composition, are essential and should remain a major responsibility of the government.

In the course of the debate on privatisation, two issues have been raised. First, the pace has been a matter of contention. In spite of the declared policy of the government, there seems to have been some tardiness in the way of privatisation in industry, finance, and infrastructure. The issue has been most salient in respect of privatisation of the nationalised industries, which have been continuously suffering heavy losses.

The slow pace in the privatisation of industries has been ascribed to the political risks of privatisation. Upon privatisation, a reduction of the labour force in the overmanned and overstaffed public enterprises is most likely. The discontent, public agitation and strikes on the part of unemployed workers and employees could cause political destabilisation.[5] Moreover, corruption and collection of rents by management contribute to the losses of publicly owned industries; rents are shared with troublesome labour leaders and, in some instances, with political party workers and leaders (a sort of ransom or protection money extracted by the latter). All participants in the process of corruption and rentseeking constitute vested interests against privatisation.

Those who gain from the prevailing state of affairs have to be paid off or compensated financially or otherwise. The employees can be compensated. How does one compensate for the illegal gains of labour leaders and political activists? One can find for them alternative income earning opportunities. The costs of compensation by the government are expected to be outweighed in many cases by government savings

---

[5] The unions of industrial workers have always been a potent instrument in the hands of political parties for organising demonstrations and strikes against the incumbent government, irrespective of whichever party may be in control. They help in ensuring large attendance at political rallies and meetings as well as in managing or interfering in elections in favour of the party to which they are affiliated.

from privatisation or even from closure of such enterprises. In addition to the excessive labour force, the problem of restructuring the accumulated past debt also creates a hindrance to privatisation. The private buyers are unlikely to bear such extraordinary costs or to face possible agitation by displaced workers.[6]

The main hurdle in the way of privatisation has been the lack of commitment and initiative on the part of the political leadership to mobilise public opinion in its favour. They need to explain to the public how and to what extent subsidies to the loss making public enterprises impose costs on the general population and what benefits will accrue to them from the savings following privatisation. How would the savings from a policy of privatisation be used for socially beneficial purposes? Nor has an adequate explanation been provided as to the various reasons why specific industries have been sustaining losses and who are the gainers and losers from the prevailing system. It is necessary to prepare public opinion in favour of privatisation by explaining the benefits and the costs of proposed reforms.

As a general proposition, privatisation has a greater chance of success when there is a dynamic and vibrant private sector, which provides employment to the displaced workers and generates adequate financial resources for the purchase of denationalised industries. An important requirement for generating confidence among the prospective private investors in the policy of privatisation is to make the process very transparent; the process of selection of buyers and the terms and conditions of sale should be widely known. Throughout history, in many countries, the act of privatisation has been smeared with accusations of cronyism, favouritism, and corruption. The most egregious recent example is the privatisation process in Russia. Historically, this also characterised the process of privatisation in Japan in the interwar period.

With the growth of the private corporate sector in Bangladesh, both financial and nonfinancial, corporate governance needs to be

---

[6] The recent closing down of the Adamjee Jute Mill, the largest jute factory in the country and a few other mills, has demonstrated that it is possible to meet all these eventualities with success, provided the political leadership is committed to such a course of action. In fact, the debates on the closing down or privatisation of this enterprise, including arrangements for compensating the workers, have been going on since the early 1990s. Therefore, to a large extent, public opinion in a way was prepared for it. It did not come as a very great surprise.

strengthened. The challenges associated with governance in the financial sector are illustrated earlier in this section. Analogous problems exist in the nonfinancial sector. The interests of multiple stakeholders ranging from shareholders to lenders, to customers and employees have to be reconciled and protected. Otherwise, sources of private investment funds may dry up or be withdrawn. Regulations are to be framed to prevent the misuse of investors' resources and to protect the fortunes of employees. They should cover functions and responsibility of the Board of Directors, its relationship with management, auditing rules, appointment and oversight of auditors, credit rating agencies, investment advisers, or managers. There are possibilities of conflict of interest in respect of each of the above functions that have to be avoided.

The essential condition of market efficiency is competition. Therefore, there is no social benefit or efficiency gain if privatisation leads to the substitution of public monopolies by private monopolies. Private monopoly, in addition, can have adverse income distributional effects when it exploits market power at the cost of consumers and employees. These considerations are specially relevant in the case of public utilities such as power generation, transmission, communications, and railways. Privatisation of these activities has become a live issue and requires serious examination. With technological innovations in recent years, there are selected activities in such sectors which can be operated on a small scale, affording opportunities for multiple enterprises competing in the market place. For example, there could be competition in the distribution of electricity if not in the field of transmission and generation. Privatisation of the distribution of electricity can take place in a competitive framework. Whenever competition is unlikely and the possibility of one or a few firms achieving market dominance is high, a well designed, efficient regulatory system for private enterprises relating to prices, quality, and quantity of services is necessary. Admittedly, the required institutions, regulations, and rules are not easy to devise and implement. How to avoid inefficient public monopolies which have their losses met by an unlimited access to public revenues, on the one hand, and exploitative private monopolies, with inadequate and inefficient regulation, on the other, is a challenge to the skill and competence of the policymakers. Regulating the market requires significant improvement in the quality and efficiency of the government. An inefficient but essential regulator/manager of the market combined with market failures could produce the worst of both the worlds.

Whenever the size and structure of the market permit, both public and private enterprises can be allowed to coexist and exercise competitive pressures on each other. This already happens in health, education, and related social services in Bangladesh. Not only the private sector but also the NGOs operate simultaneously with the public sector in the provision of services. The nonformal education programme of BRAC, an NGO, complements the provision of primary education in the public sector. Similarly, in the health sector, services are provided by the private sector at the higher end of medical care and by NGOs at the lower end of the primary health care. There is, of course, a need to avoid some undesirable unintended consequences of the coexistence of the public and private provision of services. As the affluent classes attend the private health and education services, the public institutions cater largely to the poor and the less affluent. While the affluent users and customers can exit from inefficient public services to avail themselves of more efficient and expensive private services, the public sector languishes and suffers in quality for lack of attention. Competent employees in public institutions are either enticed away by the attraction of higher incomes and incentives in the private sector or continue work in both sectors, reducing the intensity of work in the public sector. The poor, with no or limited voice, can exercise no political pressure for the improvement of public services.

Economic policy reforms, such as privatisation, efficiency in public enterprises, and improved rules and regulations governing the market, require broad national consensus and mobilisation of support of the gainers and compensation for the losers. In democratic societies, there is no alternative to consensus building on major policy issues through consultation and compromise. Otherwise, reforms proposed by the government in power are likely to be obstructed by the opposition party, which will impede implementation by exaggerating the costs of reforms. Consensus building does not imply unanimity of views. It implies that the majority considers seriously and demonstrably the views of the minority through debates and discussions in Parliament and other forums and that it is willing to make concessions or compromises, whenever feasible. The minority under the circumstances would not feel strongly enough about its reservations or views to reject the majority decision altogether. Since in a democracy, today's minority is likely to be tomorrow's majority, it will have to live by the same rules when next time it comes to power.

In Bangladesh, the major political parties are in state of perpetual confrontation, bent on denigrating or opposing whatever the other party has done in the past or intends to do. Either party in power is reluctant to take reformist measures even when its support may be ensured in Parliament. This is because it is apprehensive that the opposition party will mobilise those who may suffer losses from reforms and will try to frustrate its efforts. One way of overcoming such a deadlock is to require that both the parties face the bar of public opinion and explain clearly the reasons for their support for or opposition to different policies of national importance. It is only when the pressure of public opinion, reinforced by an active civil society, becomes strong and relentless on the political parties that they may seek compromises and retract from a perpetual state of confrontation.

16.5 NGOS: AN INTERMEDIATE REGIME

In Bangladesh, there is yet another sector, intermediate between the state and the private sector, which plays an important and growing role in the economy. This sector consists of a wide variety of Nongovernmental Organisations (NGOs). First, they implement development projects with resources provided by donors and the government and supplement the efforts of the government. In their role as contractors/agencies for the implementation of development projects, they compete for resources, which could otherwise be used by private sector contractors. Second, a few bigger NGOs have extended their activities to include investment in and management of commercial enterprises. They finance such investments partly from income earned in their grant-financed activities and partly from recourse to the private capital market, including borrowing from commercial banks. They play a role in the market economy in the same way as the private corporate and noncorporate sectors. Profits earned in the commercial ventures are intended to provide resources for their nonprofit activities. To the extent that they run commercial enterprises they are no different from the private sector and require the same kind of legal and regulatory oversight as is exercised over the private sector.

There are a few other functions which NGOs have considerable potential to perform but to date do so only to a limited extent. First, they can contribute towards improved governance of the market as well as of the state. They can serve as watchdogs over both the public and corporate sectors. With regard to the corporate sector, NGOs can raise awareness among the public about its exercise of market power to thwart competitive forces in the market for output, input, and labour. They can warn about its negative externalities such as adverse effects on health, safety and environment. Also, they can monitor and evaluate the performance of the public sector in its regulatory functions as well as in the provision of goods and services. Second, NGOs can inform and educate the public in securing access to and effectively utilising public services. They are able to mobilise and organise citizens' groups in order to exercise pressure on the government for the improvement of efficiency of services. Third, they can act as advocacy groups to espouse issues or causes of public interest responding to felt needs, values and aspirations of society such as human rights, women's empowerment, environmental protection, peace and religious freedom.

The foregoing illustrates the various ways in which NGOs, as a dominant group in civil society, can organise countervailing power against the abuse of market power by the private sector and misuse of political and administrative power by the government. In general, they can contribute to transparency and accountability in social and political transactions. It is true that they lack the kind of legitimacy conferred by democratic political representation. But they supplement the role of the political representatives by providing an additional channel for representing various interest groups as well as coalitions of private individuals, some of which lack organisational capacity or strength of their own. They represent the essential constituents of a pluralist democracy. In a democracy, they have a right to be consulted by government agencies in both national and local governments.

Most of the NGOs in Bangladesh are so overwhelmingly involved in the delivery of services and in the implementation of the donor funded and government approved or government funded projects that they may not be well suited to perform the oversight and advocacy functions. In some cases, there are possibilities of conflict of interest between their civil society functions and their responsibilities as contractors or development agents. Moreover, the methods of operations and organisation as well as the range of skill and expertise that are required for the functions of service delivery and project implementation may not be appropriate for their civil society activities and objectives.

NGOs depend overwhelmingly on funding by donor agencies; they are accountable to donors for the efficient use of resources as well as for the achievement of the goals set by donors. Currently, no less than 25 percent of the total development assistance to Bangladesh is channelled through NGOs, both national and international. It is the donors who monitor and evaluate their performance. Donors, in general, seem to prefer NGOs as implementing agents for development projects for a variety of reasons. They are perceived to be more flexible in their operations in meeting the requirements of particular projects and are quick to implement them. In addition, they operate at the "grassroots" level, reach the poor relatively easily and promote greater people's participation in the design and implementation of projects. However, as NGOs, both credit and noncredit, grow in size, handle many and big projects, and extend geographically, employing a large number of people, they may tend to acquire a few of the features, managerial and operational, which characterise large scale government agencies. A challenge for them is to avoid the pitfalls and shortcomings of large scale public sector organisations; they face the task of devising innovations to overcome them. Learning from each other, it is conceivable that the public sector and NGOs may improve the overall state of governance.

NGOs are in a state of evolution with respect to the range of their functions and activities. An example is the expansion of their commercial activities. One may wonder whether overlapping between the two sets of operations, i.e. non-profit and commercial activities, may not occur over time unless strict vigilance is exercised. Even though their operations are kept administratively and legally separate, the ultimate leadership — even if it is one step removed — and the guiding spirit remain the same. In the current sociopolitical context and ethically deficient business environment, one is not sure whether the fallout effects of their commercial activities may not seep through to the nonprofit sector. At present, their credibility in the society and in the donor community is due to the perception that, in general, they demonstrate greater efficiency and integrity or less exploitative tendencies than the public sector and certainly more integrity than the private sector. Public perception is always fragile and a small incident or misstep can damage it. Moreover, the risk is high that once the reputation of a few is adversely affected the whole group will suffer.

NGOs' involvement in commercial enterprises has been justified on the basis that they will eventually become independent of donor or government resources. Their nonprofit activities in the long run will be financed by the profits from commercial enterprises. In this scenario, their commercial activities have to substantially expand to generate income large enough to finance their nonprofit activities on a scale comparable to the present. However, NGOs, which remain predominantly credit agencies, and decide to gradually move upscale to finance the not so poor and middle level borrowers and other small scale income generating activities, may perform on a self sustaining basis without any public resources or hidden subsidy.

As in the past with micro credit, they may yet end up producing a new model combining commercial and noncommercial enterprises for the others to emulate, and to dispel the concerns of the doubters. It appears that the large NGOs in Bangladesh are a breeding ground for innovators and entrepreneurs. Many leaders of NGOs are drawn from the professions, including civil services of all varieties. There are individuals with entrepreneurial spirit or managerial competence who seem to be more readily attracted to NGOs. Compared to the private sector, freedom of entry to the NGOs' sector is likely to be greater with fewer bureaucratic hassles to overcome or regulations to encounter.

Relatively limited involvement of the government in the affairs of the large NGOs, which remain primarily a concern of donors, creates an undercurrent of tension between the government and NGOs.[7] The prevailing system of donor-NGOs relationship seems to contradict the recent emphasis by donors that development policies, priorities and projects should be "owned" i.e. chosen and designed by the government in cooperation with the various sections of society. How to improve the climate of relationship between NGOs and the government merits attention. For one thing, donors and the government may devise a different system for channelling external resources to NGOs. The model used by PKSF (Palli Karma-Sahayak Foundation) to channel external financial and technical assistance to the small microcredit NGOs may be relevant in this context. Under this system, an intermediate national agency is established by the government, which borrows from the World Bank to lend in turn to the NGOs. The latter selects NGOs on the basis of agreed criteria and lends to them on the basis of their programme of activities. It undertakes to monitor and evaluate the functions and the performance of the NGOs, their method of governance and impact on the beneficiaries. NGOs are accountable to PKSF for their successful operations as well as for the achievement of agreed targets for reaching the beneficiary population. They receive technical assistance from PKSF for improving the quality of management and for expanding the volume of their operations. PKSF is governed by a group of independent professionals of reputable ability and integrity appointed by, but operating independently of, the government and free from political interference. The World Bank, the donor, in turn, evaluates the performance of the intermediate agency (PKSF) in promoting, leading, and assisting NGOs to operate with efficiency and integrity.

Growth of democratic pluralism in Bangladesh requires further development and strengthening of the second category of NGOs with focus on civil society activities i.e. oversight, monitoring, and mobilisation and advocacy. However, their sources of financing, both domestic and international, are more limited than what is available to the first category of NGOs. Naturally, the government is not anxious

---

[7] The government, on the other hand, adopts a more relaxed attitude towards international NGOs located in the donor country and contracted by donors to implement programmes in Bangladesh, in the same way it accepts the foreign private consulting firms or contractors which are commissioned by donors to implement their projects, it is alleged, with nominal approval of the government.

to finance the type of activities that include judging and evaluating its own performance. In order to promote their civil society functions they need access to finance, which is independent of the government. In developed countries, they derive their finances from membership fees, private philanthropies, and nonprofit foundations. At present, foreign philanthropic organisations, private foundations abroad, and the international NGOs appear to be their main sources of financial support. In view of their expressed emphasis on the improvement of governance in Bangladesh, one would have expected a more vigorous support of donors for NGOs of this category. The donor community, in general, prefers to use them as agents for the implementation of development projects. In course of time, only when the government is convinced of the value of democratic pluralism, it will readily recognise the civil society functions of NGOs. In the medium term, reliance on the international donor community will remain the major source of finance. External assistance could be channelled through an independent organisation, as in the case of PKSF for the microcredit NGOs, outlined above.

It is essential that NGOs conduct their affairs in such a manner as to be credible. They should be independently governed and should be objective in their watchdog and advocacy functions. They need to be transparent in their operations; their finances should be audited by independent and reputable auditors, and should be widely available for public scrutiny. Their ultimate accountability is to the people they serve, provided their operations and financing are totally open and above board. Public opinion is the greatest judge of their integrity and credibility. International NGOs, which may be financing or cosponsoring the operations of national NGOs, have also the obligation to be transparent and open to public scrutiny.

Questions have been raised recently about the alleged participation of NGOs in political activities, associating with or helping the cause of political parties of their choice. Are political parties members of civil society? There is a basic distinction between NGOs and political parties. NGOs either as development agents or in their civil society role have the basic responsibility of influencing and changing government policies and actions. Political parties, on the other hand, have as their agenda and objective the capture of political power for themselves and the control of government. NGOs are expected to remain outside the political and administrative structure of the government and not to aspire to capture political power. Therefore, any close identification or association of NGOs with political parties subverts their very *raison de etre* and jeopardises their independent role as agents of development or as elements of the pluralist democracy providing for the participation of people, one step removed, in the governance of society at large.

It is imperative that leaders of NGOs strive hard to keep their political preferences strictly separate from or independent of their role as the functionaries of NGOs. This is not an easy task under any circumstances. In the context of the confrontational politics in the country, characterised by adversarial relationships and complete lack of trust between political parties, one is always under a shadow of doubt. To make it worse, society at large is also highly politicised and polarised. In this climate of opinion to demonstrate clearly that an NGO leadership is apolitical gets more complicated than usual. As NGOs develop extensive and countrywide operations with considerable resources, they are liable to attract the attention of political parties and groups. They appear as a potential source of help for mobilising public support in the interest of competing political parties. This is all the more reason why NGOs must do their best to avoid any appearance of political preferences or associations. In the interest of the future of NGOs in the country, it may be advisable that those with strong political preferences avoid leadership roles of NGOs.

16.6 CORRUPTION, MARKET, AND STATE

In its broad interpretation, corruption implies violation or contravention of rules, laws and regulations. In the government it involves misuse of public power or resources for private gain. In the private sector it involves violation of contracts by breaking or bending rules and regulations to enhance personal gain at the expense of partners or stakeholders in market transactions.

A market economy is jeopardised by corruption in market institutions and in government. Corruption is aggravated by poor state of the law and order situation.[8] Corruption adversely affects the functioning not only of markets but also of the public sector. It creates uncertainty and unpredictability of the results of economic transaction, and by increasing the risks of business it discourages long term investment. Illegal extortions or toll collections by *mafia/gangs* flourish in the absence of effective enforcement of law and order. This also adds greatly to the costs of economic transactions and reduces the returns on investment. Bureaucratic harassment, corruption, and organised violence — all combine to impose barriers to entry, hinder competition, and create market power for the few. The high costs of inefficiency and misallocation of resources imposed by corruption and violence are in the ultimate analysis borne by the population at large through high prices and low investment and growth. Furthermore, they aggravate inequity; the poor do not have access to political power nor resources to circumvent the obstacles placed by corruption.[9]

Admittedly, there are "niches" in the economy, which for some period may escape the adverse consequences of corruption. These sectors may manage to shield themselves for a while from the depredations of the corrupt and inefficient "visible hand" of the government or from privatised violence. The activities in the informal rural sector may fall in this category. Small nonfarm enterprises in rural and small towns are likely to be less affected than large and medium urban enterprises. However, in this general economic climate, they cannot grow and get integrated with the formal sector in a dynamic process of inter-linkages. Their long run growth remains stunted.

---

[8] Deterioration in the law and order situation is partly related to the way in which electoral politics is financed and conducted in Bangladesh. Money and "muscle power" play an important role in winning elections. The goons affiliated to political parties or electoral candidates terrorise the voters and generate fake or bogus votes. They get paid through tolls or extortions from their victims. Financiers of the respective candidates expect to be repaid by politicians through the offer of lucrative government contracts or other favours. Politicians require resources to finance the goons; when elected, they have to recoup expenditures incurred during elections and repay debt incurred to the financiers, who are the traders and industrialists. They try to accomplish this through abuse of power and misappropriation of public resources. As a result, a vicious circle sets in. Financing elections, corruption, and the use of goons/*mafia* for electoral advantage are interlocked. How to get out of this vicious circle is the challenge. To some extent, the financing of elections through public funds can help. But implementation problems of the public funding of elections are not easy to solve. Should the elections be financed by both private and public sources and if so, how does one combine them? In many countries, both developed and developing, this is a live question.

[9] See discussion on governance in Chapter 17.

The garment industry in Bangladesh has grown in spite of the failure of governance. This is a sector in which government intervention has been limited; also it has been more supportive rather than restrictive. In the beginning, the pioneers in this industry were people with influence and affluence. Many of the early entrepreneurs were drawn from the rank of retired civilian and military officers or active politicians who were able to neutralise the obstacles placed by bureaucratic regulations and political interference or even bend them to their favour. Eventually the industry attracted a large number of small and middle level entrepreneurs. Over time, a tradition of a supportive environment has been established. Moreover, very high profitability generated by quotas in the export markets has attracted a large number of enterprises. However, an adverse law and order situation, extortions by the *mafia/gangs*, the poor state of infrastructure, including bottlenecks at the seaports, have taken a toll on this sector in recent years.

As illustrated in the previous discussion on regulations governing the corporate sector, both financial and nonfinancial, temptations and opportunities for graft and corruption are ever present. If unchecked, this may lead to a collapse of confidence in the integrity of the corporate sector and market economy. Private entrepreneur, driven by the motivation of profit maximisation, seeks the highest profits mostly through innovation and enterprise and on occasions, by exploiting loopholes in rules or even risking the violation of rules and regulations.[10]

---

[10]Recently, in the recent corporate scandals in the United States and elsewhere, questions have been raised about the nature of and limits to the pursuit of maximisation of private profit as the prime mover or the mainspring for the maximisation of society's wealth and income. In this debate the pronouncements of Smith, the prophet of the private capitalist system, are invoked. Adam Smith emphasised the need for virtue as well as wealth. He was wary of high profits. "They destroy parsimony which in other circumstances is natural to the character of the merchant. When profits are high, sober virtue seems to be superfluous, and expensive luxury suits better the affluence of his situation." "The owners of the great mercantile capitals are necessarily the leaders and conductors of the whole industry of every nation, and their example has a much greater influence upon the manners of the whole industrious part of it than that of any other order of men." The kind of behaviour that is induced by exorbitant wealth and celebrity status tends to create easy pickings for alert, hungry commercial competitors. But leadership requires much more. Real leadership requires a commitment not only to capital but also to community. A century later, Marshall gave a name to the trait necessary for effective leadership: economic chivalry. "Chivalry in business includes public spirit, as chivalry in war includes unselfish loyalty to the cause of prince, or of country or of crusade. It includes a scorn for cheap victories, and a delight in succouring those who need a helping hand. It does not disdain the gains to be won, but it has the fine pride of the warrior

The risk of collusion between the regulators and those who are the subject of regulations is ever present. Who regulates the regulators is a crucial question? The answer is transparency and wide dissemination of information relating to actors in and regulators of the market. In a democratic political system with a representative Parliament, regulators are answerable to the executives who appoint them. Legislators need to exercise an oversight function over executives in all branches of the government. The ultimate responsibility of safeguarding public interest rests on them. The role of the media and an active civil society in this context cannot be overstressed.

Those who enforce the legal framework and market regulations have to be honest. In any society, there needs to be a basic minimum foundation of ethics, norms, or morals, which govern human transactions and interactions. Ethics affect economic activity in a fundamental sense. Ethical conduct creates the valuable quality of trust. At the most basic level, ethics are a low cost substitute for internal control and external regulation. Truth telling and loyalty create externalities. Though they cannot be traded in markets, these qualities have a real value that increases the efficiency of the economic system. Trust reduces monitoring and transaction costs for individual enterprises and in the wider economy. In the field of governance, without ethical behaviour, regulations beyond a point become exorbitantly costly and are difficult to enforce. The burden on the law enforcing mechanism becomes unwieldy if there is no minimum moral foundation of human transactions.[11] A core system of values makes it easier for the regulatory system to operate. Restoring values is, of course, more difficult than passing laws and introducing regulations. Yet the ethical climate clearly matters.

---

who esteems the spoils of a well fought battle, or of the prize of the tournament, for the sake of the achievements to which they testify, and only in the second degree for the value at which they are appraised in the money of the market." The fine pride of the warrior is a tough trait to capture on a balance sheet or in a compensation plan. *Financial Times*, 25th November 2002, Peter Doughtery.

[11] Where rules and regulations are flouted transaction costs go up. In markets where informed speculators are known to be extracting gains at others' expense, markets will widen their spreads to protect themselves, causing the cost of dealing to rise. As shown by recent examples of auditors and directors of private corporate sector in USA and elsewhere, regulations are not enough. Ethical conduct is necessary in both cases. It is difficult to plug all the loopholes and to enforce all regulations fully without the additional help from ethical values. *Financial Times*, 2 December, 2002, p. 13: Capitalism and Ethics, John Plender.

Civil society and its various constituents can serve as agents or guardians and advocates of such values. In the ultimate analysis, it is "people power" mobilised and activated in some way that is not at all now obvious, which can make a major assault on the prevailing system of misuse of power, corruption, and violence. This may happen when a growing and a very large proportion of the population feels a significant adverse impact on their well being and safety. They would perhaps combine, possibly sporadically and in small groups in the beginning and, later on, in larger groups, vigorously demanding a change in the status quo. Also, as the threshold of tolerance of the general population is crossed, civil society, consisting of different segments of the population organised in groups/associations, might exert increasing and ultimate pressure on political leaders for a decisive action.

Chapter 17

UNEQUAL PARTNERS
IN DEVELOPMENT

17.1 INTRODUCTION

Following the liberation war of 1971, Bangladesh started out as an independent state heavily dependent on foreign aid. She needed assistance to meet urgent needs for reconstruction and rehabilitation as well as for long term investment requirements. This reliance continued in the years to follow. At times, it appeared that maximisation of foreign aid was the overriding objective of Bangladesh's external economic policy. The success of a Finance or Planning Minister was judged by his ability to obtain large commitments of aid at the annual World Bank Consortium meeting. Much greater attention was devoted to increasing the flow of aid rather than mobilising domestic resources and making their efficient use or, for that matter, expanding export earnings. Bangladesh found it relatively easy to mobilise large volume of resources from foreign aid, by pleading poverty and espousing her cause as one of the least developed countries, rather than mounting determined efforts to mobilise domestic resources.

Over the years, aid as a percentage of GDP or public expenditures has declined. In the early 1970s, aid was about 10 percent and it went down to 4.8 percent in 1990 and 2.4 percent in 1998. During the late 1990s, aid financed between 45 percent and 40 percent of annual development expenditure as against 85 percent in the early 1980s.[1]

---

[1] The annual average level of total aid flow during 1998-2000 has been around US$1.5 billion. It was overwhelmingly composed of project aid; food and commodity aid constituted around 30 percent. The pipeline in project aid, accumulated from past commitments and unutilised,

The importance of aid as a source of foreign exchange also diminished and by the late 1990s it provided no more than 10-12 percent of foreign exchange resources. Remittances from workers abroad registered a rapid increase and by the late 1990s, exceeded estimated annual aid disbursements. In spite of a relative decline in the importance of foreign aid as a source of investment and foreign exchange resources, it is still significant enough to call for a strategy for its appropriate management.

Since the beginning in the early 1970s, the relationship between donors and Bangladesh has ebbed and flowed. Not surprisingly, it has depended upon how donors judge Bangladesh's implementation of policy reforms they advocate. In recent years, aid relationship has seemed uneasy or even tense. Donors complain. First, slow disbursement of aid has resulted in a large pipeline. This is due to administrative bottlenecks and procedural complexities, such as delays in competitive bidding, approval of contractors/consultants, and disbursement/release of funds to the executing or implementing agencies. Second, donors are reluctant to make new aid commitment because the government is unwilling to undertake policy reforms and institutional changes they consider essential for improved economic performance. In some cases, they commit aid on the undertaking that the agreed upon conditions are implemented at the required pace. Disbursement from the committed aid stalls when such conditions are not met.

Bangladesh argues that policy conditionalities required by donors are either inappropriate or unnecessary. The government considers the conditions as too invasive i.e. they intrude heavily into the government decision making and implementation process. Moreover, they do not take adequate account of the socio-cultural-political constraints. Policy reforms, which donors seek to promote in Bangladesh, extend over all major sectors such as industry, agriculture, banking and finance, energy, transport, and communications. These also cover macroeconomic policies and institutional reforms, including administration, judiciary, and legal system. Perception is widespread that Bangladesh, under the pressure of donors, is obliged to sacrifice its freedom of action in policymaking. Development policies, many in the country feel, are basically formulated by donors.

---

has been around US$5-6 billion. IMF, *Bangladesh: Selected Issues and Statistics*, Appendix, April 15, 2002.

It is alleged that government officials frequently enter into aid agreements with a stipulation of a large number of conditionalities, without fully appreciating their implications and consequently underestimating the challenges posed by the proposed reforms. They frequently overestimate their capacity to implement reforms in the face of resistance by vested interests. Alternatively, it is assumed that once aid is committed and starts to be disbursed, donors will not be enthusiastic about cancelling or withdrawing the ongoing aid. They could be persuaded to change the original conditions in the light of new circumstances. In some cases, donors do indeed modify the conditions. In any case, under both scenarios, there is a strong likelihood of tension with donors. This experience makes donors wary and consequently unwilling to commit new aid without a firm assurance that the government is willing and able to implement the reforms. Also, they have in recent past resorted to the cancellation of credits when agreed conditions have not been implemented.

17.2 POLICY DIALOGUE AND DEVELOPMENT STRATEGY FRAMEWORK

Policy dialogue and conditionalities are not new in the history of development assistance in South Asia and possibly in other developing countries. They have all along been a feature of aid relationship in one form or another. Right from the 1960s, donors emphasised that effectiveness of aid in promoting development depended not merely on increase in investment but, much more importantly, on appropriate macro and micro policies that promote efficient allocation and use of investment resources.

During the 1950s and 1960s, many developing countries produced medium term development plans setting forth targets, objectives and priorities for economic growth but also policies, investment allocations and institutions required for their realisation. Plans provided estimates of total domestic investment resources and requirements as well as the gap to be filled by foreign aid. Many South Asian countries such as Pakistan, India, and Bangladesh, after independence, produced Five-Year Plans. In the early days of development assistance, donors considered Five-Year Plans as a necessary framework for the provision of aid. Within this framework donors used to seek and find

their choice of sectors or projects for assistance as well as carry out
dialogue with recipients on policies and priorities. Recipient countries
often made modifications or adjustments in their plans in the light of
discussions and dialogue with donors.[2] In the course of time, donors,
in fact, not only encouraged the formulation of Five-Year Plans but
also extended assistance for building up planning institutions in
many developing countries, including South Asia.

That was then. But now the concept and the practice of planning
are out of fashion. It was replaced in recent years at donor's request
by what was called Policy Framework Paper (PFP) as a framework
for aid negotiations. As distinguished from Five-Year Plans, the PFPs
were considered to be more focused and shorter statements of country
objectives, priorities and investment programmes, overall and sectoral.
The Bank provided assistance to recipient countries in the preparation
of such PFPs. It was alleged that in several cases, such as Bangladesh,
PFPs were drafted by the Bank. Bangladesh, like many such countries,
accepted the PFPs prepared by the Bank with modifications, if
considered very essential. Obviously, the Bank staffs had discussions
with the officials while preparing PFPs so as to avoid surprises in the
final report. It is the World Bank, in cooperation with the IMF as
well as the regional banks and bilateral donors, that conducted or
coordinated the process of dialogue based on PFPs.

Very recently, PFPs have been replaced by a different type of
document as a basis for aid negotiations. They are the Poverty
Reduction Strategy Papers (PRSPs) to be prepared by Bangladesh.
The focus is now explicitly on poverty reduction. Investment priorities,
programmes, and policies are to be linked expressly to the objective
of poverty reduction. Looking back in history, this seems to be
exactly similar to the situation that prevailed in connection with the
massive effort all over the aid seeking developing world in preparing
Five-Year Plans. How and why it is different? Is it one of the "fads
and fancies" of donors which like all the others are destined to rise
and fall?

The PRSP approach or the formulation of a poverty reduction
strategy paper is expected to be "country driven, result oriented,
comprehensive and long term in perspective, and to foster domestic

---

[2] The experience of Bangladesh in this regard is detailed in Chapter 11.

and external partnerships." PRSP has to be an integrated and consistent document involving all sectors as well as policies, both macro and sectoral. In view of interlinkages and interdependences between sectors and programmes, consistency amongst them as well as with overall resource availability has to be ensured. After all, this was exactly the same assumption that was at the basis of Five-Year or shorter term Plans that had been traditionally produced by many developing countries. What is new? PRSP seems to be rediscovery of the old wine in a new bottle of poverty reduction. The most important characteristic is its preparation and ownership by a country. It is not to be a set of conditionalities on policies, programmes, and institutional reforms to be imposed by donors and to be implemented by recipients. After more than 50 years of experience, donors have concluded that for aid to be effective in promoting growth and poverty alleviation, national development objectives and strategies should be formulated by a country on its own initiative. Furthermore, a country should be convinced that appropriate policy reforms are needed for their achievement; it must demonstrate its commitments and capacity to implement necessary reforms.

It is suggested that the most important element of novelty lies in the process. The document has to be initially prepared by the government through an intensive consultation and agreement among different Ministries and agencies. The policies and programmes in different Ministries, directly and indirectly, have implications for growth and poverty reduction. The PRSP development strategy should not only represent the output of consultations among the government Ministries and agencies at political and administrative levels; it should also involve consultations with and reviews by various segments of civil society, extending from private think tanks or experts to business associations, farmers, labour unions, NGOs, and a widest possible variety of peoples' associations. The participation by all the actors involved in the country's socioeconomic development provides an opportunity — almost a compulsion — for policymakers, administrators, and the public to concentrate their minds about the development strategy and policies. This process of preparing PRSP through countrywide consultation with all stakeholders and segments of society is expected to establish and demonstrate its ownership.

There is an aspect of the nation wide and multilevel consultative process of PRSP that seems to have been ignored. Not all development issues or policies can be discussed fruitfully or productively at all levels and by all groups. It is necessary to determine the appropriate agenda for consultation for each group of participants. For example, at the local level the issues for dialogue and discussion have to be oriented to local problems and interests as well as to capabilities of local populations.

Monitoring and evaluating progress in the implementation of PRSP and its impact are expected to be a similar participatory process. The irony of the situation is that this participatory process of preparing a country's development strategy is being undertaken at the behest of donors. Should not nationwide dialogue, debate, and discussion on development programmes, including Five-Year or Annual Plans, now and in the past, have occurred in any case without prodding by donors and without being a prerequisite for development assistance? Does it not appear that the participatory process itself is not owned by countries but is enjoined by donors? One wonders whether the PRSP process in Bangladesh would end up being a once-and-for-all exercise and not a regular system for formulating development programmes and policies as they are elaborated over the years. To be meaningful, the process had to be an integral part of the policymaking system and not an exceptional ritual of going through the motion of participation that is required by donors. It has to be the outcome of felt need or conviction and genuine appreciation of the value of the participatory process. Till today, development programmes or policies of Bangladesh have been seldom debated in an organised and systematic way in the Parliament and in the forums of political parties — a minimum requirement of policymaking process in a democratic society. This seldom happens in Bangladesh.[3]

---

[3] See Chapter 15. The right to know and access to information are the basic foundation of transparency and accountability in government. The tradition or habit of secrecy, even when it is unnecessary and counterproductive, inherited from the nondemocratic past and archaic bureaucratic practices, dies hard in Bangladesh. The control of information confers power on those who exercise authority. But then secrecy breeds rumours and speculation which have to be fought or counteracted, not always successfully, because secrecy at the same time breeds lack of public trust in the government. Furthermore, it perpetuates ignorance and makes a mockery of any limited attempt at the participatory process.

The avowed purpose of the PRSP exercise is to establish country ownership of development strategy, which is not imposed by donors from outside. But PRSP will be submitted to donors for their examination and as a basis of discussions and dialogue with them. Their agreement with its content is a precondition for the provision of development assistance. Therefore, country ownership is only a necessary but not a sufficient condition for the flow of aid.

The next relevant question is whether the content of PRSP, apart from the process, is very different from the strategy for growth and poverty reduction that has been evolving over the past several years among development thinkers and practitioners? It may be worth recalling a few landmarks in the evolution of development thinking. First, in the early 1970s, the Bank and donors suggested that a development project should be so formulated as to indicate how many of the beneficiaries are poor and how much their poverty is reduced as a result of its implementation. It became a great preoccupation of donors following the Bank's lead to identify the poor among the beneficiaries of aid projects and to quantify the impact on their poverty. This was relatively easy to accomplish in the case of projects which were meant for and directed towards the poor such as micro credit, irrigation projects for small and poor farmers, food subsidy, and feeding or special employment programmes for the poor. In view of considerable difficulty of demonstrating the direct impact on the poor for every project in all sectors, this exercise in many instances became a command performance. It led to the proliferation of imaginative and, sometimes, fictitious ways in which the target group of the poor was identified and direct and indirect impact on poverty was presented. In a wide range of sectors and in a variety of directly productive and infrastructure projects, the impact on the poor was indirect. It was difficult to clearly identify and link directly the poor beneficiaries to many such projects. That overall economic growth should expand income and employment opportunities in which poor would participate was inadequately recognised. It was necessary to ensure that growth took place in sectors in which the poor were mostly engaged in earning their livelihood, using technology that employed them.

Second, throughout the 1980s, development strategy in its content and coverage expanded and relative emphasis on its various components kept on changing. A series of UN conferences, deliberations by the Bretton Woods Institutions and results of research, originating mostly in developed, donor countries, spawned a wide ranging, cumulative agenda for development. Over the years, priorities have ranged from basic needs, poverty, human development (a repackaged amalgam of basic needs and poverty) to environment, gender, children, youth, to participation, social inclusion, human rights and political freedom. The content and coverage of the strategy have thus become overloaded over time. The integration of such a wide variety of concerns in the consistent framework of a development strategy is a challenging task. In addition, to seek to incorporate multiple elements in each individual project and programme greatly complicates the task of project formulation and implementation.

By the 1990s, a sort of consensus seemed to have emerged that the poverty reduction strategy should have broadly three components: first, overall economic growth with emphasis on labour intensive, employment oriented projects and sectors, such as small farmer agriculture and small scale industries and services; second, human capital formation through education, health, social services, population and nutrition programmes; and third, social safety net programmes, such as specialised credit, employment and subsidy programmes that make a direct assault on poverty. At least three, if not more, refinements in the above strategy followed. It was suggested that, as far as possible, different groups of the poor, such as women, children, old, disabled, marginalised or socially excluded, ethnically disadvantaged and geographically isolated groups, should be differentiated. Programmes and policies for poverty reduction should be based on their distinct characteristics and should meet their specific needs. Second, safety net programmes should be designed not only to deal with endemic poverty but also to protect the poorest from vulnerability i.e. unanticipated declines in income and assets.[4] Third, the poor should be involved in the decision making process, specially in the preparation, monitoring, and evaluation of projects and policies. Policies and institutions that ensure such a participatory process constitute

---

[4] Vulnerability arises from exposure to shocks such as sickness, death, disability, natural disasters including crop failures, famine, floods, and drought as well as economic recession caused by internal or external economic fluctuations.

an important part of the strategy. These include decentralisation of the political and administrative system and organisations of the poor — all designed to make their voices heard in the decision making process.

PRSP embraces all the above components. To some extent it seems to be a culmination of the process in which all the strands of ideas or objectives of development are merged. It is as if all the "old and new wines" have been put together in a king-sized shaker. It professes to be both a growth promoting and a poverty reducing strategy. In addition to all the different poverty reducing measures, it encompasses policies that would accelerate growth and thus make the reduction in poverty sustainable in the long run. A strategy for growth requires a whole range of macro and sectoral policies and programmes to achieve macroeconomic stability and to increase savings and investment. In the area of macroeconomic management, PRSP stresses the crucial role of public expenditure, including its design, size, and composition as well as the system of budget control and monitoring. Also, needed are structural reforms and sectoral adjustments, including open market and trade liberalisation that would ensure greater efficiency of use of resources. In addition, growth strategy has to be propoor. In other words, investment programmes and policies for stimulating growth should be such that benefits of growth should accrue more to the poor than to the rich. This requires that investment in sectors, which contain large concentration of the poor and are the sources of their income and employment, should receive priority. In general, if inequality in the distribution of income or assets can be reduced in the process of growth, the impact of growth on poverty reduction is enhanced. Above all, good governance and healthy institutions are essential for both achieving growth and reducing poverty.

A few questions are relevant in the context of the PRSP exercise currently under way in Bangladesh and other developing countries. First, how far the wide ranging agenda meet the criterion of ownership by Bangladesh or for that matter other developing countries? To what extent they represent a set of felt, home grown aspirations and objectives of the mainstream development thinkers and policymakers in Bangladesh? One may argue that it is not necessary that ideas on development strategy must always originate in a developing country or countries. In the course of time through a process of increased understanding, interaction and exchange of ideas and experience across nations, policymakers in developing countries, as members of the international community, have in the past and will in the future come to accept a range of ideas as their own. After all, the process of globalisation occurs not only in respect of technology and institutions but also in the realm of ideas. It is difficult to test whether this has, in fact, occurred in Bangladesh. The PRSP process itself may sensitise the policymakers about a wide ranging development agenda.

Second, the involvement of all segments of society, advocacy groups and constituencies in the broadest possible participatory exercise, makes the choice of priorities among objectives and programmes very difficult, if not impossible. It greatly increases the likelihood that the full range of issues contained in each of the components of the ever-expanding development agenda will be included. Priority setting in a large assembly of all variety of groups, at all levels from the local to the national, gets much more complicated than in a representative Parliament. Compromises and trade offs that are necessary, if consensus is to be reached, are not easy to negotiate in such an environment. It demands a great deal of leadership and negotiating ability. PRSP runs the risks of either producing a long shopping list or overriding and overlooking many issues and thus, facing complaints that people's wishes have been neglected.

Third, there is no unanimity among donors in respect of their preferences or priorities. They are the most crucial group of participants in the process and would decide whether and how far PRSP is to be used as a basis for foreign assistance. While the general objective of growth and poverty reduction is accepted, the relative emphasis by different donors on various components or subcomponents of the strategy varies.

To illustrate, even within the range of direct poverty reducing measures there are choices to be made. Is vulnerability more important than endemic poverty? How important is empowerment? Is special employment programme for destitute men and women in the short run more important than long term programme for organising self help associations or for raising their awareness of potentials and responsibilities? How important is immediate relief of poverty as against institutional reforms that in the long run impact favourably on the poor? Also, how one is to determine priority among groups? Do children demand greater priority than women? Moreover, how and to what extent donors meet the investment requirements of PRSP depend on sectors and projects they choose to finance. Donors have different preferences. Investments in sectors, which do not have direct impact on the poor but are nonetheless essential for laying the foundations for growth, are not any more preferred areas of assistance for most donors.[5]

The preparation of PRSP with all its components and specification of interrelationships between them, as delineated in the guidelines laid down by the Bank, is a complicated task.[6] For example, to formulate the poverty reduction components of PRSP, the requirements are: collection and analysis of data on various aspects of poverty and characteristics of different poverty groups; identification and design of appropriate policies; analysis of the impact of macro and sectoral policies, including public expenditures, on poverty in all its dimensions as well as estimation of their costs and benefits.[7]

Domestic capacity of the government in Bangladesh like in many other developing countries is deficient for implement such a mammoth undertaking.[8] Whatever limited capacity there is, it is over employed in ongoing activities and day-to-day administration and has no time to devote to longer term exercise. In a way, the preparation of PRSP would involve learning by doing. It is argued that the beginning of

---

[5] With the new policy of privatisation and market liberalisation, financing of physical infrastructure, energy, irrigation, agricultural production, and marketing, natural resource exploration and development is left to private enterprises, both domestic and foreign. Private financial markets, domestic and international, are expected to provide financing for private entrepreneurs, both domestic and foreign. The emphasis, therefore, is now on efficient domestic financial markets and investment climate that stimulate savings at home and draw financial resources from abroad.

[6] This is amply recognised in the document "Review of the Poverty Reduction Strategy Paper (PRSP) Approach: Main Findings," prepared by the Bank and Fund for the Development Committee March 22, 2002.

[7] The poverty and social impact analysis of policies and programmes bristles with methodological problems. The link between action and outcomes is frequently imprecise.

[8] The donors are expected to assist, if requested, in the process of the national debate and deliberations by drawing upon their own independent analysis of relevant policy issues and experiences of other similarly situated countries. This should be available in the so-called "knowledge bank" of the donor institutions, such as the World Bank, the IMF, regional banks and in some cases, the bilateral donors.

the exercise, however limited, by revealing inadequacies would stimulate efforts by the government in building capacity, if necessary, with the assistance of donors. This is going to be a long drawn time consuming process. Given the limited capacity in the government, it is likely that the task of formulating PRSP would be assigned to one or two consultants outside the government. In this way, the process of learning-by-doing would not even be started in the government. Without a serious engagement in analysis and in wide ranging debates by the Planning, Finance, and other sectoral Ministries, it is not possible for them to claim ownership of such a strategy in the real sense. Building capacity in civil society organisations and at various levels of governments, including local government, is no less crucial for undertaking such a wide ranging participatory exercise. One wonders whether building up such capacity should not have preceded the exercise.

17.3 OWNERSHIP AND DIALOGUE

The prevailing practice in Bangladesh with regard to all forms of assistance often has been for donors to take the initiative, specially in respect of policy and institutional reforms. The government has usually reacted passively to the findings of donors' analysis and accompanying policy proposals. In the context of new environment for development assistance, as reflected among others in the PRSP approach, the roles of donors and the government are expected to be reversed with the government taking the proactive role and donors reacting to the government programme.

PRSP in Bangladesh is expected to indicate priorities in terms of overall and sectoral investment programmes as well as policies and institutions. This would provide the framework within which macro policy reforms, structural adjustment and related sectoral policies would be negotiated with donors, specially the Bank and the Fund. Other donors are expected to follow this agreed framework. Policies, priorities, and programmes proposed by Bangladesh, as a basis for policy dialogue and negotiations for development assistance, may, however, not be agreeable to donors in all its aspects. Donors may not agree with the findings of the government's analysis or its policy proposals. Under the circumstances, there is scope for discussions and dialogue in the true sense of the term between Bangladesh and donors. This will replace the monologue that takes place currently, in the name of dialogue, when the government reacts often on an *ad hoc* basis to the recommendations and proposals of donors. There could, of course, be legitimate differences of opinion between the government of Bangladesh and donors. Economic policy analysis and suggestions, based on such an analysis, are not in the nature of exact science. Examples abound of economists and social scientists having made mistakes in their diagnosis of economic problems and policy prescriptions. Policy decisions by their very nature have to be made under conditions of uncertainty. Moreover, not all the consequences or effects unfolding in the process of implementation are discernible ahead of time; unintended or unforeseen consequences are not uncommon.

Under the new scenario of aid relations, it is the recipient that is expected to be initiator and owner of the strategy in all its dimensions. Therefore, it is necessary that the views and the judgement of the policymakers of Bangladesh, based on their detailed knowledge of the socioeconomic circumstances of the country, deserve serious consideration. Such knowledge and insight are not likely to be possessed by donor institutions. The prerequisite for such a dialogue is mutual respect. Since the relationship between a donor and a recipient is unequal, there is a danger of the dialogue degenerating into creditors assuming a superior position vis-à-vis debtors. With a greater bargaining power, donors frequently develop a false or unjustified confidence in their policy analysis and proposals.[9]

---

[9] The operative question in the traditional policy dialogue is whether a donor can admit doubts and uncertainty in its recommendations without losing the sanction that the offer of credit brings. It is felt by donors that to depart from an absolute certitude of recommendations weakens the force and acceptability of recommendations. This situation is more than usually complicated in the case of younger donor representatives with limited acquaintance with policymaking in a country as was demonstrated in Chapter 11 in the case of Bangladesh. Barring exceptions, a young expert with impeccable academic accomplishments but without direct or /indirect acquaintance of developing country circumstances might miss out the limitations of his analysis. Such an expert feels more certain in his analysis and is more dogmatic in his recommendations. Knowledge and experience can be substitute for each other only in exceptional circumstances. Both are needed. With experience, one begins to see with some objectivity different points of view and the limitations of analysis in arriving at absolutist conclusions in the context of a highly complex reality. This is all the more reason why a great deal of attention has to be paid to the institutional constraints and socio-political limitations in the particular circumstances of a country. To admit mistakes *ex post* — many years after the fact as is done in the standard evaluation reports — is nowadays often popular. What is needed is willingness or capacity to modify and re-examine the recommendations in the course of an ongoing aid relationship or

How does one resolve the legitimate, unresolved differences of opinions between the government and donors? In order to minimise the possibilities of misdiagnosis or inappropriate recommendations and to strengthen the element of objectivity in the process, it is advisable to resort to an independent panel of experts. The panel would evaluate the analysis and policy proposals of both the government and donors and provide their own recommendations. In the above scenario, the panel acts as an "umpire" between the contending parties (donors and Bangladesh), and provides an independent answer to the issues under controversy and in the process it may reconcile their divergent views.

There could be two alternative ways of responding to the opinion or judgement of the panel. Under one alternative, both donors and Bangladesh agree in advance to accept and abide by its decision or recommendations. Under the second alternative, neither party is committed in advance to accept the panel's opinion or decision. However, it gives a way out to either party to modify its position by providing a room for second thoughts and for a subsequent round of negotiations for reaching an agreement. Under this system, "conditions" that eventually emerge in negotiations are those which are voluntarily and consciously chosen by Bangladesh. In the ultimate analysis, these policies should be worth implementation on their own even if they are not the conditions for the grant of aid.

An independent panel in the above scenario will be giving its judgement and expert opinion on the policy issues, both macro and sectoral, as well as the programmes and priorities on which disagreements occur between donors and Bangladesh. Irreconcilable differences of opinion may also arise on the detailed operational issues or specific policies that are attached as conditions for particular projects. In the case of projects, which involve large investments, specialised external panels with expertise in particular projects may be appointed in order to adjudicate between donors and Bangladesh and provide recommendations. There are some precedents in this respect. For example, in the case of a few large scale water control and irrigation projects, involving construction of dams, as well as oil pipeline projects,

---

negotiations. And also, if mistakes in the end occur, it is for both parties to accept them as one of the occupational hazards and not to apportion blame.

independent panels have been appointed in response to pressure from nongovernmental organisations. They provide their own assessment, specially with respect to environmental implications, as a guide both to donors and the recipient country.

The involvement of independent panels in any of the above variants will overcome temptation to apportion blame, when mistakes occur, as well as help save the face of both donors and the government. The decision on policies and priorities thus becomes a joint responsibility. All parties involved in the process are assumed to share responsibility and learn by doing.

An additional and useful element can be introduced in the process of policy dialogue by providing the policymakers in Bangladesh with direct exposure to the experience of similarly situated developing countries. This can be done in two ways. First, the panel of independent external experts may include members from developing countries with experience in policy issues or programmes that are similar to those in Bangladesh. Second, policymakers of Bangladesh may be invited to visit a country with similar experience and to engage in an exchange of views and share lessons of experience with their counterparts.

A few questions may be raised in connection with an independent panel. For example, what would be the trigger for the use of the new mechanism and at whose request would it be established? The initiative should be with Bangladesh to invoke the new mechanism if it wants to argue out its case before an independent panel. This is in conformity with the widely accepted, current emphasis by donors on national ownership and initiative of borrowers. Who would decide the composition of the panel? Both the parties can each nominate an equal number of members. Since the panels' recommendations would be, to a large extent, a matter of their judgement, is it necessary that some uniform criteria are used in the exercise of judgement by different panels in different countries? Currently, this is what is anyway expected to be ensured by officials of donor institutions in their analysis and recommendations. It is not necessary to provide such criteria for use by panels. The panel members are expected to be experts with wide experience and knowledge of development programmes and policies. The very case for an independent panel is based upon the assumption that in the choice of country programmes and policies there is no absolute truth and no scope for rigid certainty and that one size does not fit all. Therefore, a group of wise men and women are called upon to exercise their judgement in the particular circumstances of a country in the light of the arguments and facts presented by both sides.

How does one avoid the use of the mechanism for every instance of disagreement between Bangladesh and donors? After all, the use of a panel has an opportunity cost for Bangladesh and lenders — in fact, more for the former than for the latter. It involves expenditure of time and effort in the preparation and presentation of arguments for its case. This cost should help discourage an indiscriminate use of the mechanism. Yet another restraint on its excessive use is that Bangladesh has to obtain donors' agreement for a panel to be established. On the other hand, in order to discourage donors from being obstructive or noncooperative, a safeguard may be introduced. For example, if donors are unwilling to accept the request, Bangladesh, if she feels strongly aggrieved at such a refusal, may seek to exercise moral "suasion" on them by deciding to give wide publicity about the matter among the development community. Alternatively, Bangladesh could finance such a panel on its own and use its recommendations in negotiations with donors. In case of the World Bank or the Regional Banks, the case for establishing an independent panel can be placed before their Executive Boards by Bangladesh.

17.4 HUMAN FACTOR IN AID NEGOTIATION: A DIGRESSION

In this context, it may be relevant to digress into a particular, often neglected and seldom discussed, aspect of the diplomacy of aid negotiations. How important is the human factor in aid negotiations i.e. the way donors and Bangladesh officials interact with each other? In the course of the long history of relations with donors in Bangladesh, there have been occasions when tension and uneasiness might have developed due to the personal factor i.e. personal chemistry between an important donor representative and a Minister or a high official.[10] To many, it may seem a very minor or irrelevant

---

[10]See Chapter 11.

question. Surely, in aid negotiations, one can argue that there can be no scope for any other but strictly professional considerations. Personal likes and dislikes cannot and should not influence judgement or decisions. Unfortunately, human factor matters and sometimes matters a great deal. Personal slight or indifference, perceived or real, affects in some degree the outcome of negotiations even without the individuals being conscious of it. After all, one is dealing with human ego and perceptions which are fallible. Frequently, cultural differences cloud the possibility of objective determination. This emphasises the importance of negotiating skill and capacity to conduct interpersonal relations on the part of both donor representatives and recipient country officials.

How important is the extent of deference and respect with which the donor officials are treated a factor in the harmonious conduct of negotiations? Considerable power is perceived to be in the hands of a donor official. After all, his recommendation often influences decisions on aid and, therefore, is considered critical by the recipient. What is considered an appropriate degree of "respect" to be shown to a donor official is often determined by what is customary or what one is used to receiving in other countries. This issue frequently comes up in connection with the visiting high officials, particularly from the World Bank, which holds a very special position among donors and its judgement exercises considerable influence on them.[11]

---

[11] The degree of welcome or courtesy extended to a visiting donor official may be reflected in such simple things as the manner of reception at the airport, the level of protocol facilities, the quality of transportation and level of hospitality. Some countries tend to treat the Bank officials as if they are the highest level of visiting dignitaries. There is a competition among the smaller South Asian countries in the extension of the VIP treatment to the Bank and other aid officials. There is the story of a Vice President of the Bank who used to be received at the airport in a South Asian country by not only a Minister but also, in addition, by a representative of the office of the Prime Minister. One of the Prime Minister's cars was always placed at the disposal of the Vice President, who would also be "wined and dined" by the Prime Minister. It was reported that the Bank official's opinion of the country's economic performance gained not insignificantly from this strategy. It was difficult to confirm how far it was true or just a wild rumour. But the fact that such a perception prevailed in the aid community in the neighbouring countries was important enough to influence the behaviour of other recipients.

Bangladesh has not consistently followed that route. During the early 1970s, she wanted to strike out a more business-like relationship with donors, including Bank officials, at a level of normal, and not profuse, courtesy and hospitality. But there was no evidence that this had any adverse impact on the aid flow, though it might have influenced their judgement or opinion of the Bangladesh policymakers. It is possible, in the early 1970s, that because of the special

How important is it that donor officials, even the middle level ones, are able to conduct negotiations or discussions at as a high level of the government hierarchy as they possibly can? Sometimes an aid official considers it important that he has discussions with the Ministers and, most importantly, with the head of the government i.e. the Prime Minister. Such inclinations run against the fact that, after all, substantive discussions can only be carried out fruitfully at the level of officials or at best with the Minister, if the latter happened to be a professional person. It is often suggested that donor officials may want to impress their superiors and advance career prospects by demonstrating their access to the higher or the highest level of the political leadership. It is sometimes argued that decision making is so centralised in Bangladesh that all decisions, big and small, are in the hands of Ministers or the head of the government. Moreover, Bangladesh officials are unable to obtain with their own efforts a decision from the higher or the highest authority. Therefore, there is no choice for donor officials but to have discussions at higher levels in order to obtain any decision whatsoever.

This perception is most likely wrong in the large majority of cases. It would be difficult to demonstrate that, in Bangladesh, particular meetings or discussions with the head of the government, for example, resulted in important policy decisions which have been followed through and implemented — and this is the critical criterion — and which would not have been obtained through dialogue and discussions at the level of Secretaries or Ministers. There may, of course, be an occasion when a Minister does not accept the advice of his Secretary, or Prime Minister that of his Minister, on a subject on which both donor representative and Secretary or Minister are in agreement. On such an occasion, donor representative might like to raise the subject at a higher political level (i.e. Prime Minister) to press the urgency of the issue and the desirability of a positive response from the government.

There is an aggravating factor in the situation in that Ministers or the head of the government may feel that by dealing directly with donor representatives they are facilitating the flow of aid. This assumes that the opportunity cost of their time and effort is low. It may even mislead

---

circumstances under which Bangladesh was born, there was a general sympathy towards the country so that lack of a high level of deference on her part was overlooked.

donor officials in that a superficial discussion with a Minister may appear to have substantive implications. Ministers may not and frequently do not have the time and specialised knowledge to deal with the matter under discussions. It may, on occasions, have negative implications for officials in that the superficial comments by Ministers may be misinterpreted by donor officials and country officials have to make additional efforts to untie the knot. The process may undermine or compromise the authority and ability of officials to negotiate.[12]

The obvious solution to the problem lies in the delegation of authority in the government to the level where it appropriately belongs. Even when the final decision is centralised in the hands of Ministers or the head of the government, officials or Ministers, as the case may be, should have the responsibility of securing decisions of their superiors. This issue is indeed related to the wider problem of efficiency and accountability in the administrative structure. In the government hierarchy, the delegation of decision making authority and assumption of responsibility go together. Lack of authority and evasion of responsibility reinforce each other.

In India, visiting aid officials in general are known not to expect deferential treatment or to insist on discussions with the higher level of political authorities. This seems to be the case in spite of no significant difference in the bureaucratic procedures and decision making process between India and other countries. The answer to this anomaly appears to be that India is too important a country or a client for aid officials to expect such a deferential treatment. Absence of substantial lending by a donor, for example, the World Bank, to a big country like India may reflect unfavourably on the Bank's own performance and, therefore, it is in the aid officials' interest to do their best to generate projects and programmes in India.

---

[12]It is alleged that negotiations on and approval of aid financed investment projects are different from those on policy issues. A project involves foreign suppliers as well as domestic contractors/consultants for its implementation. When illegal and mutually beneficial financial arrangements are involved and the higher authority such as a Minister is a party to the deal, the approval of project is concentrated in the hands of the higher authority to make such a deal effective. An intervention by a donor representative with the Minister, for example, helps expedite the approval of the project. It is further alleged that donor officials or even diplomatic representatives of donor countries are not totally disinterested observers of this process of deal making. Such interventions with the higher authority in favour of a particular supplier become all the more necessary or expedient, if aid is untied, in view of competition between exporters/suppliers of different countries for the project.

They concentrate in a business-like manner on negotiations with their professional counterparts, without too much concern about the "respect" with which they are treated or how warm a welcome or hospitality is extended to them. Moreover, they rely on negotiating and reaching an agreement at the appropriate level, leaving it to the latter to seek approval from the higher authorities or Minister, as the case may be. In a way, this strengthens the hands of government officials in seeking negotiating authority from their Ministers.

As the smaller recipient countries vie with each other in encouraging the prevailing practices, they perpetuate inefficiency in the decision making process and the misallocation of the time of higher officials or Ministers. It may appear to some that this is not an important enough issue to even bother to analyse. In isolation it may be true but conceived in the overall framework of Bangladesh's desperate and aggressive search for aid, this may be relevant. In the end, the prevailing practices, for whatever they are worth, reflect on the honour, dignity and image of a government in the eyes of donors, its own people and administrators. This makes it incongruous for the same Ministers to seek to meet and negotiate with the highest level officials or political leaders in the headquarters of donor institutions or capitals of countries. An improvement in the decision making process and bureaucratic procedures in Bangladesh and clear signals to donor officials would provide a reasonable middle course.

17.5 TECHNICAL ASSISTANCE: A REAPPRAISAL

The range of tasks starting from the preparation of the strategy document on development perspectives and policies as well as its implementation, to conducting and organising nationwide debates and discussions on development issues, to engaging in dialogue with donors and independent experts or umpires requires a very considerable domestic capacity. At the present level of expertise, experience and skill, Bangladesh is unequal to the task.[13]

It is in this context that the role of one type of development assistance, i.e. technical assistance, assumes some relevance. The major objective of technical assistance is to promote capacity building. In the debate

---

[13]This issue is taken up in Chapter 15 on institution building.

on aid in Bangladesh, this subject has not received as much attention as it deserves. The manner in which Bangladesh utilises technical assistance is a good indicator of how it owns and manages its development programmes and priorities. Technical assistance is often tied to project or programme assistance and foreign experts are expected to facilitate their efficient implementation. Secondly, it provides overseas training to nationals in order to improve their skills and expertise. Thirdly, it helps to establish national institutions which, in their turn, build up national capacity.

Several issues are raised in this respect. One, donors often include technical assistance components in projects or programmes, even when they are not needed, sometimes, it has been alleged, in order to provide employment for their national experts/consultants. Moreover, experts are inordinately expensive and absorb a significant proportion of the project or programme assistance.[14] In some cases, the presence of foreign experts, however unnecessary they are, is an unavoidable condition attached to a project. If it is a grant then it has no cost to Bangladesh, unless the use of foreign experts themselves imposes an additional burden on the administration of the project. The imposition of redundant or unqualified experts by donors can be avoided if Bangladesh insists on either the rejection or modification of such assistance to suit its own requirements.[15] Experience in other countries has shown that negotiation on a project has seldom broken down because of disagreement on the technical assistance component.

Second, it is alleged that the quality of foreign experts has deteriorated over time and hence there is no addition to the level of expertise available at home. However, it may be argued that even if foreign experts are no better but are only as good as national experts and if there is a scarcity of national experts, they fill a void. This is a net gain. The strategy should be to avoid foreign experts who are inferior to national experts or unsuitable for the jobs they are required to do or unable to function effectively in an unfamiliar environment with different customs and procedures.

---

[14] It has been suggested that, sometimes, external experts are placed as watchdogs to watch and report on the implementation of aided projects as well as to check misuse of funds.

[15] Resident experts, when they are competent, do serve a very useful purpose in that they provide on-the-job training to their local counterparts.

Long run deterioration in the quality of foreign experts has been a universal phenomenon. The idealism and the challenge of experience in poor countries that attracted experts from donor countries in earlier decades have worn out over time. During the 1950s and 1960s, a high point was reached in the level of interest in overseas development among professionals, researchers, and academics in the developed world. Since then research grants and attractive employment opportunities in the field of development have suffered a considerable decline. Interest in donor countries has shifted to the domestic problems of poverty, urbanisation, violence, and crime or to countries in which they have strategic or political interests. The United States was preeminent in research and training in economic development during the earlier period. The decline in interest in the problems of developing countries has been the sharpest among professionals in the United States.

The second component of technical assistance is the training of nationals in developed countries. In this respect, long term training programme for postgraduate or graduate training has been replaced in recent years by short term training. In fact, there has been a great increase in short term study tours and training programmes. This is more an economy measure for donors rather than an efficient choice. A given amount of finance can train a much larger number if it is spent on short term rather than on a longer term training. In recent years, this has been the pattern of technical assistance in most developing countries. Bangladesh is no exception. A large number of trainees or visitors under technical assistance programmes in Bangladesh add to the visibility of particular donors. There is very little scrutiny or examination of the needs for such short term programmes. Short and medium term foreign training and study tours are frequently the result of an alliance between donor officials, who have the responsibility to disburse a certain amount of assistance, and the government officials who like to dispense favours to their colleagues or avail themselves of foreign trips. For donor officials, it is an excellent way of improving working relationship with Bangladesh. A liberal provision of study tours to government officials helps elicit their cooperation on a whole range of bilateral relationships covering political, strategic, and economic issues. At the same time, they provide an easily available resource for the distribution of patronage in the hands of the government. The selection of trainees is often unrelated to the qualifications of the candidates and to the requirements of their jobs. Short term training/ study tours are considered as a type of tourism.

There is an urgent need for policymakers to reappraise the technical assistance programme as it is currently used. To accept an offer of technical assistance, whatever its nature or form or whether it meets any need or not, serves no useful purpose. Technical assistance is best used when it is in response to a felt need. I recall an instance when I was at UN/FAO and was the head of the department responsible for providing technical assistance for capacity building in food and agricultural policy analysis. We explored the possibility of such assistance to the Bangladesh Agricultural Ministry, which expressed an interest in such a project. It agreed to send within a short period a request to FAO delineating the nature and extent of assistance that was required. Several months passed and no request came. By that time the FAO officer in charge of the programme was very anxious because the financial year was coming to a close and the budgetary provision he made on account of the Bangladesh project would lapse. It would reflect badly on his performance since it was linked to his delivery of adequate volume of technical assistance services every year. He, therefore, developed a strong personal interest in the project. He made repeated enquiries from Bangladesh and found out that the Ministry had no officer to spare time to write down such a proposal. Being more anxious than the government for having the project finalised, he offered to send a consultant out to write up the project proposal. The Ministry readily agreed to accept such help. The consultant went and wrote up the proposal. But then the Ministry did not follow it up and send it to FAO requesting assistance on the basis of the proposal. This was in spite of the fact that the FAO country representative in Dhaka tried on several occasions to persuade the government to follow up. The Secretary of the Ministry could not care much for such assistance and he might have agreed, at a moment of polite conversation with the FAO officer visiting from the headquarters, that he would like such assistance. The FAO officer having invested some funds in preparing the proposal did not give up. He again provided for the project in the next year's budget and the Ministry apparently welcomed his suggestion. The experience was repeated next year and the project never came through.

There were two aspects of this abortive attempt in technical assistance. First, there was no real interest in such capacity building in the Ministry because the Secretary did not think that he needed any more capacity for policy analysis than he had already at his disposal. Secondly, the idea behind the FAO project was not very attractive. It was an institution building project. It involved building up a unit in the Ministry for policy analysis and monitoring of developments in the food and agricultural sector. It would require the Secretary successfully negotiating with the Establishment Ministry for the recruitment of additional staff to build up the unit. The FAO project was designed to train the Bangladesh staff abroad and to send foreign experts to provide on the job training as well as to provide analysis and advice on policy issues. All this sounded too long term and of no immediate benefit to the high officials of the Ministry. It did not provide for several trips abroad for the high officials.

But for the FAO official's compulsion to show that he could deliver services to a very large poor country in Asia that would have gone to his credit, this project should never have been pursued so tenaciously by him. This was an example of assistance guided by the incentive systems for the aid bureaucrats rather than by the demand of the recipient. This was a case of supply driven rather than demand driven foreign assistance.

Several years later a similar technical assistance project was provided to the Bangladesh Ministry of Food by USAID and was implemented by IFPRI. After a few years of strenuous efforts and persuasion by USAID and IFPRI, the small unit in the Food Ministry was expanded and a few officers were transferred to the unit from the rest of the government, even though they did not have the qualifications and experience necessary for the assignment. Even this modest progress was due to the fortuitous placement of a Secretary in the Ministry who became interested in the project. Moreover, this project had the benefit of pressure from a powerful food aid donor. This was a technical assistance project linked to and conditional upon the receipt of food aid by Bangladesh. A part of the incentive package in the project was the availability in Dhaka of expatriate economists at the disposal of the Secretary for advice and written policy briefs for his use. This was also basically a supply driven project, made attractive by the provision of direct advisory services to the Ministry. The long term objective of building up a unit in the Ministry was only partially, if at all fulfilled.

This project, therefore, had a long history. The idea that a unit for food and agricultural policy analysis in the government was badly needed, was first broached about 25 years ago by various visiting experts and donor agencies, both bilateral and multilateral. It was after a lapse of 15 years that a foreign assistance project was started with the objective of promoting research on food policy issues. It continued for 10 years. For the first five years, there was no commitment on the part of the government to build up or upgrade the policy analysis unit. It was primarily a research project under which expatriate researchers were to undertake research in collaboration mainly with nationals. It did provide training to local professionals, most of whom were outside the government, in the conduct of surveys on food policy and poverty issues and in the analysis of data and thus added to the pool of professional in this field. It was only in the second phase of additional five years that the government decided to train a number of the Food Ministry officials through "on the job" as well as overseas training and, in order to give it an institutional basis, it agreed to strengthen the special unit in the Ministry for the purpose.

Many years ago there was an instance of an effective technical assistance project, which was driven by urgently felt need on the part of the government. Immediately after independence, Bangladesh was faced with the task of negotiating and managing a large and wide variety of foreign assistance from a multiplicity of sources, multilateral and bilateral. There was no procedure of keeping systematic records of such assistance with their necessary details and in an appropriate financial accounting framework. The Planning Commission, at that time, had the responsibility of managing foreign assistance. It was important to know the amount and the time profile of the inflows as well as the repayment obligations in respect of loans, which were being built up. We had no expertise to construct such a system. I desperately went around looking for such assistance, which was needed within the shortest period of time. It was a very urgently felt need, which could be elaborated in technical terms with some initial external advice. We negotiated successfully with the Bank and UNDP a package of assistance which was implemented forthwith. We assigned staff for the unit in the Planning Commission, who had experience in audit and accounts as well as some familiarity with the foreign aid project documents. There were short term visiting foreign experts and training for the local staff. After having built up the unit, we made arrangements that foreign experts would periodically visit and monitor the working of the unit and provide additional on-the-job training. It was a success because the need was acutely felt; assistance was urgently sought and clearly articulated by the recipient organisation i.e. the Planning Commission. What was equally important was the government's firm commitment to the implementation of the project by providing necessary local counterparts and resources.

It is possible that there were other technical assistance projects, which might or might not have met all these criteria to the same extent but were also successful. It will be useful for future policy guidance to derive lessons from their experience. The evaluation should cover all types of technical assistance i.e. development project related and other types of assistance for training or institution building. It should examine the objectives and achievements of the technical assistance projects. It should include an assessment of training of nationals abroad and use of expatriate experts. The lessons derived from it would provide the basis for the formulation of future requests for assistance by the government. This will help provide guidelines to the government for an examination of the needs for technical assistance. Periodic evaluations or assessments carried out by donors cannot, with the best of intentions, escape the conflict of interest. Nor the assessment by government agencies would be totally objective. The evaluation should be genuinely free of bias. Therefore, it is important that such an evaluation of ongoing and past technical assistance projects should be undertaken with the help of independent experts, national and foreign.

For technical assistance to be appropriately designed and effectively utilised, it is necessary that the government should determine the gaps in training and identify institutions abroad where the required training should be sought. Bangladesh by now has a sufficient complement of trained experts at home and abroad to identify the best technical facilities overseas. Similarly, they would be able to locate foreign experts of high quality and experience that Bangladesh needs. In this context, there is no reason why the government should not negotiate to obtain the services of the Bangladeshi experts resident abroad under technical assistance programmes. This process will enable the government to negotiate on the basis of concrete, well thought out requests for assistance, which should be so designed as to meet clearly felt needs.

Technical assistance can play a valuable role in establishing training and educational institutions at home. This used to be an important area of assistance during the 1960s and 1970s. But this form of technical assistance requires long term commitment on the part of donors because institution building is time consuming and an arduous task. Again, in this instance as well, the government should take the initiative, do the preparatory work and ask for long term commitment from donors. One well equipped and properly manned national institution for advanced training is worth a large number of short or medium or even long term overseas training programme/study trips for several years. It may be necessary to combine assistance from several donor agencies, both bilateral and multilateral, to build high quality institutions of learning. The kind of approach suggested above cannot be implemented without decision at the highest level of the political leadership. There are too many powerful vested interests at all levels eager not to change the existing system.

17.6 GOVERNANCE AND FOREIGN AID: STICK OR CARROT?

In recent years, in the course of dialogue with donors, the role of governance in development has drawn considerable attention. Governance in a wide sense includes the systems, rules, and procedures that determine the functioning of the various branches of the government i.e. executive, legislative, judiciary, and their interrelationships. How well designed development policies and programmes are and how efficiently and with how much integrity they are implemented, depend crucially on the state of governance. Improvement of governance, for example, accountability and transparency at each level and branch of government, enforcement of contracts, rule of law, and prevention of corruption may reduce the need for or enable effective compliance with macro or project related conditionalities about policies and institutions. Inefficiency and corruption inflate the cost of projects and hence increase debt liability. Cost savings on projects increase resources for development. Improved financial management and rigorous monitoring and auditing of public expenditures will reduce wastes and inefficiencies in the public sector, reduce fiscal deficit and improve macroeconomic balance — an important policy conditionality for aid. Integrity of tax administration would increase tax revenues. Tax payments due to the government are now spent in bribes and ransom money. Reduction or elimination of illegal payments to the tax officials, on the one hand, and of extortions by the *mafia/gangs*, on the other, will result in improved tax collection. Nonpayment of charges or fees for public utilities, diversion of their services to unintended users, and losses inflicted on public enterprises through manipulation of accounts by an unholy alliance of labour leaders, managers, and political agents — are all examples of poor governance.

Appropriately, therefore, it seems that the most important conditionality donors might seek to attach to development assistance in Bangladesh should relate to the improvement of governance. Unless the state of governance improves detailed conditionalities about institutions and policies are unlikely to be met or met effectively. Moreover, in the context of poor overall governance, many sectors/project specific conditionalities, designed to realise project objectives and expected returns, tend to be too numerous, verging on micro management. They tend to be too complex and difficult to monitor or supervise. To use a much-maligned metaphor, conditionality relating to overall/macro governance is the "mother" of all conditionalities.

Concerned with the poor state of governance in Bangladesh, donors have been extending assistance for improving rules and regulations as well as management and organisation in a number of institutions. For example, the World Bank *Country Assistance Strategy* document for Bangladesh as of February 2000 indicates, among others, the following priority areas of financial and technical assistance — public sector management, financial management and civil service reforms; empowering communities and vulnerable groups, including decentralisation and local capacity building; judicial and legal reforms; human capital improvement, including primary, post-literacy, secondary, informal education; health and nutrition improvement and population programmes; and rural development, including rural roads, transport, rural energy, water supplies, and arsenic control.[16]

Many of these aid projects or components of aid projects in education, health, and rural development concentrate on capacity building or strengthening of local institutions. They include sectors or areas of the economy or the society such as legal and judicial system, decentralisation, civil service system, administrative procedures and empowerment, in which traditions and societal norms often play a dominating role. To change them in a way that is conducive to development is a long drawn process. In fact, it is partly a task of social transformation. It requires increase in awareness and consciousness among policymakers and public about the need and direction of reforms. These are precisely the areas in which the political and social leadership plays a crucial role.

To be effective, external assistance for the improvement of governance and for ensuring transparency and accountability in such areas as judiciary, law enforcement, legislative and administrative systems or procedures should take into account a few considerations. First, in various aspects of governance, Bangladesh can learn from similarly situated developing or relatively advanced developing countries more than she can from developed countries. This is because in respect of social norms and traditions as well as political institutions, Bangladesh bears closer resemblance to them than to developed countries. Donors' assistance for the Bangladesh policymakers to learn from the experience of successful reforms in regulations, organisation and management in the comparable countries is likely to be useful. Second, in some respects, solutions to the problem of misgovernance are better found by local experts and practitioners in their respective fields. Those who implement policies and administer public sector programmes and agencies know best where the problems are and frequently have practical ideas about how to solve them. Mostly they lack the incentive to do so. They would be able to suggest solutions if they are engaged in problem solving exercise and appropriate questions are posed in a constructive manner. For example, tax officials know best where the

---

[16]World Bank, *Country Assistance Strategy*, Washington, D.C., World Bank, 2001, p. 5.

loopholes are to avoid taxes and how to evade taxes. Also, lawyers and judges at the lower courts — an area reported to have suffered a loss of credibility — together know well the incentives (rewards and penalties) needed for advancing the integrity and efficiency of the lower judiciary. Donors can play a catalysing role, so to speak, in bringing together local executives, administrators, and policymakers in order to jointly concentrate their minds and to examine in a focused manner the problems at hand and explore solutions. External experts can participate and help in this process by bringing the experience of other countries to bear on their deliberations. In most cases, solutions to the problem of bad governance have to conform to the cultural and social traditions of Bangladesh. Under these circumstances, a process of well structured national consultations in Bangladesh, guided and aided by experts from abroad, is the best way of finding appropriate solutions.

The World Bank refrained from providing new loans in the energy and water sectors due to their concerns about misgovernance and absence of the government's sustained efforts to reform and improve. Bilateral donors, on the whole, have not gone so far, at least overtly, to stop new commitment, with the exception of Denmark, which most recently withdrew aid from a particular project after complaints of corruption. However, all donors combine together in expressing periodically their concerns about the poor state of governance. They have often called upon the government to take urgent steps to improve the law and order situation and to combat corruption. Both these factors impose serious constraints on development. Improvement in them requires a significant change in the way politics is managed and administration is run.

How far donor pressure can bring about a change? To some extent, donors and recipients of development assistance are prisoners of each other. To disengage or disentangle imposes costs not only on recipients but also on donors. For one thing, the aid bureaucracy in donor agencies, both national and international, has a vested interest in the continuation of aid. Second, rich countries in any case provide annually a certain amount of overall development assistance due to a multiplicity of considerations i.e. humanitarian, developmental, political and strategic. Also, given the general climate of international public opinion, the poorer or the poorest countries receive priority in the allocation of aid. Bangladesh, one of the least developed countries in the world, invariably appears high on the list of recipients. When donors take a global view of the relative aid-worthiness of poor countries and consider the state of economic performance, governance, and corruption, they do not find that Bangladesh presents the worst-case scenario. After all, not many poor countries have grown at 4-5 percent per year in recent years — a rate at which Bangladesh has grown in recent years. There are other poor countries, such as those in Africa, which are possibly worse performers; they are not able to absorb much aid. They have limited capacity to implement a substantial programme of development assistance.

The frustration of donors with Bangladesh arises not because she is the worst performer among the aid recipients but because her potentials are greater than her actual performance. Also, they believe that her performance can be improved, and in some areas significantly, if there is greater political commitment and decisive action to improve governance. Many in Bangladesh outside the government share this view. Bangladesh has developed a very vibrant civil society. The performance of the Bangladesh NGOs in a wide variety of development programmes bears testimony to the potentials for achievement by various actors in the economy, if only opportunities are open to them.[17] In the field of microcredit for the poor, through the example of Grameen Bank and similar institutions, Bangladesh has led the developing world in successful institution building for delivery of credit and related services to the poor. The remarkable performance of the garment industry in Bangladesh which has earned an important place in the world textile market is yet another instance. All the above factors persuade donors that Bangladesh may yet make good progress with foreign assistance. Moreover, bilateral donors have political, historical and above all, commercial interests of exporters, contractors and consultants, which they cannot ignore. Multiplicity of considerations such as these weigh with donors in order for them to provide Bangladesh a continued access to an annual development assistance to the tune of US$1.5 billion in most recent years — even

---

[17]One may argue about the shortcomings of NGOs. They are not perfect or above controversy. Nonetheless, there seems to be a consensus among donors that they have on the whole demonstrated greater efficiency and integrity than the government agencies. Several issues in this connection are discussed in Chapter 16.

though it is less than what she used to receive earlier during the 1980s and early 1990s.

Under these circumstances would donors use the penalty of withdrawal of aid to improve governance? Would all of them take concerted action to reduce aid and reduce it significantly? Assuming that donors take such action, would there be positive consequences? Would governance improve and desirable policy reforms be implemented? It depends and it is difficult to predict. One can only speculate about the ways in which consequences of the stoppage of aid flow may work out. Roughly, there are several groups of beneficiaries of foreign assistance. The domestic indenters, agents of suppliers, national contractors, and consultants gain from expanded business opportunities. Secondly, there are the "rent seekers" in the administration and implementation agencies that deal with the first group of beneficiaries and share in the income generated from their contracts and business. Thirdly, there are the ultimate beneficiaries of development projects, who gain in income and employment opportunities. The first and second groups of intermediate beneficiaries constitute a significant number but are not very large. But they have an important place in the sociopolitical power structure.

If aid flow declines or stops, the second group i.e. rent seekers, could try to increase their "take" or share in the rest of the government expenditures and contracts that are financed by domestic resources. The rate of their rent collection per unit of transactions might go up. What will be the socio-political consequences of such an increase in corruption? How would the rest of the society react and how would the government respond? One does not know. For one thing, it depends on how serious will be the effect of their rapaciousness on the rest of the society.

The first group will be net losers. The loss of business on the part of the first group cannot be compensated unless the government avoids wastes and improves inefficiencies and saves resources to expand development projects from which they would gain income earning opportunities. The losses incurred by the first group and also by the second groups, in case the latter cannot increase their share in income or "rent" from other public expenditures, and the indirect impact on sectors or groups interlinked with them may be significant.

They constitute high and middle income groups who are likely to sustain losses as a direct consequence of a fall in aid. To the extent that the ultimate beneficiaries of development projects are poor, they will also be among the losers. Moreover, a large proportion of aid now goes to social sectors i.e. health, education, nutrition, and related programmes; also rural infrastructure, transportation, and energy receive some assistance. Would political leadership reallocate domestic expenditures in such a way as to reduce wasteful, low priority expenditures or withdraw resources from the rest of public expenditures to maintain social services at an unchanged level in order to avoid adverse impact on the poor? The poor are not organised enough to put great pressure on the government either to effect a reallocation of public expenditure in their favour or to improve the efficiency and integrity of resource use. More important, it is unlikely that under the present circumstances direct impact of a reduction of aid on the poor would be widespread and large enough for the government to respond by undertaking such a resource reallocation.

What would be the possible impact on the poorest? As various studies have demonstrated, the poorest do not gain much benefit from social expenditures. Therefore, it is likely that the poorest will not suffer much deprivation as a direct consequence of a decline in aid. They are not directly involved or engaged in sectors or activities that are significant users of assistance. Under the worst of circumstances, aid for few direct poverty reducing measures such as feeding, employment and nutrition programmes directed to the most vulnerable groups and in the poorest areas, could be probably maintained or restored. We have travelled a very long way from the early 1970s when there was a famine due to a combination of circumstances described in Chapter 10. With significant progress in the food and agricultural sector, domestic food availability has improved; income and employment opportunities in farm and related nonfarm occupations have expanded.

Even though a large part of foreign assistance is project aid, projects in the social sectors are not import intensive and provide untied foreign exchange resources to finance imports. A decline in the availability of such untied foreign exchange resources might cause exchange rate depreciation and a rise in the cost of imported inputs, including possibly for the small industry sector, an important source of employment of the poor. This by itself would not cause any significant or widespread impact on the poor. In any case in the very unlikely event of a significant and visible deterioration in the conditions of the poor, it is expected, if past experience is any guide, that the government would take remedial measures directed towards the poorest by reducing other expenditures.

It is difficult to predict the end result of the diverse, direct and indirect, implications of such a no-aid scenario. The above is a very sketchy analysis. It is obvious that different groups in society will suffer to a varying extent. The middle and upper income groups, who will lose, are important in the power structure. How significant will be their loss, how they would react to such loss, and how the government would respond to their reaction are difficult to assess without a more detailed analysis. First, one needs to delve deep into the existing composition of the aided projects. Second, assuming an unchanged pattern of government expenditures as well as fiscal, trade and exchange policies, one can examine the interrelated consequences for the overall economy as well as their distributional impact. Third, one can then introduce the second round effects of changes in exchange rate and related policies that follow the stoppage of aid. A more rigorous and exhaustive analysis of a no-aid scenario, without compensating domestic resource mobilisation, can only be carried out within a comprehensive general equilibrium framework.

It is conceivable that there is an indirect consequence of the withdrawal of aid, which is not related so much to the question of the quantum of aid. It is more a question of its psychological impact on the economic actors in the country and abroad. In the present climate of dependence on aid, when donors' approval or appreciation is considered a crucial test of Bangladesh's economic performance, the withdrawal of aid may adversely affect the confidence of the public and the international community in the economy and its prospects. It may be considered a vote of no confidence in the credibility of the government, adding to the adverse impact already caused by the recent ranking of Bangladesh as the most corrupt country by *Transparency International*.

It is difficult to be certain about the ultimate economic consequences that may follow. Depending on the degree of loss of confidence or the psychological shock, it may discourage domestic and foreign investors and, in the extreme case, cause a flight of capital, a fall in foreign exchange reserves and deterioration in the fiscal and monetary situation. The cumulative effect of all these factors may not leave the status quo unaffected and it may not be "more of the same". For example, it is possible that middle classes will become more vocal and active and the civil society and those who are adversely affected get organised so that the pressure for improvement in governance may become irresistible.

The pragmatists argue that, in the past, consistent pressure by donors, accompanied by conditionalities on aid, has led to some reforms in macroeconomic policies as well as in one or two sectors, even though improvement has been slow. The misuse of resources is probably less in the donor financed projects than in the projects financed by domestic resources, because of the monitoring and supervision by donors. Therefore, there is no need to use the blunt instrument of the withdrawal of aid to mount heavy pressure for major policy reforms and better governance. The direct and indirect consequences of such a policy may in the end not bring about the change and improvement that is desired. The pragmatists suggest that men of practical affairs should strive to do as much as they can to improve upon the status quo. This view in favour of the status quo does not seem to offer a way out of the impasse facing Bangladesh today. Since the poor is not likely to suffer much, if at all, and in any case any serious impact on them can be offset, one tends to opt for the no-aid scenario for the next few years to push the policymakers and the political leadership out of the state of inertia and inaction. This would provide an occasion for concentrating their minds and spur them to improve governance and to undertake reforms.

In any case, all, including the pragmatists, agree that Bangladesh should seriously prepare on its own for a reduction in dependence on aid. After all, few deny that aid relationship is not an honourable or an equal relationship. It creates a dependency syndrome and discourages attempts at self reliance. Moreover, overall development assistance globally will either stagnate or increase very slowly in the coming years. Bangladesh is, thus, unlikely to be able to secure much larger aid sustained over a longer period. How does Bangladesh raise investment and growth rate as well as reduce poverty, consistently with a current or at best a very slow increase in the volume of aid? Bangladesh will need to greatly intensify the mobilisation of domestic savings and expand foreign exchange earnings. Much has been said about wastage and loss of resources in the public sector due to inefficiency and corruption. The losses in just two sectors, i.e. nationalised industries and commercial banks, are estimated to amount to an average of about 1.5 percent of GDP during 1997-2000 whereas the disbursement of foreign aid was about an average of 2.5 percent of GDP.[18] This does not include wastes and inefficiency in the rest of the government; a small fragment of such wastage reported in a recent Auditor General's report on a limited segment of the government, i.e. the 15-20 percent of the government transactions, amounted to about US$3 billion over a period of seven years. Reduction of wastage and inefficiency will also save foreign exchange expenditures. Combined with appropriate monetary and exchange rate policies, concerted efforts for export expansion and diversification, would increase foreign exchange earnings. In most recent years, the contribution of worker's remittances to foreign exchange and investment resources has, indeed, been significant. However, the prospects of its substantial increase are uncertain. Antiforeign bias and competition from other labour exporting countries will act to restrain its growth. Efforts to diversify the destination of labour migration need to be intensified.

It is recognised that a much larger reliance on foreign direct investment will be necessary. In view of donors' pronounced preference for social sectors, external resources for investment in physical infrastructure such as transport and communications, ports, energy, and natural resources will have to be sought mainly, if not entirely, from foreign direct investment. All the well known factors that contribute to improvement in the investment climate for domestic investors will also attract foreign investment. The policy framework of incentives and facilities for foreign investment in Bangladesh are

---

[18]IMF, *Ibid.*

very liberal. But the real obstacle remains, as elsewhere in the economy, in the lack of well functioning institutions and policies. They remain crucial for attracting foreign direct investment as well as for the efficient utilisation of aid, specially in social sectors. This brings us back full circle to the primary role of governance.

Chapter 18

LIVING WITH A BIG NEIGHBOUR

18.1 INTRODUCTION

Bangladesh is in the throes of integrating with world economy. The process will continue at varying paces in various sectors under the compulsion of changing domestic and external circumstances. Within the broad framework of the process of globalisation, Indo-Bangladesh economic relations loom very large.

The challenge facing Bangladesh is how to develop a range and pattern of economic relationship with India that will help Bangladesh achieve a high rate of efficient growth. Evidence in all regions of the world confirms that economic relationship or interdependence is the closest between neighbouring countries. The current state and future prospects of Indo-Bangladesh economic relations have to be viewed in the context of their overall relationship, including historical, political and strategic aspects. There is an interdependence between economic and political relationships. In most cases, good political relations fostered by identical values, common problems and similar experiences as well as common foreign and regional policy concerns tend to promote close economic relations. It is conceivable that growth in bilateral economic relations may promote, in turn and over time, friendly political relations. This requires that political relationship is not characterised by distrust or suspicion but is generally congenial and friendly enough to allow first steps in economic relationship to be taken, which would then expand and generate a second round stimulus. Over time, interest groups which participate in and gain from trade, investment, and other bilateral economic transactions may act as a positive influence on the development of friendly political relations. However, in fact, in most cases the progression has been from close political relations to the deepening of economic relations. History is replete with examples of friendly or amicable political relations providing the incentive and climate for forging closer economic relations. Experience ranging from the birth of European Union (EU) in Europe to North American Free Trade Agreement (NAFTA) in North America, to the Mercosur, and the Andean Pact in Latin America — all seem to lend support to such a hypothesis.

The overall relationship between India and Bangladesh has often been affected by varying political complexion of the governments in two countries. For example, whenever the influence of the rightist parties in either country has waxed or waned, there has been a corresponding side effect on bilateral relations. In addition, there is an important historical factor that has influenced India's relationship with Bangladesh. Since 1947, India and Pakistan had recognised each other and were also recognised by the rest of the world as equal, competing rivals. The rivalry and confrontational relationship with Pakistan, marked by several wars, had its effects on India's relationship with Bangladesh. The post-1973 restoration and gradual improvement in Bangladesh's relationship with Pakistan had cast a shadow on India's relationship with Bangladesh. Since 1976, there had been periods in the political evolution of Bangladesh when she had been close to Pakistan, politically and strategically. From the point of view of India, this had not been a very comfortable or very welcome development against the background of India's relation with Pakistan and her supporting role in the war of independence of Bangladesh. The more Bangladesh felt that India tended to dominate in bilateral relationship or constrain her freedom of manoeuver, globally or regionally, the more she wanted to offset it by moving closer to Pakistan. The more that happened, the more India considered it unfavourable to her interests and felt unhappy.

Because of size, economic strength and potential, military power, geography and history, India has emerged as a regional hegemon, i.e. a regional power, and it tends to behave as such.[1] It seems, however,

---

[1] An Indian official with experience of dealing with the Indo-Bangladesh relationship makes the point very succinctly. "India is too overarching and too proximate to be ignored. It is also

that she has not been able to develop a strategy that would clearly identify her responsibilities in order to play that role. All power brings responsibilities and obligations. There is a distinct impression in Bangladesh that India is more conscious of her position as a regional power than of her responsibilities to her neighbours. For example, India seems to feel uncomfortable or uneasy if neighbours develop close political and strategic relationships which do not conform with her regional or national interests or with countries with whom India does not have a close and friendly relationship. India wishes that her neighbours facilitate, if not cooperate, in arrangements that enhance her political and strategic interests in relation to other countries such as India's defense arrangements, for example, vis-à-vis China. But she does not seem to appreciate that such political or diplomatic cooperation of neighbours requires visible gestures or concessions towards them. India may consider the above perceptions about her to be exaggerated. But then in politics and interstate relations perceptions matter a great deal.

As an aspiring regional hegemonic power, India has the responsibility to understand and respect the sensitivity of a small neighbour such as Bangladesh. To promote goodwill by being generous and to refrain from maximising short term advantages in her relations with Bangladesh may not have an immediate and visible payoff. However, it is in India's long term interest to have a cooperative and friendly neighbour with a large population; a disgruntled neighbour, however weak, may cause difficulties in the way of her pursuit of long run regional or global interests. In these days of globalisation and interdependence of crosscutting interests among nations across continents, no country, however big, can carve out a exclusive sphere of influence. At the same time, Bangladesh has to face the challenge of living with the reality that India is a regional power with global and regional geopolitical interests and that it is not easy to build bilateral economic

---

a too proximate and asymmetrical identity to have close relationship with" (see, J.N. Dixit, *Liberalization and Beyond: Indo-Bangladesh Relations* (Dhaka: The University Press Limited, 1999, p. 280). This is a predicament which invariably characterises Indo-Bangladesh relationships. Bangladesh is surrounded on three sides by the Indian territory; its access to Bay of Bengal has to reckon with the dominant presence of the Indian Navy. India has her Northeastern states cut off from the Indian mainland without a convenient direct route and the easy access is only through Bangladesh.

relationships in a political and strategic vacuum. Economic and political negotiations or concessions may, indeed, on occasions be interrelated. The trade off or balancing of costs and benefits on two fronts, economic and political, is a very delicate task and does not admit of a very neat solution.

That unease and tension frequently characterise the relations between big and small neighbours is common throughout the world. This occurs in the case of the United States in interactions with her neighbours in the north and in the south. Similarly, this is true of Brazil's relation with her neighbours in South America and is comparable to Nigeria's experience vis-à-vis adjacent countries in West Africa. Inequality between India and Bangladesh in respect of economic and technological strength, with India enjoying significant superiority in all respects, is a factor which affects economic relationship between the two countries. In bilateral negotiations, as it appears to Bangladesh, India seeks to gain the maximum advantage in view of her greater economic strength. At the same time, Bangladesh is highly sensitive to the possibility of her yielding more than what she perceives as necessary or warranted. Also, Bangladesh expects India to make unilateral concessions without reciprocity from Bangladesh. She assumes that India would find it feasible to do so since the cost of such concessions is negligible, given her much larger economy with a diversified resource base. Contrary to Bangladesh's expectations, India is not very amenable to making such special or preferential gestures or concessions to Bangladesh. In economic negotiations, India does not view generosity as a relevant criterion, however small is the cost of such concessions. Bangladesh has to wake up to this reality. In the last analysis, she has to build up self confidence as well as greatly improved competence and knowledge on all aspects of Indo-Bangladesh economic relations.[2]

The disparity in the size of their respective economies has implications for the distribution of gains from economic cooperation. Because of the size of the Indian economy as well as its larger base

---

[2] In the long run , the best answer to the " small or weak neighbour "syndrome is for Bangladesh to realise her economic potentials and to build up a self confident nation on a sound economic foundation. There is nothing like economic performance in generating self confidence and optimism.

of resources and population, a given amount of absolute gain from bilateral cooperation is small on a per capita basis or as a proportion of her aggregate economy; the same amount of absolute gain brings a proportionately greater benefit to Bangladesh on a per capita basis or in relation to the size of her economy. This asymmetry reduces the urgency on the part of India to seek reciprocal concessions from Bangladesh. The task for Bangladesh is to identify and seek concessions from India in areas where Bangladesh gains substantially in return for reciprocal concessions in the related or other areas in which India perceives her gain to be large.

In this context, there is an additional consideration that is relevant for Bangladesh. There are fields of cooperation with India in which gains to the Indian states bordering Bangladesh are significantly higher than to the economy of India as a whole. However, Bangladesh conducts negotiations with India at the level of the central government. How forthcoming India would be in making reciprocal concessions to Bangladesh in the interest of her border states, depends upon the weight she attaches to the gain that accrues to the latter. It is, for example, widely believed that in the latest agreement on the sharing of the Ganges waters at *Farakka*, West Bengal had an important supporting role to play. Therefore, it is in the interest of Bangladesh to engage the border states of India in dialogue and discussions in exploring mutually advantageous economic relationships. If they perceive gains from such cooperation, they could exercise influence on the central government of India to assign priority to their concerns and to provide concessions to Bangladesh.

The prevailing and potential economic relationships between the two countries cover, among others, trade, investment, labour migration, water resources in the common rivers, and exploitation of natural resources. There are mutual gains from cooperation in many of these areas which are interrelated. However, the gains in each and every case are unlikely to be equal for both participants. Bangladesh might gain more than India in some areas; reverse might be the case in other areas. To evaluate the differential gains for each country in disparate areas or sectors to reach a reasonably acceptable overall balance is not an easy exercise. It is a challenge to the skill in negotiations and to the capacity to appraise and offset short and long term gains.

Within the confines of the prevailing overall bilateral relationship, this chapter explores a few selected areas of economic cooperation with India with focus on trade, investment, and labour migration. The very important area of water resources development is left out. The gains from cooperation in water resources development may have enormous implications not only for development of forestry, fisheries, and crop agriculture, but also for ecological sustainability of the entire region in the long run.[3]

18.2 INDO-BANGLADESH TRADE

Since independence of Bangladesh, trade between the two countries has been growing rapidly. The pattern of Bangladesh's trade with India has been marked by two significant characteristics: a large volume of illegal trade and a large deficit in the balance of both legal and illegal trade of Bangladesh. Imports from India have been growing rapidly; she has emerged as the largest single source of imports for Bangladesh. Between 1996-97 and 2000, the share of India in total recorded imports of Bangladesh varied between 11-15 percent. Legal imports from India amounted to US$1,000 million whereas exports of Bangladesh average about US$100 million. Geographical proximity, low costs of transport, close knowledge of the Bangladesh domestic market, easy comparability of or familiarity with each other's products/processes, and comparative cost advantage coupled with large production capacity in India have all contributed to the growth of imports from India.

In recent years, starting in the 1990s, rapid growth in imports from India was greatly stimulated by a fast pace of import liberalisation in

---

[3] The past history and current state of negotiations on water resources are partly discussed in Chapter 13. Cooperation in water resources development by its nature involves much more common efforts and collaboration than is needed in trade and investment relations. One of the outstanding questions here relates to the augmentation of water supplies in the *Ganges* at *Farakka*. Differences persist between the two countries in their approach towards the sources and methods of augmentation. For example, should water be drawn from the upper reaches of Nepal involving tripartite collaboration or should it be from *Brahmaputra* flowing from the Indian state of Assam to Bangladesh? There is an interesting aspect of Indo-Nepalese cooperation in water resources development. India's disadvantage, as a lower riparian vis-à-vis Nepal, is more than offset by her bargaining advantage, Nepal being a land-locked country. Given the current state of relations between Bangladesh and India, one can take the view that development of economic relations in other areas such as trade, investment, and labour mobility may over time contribute to the improvement of trust and cooperative spirit and facilitate common efforts in water resources development.

Bangladesh.[4] Large scale import liberalisation within a very short period during the 1990s had exposed the industries in Bangladesh to strong competition from India. It has been argued that the process was too sudden for the long protected industrial sector without any time to prepare for such a measure. There is some force in the argument. However, to ascribe the losses suffered by the Bangladesh industrial enterprises wholly to the surge of competition from the Indian imports would be an exaggeration. It was more likely that, in many cases, import competition laid bare the factors that contributed to inefficiencies and high costs of local enterprises. In fact, a number of well known factors have contributed to the high costs of almost all the productive sectors in the economy. They include deficiencies in infrastructure of transport and communications, bottlenecks at seaports, frequent interruptions in power supply, and inefficient and heavy debt structure, and excessive labour employment plagued by indiscipline and the poor law and order situation.

To use blanket trade protection to compensate for economy wide inefficiencies or for sector wise cost disadvantages, is self defeating in the long run as it weakens the incentive or sustained pressure for improvement in productivity. Secondly, in a few industrial sectors, in spite of the stiff Indian competition, several units not only survived but, in fact, prospered while others stagnated and suffered. As elsewhere in the world, there were always significant differences among different enterprises producing the same or similar products. Enterprises that responded to the challenge of competition and improved efficiency prospered. At the same time, it could be argued legitimately that

---

[4] Though Bangladesh and India have been unilaterally liberalising trade during the 1990s, the speed and extent of liberalisation have been higher in Bangladesh than in India. By 2000-01, the average customs duty was 30% in India and the maximum rate was about 41.3% (35% customs plus special additional duty). The average customs duty was 17% in Bangladesh and with the addition of various supplementary taxes, fees, and duties (infrastructure development surcharge, license fee, and other duties, etc.) reached the level of 22%. The maximum duty was about 37.5%. In addition, India uses antidumping duties extensively more than other member countries of WTO. Further, she has nontariff barriers such as technical standards requirement as well as sanitary and health regulations affecting trade. Bangladesh, though has generally eliminated the system of import quotas, still imposes ban on imports of a few items such as all varieties of fabrics, cotton, synthetic, and silk, nylon, polythene; she also restricts imports of such items as cement, paper bags, chemical fertiliser, etc. See, G. Purcell, "Trade Policies and Regional Trade in South Asia," draft Concept Paper, World Bank, February 2002; Arvind Panageria, "Dump Anti-Dumping?" *Economic Times* (May 7, 2002), Delhi, India.

liberalisation at a slower pace, if followed in a determined manner by a systematic deepening of the liberalisation process, could have provided some breathing space for an adjustment in the import-competing industries. This would have required an assurance that there was no back sliding from the path of liberalisation and no "stop and go" policy to ensure that the process of liberalisation was inexorable and would continue.

Given import competition from India in the Bangladesh domestic market, two alternative policies can be considered. First, Bangladesh can raise duties on imports, which threaten her industries in which she has long run comparative advantage. The highest level of tariffs would have to be in any case below the level of bound tariffs agreed by Bangladesh under WTO and would have to be applied on a multilateral basis to imports from all countries. Such a rise in tariffs might also raise objections from the Bretton Woods financial institutions. There is also the possibility of Bangladesh imposing temporary protective duties under the "safeguard clause" of WTO. In any case, in whatever form they are feasible, the tariffs should be time bound, with a preannounced schedule of reduction over time to be unflinchingly enforced. However, the identification of infant industries requiring protection is a tricky affair and as past experience in all countries has shown, it is prone to abuse by the vested interests. The decision on such protection should be taken as a result of an open, transparent process of inquiry and consultations by the Tariff Commission, with a careful evaluation of the viewpoints of and evidence from relevant interest groups. The groups should include importers, traders, consumers, and users of protected products who gain from liberalisation as well as import competing industries who claim protection. Alternatively, instead of tariff protection, which may create strong resistance from donors, an alternative measure is to provide production subsidies, time bound with a preannounced schedule for reduction over time, to compensate for cost disadvantages. The implementation of such a measure should follow the same procedure of open consultations and inquiry as in the case of tariff protection.[5] Also, as Bangladesh

---

[5] A question may be raised as to whether production or export subsidies for manufactured goods are permissible under the WTO rules. Bangladesh has a longer period before she is obligated to implement the WTO obligations. Moreover, excessive exports to a particular

improves her investment climate as well as physical infrastructure, power supply, labour and financial markets, she would gain competitiveness and be able to exploit her comparative advantage in respect of cheap and abundant labour.

Exports to India have grown very slowly with a widening gap between imports and exports. The dominant view in Bangladesh is that high tariffs and nontariff barriers in India constrain the expansion of Bangladesh's exports to India. It is not that India has a discriminatory trade policy against Bangladesh. Tariffs and nontariff barriers on imports from Bangladesh are no higher than those on exactly the same category of imports from the rest of the world. One could, therefore, argue that constraint on exports to India under the circumstances is either Bangladesh's low competitive ability vis-à-vis the third country exports or her limited production capacity. This argument could be misleading in some respects because the devil is as usual in the details. Many items of current or potential exports of Bangladesh, specially manufactured goods, which carry high tariffs in India are very different from those for which India has negotiated, with her main trading partners, reciprocal trade liberalisation on a most-favoured nation basis. These commodities, which are not of export interest to her main trading partners in North America, Europe, and Japan, have been left out of her multilateral trade liberalisation process. This is the standard process or the way in which trade liberalisation in manufactured goods is carried out under the WTO rules. While average rates of duty on broad categories of imports of India have been reduced over time, there are many specific items, which are the potential exports of Bangladesh, that enjoy a relatively higher margin of protection. However, high protection tariffs on these commodities apply irrespective of the source of imports i.e. whether they are from Bangladesh or from any other source.

As a result, while India exports to Bangladesh a wide variety of manufactured goods, i.e. consumer, intermediate and capital goods, Bangladesh exports only a few traditional commodities like raw jute,

---

importing country, which may invite retaliation, are most unlikely to occur in the case of Bangladesh. After all, the subsidy receiving industries are those which are identified as struggling for survival under severe import competition. Nor her exports are likely to exceed 3.5% of world exports of the commodity in question.

tea, fish products, fertiliser, jute manufactures, and leather products. Manufactured exports from Bangladesh are few and relatively small in volume.

Another factor inhibiting the expansion of Bangladesh exports to India is likely to be the limited access of Bangladesh to the Indian marketing and distribution channels. Moreover, India reaps significant economies of scale in both production and marketing because of a large domestic market. Consequently, marginal marketing costs of the Indian producers in exporting to Bangladesh constitute a very small fraction of their total marketing costs. On the other hand, the costs of marketing for Bangladesh's exports in India could be significant as total sales are small. Bangladesh does not enjoy comparable economies of scale in production or marketing because of the small size of the domestic market. She can expect to reap comparable economies of scale only after and not before she gains access to the large Indian market.

To make matters worse for Bangladesh, India also imposes, from time to time, antidumping or similar countervailing duties on imports. One recent example was that of antidumping duties on Bangladesh exports of batteries. India has been one of the most prolific users of antidumping duties among the members of WTO. If this is the harbinger of things to come as India reduces her general level of tariffs, this is a bad omen. Antidumping duties are country specific and commodity specific, a very damaging exception to the multilateral and liberal trading regime of WTO. In the case of batteries, it is unlikely that Bangladesh is able to resort to a large scale selling below costs in order to oust the competing producers in or exporters to India, and thereby to establish a dominant position in the Indian market and thereafter, raise prices. This is the motivation in the traditional, standard case of dumping. If Bangladesh sells below domestic price or costs in order to get rid of short term surpluses as a temporary measure, the imposition of the antidumping duties should likewise be a temporary measure. In such a case, such duties could have been imposed by India under the "safeguard clause" as permitted by the WTO rules. If it is a short term phenomenon, it is unlikely to inflict a long run damage on the Indian industry to justify antidumping duties. If, on the other hand, the Indian battery producers are unable to compete on a sustained basis with the batteries imported from Bangladesh — a country which is far less advanced than India, industrially and technologically — then this is a case in which India, indeed, may suffer from distinct cost disadvantage. In such a diversified industrial economy as India's, reallocation of resources to other sectors would be a relatively easy and efficient solution.

Illegal trade, facilitated by long and porous border with India and stimulated by trade restrictions on legal trade, has been salient in the bilateral trade. In addition to high protective tariffs, procedural complexities and bureaucratic hurdles in legal trade provide an incentive for illegal trade. The dominance of livestock, textile products, food products, both processed and unprocessed, among the illegal imports of Bangladesh testifies to the importance of both these factors. In fact, on such imports of Bangladesh as livestock, there are or used to be bans on exports from India, thus providing added incentive for illegal trade. There is no official estimate of illegal trade. Private estimates by researchers indicate that illegal imports from India are at the levels of legal imports. Illegal exports to India are considered to be no more than legal exports. It is widely believed that illegal trade deficit is at least equal to the amount of legal trade deficit which is about US$900 million in recent years and on the basis of this assumption the total deficit might be around US$1800 million. The indirect estimates of researchers seem to indicate that the deficit is financed by remittances from Bangladeshi workers abroad as well as by illegal transfers of gold.

A relevant question is, if Indian traders can circumvent Bangladesh's import restrictions as well as India's export restrictions in order to expand illegal exports to Bangladesh, how is that Bangladeshi traders cannot circumvent India's high import restrictions and resort equally forcefully to illegal exports to India? Are the Indian border controls more restrictive on imports to India than on exports from India or are Bangladesh border controls more restrictive on exports than on imports? There is no logical reason for this asymmetry. However, it is possible to argue that the characteristics of most of the potential exports of Bangladesh, constrained by India's import restrictions, are such that they are not suitable for smuggling or shipment through illegal channels. This limits her illegal exports. In other words, their total transaction costs, including costs of handling and shipment through illegal routes plus the burden of penalty in case of detection by the border control force, are higher than the transaction costs plus tariff rates involved in legal exports. This is an empirical question to be explored. As tariff rates are lowered in both countries, the incentive for illegal trade will diminish and favourable impact of such an action on legal trade would be further strengthened if the transaction costs in terms of bureaucratic regulations are also reduced.[6]

While evaluating bilateral trade, several studies have found significant productivity differences between India and Bangladesh for a range of commodities, with productivity in India being higher than in Bangladesh but in varying degrees or proportions. This opens up possibility of mutually advantageous trade, if exchange rate is in equilibrium and if trade restrictions are lowered. Indo-Bangladesh exchange rate (Taka-Rupee) reflects the exchange rate of Bangladesh vis-à-vis the rest of the world. However, India has lately depreciated more than Bangladesh vis-à-vis dollar, thus conferring a comparative advantage to India over Bangladesh.[7]

During the next round of the WTO negotiations on agriculture, India would be required to liberalise the agricultural sector, which is at present heavily protected through an array of heavy domestic subsidies and tariffs. Bangladesh might benefit from such a liberalisation even though the prospects of a substantial reduction in domestic agricultural subsidies under the WTO negotiations are not very bright.

If Bangladesh is to follow the path of multilateral trade liberalisation with India, she needs to concentrate on items in which she has substantial export potential to India. However, India may not have much interest in liberalising on a multilateral basis tariffs on commodities of export interest to Bangladesh. This is for two reasons. First, this would require her to open the door to the import of same commodities from third countries with the same export structure as Bangladesh. Secondly,

---

[6] It is pertinent to note that the expansion of illegal exports does not provide the stability and predictability that legal trade confers. Uncertainty, risk and unpredictable changes in the scope for illegal transactions inhibit the long run investment in production and trade. Legal trade, specially under the auspices of the multilateral regime, enjoys greater predictability.

[7] Z. Eusufzai, *Liberalisation in the Shadow of a Large Neighbour*. (Dhaka: The University Press Limited, 2000). S. Ahmed and Z. Sattar, 'Trade Liberalisation, Growth and Poverty Reduction: The Case of Bangladesh', Draft, World Bank, May 2003.

most probably there are only a few commodities, if any, for which India would like further import liberalisation by Bangladesh, beyond the very significant import liberalisation that Bangladesh has already implemented. India's gains from additional access to the Bangladesh market in competition with other countries may not be large enough to justify her import liberalisation.

In case Bangladesh, as part of her over all long term trade strategy, undertakes further liberalisation of imports on a multilateral basis, in line with most developing countries, India will be able to expand her exports to Bangladesh. In view of her diversified production structure, India has the capability for meeting the import needs of Bangladesh on a very wide range of commodities. Secondly, in the long run, as and when a progressively more liberal trading regime evolves in India, Bangladesh should explore and exploit her comparative advantage/export potential in the range of commodities for which India undertakes multilateral liberalisation. It is possible that even under a more liberal multilateral regime in India, resulting in a reduction of average rates of tariffs on commodities of export interest to her major trading partners, specific commodities of export interest to Bangladesh might still continue to carry high tariffs. This may happen, as it did in the past. In any case, the timeframe for further multilateral trade liberalisation by India in respect of manufactured goods is unknown.

Bangladesh's need for larger market access to India is of some urgency. The alternative under these circumstances is for Bangladesh to seek faster trade liberalisation on a bilateral basis with India. Unless such bilateral liberalisation involves sectors and commodities across the board, it might end up liberalising trade in respect of commodities in which they are least likely to compete with each other. This will not lead to much expansion of trade, given the structure of their economies and resource endowments. The list of commodities that so far have been discussed among the South Asian Association for Regional Cooperation (SAARC) countries under the South Asian Free Trade Agreement (SAFTA) confirm this pattern of time honoured behaviour.[8]

---

[8] The role of regional integration in the WTO agreement is supposed to be outward looking and trade creating rather than trade diverting. Increasingly, WTO is expected to assess the regional agreements with a view to ensuring that they are steps towards and not away from

Would Bangladesh welcome a free trade agreement with India? As earlier described, Bangladesh currently complains that due to her fast pace of import liberalisation in the past, she faces strong competition from a wide range of manufactured and agricultural imports from India. This is further aggravated by competition from illegal imports. If the threat is from illegal imports, then it already approximates free trade in imports. If competition is with legal imports, a free trade agreement will intensify the scope and extent of competition. The relative importance of illegal and legal imports in creating the competitive pressure on the Bangladesh economy is not known. Therefore, it is not clear without a detailed examination how serious will be the impact of unrestricted imports from India on the economy of Bangladesh. Would the gain in increased exports to India be large enough to compensate the losses in domestic production from increased import competition from India? A free trade regime with India will test as to what extent and how severely India's import restrictions constrain the exports to India. Given the broad similarity in the labour intensive segment of the industrial and service sectors, there is likely to be a scope for an inter and intrasectoral reallocation of resource to promote specialisation and division of labour between the two economies. It is difficult to foresee and quantify, at the start, the extent of such reallocation. In the high technology and capital-intensive sectors, India is likely to have comparative advantage in most cases.[9]

Of course, there will, necessarily be short term losses and dislocations in the process of adjustment. In the short or medium term, the adverse trade balance of Bangladesh with India is likely to be aggravated. Free trade agreement is best combined with or facilitated by free movement of capital between the member countries. An increase in the flow of capital from India to Bangladesh will help finance an increase in the trade deficit of Bangladesh. Would India's additional

---

the goal of the multilateral reduction, if not a total elimination, of trade barriers. Regional trade agreements that are likely to be frowned upon by WTO are those, which do not involve across the board but only free trade in selective commodities in which they do not compete each other.

[9] A genuine free trade agreement in this context is meant to be a very wide and across — the board elimination of tariffs and other non-tariff barriers, not watered down by (a) large negative list (excluding, competitive items), (b) restrictive rules of origin, and (c) overly demanding technical standards and complex customs procedures.

gains from an enlarged access to the Bangladesh market be large enough for her to welcome such a step? India may not be overly enthusiastic about it since she already has substantial access to markets in Bangladesh. In SAFTA, such a possibility is contemplated in the medium term. The progress in negotiations on SAFTA has been very limited to date.[10]

In the meanwhile, Bangladesh seeks preferential access for a list of her exports to India on a unilateral basis. The grant of unilateral or nonreciprocal preferences by India is consistent with the WTO obligations. In fact, India like other developing countries has, in general, agreed as a part of the WTO agreement to consider giving on a voluntary basis preferential market access to the least developed countries but they are under no legal obligation to do so. This is not part of the WTO treaty obligation. In relation to Bangladesh, India does not seem to be eager to follow WTO's lead in this respect. From all indications, it appears that India is reluctant to grant preferential access on a significant scale unless Bangladesh reciprocates by concessions in other ways or sectors.

A system of preferential access yields optimum results only if it is part of a long term agreement. Otherwise, it runs the risk of being withdrawn or modified at the discretion of the preference-giving country, creating uncertainty which discourages long term investment and production decisions. Secondly, unless it is very wide ranging in coverage, it freezes the current pattern of trade as preference remains tied to a specific list of commodities. Ideally, it should be a part of a movement towards widening the list and coverage of commodities.

Why should India agree to provide preferential access to Bangladesh on a wide range of her current and potential exports of Bangladesh? One could argue that India should have a long term interest in a prosperous Bangladesh, which will provide a large market for India's exports and investment. It will help promote stability in her eastern borders. The case for decisions based on long term considerations

---

[10]As a least developed country Bangladesh seems inclined to seek special market access and lengthier time frame for restructuring the tariffs under the SAFTA regime. She also seeks rapid reduction or elimination of tariffs and non-tariff barriers by the three developing countries in SAARC (India, Pakistan, and Sri Lanka) on imports from four least developed countries (Bangladesh, Bhutan, Nepal, and the Maldives). *The Daily Star, Dhaka*, 26th November, 2002.

and enlightened self interest in such a broad sense is strong in the context of evolving Indo-Bangladesh relations.

Are there immediate or intermediate term gains for India? An issue of considerable interest to India is the grant of transit facilities to the northeastern states of India through land routes and seaports in Bangladesh. This subject has created a great deal of controversy in Bangladesh, involving both political and economic considerations. This issue is worth serious consideration and deserves an empirical indepth evaluation of costs and benefits, if Bangladesh is to strive for preferential and ultimately free access for her exports to India. India's major concern is to provide an easy access for Indian products to the northeastern states and to reduce their transport cost from the rest of India. To ease the problems of their access to imports, Bangladesh could invite Indian investors to establish enterprises in Bangladesh for export to the northeastern states, preferably in collaboration with the Bangladesh private sector. This does not have to be in lieu of but could be in combination with the grant of expanded land routes, to begin with.

It is conceivable that the cost of imports from the rest of India through land routes in Bangladesh would be higher than that obtained from enterprises in Bangladesh, even if it is necessary to expand existing or establish new capacity to meet the import needs of the northeastern states. This is likely to be specially so if at the same time the grant of transit facilities is combined with trade preferences. In fact, free or preferential market access to India will be an attraction for Indian investment in Bangladesh.

Should transit facilities to India through expanded land routes in Bangladesh be combined with the grant of transit facilities through India for Bhutan and Nepal to get access to the seaports in Bangladesh? In fact, very recently India has agreed to grant transit facilities to Nepal.[11]

---

[11]This is expected to boost trade between Nepal and Bangladesh. In 1997, Bangladesh established a land port in the North of Bangladesh to provide transit facilities to Nepal through Bangladesh to Mangla, the country's second seaport. However, it could not be effective due to the lack of transit facilities for Nepal through India. The access of Nepal to the Bangladesh land port passes through the Indian territory, which was not made available to Nepal by India until late 2002. With India's agreement to do so, the government of Bangladesh has now decided to expand the infrastructure at the land port for facilitating transit trade. Moreover, Bangladesh

To what extent Indian private investment in Bangladesh for exports
to the northeastern states and the rest of India under preferential or
free trade agreements would be profitable needs examination by both
countries. If transit facilities through land routes combined with Indian
investment in Bangladesh for exports to the northeastern States are
inadequate to meet the latter's import needs, additional facilities through
seaports are worth consideration. In the meanwhile, questions have
been raised as to whether the existing infrastructure of roads and bridges
requires improvement for carrying the additional burden of heavy
traffic involved in transit trade. If so, investment in the improvement
of the land routes will be needed. The transit facilities through seaports
would require additional investments on a much larger scale: first, to
upgrade and expand port facilities in Chittagong; and second, to expand
associated transport facilities from the port to the northeastern states.
Given the volume of trade that will be generated by the import needs
of the northeastern States, it is not quite clear whether the rate of
return would be high enough to justify such investment. Empirical
studies, including appropriate cost comparisons, do not appear to
have been made, at least it is not in the public domain. In case
necessary investment is not fully financed by India, there would be
need for foreign investment and the returns have to be attractive
enough for inviting such necessary investment.

18.3 INDIAN INVESTMENT IN BANGLADESH

As earlier mentioned, an important aspect of trade relationship with
India is the persistent and large trade imbalance of Bangladesh. The
large bilateral trade deficit of Bangladesh should, by itself, be of no
serious concern to Bangladesh.[12] A bilateral balancing of trade in a
multilateral world is neither possible nor efficient. The global balance
of payments deficit of Bangladesh might be a matter of concern if it
is not financed by capital inflow, both development assistance and
private capital. Flow of the Indian capital to Bangladesh is one way
of financing the payments deficit with India. Anxious to invite foreign

---

has agreed to provide 50 percent discount to Nepal on the charges for the use of the transit
and port facilities in Bangladesh (*The Daily Star*, 10th October, 2002).

[12]During the same period, the trade deficit of Bangladesh was US$821 million with China and
US$523 million with Japan (*The Daily Star*, 26th August, 2002).

direct investment in general, Bangladesh has greatly liberalised domestic regulations and offered substantial fiscal and financial incentives. Despite such liberal policy framework, not much foreign investment has come to Bangladesh. Bureaucratic hurdles, poor infrastructure and governance have been cited among the causes inhibiting foreign direct investment, apart from competition from more attractive investment opportunities elsewhere in the region and in the rest of the developing world. Also, there has not been much Indian investment in Bangladesh. The poor state of investment climate may equally discourage both Indian and other foreign investment. However, one would have expected Indian investors to be less daunted by them. They should have found it easier to do business in Bangladesh in view of similarity of and familiarity with laws, regulations, bureaucratic practices, business traditions and customs. Also, they should be able to interact more easily with industrialists, traders and with society in general.[13] It is not easy to know how far it is the lack of enthusiasm in India or lack of interest in Bangladesh that inhibits Indian investment. It will be worthwhile to examine whether it is the supply or demand constraint that might have limited the potential Indian investment in Bangladesh. On the supply side, it also depends on how restrictive India's policy is regarding the outflow of Indian capital abroad, including neighbouring countries. Would unrestricted or preferential access to the large Indian market act as a powerful incentive to attract the Indian private investment? Experience in other countries, including Sri Lanka's experience vis-à-vis Indian investment, seems to confirm such a favourable impact.

It is alleged that there is an attitude of ambivalence in Bangladesh towards the Indian private capital. The underlying popular sentiment is possibly not one of unqualified welcome but one which is partly tinged with fear of domination, both economic and political. This is the kind of sentiment which is fairly common in all small countries in relation to direct investment from a big and powerful country, be it a developing or a developed country. This was the case in Canada

---

[13]There is some Indian private investment in Bangladesh. Many foreign buying houses procuring garments in Bangladesh are Indian enterprises; many enterprises of the Indian origin are registered in Southeast Asia with buying houses in Bangladesh. There is an increasing employment of Indian managers/technical experts in Bangladesh.

and Mexico even as late as the 1960s and 1970s in relation to the US investment.[14]

The fear of interference or dominance is considerably reduced when direct investment flows between countries which are not at substantially different stages of development. Even in a host country, which is economically weaker than the home country, the fear is likely to be less pronounced if there is stable and strong government with a well functioning democracy that ensures transparency and accountability. Past experience around the developing world indicates that such dominance is likely in countries which are politically unstable and have weak, inefficient and corrupt governments.

Moreover, the state of corporate governance is critical. It is necessary that the operations of private enterprise, both foreign and domestic, are carried out in the open and are subject to public scrutiny.[15] An active and free media as well as a vibrant civil society provides some antidote to the possibility of undue influence by foreign direct investment. Clandestine operations outside the range of public scrutiny, involving ruling or governing classes and foreign enterprises, frequently open the door to undue or dominant influence on policies and actions in host countries.

Admittedly, the risk can never be eliminated. Moreover, often governments of home countries of foreign investors intervene to promote the interests of their investors in various ways. For example, US government officials were reported to have interceded and canvassed with politicians and officials in India regarding the affairs of the now discredited Enron Corporation. This tends to complicate the situation since it projects matters relating to the relation between the host country government and private investors to the wider realm of interstate political and economic relations.[16]

---

[14]If foreign investors such as multinational corporations with "global reach" are very large in relation to the economy or industrial sector of the host country, and have far-flung interests, they may and do influence the policies of the host country with regard to domestic and foreign economic policies.

[15]See, Chapter 16.

[16]For decades, attempts have been made at the international levels to formulate codes of conduct for foreign direct investment in order to set guidelines for governing the relations between host country governments, foreign investors and home country governments. Attempts have so far signally failed. At the same time, there is a vigorous competition among the developing countries to attract foreign investors. This strong act of revealed preference confirms that the

Generally speaking, when a country has a strong thriving and dynamic private sector of its own, she happens to be more confident in her attitude towards the presence of foreign enterprise in the economy. The growth of a dynamic and efficient private sector in Bangladesh will help develop confidence in the country's ability to invite and deal with the presence of foreign private enterprise. It will not only help attract foreign, including Indian, investment but also confer the advantages of transfer of technology, managerial as well as technical, through joint enterprise or otherwise. It allows foreign investment to reap the benefits of external economies flowing from the availability of a pool of skilled labour as well as middle level professional managers. Ready availability of various servicing facilities and infrastructure are additional benefits that result from a thriving private sector in the host country. Frequently, foreign enterprises prefer on their own to start joint enterprises in the host country; they spread the risks of investment in an alien socio-political environment and facilitate access to the domestic regulatory system. These considerations should equally apply in the case of Indian investors in Bangladesh.

Indian direct investment should be encouraged to engage in sectors, which could develop export markets in India in the future. This could help open up the Indian market. Foreign direct investment frequently serves as a positive force for trade liberalisation in and market access to the home country. It may be advisable in the initial stage to encourage foreign enterprises, whenever feasible, which combine Indian and nonIndian capital and enterprises. This would dilute whatever reservations exist in popular mind about the dominant role of Indian investment. Access, specially if it is preferential access, to the Indian market might also attract nonIndian foreign investment to Bangladesh in order to exploit opportunities of export to India.[17]

There is yet another way in which nonIndian foreign and Indian investment might get intertwined in Bangladesh. Many nonIndian foreign enterprises may find investment in Bangladesh an economic and efficient way of expanding their existing or planned investment

---

benefits of direct investment are so considerable as to more than offset and override doubts or hesitations in the minds of the recipient countries regarding any limitation that foreign investment might place on their freedom of action.

[17]This would require that India sets up "rules of origin" for exports from foreign enterprises in Bangladesh to India.

in India. Their investment in Bangladesh may be in the same or related activities, depending on cost advantages, and may enable them to expand the scale and scope of operations when the market in Bangladesh is added to that of India. Already many of them export to Bangladesh products of their enterprises in India. The latter could act potentially as their regional headquarters for extending and managing their investments in the rest of South Asia and beyond. This happens in the case of many foreign investors in Singapore in relation to their investments in Southeast Asia. In this scenario, foreign investors may split activities between their enterprises in India and their counterparts or associated enterprises in Bangladesh. Thus, firms in the two countries may supply each other with intermediate inputs, spare parts and components; they may engage in different stages of assembling operations. A close interlinking of the operations in the two countries will lead to an increase in the interfirm trade across borders and hence in the bilateral trade flow.

An example of foreign investment in Bangladesh being linked to trade with India is the widely debated case of export of gas to India, produced by foreign companies in Bangladesh.[18] Foreign gas companies, which have entered into production sharing agreements with the government of Bangladesh are concerned that the limited domestic market of Bangladesh constrains the exploration and utilisation of gas in Bangladesh. Moreover, they worry that the government would not be able to make regular payments to them in foreign exchange for its purchases under the production sharing agreement unless it earns foreign exchange from the export of gas. Under the circumstances, they advocate the export of gas; the only market available for the export of gas through pipelines is India.

The answer to the question whether gas should be exported or not depends upon the optimum rate of utilisation of gas reserves and on whether it would yield an annual rate of output that exceeds domestic demand. In the case of Bangladesh, demand is not a constraint on the rate of utilisation so long one is indifferent between export and domestic market. The optimum rate of utilisation in its turn depends

---

[18]This is reminiscent of the debate in the 1970s about the export of fertiliser from Bangladesh to India, from enterprises jointly financed by Bangladesh and India and based on the utilisation of gas in Bangladesh under a long term agreement with India.

on expected revenues and costs of exploitation, on the one hand, and the social discount rate, on the other. Given the current state of poverty in Bangladesh, the social rate of discount is likely to be high.

Within this framework of analysis, the suggestion that export should only be considered if gas reserves exceed what is required to meet the expected domestic demand over a period of 25 years has no logical foundation. What happens if gas reserves are exhausted before 25 years? In that case, gas or its substitutes can be imported. After all, Burma is reported to have enormous gas reserves on and offshore. It is suggested that oil, the obvious substitute, is more expensive, apart from being environmentally unsafe. However, by that time, the capacity of Bangladesh to pay for higher oil price will also increase as she would have a higher income. After all, the whole logic of the utilisation of gas today is to increase investment and accelerate income growth in the future. Moreover, there are prospects of technological innovations and new sources of energy in a few years' time. Also, more importantly, there could be more energy efficient technology.

The export of gas, which is a nonrenewable, exhaustible resource, raises the kind of emotion that is associated with the selling of "family silver." The range of uncertainty in the determination of the extent of gas reserves is wide.[19] In view of the uncertainty of supply prospects of gas in the future, one alternative would be to investigate whether it is possible, tentatively, to put a cap on the extent of utilisation of the currently "proven and probable" gas reserves so as to limit export to the extent that is minimally necessary for cost effectiveness, i.e. to make the minimum investment in exploration pipelines and infrastructure that pays adequate returns. Sufficient flexibility should be kept for a change of policies and plans in the future.

Two extraneous factors complicate the decision on the optimum rate of utilisation. First , it is alleged that all the high potential gas fields have been already covered by production sharing agreements with the international companies who would only undertake investment in exploration if they are assured of market. Under the agreement, they are entitled to delay exploration activities and wait for five years or

---

[19]The nonspecialists get overwhelmed by the arcane concepts, such as "proven," "probable," and "possible" reserves, to mention only one of many distinctions and definitions. A piece of conventional wisdom seems to indicate that estimates of gas reserves are themselves a function of exploration; as one continues exploration, estimates of gas reserves go up.

so. The multinational oil companies prefer a fast rate of exploration and exploitation for immediate export; they are interested in maximising current profits and their rate of discount is high. There could be a divergence of interests between foreign investors and Bangladesh, if their private rate of discount is found to be higher than Bangladesh's social rate of discount.[20] Second, in the meantime, the home country governments of the international gas companies are alleged be advocating to the government of Bangladesh the case for export of gas to India. This introduces diplomatic and political element, in an already complicated situation, specially since Bangladesh seeks aid and trade concessions. One wonders how far an objective assessment of policy alternatives is possible under the circumstances.

The question of export of gas to India should be considered within the framework of a national policy for the exploration of gas based on such considerations as outlined above. Export of gas to India would involve construction of pipelines in Bangladesh to the border as well as the corresponding investment in India in pipelines for distribution of gas. Prerequisites for making such investments worthwhile are: the amount of gas export has to be large enough and has to last for a sufficiently long enough period of time to yield an adequate return on related investments.

The skeptics on the issue of export to India raise additional but unspoken questions which may lie behind their attitude of ambivalence. Some argue that in the light of large and long term investments for the export of gas from Bangladesh and India's dependence on such supplies, it will be in India's interest to ensure that there are no interruptions in gas supplies. In case of interruptions of supplies due to various reasons such as internal civil disturbance, law and order breakdown and labour indiscipline, would India want supplies to be diverted from domestic uses in Bangladesh to meet export commitments to India? India might exercise economic and political pressure on Bangladesh in order to ensure the supply of gas. This might cause tensions and frictions. This concern is further aggravated by the

---

[20] There was a time when investment in natural resource exploration and exploitation was considered to be a primary field for the public sector investment supported by international development assistance. In view of the possible divergence between the social and the private rate of discount, this sector was traditionally conceived as an area of public intervention. This is no longer true; donors want multinational private companies to undertake such investment.

prospect of the convergence of interests between a big, unequal neighbour and foreign governments acting on behalf of their gas companies. Secondly, the Indian company or agency importing gas may not be able to pay on time and in agreed instalments. This is because of problems in collecting fees from its customers within India, as exemplified by the inability of the Indian electricity/power corporations to meet their financial obligations to Enron. To reduce the possibility of such conflicts or frictions, the agreement with the gas companies could be so designed as to provide for such contingencies, including possibility of mediation by a third party. Experience of other countries in this respect could be drawnupon, even though there can be no foolproof arrangement that difficult problems will not arise.[21]

18.4 BANGLADESH LABOUR IN INDIA

Besides trade and capital investment, there is the issue of migration of labour from Bangladesh to India. Unlike trade and investment issues, this is one aspect of the Indo-Bangladesh relationship which does not figure much in the public debate in Bangladesh. However, the Indian media frequently provides wide publicity to the case of the Bangladeshi migrant labour in India. This raises sensitive politico-religious issues. There are two aspects of the problem of migration: one is the migration of the Hindu minority from Bangladesh to India, which is often permanent migration; second is the migration of the members of the Muslim community. The second is largely, if not entirely, in the nature of temporary migrants in the same category as the migration of labour from Bangladesh to the Middle Eastern and Southeast Asian countries. In the latter case, most migrants go back and forth. They migrate in search of employment opportunities and higher earnings. While the migration of the Bangladesh labour to other countries is largely legal, the migration of labour to India is illegal.[22]

---

[21] If the environment of an overall relationship with India is characterised by a lack of trust and a sense of insecurity, any cooperative project carries some risks. It is for the political leadership to assess the extent of such risks and take decision.

[22] A recent analysis by a very distinguished policymaker in India can be quoted on the post-1971 movement of population from Bangladesh to India. See, I.G. Patel, *Glimpses of Indian Economic Policy: An Insider's View.* New Delhi: Oxford University Press, 2002, p. 146. "For Bengali Muslims, India was a land of opportunity. A new chapter of migration from India to Bangladesh began. This has not yet ended and has created a new set of tensions in the northeast where

India has expressed concern on this subject on more than one occasion; it has come up in bilateral intergovernmental discussions. This portends to be a subject of bilateral tension in the future, with possible implications for communal conflicts and tensions, and unfavourable consequences for the overall Indo-Bangladesh relationship. Not much data have been collected nor any analysis of the problems of migration of labour from Bangladesh to India is available. India estimates that the number of migrants run into hundreds of thousands. It is a subject which does not lend itself easily to statistical analyses since migrants are difficult to identify and, in most instances, are indistinguishable from the local population. However, India considers that the size of the migrant labour from Bangladesh is large enough to be a matter of concern. It is a world wide experience that large economies with a growing demand for labour, which have small neighbours with a large population but limited employment opportunities for the unskilled labour, always serve as a very strong magnet of attraction.

This is one aspect of the Indo-Bangladesh relationship that should provide an incentive — a very strong rationale — for India to adopt measures vis-à-vis Bangladesh, which make migration less attractive. As income and employment growth accelerate in India, while Bangladesh stagnates, the greater will be the scope for employment opportunities for Bangladeshi labour in India and greater will be the outflow of labour. Moreover, to the extent there is Bangladeshi labour in India, their earnings provide one of the means of payment for Bangladesh's large deficit on account of illegal trade with India. The decline in or stoppage of any such earnings of the migrant labour will constrain illegal imports from India. In fact, one way for India to reduce her illegal exports to Bangladesh is to recognise the movement of Bangladeshi labour as necessary for meeting pockets of labour scarcity in India and to make it legal. Their earnings in India would then be remitted through official channels and deprive the illegal traders of a means of payment.

---

the indigenous people are up in arms against what they see as cultural annihilation by alien people. That the Congress Party often turned a blind eye to this influx for electoral reasons has added fuel to the fire of insurgency. This particular outcome of the Bangladesh war was not obvious to us then. Pakistan had effectively sealed the border for ideological reasons. Now that India has a friend in Bangladesh, the borders difficult as they are to maintain in any case became rather porous."

Export of labour from Bangladesh to India in a way can be seen as
a substitute for export of commodities. In view of relative scarcity of
capital vis-à-vis labour in Bangladesh, Bangladesh can export either
labour intensive goods or labour. The phenomenon of labour migration
from Bangladesh to India is similar to what the United States faces
vis-à-vis its southern neighbours, specially Mexico. All the sophisticated techniques of border surveillance, including a large border
control force, have not succeeded in substantially reducing the flow
of illegal immigrants to the United States. One of the principal rationale
and expected benefits of NAFTA and associated measures to promote
investment in and to greatly expand exports from Mexico was to
increase employment and income opportunities in Mexico.[23] In a
similar manner, a prosperous and a fast growing Bangladesh economy,
in the long run, will discourage any labour migration from Bangladesh.
Higher economic growth in Bangladesh can be facilitated by a liberal
access of Bangladesh's exports to India.

Unfortunately, long term considerations seldom determine the
priorities of politicians. Construction of fences/wires and other
obstructions, including the use of force at the border by India, unless
they are on a very substantial scale, are unlikely to totally eliminate
the flow of labour. On the other hand, such stringent measures might
exacerbate tensions in bilateral political relationship and may cause
border conflicts. One sees an important role for civil society in India,
including the media, professional associations, and employers' and
labour organisations, to debate a rational and constructive way of
meeting this problem.

On a broader level, the role of public opinion and civil society in
both countries in forging viable and cooperative relations over the entire
range of economic and political issues cannot be over emphasised.
In Bangladesh, discussions on the various aspects of Indo-Bangladesh
relations do occupy an important place in newspapers and related
media. But the pros and cons of the Indo-Bangladesh economic

---

[23]In fact, this is exactly what has happened to some extent already but the stimulus to the
Mexican economy has not been large enough for a sufficient length of time to make as yet a
considerable impact on labour flow out of Mexico. One has to add to it the strong pull of the
demand for low paid labour to work on menial jobs not acceptable to the US labour. Of
course, there are a wide range of other internal and external policy measures which constrain
the growth in Mexico. NAFTA was only one of the supporting measures.

cooperation in different or related areas are seldom discussed in public fora in a way in which the conflicting viewpoints are fully aired.[24] There need to be active debates on such controversial issues as gains and risks, including political risks, of Indian private investment in Bangladesh, countervailing measures against import competition from India, different types of transit facilities as well as labour migration. The debates should be based on good empirical analysis; they should appraise both the possibilities and limitations of Indo-Bangladesh relations. There is an urgent need for the education of public opinion on various aspects of Indo-Bangladesh economic cooperation. Above all, it is only through a process of national debates and discussions that Bangladesh should arrive at a broad consensus on the appropriate strategy in respect of both political and economic relations with India.

The extent and range of discussions and debates among different groups of civil society in India about the various aspects of Indo-Bangladesh relationship have been much more limited than in Bangladesh. Like in any country of a continental size, the government of India is focused on its internal problems and on selected external policies only so far as they relate to the major powers. This is also the governing occupation of the media, think tanks, academia, and professional associations of all types — in all of which India is singularly rich. Exceptions occur only when something sensational or egregious happens.

Some sections of the Bangladesh civil society have been engaged in stimulating and promoting contacts, dialogue, and debates with their Indian counterparts on selected aspects of Indo-Bangladesh relations. There has been increasing contact in recent years between traders of the two countries — less so among industrialists mainly because there are few industrialists in Bangladesh. There is probably a case for Bangladesh to take the initiative through multiple channels in increasing awareness and interest in India about the crucial aspects of Indo-Bangladesh relations. For example, how significant is the gain to India if Bangladesh is a peaceful, stable, prosperous country, and above all, a cooperative and friendly neighbour? Why it is better

---

[24]There are one or two "think tanks" which deal occasionally with the subject in a noncontroversial manner. The controversial debates take place mostly in the living rooms or private gatherings and are not vigorously pursued in the public domain.

for India to invest in the goodwill of a neighbour rather than extract cooperation by the weight of her superior bargaining strength, politically and otherwise? Bangladesh civil society has to engage their counterparts in India in debates and dialogue as to why and how India needs an assessment of her policy towards Bangladesh in the context of her role and responsibilities in the South Asia region. Efforts have to be made to spur debates and discussions within India among the broad spectrum of public opinion with differing and conflicting viewpoints. The current contacts between think tanks and professional groups or members of civil society seem to be among the like minded groups in the two countries; it is like "preaching to the converted". The network has to be widened to include those who are either skeptics, ignorant, indifferent, or even critically opposed to any significant expansion of Indo-Bangladesh economic cooperation.

Index